THE ENVIRONMENT AND THE LAW

Fire and Water

A PRACTICAL GUIDE

The memory and example of my parents
The future of my grandchildren and all grandchildren everywhere.
Martin

To the memory of my parents
Simon

THE ENVIRONMENT AND THE LAW

Earth Air Fire and Water

A PRACTICAL GUIDE

Martin Polden
and
Simon Jackson

Solicitors

LONGMAN

© Longman Group Ltd 1994

ISBN 0 75200 0004

Published by
Longman Law, Tax and Finance
Longman Group UK Ltd
21–27 Lamb's Conduit Street London WC1N 3NJ

Associated offices
Australia, Hong Kong, Malaysia, Singapore, USA

Printed and bound in Great Britain by
Biddles

CONTENTS

ACKNOWLEDGEMENTS

The authors have many to thank for assisting them on the stony path from the initial bright idea of writing this book to its reality.

First, acknowledgement and thanks are due to those who have written parts of the text subject to the authors final editing. Simon Payne, who contributed the parts of Chapters 1, 2, 4, 5 and 9 that concern air pollution. Peter Carty who wrote parts of the same chapters relating to the pollution of land, and who also provided the chapter on European law. Finally, Reuben Taylor who was responsible for the chapter on planning and the environment.

The authors are grateful to Neville Jones, Kate Harcourt and Geoff Taylor who contributed sections on water, land and air respectively, in the basic science section of Chapter 9.

The patience and encouragement of Anne Place and Jeffrey Boloten at Longmans must be recorded, together with our recognition of their willingness to back a new style practice book: our appreciation also to our editor Mary Kenny for her fortitude.

Our thanks to Sarah Rodger who cheerfully and efficiently bore the brunt of updating and editing the numerous drafts of the text and generating the final manuscript and to Rickie Hoole who provided timely support often at unsociable hours and short notice, with the typing of the text.

We are grateful for encouragement from the Executive Committee of the Environmental Law Foundation and particularly to Diana Schumacher, founder member of ELF and its Deputy Chair who ensured that we kept the environmental perspective well to the fore; to John Bates, former Chair of UKELA, who kindly read and commented on drafts of Chapters 2 and 7.

Our appreciation for the support forthcoming from Leonard

Ross and his partners at Ross & Craig, to Hugh Barrett of the Land Regeneration Unit of that firm for guidance on land contamination and to Kitty Mather for her research.

Martin thanks his wife Margie and family who have had to live with him through the writing experience and for the professional editorial input of his daughter Sarah. Simon could not escape to the bosom of a family but has to acknowledge the sympathetic ears of innumerable friends and relatives to whom he has complained of the rigours of authorship over the last year.

For all the hard work it has proved a rewarding experience conscious as we have been of breaking new ground in the presentation of the subject. We hope that both the material that appears in book form for the first time as well as the treatment of more familiar material will be of value to lawyers and others involved in the protection of the environment.

MAP
SRBJ
LONDON,
OCTOBER 1994

ABBREVIATIONS

ACA	Anglers Conservation Association
ADR	Alternative Dispute Resolution
APC	Air Pollution Control
BATNEEC	Best Available Technology Not Entailing Excessive Cost
BMWP	Biological Monitoring Working Party
BNFL	British Nuclear Fuels Ltd
BOD	Biological Oxygen Demand
BPEO	Best Practicable Environmental Option
CCW	Countryside Council for Wales
CEDR	Centre for Dispute Resolution
CITES	Convention on International Trade in Endangered Species of Wild Flora and Fauna
COD	Chemical Oxygen Demand
COREPER	Committee of Personal Representatives
CPO	Compulsory Purchase Order
CPRE	Council for the Protection of Rural England
CUT	Clean Up Tax
DLT	Development Land Tax
DoE	Department of the Environment
EC	European Community (formerly EEC—European Economic Community)
ECJ	European Court of Justice
ECSC	European Coal and Steel Community
EEA	European Environment Agency
EH	English Heritage
EIA	Environmental Impact Assessment
ELF	Environmental Law Foundation

ENDS	Environmental Data Services Group
EPA	Environmental Protection Act 1990
EU	European Union
EURATOM	European Atomic Energy Community
FOE	Friends of the Earth
FRU	Free Representative Unit
GDO	Town and Country Planning (General Development) Order 1988
GL	Guide Level
HMIP	Her Majesty's Inspectorate of Pollution
HSE	Health and Safety Executive
ICRCL	Interdepartmental Committee on the Redevelopment of Contaminated Land
IPC	Integrated Pollution Control
IPM	Inhalable Particulate Matter
IPPM	Integrated Pollution Prevention and Control
LAWDC	Local Authority Waste Disposal Company
LBCA	Planning (Listed Buildings and Conservation) Areas Act 1990
LDA	Land Drainage Act 1991
LWRA	London Waste Regulatory Authority
MAC	Maximum Admissible Concentration
MAF	Minimum Acceptable Flow
MAFF	Ministry of Agriculture, Fisheries and Food
MRC	Minimum Required Concentration
NCC	Nature Conservancy Council
NERC	Natural Environment Research Council
NGO	Non-Governmental Organisation
NRA	National Rivers Authority
OECD	Organisation for Economic Co-operation and Development
OFWAT	Office of the Director General for Water Services
OJ	Official Journal of the European Communities
ONB	Outstanding Natural Beauty
PPG	Planning Policy Guidance note
ppm	parts per million
REVOLT	Rural England v Overhead Line Transmissions
RFAC	Regional Fisheries Advisory Committee
SEA	Single European Act 1986
SFFA	Salmon and Freshwater Fisheries Act 1975

SSSI	Site of Special Scientific Interest
UKELA	United Kingdom Environmental Lawyers Association
WCA	Waste Collection Authority
WDA	Waste Disposal Authority
WFF	Worldwide Fund for Nature
WIA	Water Industry Act 1991
WMP	Waste Management Paper
WQO	Water Quality Objective
WRA	Waste Regulation Authority
WRA	Water Resources Act 1991

TABLE OF CASES

TABLE OF STATUTES

Table of Statutes

TABLE OF STATUTORY INSTRUMENTS

xxix

TABLE OF EUROPEAN PROVISIONS

INTRODUCTION

*Modern Man does not experience himself as a part of nature
but as an outside force destined to dominate and conquer it.
He even talks of a battle with nature, forgetting that, if he won
the battle, he would find himself on the losing side.*
                                    E F Schumacher in *Small is Beautiful*

The environmentally committed lawyer is a recent phenomenon.
Fortunately, unlike most rare species, the numbers are growing
rather than falling into decline.

The purpose of this book is to highlight for the busy practitioner,
citizens and groups involved in environmental issues, the essentials
of the law to applicable casework. In so doing, the authors have
drawn on the experience of the Environmental Law Foundation
(ELF), established at the beginning of 1992 and now a focus for
practitioner case activity.

The concern is with the practicalities required to construct a
working shelter for the environment. As part of that study, the
authors offer the proposition that the practitioner engaged in
environmental casework should be knowledgeable about the environment and also be alive to the aspirations, standards and expectations of those likely to appear as clients. Today's man on the
Clapham omnibus may be travelling a route similar to that of
his horse-drawn ancestors at the turn of the century, or even his
diesel-driven predecessor of the 1950s but his experience and
outlook are different, as must be the value judgements exercised on
his behalf.

1

EARTH, AIR, FIRE AND WATER

In 340 BC, Aristotle, in identifying the constituent elements of earth, air, fire and water, was expressing an interpretation and understanding of the make-up of the world and its place in the universe as known to him. His world was a less complicated place than ours and yet the Rio Conference of 1992 curiously echoed those primal elements and their application and focus for today.

EARTH

The use, or misuse, of land is a major factor in the case load of the environmental lawyer. Interference with habitat, constant pressure on sites of special scientific interest (SSSIs) and the failure to value biodiversity carry the same message from Rio whether it be in the Brazilian Rain Forest or on the Hampshire Downs. Ecological imbalance and the impact on landscapes created by quarries and gravel pits, landfill sites and deforestation reflect the dangers brought about by the misuse of resources.

AIR

Pollution of and through the air we breathe, the medium for the flow and movement of harmful substances, and atmospheric change, constitute a growing area for legal intervention. Noise, similarly transmitted, is a social problem, causing distress and nuisance at an increasing rate.

FIRE

In classical thinking fire was regarded as the outflow of energy, and has similar significance in our time. The increase in carbon emissions generated by escalating consumption of energy resources, the consequences of CO_2 upon climatic changes have local, leading towards global, importance. The health implications of lead discharged from the internal combustion engines of motor vehicles and the toxic impact of ill-designed or badly sited incinerators and dirty industrial processes; acid rain resulting from all such emissions and emissions producing profound ecological changes throughout the world; forests, lakes, coastal waters and finally buildings—all bear the marks of twentieth-century energy excesses. Nuclear power, the most dramatic of fire power, has created its own concerns to the practising lawyer and to society.

WATER

Pollution of our inland waterways and coastal waters has direct impact upon the nation's health whether the water be used for drinking or recreational purposes. The indirect implications can be no less serious: whatever toxic matter is absorbed by fish (and shell fish), livestock (farm reared and wild) as well as vegetation (cereals and fruit), eventually finds its way to people. Degradation of the food chain is thereby perpetuated. Most readily identifiable are noxious substances fed directly into rivers or discharged near beaches. Less easily found in time is the insidious seepage into the water table of toxins from the injudicious use of chemicals on farm land or industrial or other hazardous waste deposits.

THE RISE IN ENVIRONMENTAL AWARENESS

In recognising that there is nothing new under the sun, we can draw comfort from the fact that, in his time, Aristotle was confronting the similiar basic mysteries by which our own era is no less challenged, even though his world was a less cluttered place and largely free of mechanisation. It is a great irony that mankind, desperate for protection from the very technology it created, now looks to the law to protect itself from itself! It is arguable, alas, that the very need for a book such as this is testimony to a failed progress.

Sadly, the early warnings emerging from the modern ecology movement made little impact on governments or the world population. In 1962, the Report of the Club of Rome was published, highlighting the implications of unrestrained growth, industrial consumer demand and the increasing gap between the Western world and the Third World. In the late 1960s Fritz Schumacher was communicating his concern at the rush for unbridled growth and the consumption of non-renewable resources. The Stockholm Conference of 1972 resulted in the UN Environmental Programme and in 1973, one year after the Yom Kippur War jolted the world with the energy crisis, Schumacher published *Small is Beautiful*.

Around that time also was published the important work of Barbara Ward and Rene Dubois entitled *Only One Earth* and in America appeared *The Silent Spring* by Rachael Carson.

Of course, we are all environmentalists now! Attention to environmental issues is on the political agenda of all British parties. Accordingly, it is no less important for those practising law with an environmental content to have an overall awareness and understanding of such matters. Representing citizens whose health has been adversely affected by toxic emissions from an incinerator requires the basic skill used in conducting any claim for personal injury. Fear of the destructive impact upon a local community by a proposed motorway or industrial development scheme falls within the purview of the planning specialist. Each professional, in the tradition of the common law system, follows the empirical approach of turning his or her skills and experience to the needs of the client in pursuing the appropriate remedy.

In bringing together these strands as component parts in the pursuit of appropriate remedies, the authors urge upon practitioners the advantage to be gained from having an additional forensic weapon, in the form of the environmental perspective. With this goes the value, where possible, of working within shared-disciplinary units that draw upon the skills of the litigator as well as lawyers with expertise in planning, property, company law, and banking.

THE ENVIRONMENTAL LAW FOUNDATION

ELF was established in 1992 in response to environmentalists urging that lawyers should become more involved in environmental protection, given their special training and knowledge and professional ability to support those in need. The prodigal misuse of natural resources, to satisfy the growing expectations of society, has imposed increased demand upon the environment. The last decade or so has seen the emergence of Britain's citizenry forming action or protest groups, whether for specific local purposes or to counter perceived national and international wrongs. It is the increasing expectation (indeed the right) of such groups that they should have the equality of access to justice with equal opportunity to be heard, and have good representation and sound expert advice, at no lower a standard than that available to their corporate or institutional adversaries.

It was and remains a practical demonstration of Barbara Ward's exhortation to think globally while acting locally. Through its national network of practitioners ELF is contributing to the realisation of that commitment.

Those involved in the formation of ELF also recognised that a multi-disciplinary approach was essential. So it is that ELF includes, at its helm, and among its membership, ecologists, environmental scientists, economists, experts in planning, traffic, toxicology, biology, and lawyers. The emphasis upon the ELF experience assumes that the reader is sufficiently committed to embrace a broader long-term interest in matters environmental that goes beyond simply regarding the subject as just another legal topic.

The UK (along with other countries) witnessed an upsurge of ecological damage in the 1980s with predictable reaction from private citizens. In the 1990s that imbalance is being redressed. The emergence of ELF reflects that change and there is now greater prospect that the existing law and legal process is being more comprehensively used in support of environmental interests. Beyond that, there remains the need to encourage the extension of legal boundaries to espouse the cause of law reform. The tools of our trade are expressed in this volume. For the most part our work is of a non-dramatic but locally important nature. Each small step is part of the long trek well trodden by the early environmentalists and in whose company the legal profession appears as a late joiner, but nevertheless with a major contribution to make.

It must be acknowledged that leading ecologists, writers and commentators of long standing have a degree of scepticism towards the role of lawyers and the law when it comes to protection of the environment. The laws of nature, rather than those of mankind, are understandably their primary focus. There is growing recognition, however, that legislation sympathetic to and aimed at supporting, and not attacking, the Earth's resource base has a proper and valid place.

To take this thinking one stage further, the idea has been floated by Edward Goldsmith, founder and publisher of *The Ecologist*, of the need for a new type of jurisprudence to operate as an accepted form of universally recognised natural law for the protection of the environment. Achievement of this will be no easy task, but if ever in place it will give international authority to those basic tenets considered essential to the survival of the earth and its eco-systems. Eco-

Law has not yet found an accepted place in the vocabulary of works on environmental law writing (although argued by Professor Klaus Bosselman writing in his book 'In the Name of Nature' in Germany and New Zealand) but that opportunity may fall to be explored at another time and another place!

Environmental concern is clearly not an invention of lawyers, and the law relating to the environment cannot be in the sole domain of lawyers. Preserving the quality of life is the concern of all with dependency upon the interaction of the four elements. Monitoring the quality of those elements and being alert to changes which occur have not always been welcomed and are often viewed as needless interference. Laws are by their very nature intrusive, whether by prohibiting certain activities, or imposing standards and obligations within which activities may be permitted. Protection of person, of property, of civil order has traditionally been recognised as coming within the province of law makers. Lawyers have a natural and accepted role in its implementation. Frequently, by way of response to need, practitioners have developed their special skills and been drawn into environmental work by separate routes, academics have followed a similar path, as has the judiciary. Now there are many university centres for training in environmental law most have only been established since the early 1990s.

Practitioners (as well as academics and the judiciary) have accordingly had to construct an identifiable body of applicable law to meet the needs and demands of the public. This is a continuing process despite increasing legislative involvement. Curiously, it is the judiciary rather than Parliament to whom citizen groups have in many respects looked for enterprise and solace.

Of further significance is the fact that environmental law, as such, is not in a codified form and any serious student or practitioner must work through a number of statutes and much case law. In the 1990s there has been a remarkable growth in environmental legislation but the practitioner must continue to consider a number of parallel sources and authorities for the relevant law, as well as for the evolving concepts and developments of that law.

The responsibility and burden upon the practitioner is that she or he is directly in the forefront of any controversy. That burden is also an opportunity which can be seized by the present generation of lawyers following new harmonisation in approach espoused by ELF.

Accordingly, the law relating to the environment has to be presented as a total package. If we categorise the environment as something distinct and separate, as though it were on its own, we create an artificial entity and it becomes a topic disengaged from all the other essentials of which it is, in fact, an integral part. In so doing we allow inherently false judgements to be made as to perceived balances of convenience and the giving of alleged economic priorities.

The creation of social and economic models, and with them legal structures, are an inevitable product of communal needs and form the mechanism for the pursuit of sustainable development. These are not to be assumed automatically as necessarily hostile to the environment, but, where problems do emerge, the intervention of law and even the administration of that law becomes of increasing significance.

In that equation we see the shape of the future and the responsibility we have for our children, their children and those children's children. It is an intriguing thought that the North American Iroquois Indians live by a law that no step is to be taken or permitted unless it be in the interests of the seventh generation. We suspect these primitive people set too high a standard for the sophisticates of the late twentieth century but even to think in terms of the fifth (occasionally even the fourth) generation would really be a giant step for man.

By operating laws set by Parliament and developed by the judiciary, the practitioner is well placed to promote that which is good and identify where change or reform is needed. The pursuit of citizen suits, the protective support of communities, as well as safeguarding the individual and not forgetting that fifth (or even fourth) generation ahead, provide constant practical opportunities, for ensuring the proper balance between economic development and the sustaining of environmental need.

THE COMMERCIAL REALITY

In the mid-1990s sound environmental policies, the conducting of industry with proper respect for and in due compliance with the regulatory standards is becoming a *sine qua non* of commercial life.

There is growing recognition in the business world that small and medium-sized enterprises need guidance and direction and indeed support towards good environmental practice.

The concept of enlightened self-interest has been identified by Jonathan Porritt as a force behind much of the increasing environmental awareness of industry and commerce. By whatever route, such conversion is to be welcomed.

Banks and other funding and investing institutions, as well as the insurance industry, require the highest standards and will not approve short-term benefit at the expense of long-term liabilities. The environmental audit on company acquisition is now commonplace. For those starting in business, it is no less essential to get the right guidance at the beginning and to build in any extra cost as part of the basic start-up and business plan. Those operating in older plants or on land beset by uncertain and historical contamination face greater difficulties. It is a false economy to pretend the problem does not exist by seeking to ignore its existence. The casualness of today is the claim of tomorrow.

THE AIM OF THIS BOOK

The primary thrust of this book, and the area of law covered, focuses upon the amenities that go to make up the quality of life for communities and the citizens they comprise. In essence it covers the areas identified in s 1 of the Environmental Pollution Act 1990, namely:

> (2) The 'environment' consists of all, or any, of the following media, namely, the air, water and land; and the medium of air includes the air within buildings and the air within other natural or man-made structures above or below ground.
> (3) 'Pollution of the environment' means pollution of the environment due to the release (into any environmental medium) from any process of substances which are capable of causing harm to man or any other living organisms supported by the environment.

Accordingly while the book must touch upon issues involving interference with personal health and safety resulting in consequential claims for damages, it will be seen that this is not a major focus of this work.

The fact, however, that common law, and the system through which it operates, favours property rights, is something of a handicap in the pleading of the environmental case. Damage to the rights of individuals has frequently to be argued as an extension of rights in property and establishing such claims within the existing legal framework can require ingenuity. Similarly there is need to address the problem of the locus of the party or parties seeking judicial intervention in issues other than those that directly infringe such personal or property rights. For that reason it will be seen that, notwithstanding the broad extent of legal remedies listed in this book, there are limitations respecting those to whom they can be made available.

The onus is on the practitioner to look at the full range of remedies, legal and extra-legal, that may be available to deal with a particular problem. Equally it is incumbent on the practitioner to be innovative in the use and to be alive to the possible extension of the boundaries of those remedies. The restricted funding capability that generally characterises community groups is an incentive for the practitioner to look at a variety of ways to achieve a given objective rather than committing clients to expensive litigation: it can also, unfortunately, raise problems over the completeness of preparation that the case demands.

In practice the majority of environmental problems will raise not only the possibility of a common law action, but the questions of whether the activity involved is subject to an authorisation and/or planning consent; whether the regulator responsible for the authorisation has conducted itself properly; and whether any criminal offence has been committed. There will increasingly be occasions on which consideration should be given to the use of extra-legal remedies such as political pressure or involvement of the media. Proper advice therefore has to be based on a multi-disciplinary approach, which reflects the fact that there may be a number of ways to pre-empt redress an environmental problem, and the practitioner has to be aware of them all.

Against this background and the challenge it creates, the authors have endeavoured to structure the book in a way that it is hoped will be of practical value to those whose profession or calling leads them into day-to-day contact with environmental issues, and equally to groups and organisations directly involved in the front line. Provision has been made to cross-refer, as far as possible, to other sections that offer alternative ways of approaching the same problem—methods which may be more effective, or cheaper than the conventional remedy, or which may even present a remedy where none seemed obviously available.

The book falls roughly into two parts.

Part I covers areas of substantive law. Chapter 1 looks at the statutory framework of environmental law; Chapter 2 looks at the common law; Chapter 3 examines planning as it affects the environment; Chapter 4 deals with authorisation, while Chapter 5 looks at criminal law. Chapter 6 provides a brief summary of the influence of European law on United Kingdom law and practice.

Part II turns to an examination of remedies and practical considerations for interest groups and practitioners advising them. Chapter 7 looks at remedies through the courts, while Chapter 8 covers the many extra-legal remedies available, which can be equally as efficacious as legal courses of action, as well as often being cheaper. Chapter 9 provides practical guidance on the use of experts, expert knowledge, and the range of information available on environmental matters. Chapter 10 deals with the issues of finance and funding, areas clearly of concern to interest groups and their advisers, and discusses the priorities of governments and individuals on environmental matters.

In conclusion, the authors express the hope that readers gain both in knowledge of the subject-matter and enthusiasm for the cause represented. If there is a regret it is that, for reasons of space, some aspects are not included or are only touched upon. There remains nevertheless a great deal to absorb. If use of this book can assist in disposing of problems at local level, there will be less prospect of global damage developing, most of which has localised origins.

We bid you go forth and multiply and contribute to enhancement of the environment.

CHAPTER 1

STATUTORY FRAMEWORK

INTRODUCTION

1.1 This chapter sets out the statutory framework for environmental regulation in England and Wales, an understanding of which is essential in order to place in context the matters dealt with in succeeding chapters. It is this framework that provides the basis for the application of criminal or other sanctions for activities potentially damaging to the environment and the system of authorisations for discharges into the environment. This chapter looks first at the more general environmental legislation and regulatory institutions and then at those that are specific to water, air, and land. (Controls over the development and use of land are, however, considered in Chapter 3.) Finally attention will be given to the duties imposed on bodies for the protection of the environment as an element of their other activities and the duties imposed on environmentally sensitive industries.

The importance of understanding the statutory framework is of more than academic interest to those involved with environmental issues. Those concerned with environmental issues need to know the obligations, powers and duties of the regulators. The regulatory bodies have powers which the general public do not enjoy. They also have duties to protect and promote the environment and its use. Finally they have resources, human and financial, to exercise their powers and duties. All regulatory bodies believe themselves to be acting in the interests of the environment and the public that they represent. They may not however, always know what those interests are unless the public communicate them. This is particularly the case with single issues, as opposed to overall policy. Sometimes the public find it necessary to exert a degree of persuasion on the regulators, the more so where a conflict of interest confronts a regulator, or where the consequence of their action results in the payment of compensation. Equally, it is important to be aware of the duties imposed on environmentally sensitive industries to promote conservation and protect the environment.

A lack of resources causes many of those affected by significant environmental issues to rely on the regulators to make their point on behalf of the environment. To that end it is of great importance to understand what the powers and duties of the regulators are, and to be ready to point out to them that their powers need to be exercised. Getting regulators to take action themselves is more effective than other courses of action. Acts or omissions which are in breach of the regulatory bodies' duties may render them liable to judicial review proceedings (*see* Chapter 3).

Opportunities exist both formally and informally for members of the public to become involved in environmental policy-making processes through such means of contact as regulators' special emergency lines to deal with pollution incidents or survey work carried out by regulators where an issue of importance is identified. These are covered in more detail in Chapter 8.

A BRIEF HISTORY OF ENVIRONMENTAL REGULATION

1.2   Environmental regulation has developed in a piecemeal fashion over the last century or more. The first Public Health Act was passed in 1848. Other legislation, for example that dealing with water pollution, also emerged in the Victorian period in response to the gross and uncontrolled pollution which was a by-product of the industrial revolution. One result of this piecemeal development is the disparate group of bodies having responsibility for environmental regulation.

The present government has announced its intention to create an Environmental Protection Agency. The 1993 Queen's speech indicated a proposal to pass legislation to set up this Agency in the last parliamentary session. This did not happen and it seems more likely that the Agency will not be in operation until April 1996 at the earliest. Even then it is doubtful whether present proposals will lead to the creation of a body with a strong identity and adequate funding which will co-ordinate the variety of functions at present carried out by Her Majesty's Inspectorate of Pollution (HMIP), the National Rivers Authority (NRA), and local authorities.

In order that regulatory bodies may deal with existing environmental pollution and regulate current polluting activity, if they are to be effective, regulators must be given the chance to do their job properly. It is necessary for agriculture and industry to commit greater funds to operating in a manner that will reduce pollution. While some quarters of industry realise the value of becoming more environmentally aware, many others do not. Government, with its preference for voluntary regulation, is still prepared to listen to arguments from industry that the costs of environmental improvements are too great, to water down legislation, and to tie the hands of regulators so that they cannot achieve the aims they set themselves.

MULTI-MEDIA ORGANISATIONS

INTRODUCTION

1.3 The principal institution responsible for multi-media environmental regulation is Her Majesty's Inspectorate of Pollution (HMIP). In addition, government departments have responsibilities for regulating the regulators and operating appeal procedures. These supervisory and appeal functions are referred to later in this chapter and in Chapter 5 respectively. Some duties are imposed on ministers, who have powers that are not delegated to other agencies. These are looked at below (see para 1.8 et seq). Finally there are statutorily created bodies, such as English Nature and English Heritage, that have functions that impinge on environmental issues.

INTEGRATED POLLUTION CONTROL

Background

1.4 Integrated Pollution Control (IPC) was introduced into the UK by the Environmental Protection Act 1990 (EPA) Part I in response to the growing demands for the implementation of a number of EC Directives, in particular 84/360 on Air Pollution from Industrial Plants, 88/609 concerning Large Combustion Plants and

76/464 on the release of Dangerous Substances to Water together with its daughter directives (*see* Chapter 6 and Appendix 5). It also provides for the setting by the Secretary of State of quality objectives for environmental media or emission standards for particular substances or processes. For an example see the Municipal Waste Incineration Direction 1991.

IPC regulates emissions to all environmental media. These include air, water and land (s 1, EPA). Part I of the EPA allowed the implementation of the UK idea of 'integrated' control as well as providing a method of complying with EC obligations. Under the integrated system one body would determine the controls to be imposed in respect of several environmental media. The perceived advantages of having one statutory body administering controls concerning air, land and water are that a balanced and co-ordinated approach to control may be developed that takes account of all the effects on the environment as a whole.

It should be noted that the EPA Part I also covers local authority air pollution control. This bears many similarities to IPC but is regulated by local authorities and is concerned only with atmospheric pollution. It is considered later in this chapter. (see para 1.34 below)

Her Majesty's Inspectorate of Pollution

1.5   HMIP was established in 1987. It is part of the Department of the Environment (DoE) and does not have the independent corporate status of, for example, the National Rivers Authority (NRA). When it was established it brought together a number of existing government pollution inspectorates including the Industrial Air Pollution Inspectorate, the Radiochemical Inspectorate and the Hazardous Waste Inspectorate. HMIP has a number of regulatory and advisory functions. These include:

(a) provision of advice to government on pollution control;

(b) regulation of those premises subject to the Alkali etc Regulation Act 1906 and s 5 of the Health and Safety at Work Act 1974;

(c) regulation of some of the processes controlled under the EPA Part I—those known as Part A processes which are subject to integrated pollution control;

(d) regulation of radioactive substances under the Radioactive Substances Act 1993;

(e) regulatory oversight of the discharge of waste regulation authorities' responsibilities under EPA Part II;

(f) regulatory oversight of the discharge of local authority responsibilities under EPA Part I in respect of those processes known as Part B processes—local authority air pollution control.

HMIP is based in London and has three regional divisions. Information on the administrative operation of HMIP is included in Chapter 8.

HMIP's powers stem from each of the statutes under which it has responsibilities. These are considered separately below.

Functions of HMIP

1.6   HMIP is responsible for authorising, regulating and enforcing the controls and operating the IPC system (ss 4(2) and 16, EPA). IPC is applicable to about 5,000 processes in the UK, which are subject to IPC, are set out in the Environmental Protection (Prescribed Processes and Substances) Regulations 1991 (as subsequently amended). These regulations describe in detail a number of processes which may appear in the regulations as either Part A or Part B processes. Those subject to IPC are Part A processes. Part B processes are subject to local authority air pollution control (*see* para 1.34). The Regulations classify the processes subject to IPC by sector. The following industrial sectors are included:

(a) fuel and power;

(b) metal production and processing;

(c) mineral industries;

(d) chemical industry;

(e) waste disposal and recycling;

(f) other miscellaneous industries.

Each individual industrial sector is then subdivided into various general processes and then into very specific process descriptions.

On complex industrial sites a number of prescribed processes may be carried on. Where some processes are Part A and some are Part B, to avoid confusion the Regulations provide for the Part A processes to take precedence. Therefore control will be exercised by HMIP even over Part B matters.

The Environmental Protection (Prescribed Processes and Substances) Regulations 1991 list prescribed substances for each environmental medium. They also create a number of exceptional cases where a listed process is not subject to control. These are set out in Regulation 4. The most important of the exceptions are where there are no or only trivial emissions of prescribed substances.

IPC is gradually being phased in between April 1991 and November 1995. All new processes or existing processes which are substantially altered require authorisation immediately. Controls for other existing processes are being phased in according to a timetable set out in the Regulations.

IPC controls are based on the need for an authorisation before a pre-scribed process may be operated (subject to the transitional provisions for existing processes). Such authorisations are considered in Chapter 5. Here it is important simply to identify whether an authorisation is needed and to appreciate that the conditions attached to it are crucial to the impact of the operation of the process on the environment.

Objectors can have a substantial role in the authorisation process and in ensuring that the terms of an authorisation are complied with. The objectives that any process must use the best available techniques not entailing excessive cost (BATN.EEC) to minimise emissions and render them harmless and that Part A processes must embody the best practicable environmental option (BPEO) are both controversial and central to the controls. Chapter 5 considers the authorisation application procedure for IPC consents.

As IPC controls are based on the regulation of emissions to all environmental media other statutory regulation of emissions, for example to water and land, is suspended and all controls are vested in HMIP. There are important provisions in s 28, EPA on the overlap between IPC and other controls. In outline these require:

(1) Authorisations may not regulate the final disposal of waste on land.

(2) Water emissions are controlled under the EPA authorisation but the NRA may require conditions to be attached or new conditions to be imposed into an existing authorisation. In addition, if the NRA certifies that the authorisation will lead or contribute to a failure to achieve a water quality objective set under the Water Resources Act 1991 (*see* below) then authorisation must be refused.

Duties imposed on HMIP

1.7 HMIP is required to follow developments in technology and techniques for pollution reduction or prevention (s 4(9) of the EPA), in particular looking to what is termed BATNEEC and BPEO (*see* Chapter 5). In addition, in respect of authorised processes HMIP must review the conditions of every authorisation at least every four years. HMIP must include certain conditions in authorisations (*see* Chapter 5). Finally HMIP may serve a prohibition notice to enforce an authorisation, and has a discretion to take other enforcement action.

GOVERNMENT DEPARTMENTS

1.8 The duties and powers of government ministers stem from a number of different Acts, as detailed below.

Environmental Protection Act

1.9 The EPA imposes no direct duties on government ministers. There are, however, some powers the exercise of which is reserved to ministers. These are contained in ss 140–2 of the EPA.

(1) Section 140 gives power to issue regulations to prohibit or restrict the importation, use, supply or storage of injurious substances or articles for the purpose of preventing, *inter alia*, the substance or article from causing pollution of the environment.

(2) Section 141 gives the Secretary of State the power to prohibit or restrict the importation of waste of any description for the purpose of preventing any risk of pollution of the environment. The section contains a very broad discretion as to how this power can be exercised.

(3) Section 142 gives power to the Secretary of State to compel the supply of information on substances specified by him where that information is needed to assess that substance's potential to cause damage to the environment.

Water Resources Act 1991

1.10 The Water Resources Act 1991 (WRA) uses the expression

'Ministers', which includes the Secretary of State for the Environment and the Minister of Agriculture Fisheries and Food.

Sections 16 and 17 of the WRA contain duties for, *inter alia*, the promotion of the conservation of flora and fauna. The extent of these duties is considered at para 1.14. These duties are imposed on the ministers as well as on the NRA. Analogous duties are imposed in the Land Drainage Act.

Section 213 of the WRA gives ministers the power to cause a local inquiry to be held in connection with any of the NRA's functions. The section refers specifically to the holding of an inquiry with a view to preventing or dealing with pollution of controlled waters. Although government departments are reluctant to interfere with the NRA's exercise of its functions, this section does permit a review of the NRA's approach to a problem if it is felt that the NRA is failing to deal with it effectively.

Water Industry Act 1991

1.11 Sections 3 and 4 of the Water Industry Act 1991 (WIA) contain environmental duties which mirror those in the WRA set out above. The ministers have to have regard to these environmental duties when exercising their powers under the WIA.

OTHER INSTITUTIONS

English Nature

1.12 English Nature was created by the EPA, Part VII, which divided the former Nature Conservancy Council (NCC) into the NCCs for England (known as English Nature) and Scotland and the Countryside Council for Wales. Funded by the government and having as its main function the promotion of nature conservation, English Nature has other duties which include:

(a) the establishment and maintenance of National Nature Reserves (there are reserves in England covering 43,000 hectares) and Marine Nature Reserves;

(b) advising central government on nature conservation;

(c) commissioning nature conservation research;

(d) scheduling Sites of Special Scientific Interest (SSSIs) (there are 3,749 SSSIs in England covering 861,341 hectares); and

(e) the conservation of wildlife and natural features.

In 1990, it launched the 'Regionally Important Geological/ Geomorphological Sites Scheme' which encourages local voluntary groups to identify geological sites that merit conservation.

As the government's statutory body on nature conservation, it is able to provide advice and guidance. Unlike the NRA, however, it does not control pollution and has no enforcement powers.

The powers of English Nature are contained in the Wildlife and Countryside Act 1981 (the Act) and the Wildlife and Countryside (Amendment) Act 1985. Under s 29 of the Act owners and occupiers must give English Nature four months' notice in writing if they intend to carry out, or cause or permit to be carried out, any operation likely to damage the SSSI. Under s 29(7) an owner or occupier who does not give the necessary notice will be liable on summary conviction to a fine of up to £1,000. Section 29(9) provides for two exemptions: where the operation is an emergency; or if authorised by a planning permission on application to the local planning authority. English Nature may consent to the operation, refuse it or seek modification to it. It may also request the Secretary of State for the Environment to make a Nature Conservation Order which extends consultation while protecting the area.

The statutory exemption of the grant of planning permission appears to be a major gap in the efficiency of the powers of English Nature. However, the planning authority must consult with English Nature and take its views into account in making its decisions. Also, if an environmental assessment is required English Nature must be consulted. Nevertheless, unless greater authority is granted by statute the right to consultation conveys few real powers.

Section 38 of the Act empowers English Nature to offer various types of grants to help individuals and organisations to carry out nature conservation. These include general grants, community action for wildlife, school grants, reserve enhancement schemes (these help county wildlife trusts to manage reserves that are SSSIs), species recovery grants, churchyard schemes, voluntary marine nature reserves grants, heathland grants, volunteer action grants and rural action.

English Heritage
1.13 Originally created under the National Heritage Act 1983 as the Historic Buildings and Monuments Commission for England,

English Heritage (EH) is sponsored by the Department for National Heritage which took over this role from the Department of the Environment in 1992. It is funded principally by central government.

In the broadest terms, EH is responsible for the built environment. It manages 400 of the country's most important historic buildings and ancient monuments as visitor attractions. It also provides technical and financial advice. More specifically, s 33 of the National Heritage Act sets out the duties, powers and functions of EH. Its duties are threefold:

(a) to secure the preservation of ancient monuments and historic buildings;

(b) to promote the preservation and enhancement of the character and appearance of conservation areas;

(c) to promote the public's enjoyment of and advance their knowledge of ancient monuments and historic buildings.

Its powers include the provision of educational facilities and information, the giving of advice, helping with financial research and maintaining records. In addition, it is given powers to enter into contracts and acquire property other than land and the catch-all power to do other things as it thinks necessary or expedient. It also has certain other statutory rights and duties:

(1) Under s 1 of the Planning (Listed Buildings and Conservation) Areas Act 1990 (LBCA) the Secretary of State for National Heritage must compile lists of buildings of special or historic interest and approve any such lists compiled by EH. When compiling such lists the Secretary of State must consult EH.

(2) Under the Ancient Monuments and Archaeological Areas Act 1979 the Secretary of State must consult EH when compiling lists of ancient monuments. Section 2A of this Act places a duty on EH to inform the owner and occupier of the monument and the local authority in whose area the monument is situated.

(3) Section 3A of the Historic Buildings and Ancient Monuments Act 1953 allows EH to make grants for repair or maintenance of any building which appears to EH to be of outstanding historic or architectural interest.

(4) Under s 68 of the LBCA planning applications involving listed buildings in Greater London must be referred to EH

before being dealt with by the planning authority. Outside Greater London such referral only applies to Grade I or II listed buildings.

When EH is consulted either by a Greater London planning authority or the Secretary of State it may seek or accept representations. EH is also able to provide information on whether ancient monuments or historic buildings are scheduled under any legislation and more generally on the built environment itself.

WATER

INTRODUCTION

1.14   The principal Act concerned with the regulation of the water environment is now the WRA. The Act provides for the establishment of the NRA as the main agency for the protection of the water environment. Additionally the Department of the Environment and the Ministry of Agriculture Fisheries and Food (MAFF) have important functions, primarily as the point of appeal from NRA decisions and the initiator of regulations under which the NRA operates. The environmental duties imposed on the ministers are dealt with above.

The NRA has three principal areas of responsibility:

(a) the control of pollution of the water environment;

(b) the control of water resources;

(c) the regulation of land drainage, including flood protection.

The NRA also has significant powers under the Salmon and Freshwater Fisheries Act 1975 (SFFA), most of which concern the regulation of fisheries. Section 4 of that Act, however, contains one of the two main pollution offences, along with s 87 of the WRA.

The NRA operates on a regional basis (at present with nine regions, soon to be reduced to eight). It is an independent body which does not enjoy Crown immunity. The administrative structure of the NRA is discussed in Chapter 8.

Pursuant to ss 6–14 of the WRA the NRA has a duty to set up advisory committees for regional rivers, regional and local fisheries and flood defence. (The role of these committees as pressure groups is discussed in Chapter 8.)

Partly because the NRA's powers and duties extend beyond mere environmental protection, such as flood defence and land drainage, the WRA imposes statutory duties on the NRA in relation to the exercise of its functions. The most important of these so far as the environment is concerned is s 16, which imposes a duty on the NRA to exercise its functions so 'as to further the conservation and enhancement of natural beauty and the conservation of flora, fauna and geological or physiographical features of special interest'. Section 16 also imposes other duties in relation to the protection of historical sites and promotion of public access.

It is worth bearing these obligations in mind when dealing with the NRA. A failure to comply with these duties may form the basis for judicial review proceedings. Short of this, however, the duties remain highly relevant to the exercise of functions such as the grant of consents to discharge, particularly as the grant of a consent is discretionary whereas observation of the environmental duty is not.

POLLUTION CONTROL FUNCTIONS

1.15   Part III of the WRA sets out, in three separate chapters, the pollution control functions of the NRA. Included are the following matters.

Quality objectives

1.16   Sections 82–4 set out a framework for the introduction of a system of water quality objectives (WQOs). The scheme is based on a water quality classification which the DoE prescribes in regulations, which will be based on one or more of the following criteria: the use to which the waters are to be put; the presence or absence of specified substances and the concentrations at which they are permitted to be present; other specific requirements for the water in question.

In effect these classifications will enable the purity of rivers to be assessed. A similar informal system has been in operation for some years, but the new one will be more comprehensive, and will take into account the increasing obligations imposed on water quality by EC Directives albeit the present government are doing their best to reduce the impact of these Directives. The new system is at present in the consultation stage.

Once the classification system is in place the DoE will have the power to introduce a system of WQOs to provide not only an accurate national classification of all waters but also an effective system for improving the quality of some waters. Again, the basic policy of objectives is incorporated in earlier legislation, but it has always been discretionary and the discretion has never been exercised. It is to be hoped that this time things will be different. If properly implemented the scheme should have major potential for improving the water environment. The WRA provides for public consultation prior to determination of WQOs. The NRA has already initiated consultations on the overall philosophy. Once WQOs have been established a duty is imposed on the DoE and the NRA to ensure the objectives are observed at all times.

Pollution offences

1.17 The question of pollution offences is considered in detail in Chapter 5. This part of the Act also gives the NRA the power to grant consents to discharge, a matter which is discussed in Chapter 4.

Preventative powers

1.18 A welcome development, in view of the number of avoidable incidents of pollution, is the inclusion of some provisions designed to prevent pollution occuring in the first place.

(1) Section 92 gives the DoE the power to make regulations which can prohibit a person from having custody of polluting matter unless prescribed works and precautions are taken, and obliging a person to carry out necessary works. To date the only regulations to have been made are the Control of Pollution (Silage Slurry and Agricultural Fuel Oil) Regulations 1991. These sources of pollution constitute the vast majority of agricultural pollutions, and the Regulations give the NRA practical powers to ensure that these pollutants are stored in a manner that reduces the risk of their escape.

(2) Section 93 provides for the DoE to authorise the setting up of water protection zones, which will enable the NRA to regulate activities likely to cause pollution in a particular catchment. This is potentially a very useful power in situations where persistent pollution from disparate sources threatens the integrity of a particular river or catchment. The Welsh region are at present setting up a water protection zone in the upper Dee, a spawning area for salmon.

(3) Sections 93 to 96 set up a system for the establishment of nitrate-sensitive areas with a view to controlling the use of fertilisers in given regions.

(4) Finally s 97 gives MAFF power to approve Codes of Good Agricultural Practice. Copies of approved codes are available from MAFF offices in London, but they are of limited value, since the Act specifically states that a contravention shall not give rise to criminal or civil liability. However, failure to observe these codes is likely to be persuasive in determining liability in negligence, and, no doubt, influential in sentencing in criminal cases.

Supplemental provisions

1.19   The final sections of Part III of the Act set out sundry other provisions relevant to the NRA's pollution control functions, two of which are worth mentioning. First there is a definition of controlled waters. This is particularly relevant to the principal pollution offence which relates to controlled waters. In simple terms controlled waters are all inland waters, including water in underground strata, and coastal waters up to a three-mile limit. Thus the authorisation and criminal framework apply equally to those waters.

The second section to note is s 101, which provides that the time for initiation of any summary criminal proceedings under this Part of the Act shall be one year rather the usual six months.

Other relevant provisions in the WRA

1.20   Sections 169–73 of the WRA give NRA officers powers of entry on to land to carry out its functions under the Act. In particular power is given to take samples and to collect evidence. Most data collected by the NRA are available for inspection in public registers (*see* Chapter 9).

Section 161 entitles the NRA to carry out clean-up operations and recover the cost of so doing. The section is concerned with anticipated, actual and past pollution and enables the NRA to carry out preventative and remedial works, and to reinstate flora and fauna. It goes on to provide that the costs of such works will be recoverable from any person who caused or knowingly permitted the pollution to occur. The NRA regularly uses this provision to recover costs when prosecuting polluters. It is, however, not often used as the basis of a civil claim. Nevertheless the wording of the section is broad enough for it to be used much more positively than hitherto by the NRA, since it gives them the opportunity to tackle pollution problems and recover the cost of doing so from polluters. Sometimes a civil claim will arise where costs have not been recovered in a prosecution. However s 161 could be used in circumstances where criminal libility may not exist.

WATER RESOURCES FUNCTIONS

1.21   Part II of the WRA contains the NRA's powers and obligations relating to water resources. The NRA is responsible for operating the consent system for abstraction and impoundment of water, and this Part of the Act sets out the offences relating to unauthorised abstractions and impoundments. Chapter 4 looks at the consent system, and Chapter 5 considers criminal offences.

This Part of the Act also contains some more general provisions relating to water resources. The issue of river flows and the use of underground water was much publicised during the drought years of 1989–91. Before the creation of the NRA the water authorities were responsible for both raising revenue from water supply and protecting the environment from over-exploitation. Under the Water Resources Act 1963, which governed the water resources regime before the 1991 Act, there was an obligation to establish minimum acceptable flows (MAF) for all main rivers in England and Wales. It is an indication of priorities in that period that the government and the water authorities managed to avoid setting a single MAF before the repeal of the 1963 Act in 1989.

The purpose of establishing MAFs is to dovetail with the imposition of WQOs to provide an overall management of the water environment that will offer protection to water users and the environment.

The MAF provisions have been re-enacted in ss 21–3 of the Act, although their imposition is now discretionary rather than mandatory. These sections provide the framework for preparing a scheme and consulting with affected parties before the MAF is imposed. To date no MAF has been established although the WRA are starting consultations with parties. However, it is to be hoped that MAFs will follow the introduction of WQOs, since the assessment of acceptable concentrations of polluting inputs to a watercourse, and its general well-being, are both seriously compromised if flows are not also taken into account.

Section 19 of the Act imposes a duty on the NRA to take all such action it shall consider necessary to conserve, redistribute or otherwise augment water resources, and to secure their proper use.

There is no doubt that since the creation of the NRA the environmental aspect of water resources has been taken much more seriously, not least as the climatic conditions have brought the issue into sharp focus. Water resources had previously been treated almost as if they were available on demand. The NRA now acknowledges that this approach is no longer tenable in relation to, for example, abstractions from the chalk aquifers in the south of England. Nonetheless, the approach to the issue of water resources is still relatively low key, given the impact of low flows on the health of the environment. The views of communities where local rivers are 'disappearing' in dry weather conditions are now being heeded. But by far the largest users of water are the statutory water companies who, by virtue of existing licences, have grown accustomed to the concept of resources on demand, so that their access to water is protected even in times of drought.

In Yorkshire the NRA applied for borehole abstraction to be used to augment flows in the River Ouse to facilitate increased abstraction by the water undertaker. This application met with concerted opposition, and the NRA withdrew. The application led to consideration of issues such as the lack of any coherent policy in the previous decades for water supply in the Yorkshire area, and equally the lack of investment. Throughout the country the rate of loss of water between the point of abstraction and the tap is approximately 20 per cent. There are also inadequate facilities for distributing water around the system, and storing it. Increased abstraction will always be the easy and the cheaper option, but, as the Ouse application has shown, that option is no longer so straightforward.

LAND DRAINAGE AND FLOOD CONTROL FUNCTIONS

1.22   There are provisions for land drainage and flood control in both the WRA and the Land Drainage Act 1991 (LDA). Under the latter Act the functions are sometimes carried out by internal drainage boards in place of the NRA. These bodies exist primarily in agricultural areas where drainage is essential for the continuation of agriculture.

Section 16 of the LDA authorises an appointed drainage board to maintain, improve and construct new drainage within its authorised area.

Part IV of the WRA gives the NRA the power to set up flood defence schemes through the agency of flood defence committees.

Sections 23–5 of the LDA set out a system of consents and criminal sanctions relating to the flow of main rivers which are considered in Chapters 2 and 3.

The exercise of land drainage and flood protection functions by the NRA or internal drainage boards is subject to the environmental duties mentioned above. The LDA imposes similiar duties by ss 12 and 13.

LAND

INTRODUCTION

1.23 Where contamination of land is present in sufficient concentrations and has been the subject of past disposal, it is the subject of waste management regulation under the EPA and environmental quality regulation expressed in statute law. A particular feature of environmental law as it relates to contamination of land is the discretion given to regulators.

Liabilities arise from relatively subjective tests such as 'harm' and 'damage' to environmental targets which may vary according to circumstances and will generally need to be determined on a case-specific basis.

Waste comes from a variety of sources—household, industrial, commercial, radioactive and agricultural, to name a few. The disposal of this waste has to be controlled. Waste legislation, therefore, controls the collection and disposal of waste, sets up an administrative structure and licensing system and means to enforce those controls.

The waste management regime in the United Kingdom, at present, is undergoing substantial change. Part II of the EPA introduced a new administrative structure and management controls. The waste management licensing system was brought into force by the Waste Management Licensing Regulations 1994 (SI No 1056). Any references, therefore to 'the Act' in this section will be to the EPA.

DEFINITION OF WASTE

1.24   Controlled is defined in s 75(4) of the EPA as 'household, industrial and commercial waste or any such waste'. A more detailed explanation is provided in the Controlled Waste Regulations Act 1992 (SI 1992 No 588). Wastes not included in this definition are agricultural, explosive, radioactive, sewage and waste from mines and quarries.

REGULATORY BODIES

1.25   There are three principal bodies which operate at local government level: Waste Regulation Authorities (WRA), Waste Disposal Authorities (WDA) and Waste Collection Authorities (WCA).

Waste Regulation Authorities

1.26   WRAs control the carriage and disposal of waste. They draw up waste disposal plans which cover such matters as the amount of waste to be disposed of, methods of disposal and the location of disposal sites. These sites are licensed by the WRA which supervises their operation. WRAs also process applications for licences, charge fees and decide who, under s 74 of the EPA, is a 'fit and proper person' to hold a licence. In addition, they supervise closed landfill sites.

Waste Disposal Authorities

1.27   WDAs' functions are limited to the organisation of the disposal of waste collected in their areas and the provision of refuse amenity sites. However, these functions must be carried out by Local Authority Waste Disposal Companies (LAWDC) or private contractors. LAWDCs are companies formed by local authorities to carry out disposal as a result of the DoE's policy of separating waste disposal and regulatory functions. There will be a transitional period while these functions are transferred although WDAs will retain certain powers such as directing a collection authority to deliver waste and they will have input to waste recycling plans.

Waste Collection Authorities

1.28 WCAs collect waste from households and make arrangements to collect commercial and industrial waste if requested to do so. They also have the power to serve notices requiring the removal of unlawfully deposited waste or to collect it themselves. The waste collected by the WCA must be delivered to the local WDA or kept for recycling. The WCA must draw up a recycling plan for waste collected and has additional powers to buy waste for recycling and to dispose of the recycled waste.

The table below sets out the bodies that make up the WRAs, WDAs and WCAs in England and Wales.

	WRAs	WDAs	WCAs
England	County Councils	County Councils	District Councils
Wales	District Councils	District Councils	District Councils
Greater London	London Waste Regulation Authority	London WDAs Common Council (City of London)	London Boroughs Councils Common Council (City of London)
Metropolitan areas	Greater Manchester WRA Merseyside WRA District Councils in other regions	Greater Manchester WDA (except Wigan District Council) Merseyside WDA District Councils in other regions	

GOVERNMENT POWERS

1.29 The government department with overall responsibility for waste management and control in the United Kingdom is the DoE in England, and the Welsh and Scottish Offices in their respective countries. It supervises WRAs. To do this it may appoint inspectors and if it discovers that a WRA has not been performing its functions

properly it may make a default order against it. This directs the
defaulting WRA to carry out a specific function and states the
manner and time in which it is to be done. If the WRA still refuses
then the Secretary of State may apply to the High Court or transfer
any of the WRA's functions to his department (s 72 of the EPA).

The Secretary of State's supervisory powers include the review of
waste disposal plans and waste recycling plants and the issue of
guidance notes. The latter help WRAs in the licensing of sites, the
supervising of closed sites and the determination of who is a 'fit and
proper person'. He also has the power to direct a WRA to include
a condition in a licence, to revoke or suspend a licence, to supervise
a licence, set a schedule of fees for the grant of licences and to determine disputes between WRAs and the NRA.

INSPECTORS

1.30   To help them in their duties, WRAs, WDAs, WCAs and the
Secretary of State may appoint inspectors (s 69 of the EPA).
(Guidance on the exercise of these powers is given at Paragraph 2.32
of the Department of the Environment's Waste Management Paper
(WMP) No 4.) An inspector may enter premises which he has reason
to believe it necessary for him to enter. This wide discretion is qualified in that entry must be made at a reasonable time, although the
inspector may enter premises at any time if he thinks that there is an
immediate risk of serious environmental harm or harm to human
health (s 69(3)(a) of the EPA).

When on the premises the inspector has various powers under
ss 69(3) and 70:

   (a) to make such investigations and examinations as are neces-
        sary in the circumstances;
   (b) to take photographs, measures, recordings and samples of
        articles and substances on the premises including samples of
        land, air or water;
   (c) to require the dismantling of any article likely to cause pol-
        lution or harm to human health;
   (d) to take possession of that article to ensure that it is available
        in any proceedings under Part II of the Act;
   (e) to question any person who he thinks can give him informa-
        tion;

(f) to require the production of records whether documentary or held on computer;

(g) to seize or instruct that an article which he thinks is an imminent danger of serious pollution or harm to human health be rendered harmless even if this means destroying it (s 70).

If he is obstructed in the performance of his duties or someone does not comply with his requests that person will be guilty of an offence (s 70(4)).

All the above appears to give inspectors many powers with a wide discretion in their use. However, certain safeguards are provided:

(a) an inspector must consult the appropriate person before dismantling an article (s 69(6));

(b) special procedures must be followed when taking samples;

(c) if an inspector removes an article he must leave a notice either with a responsible person or in a prominent place stating that he has taken it under powers granted to him by the Act (s 69(7));

(d) any answers given by a person questioned will not be admissible against him in criminal proceedings (s 69(8)).

Despite this, he cannot be held liable for anything done by him in the performance of his powers if he did them in good faith and there were reasonable grounds for doing them.

WASTE DISPOSAL PLANS AND RECYCLING

1.31 WRAs set out waste policies for their area. These policies consist of waste disposal or recycling plans, in conjunction with development plans drawn up under planning legislation. (Development plans are covered in Chapter 3.) WRAs draw up the waste disposal plans and detail the current and proposed provisions for the treatment and disposal of waste in their area (s 50 of the EPA). To do this each WRA has to consider what arrangements are necessary to treat and dispose of waste and how it should operate its licensing functions in the light of those arrangements. Points that have to be considered include the volumes and types of waste that will arise, the methods that must be used to treat or dispose of the waste and the practicality of waste recycling. In essence, the plan will set out the policy of the WRA, guidance notes issued by the Secretary of State, disposal sites and equipment to be used.

In drawing up their plans the WRAs must consult others: the

NRA, WCAs, especially in relation to waste recycling, representatives of the waste management industry and the public (s 50). Finally, the draft plan must be sent to the Secretary of State (s 50(10)). The plan is open for inspection by the public and the WRA must conduct periodic revision of the plan.

A waste plan is not definitive. A planning authority can take such a waste plan into account when making decisions but is not required to follow it absolutely. It does not have the same authority, therefore, as a development plan.

WASTE RECYCLING

1.32   The WCAs are principally responsible for waste recycling (s 48(1)). It is their job to draw up the waste recycling plans referred to above (s 49). (Guidance on the preparation of the plans is provided in WMP 28.) The WCA must first make a survey of its area and find ways in which household and commercial waste can be recycled. The plan will detail the arrangements for separation, baling and packaging of waste for recycling; the types and amount of waste to be recycled; arrangements with other bodies; plant and equipment required; an estimate of the costs of recycling the waste and any savings expected to be made. The plan is sent to the Secretary of State for the Environment who may make such directions as he deems necessary. There is no public consultation procedure as with waste disposal plans but the plan, once settled, must be open to public inspection. A copy must also be sent to the relevant WRA and WDA.

The usual procedure is for WCAs to pass waste on to a WDA. If a WCA decides to keep waste for recycling itself, it must inform the WDA as soon as possible as the WDA may object, especially if it has already entered into a contract to recycle the waste. If the WDA objects then the WCA must deliver the waste to it. WDAs also have the power to acquire waste for recycling or to sell waste they have received.

The EPA has introduced a system of recycling credits to encourage recycling (s 52). Increased recycling will lead to savings because WDAs will have less waste to dispose of. The authority that makes the saving will pay a credit to the body which has allowed it to make the saving. The credit will be the amount that the WDA would have incurred to dispose of the waste less any sum it has had to pay to organise for the waste to be recycled. Thus, if a WCA retains some waste for recycling then the WDA must give it a recycling credit. If a company collects waste and retains some for recycling then, in similar vein, it must also be given a credit for the waste retained. At present, the system of credits only applies to household waste.

LITTER

1.33 Part IV of the EPA and the Litter Act 1983 are the main statutes regulating litter. Under the former, county, district and London borough councils are the principal litter authorities while the Litter Act includes parish and community councils, a joint board of any two or more of these authorities or a Park board. Overall, the Secretary of State for the Environment oversees litter controls in England and the respective Secretaries of State in Wales and Scotland.

A litter authority is responsible for cleaning the land under its control of litter and refuse. The Act does not define litter. However, at common law whether something is litter is a matter of fact—*Hills v Davies* (1903) 88 LT 464. It has been held that an abandoned motor car is litter—*Vaughan v Briggs* [1960] 2 All ER 473. Land is that land in the open air which is under the control of the litter authority to which the public has access either with or without payment. Some litter authorities have been specially designated as responsible for litter control. Transport undertakers, governing bodies of universities, colleges of higher or further education and state-maintained or grant-aided schools fall into this category.

Under the Act a litter authority may designate litter control areas. Such an order may only be made if the particular area is likely to detract from local amenities because of the presence of litter. Only certain types of land can be so designated and not land that already falls within the litter authority's control. They include camping and caravan sites, picnic areas, aerodromes, coastal resorts, car parks, places of entertainment, industrial estates, shopping centres and open air markets. The occupier of a litter control area is under a duty to keep the land clear of litter. He will be notified and given 21 days to comment on the proposal.

Litter authorities also have the power to issue street litter control notices, the purpose of which is to prevent accumulation of litter in any street or adjacent land. The notice must identify the premises to which it relates and the grounds on which it is issued. It specifies the requirements to ensure the area is kept clean such as the provision and emptying of litter bins or the clearance of all litter within a specified time. Such notices are issued in respect of commercial or retail premises used for the sale of food and drink off the premises, places of entertainment, service stations and banks or building societies with cash machines on outside walls.

AIR

INTRODUCTION

1.34   The IPC provisions in EPA Part I also form a framework of controls for air pollution control by local authorities (APC). The controls arise from the same statutory provisions and the framework is in most respects identical. The Environmental Protection (Prescribed Processes and Substances) Regulations 1991 (as subsequently amended) set out a number of processes which are identified as Part B processes and are therefore subject to local authority control in respect of air pollution. These Part B processes are regulated only by local authorities (at district level in the Shires) in respect of atmospheric pollution. If the process leads to emissions to land or water separate authorisation is required from the appropriate regulatory authority (*see* sections on water and land above and Chapter 4).

In a few exceptional cases local authorities may not exercise control over Part B processes. These exceptions include:

(a) where the Secretary of State has issued a direction under s 4 of the EPA transferring controls over a specific Part B process or APC generally to HMIP (*see* para 1.5 above);

(b) where the process includes a Part A process as well; in these cases HMIP will deal with all of the processes together;

(c) where the process is exempt from control under reg 4 of the Environmental Protection (Prescribed Processes and Substances) Regulations 1991, for example because no substance prescribed in the Regulations in respect of air is to be released or is to be released in trivial amounts.

EPA Part I refers throughout to 'enforcing authorities'. This phrase includes local authorities in respect of Part B processes and HMIP in respect of Part A processes. The statutory framework is identical.

Like IPC, APC is based on the need for processes to be authorised. The APC controls have also been phased in but all existing processes subject to APC should have applied for authorisation. APC controls require the operator and local authority to ensure the use of the best available techniques not entailing excessive cost for the reduction and minimisation of atmospheric pollution (*see* Chapter 4). There is no requirement for the process to be operated in a way that achieves the best practicable option for the environment as a whole. This is simply because controls are only exercised in respect of emissions to one environmental medium.

CONTROLS PREDATING **IPC** AND **APC**

1.35 The statutory framework that existed before the EPA still applies to some processes:
  (a) existing processes which are subject to IPC but which are not yet required to apply for authorisation under the phasing-in provisions;
  (b) processes subject to IPC or APC which have applied for authorisation but whose applications have yet to be granted or refused or if refused are subject to appeal.
The pre-EPA controls are the Alkali Works Regulation Act 1906 and s 5 of the Health and Safety at Work Act 1974. The controls under these Acts are restricted to atmospheric pollution (although of course other consents may be held in respect of water or land). Alkali works are subject to control under the 1906 Act in respect of emissions of substances listed in Sched 2 to the Health and Safety (Emissions into the Atmosphere) Regulations 1983. In addition, other processes listed in Sched 1 to the 1983 Regulations are subject to registration under the 1906 Act. The basic obligation of alkali works and other registered works is to use the best practicable means to minimise emissions of such substances.
Controls under the pre-EPA system are exercised by HMIP.

CLEAN AIR ACT 1993

1.36 The Clean Air Act 1993 consolidates the Clean Air Acts 1956 and 1968 and certain provisions from the Control of Pollution Act 1974. The 1956 Act arose out of concerns over inner city smog (particularly the great London smog of 1952 in which it is said thousands died). The 1968 Act refined and extended the provisions of the earlier Act.

The key features of the statutory framework set out in the consolidated Act are:

(a) the prohibition of dark smoke emissions;
(b) controls over the design of certain furnaces and chimneys;
(c) the use of smoke control areas; and
(d) the provisions relating to information on atmospheric pollution formerly contained in the Control of Pollution Act 1974 (these are considered in full in Chapter 9).

Local authorities (district councils in the Shires and metropolitan and London boroughs elsewhere) are under a duty to enforce the controls (s 55 of the 1993 Act).

Dark smoke control

1.37   From a practical point of view the provisions relating to the control of dark smoke emissions contained in ss 1–3 of the 1993 Act are probably the most important. The details of the controls are considered in Chapter 5 as controls are imposed via criminal prohibitions. Dark smoke is defined in s 3 as being smoke which if compared with a chart known as a Ringelmann Chart would appear to be as dark as Shade 2 or darker. It is not necessary for an actual comparison with a Ringelmann Chart to have taken place. Smoke emissions from chimneys are controlled under s 1 and from industrial or trade premises by virtue of s 2.

In addition to the controls over dark smoke emissions, s 5 of the 1993 Act and the Clean Air (Emission of Grit and Dust from Furnaces) Regulations 1971 set prescribed levels for emissions for certain types of furnace. These provisions are enforced by criminal sanctions which are considered in Chapter 5.

Controls over furnace design

1.38   New furnaces (other than domestic furnaces—on the meaning of domestic *see Re Willesden Corporation* [1944] 2 All ER 600) must be capable so far as is practicable of operating without emitting smoke when burning fuel of a type for which it was designed: s 4(2). Furnaces installed in accordance with plans and specifications submitted and approved by local authorities are deemed to comply with s 4. Notice must be given to the local authority of intention to install a new furnace in order to assist the local authority in enforcing these provisions.

The controls over the design of all furnaces (not just installations of new non-domestic furnaces) are now contained in ss 6, 7 and 8 of the 1993 Act. They apply only to the more substantial furnaces defined in s 6 (ie those which burn pulverised fuel or solid fuel at a rate of 45.4 kilograms or more an hour or burn liquid or gas at a rate equivalent to 366.4 kilowatts per hour or more) and s 8 (larger domestic furnaces).

Such furnaces may only be used (subject to a criminal penalty— *see* Chapter 5) if fitted with properly maintained and operating dust and grit arresting apparatus. The design of the grit and dust arresting apparatus is subject to prior approval from the local authority.

Certain furnaces are exempted from the requirements of s 6 by s 7 and the Clean Air (Arrestment Plant) (Exemption) Regulations 1969. In addition, individual furnaces may seek exemption by local authority approval under s 7. Such approval may be given only where the authority is satisfied that the emission of grit or dust will not amount to a nuisance or be prejudicial to health. If the local authority fails to determine the application within eight weeks a deemed exemption is granted. An exemption may be granted conditionally or unconditionally. An appeal may be made to the Secretary of State against an adverse determination.

It is possible under s 47 of the 1993 Act for the requirements of s 6 to be extended to fumes and gases by statutory instrument. This has not yet been done.

The provisions relating to the installation of grit and dust arresting apparatus and new furnaces are enforced by a series of criminal sanctions which are considered in Chapter 5.

Controls over chimney design

1.39   Section 14 of the 1993 Act controls chimney installation and use. Where any plans submitted for building regulation approval reveal the construction of a chimney (except in the case of the construction of residential buildings or offices) the local authority must reject the plans unless satisfied that the height of the chimney is sufficient to prevent, so far as is practicable, smoke, dust or gases becoming prejudicial to health or a nuisance.

In addition, for the more substantial furnaces defined in s 6 of the Act, the use of the furnace is not permitted unless the height of the chimney has been approved and the conditions concerning any approval are complied with. Approvals under s 14 are considered in Chapter 4. The provisions of s 14 are enforced by criminal sanctions which are covered in Chapter 5.

HMIP has issued guidance on chimney heights in 'Guidelines on Discharge Stack Heights for Polluting Emissions' (1993).

Smoke control areas

1.40 Smoke control areas were originally introduced in s 11 of the 1956 Act, which gave power to local authorities to declare all or part of their area to be a 'smoke control area'. The provisions are now contained in Part III of the 1993 Act.

The consequence of the designation of a smoke control area is, subject to exemptions, that if smoke is emitted from a chimney of any building the occupier of the building is guilty of an offence (*see* Chapter 5 for details). Thus controls under the Act are extended in the smoke control area to domestic premises and non-dark smoke. The designation by a local authority is flexible. It may be limited to certain classes of building or may exempt specified buildings or classes of buildings or fireplaces conditionally or unconditionally. Alternatively, the designation could be a blanket provision.

In addition, general exemptions have been created by regulations authorising certain fuels for use as being smokeless and exempting by order certain classes of fireplaces.

Subject to what is said below local authorities start the procedure for designating an area a smoke control area. Thus, if it is felt by persons in a locality that it would be desirable to have a smoke control designation the starting point must be for the local authority to be lobbied. The procedure for designating a smoke control area is set out in Sched 1 to the 1993 Act. Publicity is ensured through advertisement in the *London Gazette* and local newspapers. The proposed order must be available for inspection. Copies of the order must be posted throughout the affected area. Any representations must be considered. Once made the order must be registered as a local land charge.

Section 25 of the 1993 Act requires local authorities to make grants available for the cost of adapting or replacing domestic fireplaces and chimneys so they could be used to burn authorised fuels.

The smoke control area policy was successful under the 1956 Act but did not provide coverage over significant parts of the country where air quality was considered to be a problem. Section 8 of the 1968 Act therefore gave central government powers to direct a local authority, where it was expedient to do so to abate air pollution, to prepare and submit proposals for the making of smoke control areas. Powers were also created for the minister to direct a local authority to make an order designating a smoke control area. Over 5,000 smoke control areas have been designated and the problems of smoke from domestic properties largely eliminated. (This may of course owe more to a change in the way that homes are heated than to the Clean Air Acts.)

General enforcement provisions under the Clean Air Act 1993

1.41 Most of the provisions of the Clean Air Act 1993 are enforced by way of criminal sanctions. However, in addition to the offences considered in Chapter 5, there are other enforcement powers. Although these are not available to private individuals objectors may find it useful to point them out to local authorities in cases where it seems that action could be taken under the 1993 Act. In addition, objectors may wish to point out to local authorities their general duty to enforce Parts I–III of the 1993 Act (s 55), although whether it is possible to enforce the duty by judicial review requiring prosecution of a specific offence seems unlikely. (Chapter 7 considers judicial review and prosecution policies.)

The main provisions are:
(a) information acquisition powers under ss 12, 36 and 58;
(b) powers of entry under s 56.

CONTROL OF POLLUTION ACT 1974 AND NOISE

1.42 Miscellaneous provisions in the 1974 Act deal with noise from construction sites, street noise and noise abatement zones.

Construction site noise

1.43 Construction site noise is subject to the normal statutory nuisance provisions (Chapter 4). In addition, a local authority may serve a notice under s 60 of the 1974 Act imposing requirements as to how the construction works are to be carried out. Alternatively, the person intending to carry out the construction works can apply to the local authority for a consent. In either case if the person is dissatisfied with the local authority's determination he or she may appeal to the magistrates' court. If a consent is granted and complied with, the local authority may not take action under the statutory nuisance provisions of EPA (Part III).

Street noise

1.44   Street noise is subject to control under s 62 of the 1974 Act which prohibits the use of loudspeakers in the street between 9 pm and 8 am subject to minor exceptions. Section 62 has recently been amended by the Noise and Statutory Nuisance Act 1993 to allow the Secretary of State by order to alter the times at which loudspeakers may be used in the street so as to make them more restrictive. Schedule 2 to the 1993 Act allows local authorities by resolution to introduce a consent system which allows loudspeaker noise which otherwise would contravene s 62. Consents are subject to restrictions and may not permit loudspeaker noise in connection with any election, entertainment, trade or business. *See also* the Household Emission Noise Regulations 1994.

Street noise is also subject to control under s 79 of the EPA (Chapter 4) and Sched 3 to the Noise and Statutory Nuisance Act 1993. Schedule 3 applies to audible intruder alarms and allows local authorities to apply strict controls to those installing or occupying premises in which audible intruder alarms have been installed. Schedule 3 will only apply where the relevant local authority has resolved that it should so apply. Clearly this Schedule is designed to deal with the problem of burglar alarms which go off in urban areas and very often are not turned off for hours. If this is a concern of an interest group or residents association it may be worth lobbying the local authority to take action under Sched 3.

Noise abatement zones

1.45   Noise abatement zones may be established by local authorities in order to prevent increases in levels of neighbourhood noise or indeed to reduce such noise. After an area has been so designated the local authority will create a register of noise levels for the types of premises included in the noise abatement zone designation. The noise levels have to be measured in accordance with the Control of Noise (Measurement and Registers) Regulations 1976. All noise registers for noise abatement zones are subject to public inspection (Chapter 9). Once the register has been compiled the registered level of noise for any building included may not be exceeded. Indeed it is possible for the local authority to serve a reduction notice reducing the registered level. There is a right of appeal against a reduction notice to the magistrates' court.

Section 67 requires an acceptable level of noise for new buildings within a noise abatement zone to be entered on the register.

It is possible to seek the consent of the local authority to exceed the registered level and to appeal to the Secretary of State against their determination or non-determination within two months.

It is a criminal offence to breach the registered noise level (*see* Chapter 5).

Those concerned with reducing the level of noise pollution in a particular area might lobby their local authority to establish a zone under the 1974 Act and where such a zone has been established to serve appropriate noise reduction notices.

Statutory framework—overlaps and interactions in atmospheric pollution

1.46 There are a number of alternative regimes in operation in respect of atmospheric pollution. These are principally the statutory nuisance controls under EPA Part III, IPC and APC under EPA Part I and the Clean Air Act 1993. How do these controls interact?

The position is that:

(1) Statutory nuisance powers may not be used in respect of smoke (s 79(1)(b) of the EPA), dust, steam and smell (s 97(1)(d) of the EPA) or accumulations or deposits (s 79(1)(e) of the EPA) if proceedings could be brought under the EPA Part I, the Alkali etc Works Regulation Act 1906 or s 5 of the Health and Safety at Work Act 1974 (*see* Chapter 4). Exceptionally, statutory nuisance powers can be used in respect of these matters but only with the consent of the Secretary of State.

(2)   Clean Air Act controls may not be used if proceedings could be brought under the EPA Part I, the Alkali etc Works Regulation Act 1906 or s 5 of the Health and Safety at Work Act 1974. Exceptionally they may be so used but only with the consent of the Secretary of State.

OTHER ORGANISATIONS WITH ENVIRONMENTAL RESPONSIBILITIES

INTRODUCTION

1.47   The final section of this chapter will look at some other institutions that are not regulatory bodies but whose activities are environmentally sensitive such that they are regulated in the manner in which their activities impact on the environment.

THE FORESTRY COMMISSION

1.48   Established in 1919, this commission is a government department which reports to the Secretary of State for Scotland, the Minister of Agriculture, Fisheries and Food and the Secretary of State for Wales. It operates within a statutory framework of the Forestry Acts 1967 and 1979, the Plant Health Act 1967, the Countryside (Scotland) Act 1967 and the Countryside Act 1968 and has the specific duty to endeavour to achieve a reasonable balance between the needs of forestry and those of the environment. It differs from other government departments in that it is run by a chairman and a board.

It has a dual role: as the national forestry authority it advises on and implements government policy for all the country's forests and promotes the interests of forestry in general; as Forest Enterprise, it manages 40 per cent of the country's forests and is responsible for producing timber, providing recreation and conserving the environment of its woodlands. The commission is under a general duty to promote the interests of forestry, the development of afforestation and the production and supply of timber products. This includes the establishment and maintenance of adequate reserves of growing trees. It is obviously mainly concerned with the production of timber as indicated but this activity also involves it in wildlife and countryside management.

THE WATER INDUSTRY

1.49   The Water Industry Act 1991 (WIA) is the statutory basis for regulation of the water industry.

Sections 3 and 4 impose on water undertakers duties to, *inter alia*, so carry out their functions as to promote the conservation of flora and fauna. These duties are in the same form as those imposed on ministers and on the NRA under the WRA and considered at para 1.14 above.

Section 68 imposes a duty on water undertakers to supply only wholesome water for domestic purposes, and to ensure that the standard of water supplied from their area does not deteriorate.

Section 94 imposes a duty on every sewerage undertaker to provide, improve and extend such a system of public sewers and so to cleanse and maintain those sewers as to ensure that that area is and continues to be effectively drained.

Powers are also vested in sewerage undertakers to control the type of trade effluent received by them into sewerage works. The WIA provides that the occupier of trade premises shall be entitled to discharge trade effluent into public sewers provided that it is done with the undertaker's consent (s 118, WIA). This proviso gives to the undertaker the power to control the quality of the effluent that is ultimately received at its works for treatment.

A system for the grant of consents is set out in the WIA which has many parallels with the consent system for discharges into the water environment regulated by the NRA and described in Chapter 4. It differs, however, in that there is no obligation to advertise applications nor any right for third parties to make representations. The rationale behind this is that the trade effluent received will be subject to treatment at the sewage works before discharge into any river, and public participation is possible in relation to the issue of that consent. Unfortunately this rationale is somewhat flawed, since the ultimate consent to discharge may well not have as one of its parameters the particular substance which is regulated in the trade effluent consent even though it is in fact present in the final effluent.

The sewerage undertakers are bound to maintain a register of consents to discharge trade effluent and to have this open to the public. This requirement does not extend to the results of analyses of samples taken of trade effluent.

Section 211 of the WIA restricts the right to bring prosecutions for discharges of trade effluent into sewers without consent to the undertakers, unless the Attorney-General permits otherwise.

THE COAL INDUSTRY

1.50   This industry is currently subject to privatisation legislation. It is an industry that leaves a legacy of current and future pollution of water by reason of minewater discharges. The Coal Industry Bill does not clarify the legal uncertainty over the liability for polluting discharges from old mine workings.

The Bill does, however, contain a duty to be imposed on the new Coal Authority, similar to that imposed on the water undertakers, to have regard to the promotion of the conservation of flora and fauna when exercising its powers.

The coal industry illustrates the difficult question of liability for historic pollution. During the passage of the Bill through Parliament there has been much debate as to the extent of environmental liability and who should shoulder that liability. Potential bidders for licences after privatisation have lobbied for statutory guarantees that they will only be held responsible for problems arising from their own mining activities, and not those that arise from surrounding workings that are geologically linked with them.

In many coal fields the balance of the underground water table was upset when mining started as long ago as the seventeenth century. For as long as mining continues, controlled pumping ensures that discharges of minewater are subject to consents that control their quality. Once that pumping stops, minewater finds its way out at the first available exit and often picks up polluting material from old mine workings.

While the issue of legal liability for these discharges remains a live one, a political problem also exists. The coal industry over the last century earned large profits and sustained economic activity. No part of those profits has been put aside to deal with the human or environmental consequences of the rundown of the industry and there is a marked reluctance to pay the price of decline.

THE ELECTRICITY AND NUCLEAR INDUSTRY

1.51   Part II of the Electricity Act 1989 ('the Act') reorganised the electricity generation and supply industry. Anyone may now apply for a licence to generate and supply electricity as required under ss 4–6 of the Act and s 7 allows conditions to be imposed. National Power Plc and Powergen Plc are the privatised successors of the old Central Electricity Generating Board, while Nuclear Electric Plc retains the nuclear stations and the remainder are state owned. National Grid Plc took over transmission functions and the 12 regional distribution companies are also now privatised.

Electricity supply

1.52 Under s 3 of the Act the Secretary of State for Energy is responsible for general supervision of electricity supply. He must promote the efficient and economical use of electricity, encourage research and protect the public from the dangers involved in the use and supply of electricity. He also has to consider the effect on the environment of the generation and supply of electricity.

Under s 36(1) a generating station cannot be constructed, extended or operated except in accordance with consents issued by the Secretary of State. He may include such conditions as he thinks fit. These may include conditions on ownership and operation. Planning permission is still, however, required.

As regards the installation of electrical lines or plant in, on or over any street, s 10 and Sched 4 to the Act dictate that public electricity suppliers must do as little damage as possible and must pay compensation for any damage done as a result of such installation and maintenance works. They must also ensure that the installations do not become a source of public danger. Section 37 of the Act requires the consent of the Secretary of State for the installation of overhead power lines.

The impact of overhead power lines on the environment has attracted a good deal of public concern. The organisation Rural England v Overhead Line Transmissions (REVOLT) sought input from ELF in relation to an application by National Grid to erect a line of pylons across North Yorkshire. Advice was given to the group that helped it to achieve agreement to run the power lines underground.

The Secretary of State is also responsible for control of the development of nuclear power. His powers are contained in various statutes: the Atomic Energy Act 1946, the Atomic Energy Authority Act 1954 and the Nuclear Installations Act 1965. These include the power to authorise inspection of and entry on certain premises, to acquire property compulsorily and to control the production and use of nuclear power. The United Kingdom is also a signatory to the Vienna Convention on Assistance in the case of a Nuclear Accident or Radiological Emergency which allows states to request assistance in the event of a nuclear incident from others who are party to the convention.

Nuclear installations

1.53   The Nuclear Installation Act 1965 requires a nuclear site licence for a nuclear power station. (This is in addition to the consents required for an oil, coal or gas-fired power station set out above.) These are issued by the Nuclear Installations Inspectorate, which carries out an assessment of the proposed developments. Conditions can be imposed and will regulate the operation of the plant and may require inspections and safety checks. One of the most well-known public inquiries into a proposal to build a nuclear power station was that at Sizewell in Suffolk. A total of 13,000 formal objections were received and the transcript of evidence contained over 14 million words. Permission for construction was eventually granted in March 1987.

Liability for damage from nuclear installations is governed by the Nuclear Installations Act 1965. Section 7 imposes strict liability in respect of certain occurrences or in connection with the use of licensed sites. Section 1 requires a licence to install or operate a nuclear installation. There must be no occurrences involving nuclear matter on site and no ionising radiation emitted during the period of the licensee's responsibility from any waste discharges on or from the site. Strict liability arises where injury to a person or damage to property arises from radiation. The damage, however, must be physical and not economic loss and it must relate to tangible property, not property rights. There is a 30-year time limit to bring a claim from the occurrence giving rise to the claim. Licensees have to make funds available to satisfy claims and any claim exceeding the limits imposed must be met out of the public funds.

If a child is born with disabilities attributable to injuries caused to its parents as a result of a nuclear incident s 3 of the Congenital Disabilities (Civil Liability) Act 1976 imposes liability on the licensee.

CHAPTER 2

COMMON LAW

INTRODUCTION

2.1 This chapter looks at the common law in relation to the environment, and at the advantages and disadvantages of the use of common law in dealing with environmental problems.

Claiming damages and seeking an injunction at common law is a more direct and effective recourse than other remedies dealt with in this book. The main limitations of common law are the need to bring the aggrieved party within the relatively strict requirements as to who is entitled to sue (locus), and the difficulties of funding what can be expensive cases quite apart from the potential liability for the defendants' costs if a claim is unsuccessful (*see* Chapter 10). Chapter 7 looks at how to apply common law as a remedy.

The problem of locus in environmental cases, in particular where a class of people are affected by a given problem, has been identified in the Introduction. The limitations which common law imposes on who can bring an action are set out in paras 2.6–2.10 below. In strict liability torts, the right to sue is dependent on establishing an interest in land. In negligence claims there must be sufficient proximity between plaintiff and defendant. Although this does impose restrictions on the ability to commence actions, it should be borne in mind that successful action by one person in an environmental case can benefit a class of people. An action that reduces or eliminates noise levels, or one that stops a polluting discharge into a river, benefits not only the plaintiff but other people and the environment generally. Environmental lawyers should always have this dimension in mind when considering common law as a remedy.

Common law nuisance, in particular, is a very flexible remedy and is receptive to new forms of liability being established within existing principles. Given that environmental law is still a nascent area it behoves the practitioner to be innovative in the application of common law.

The House of Lords judgment in the *Cambridge Water Company* case (*see* para 2.16 below for more detail) follows a long tradition, dating back to the last century, of using common law in environmental cases. The genesis of such actions was the *defence* of property rights. This has extended into the protection of the *use and enjoyment* of property rights. In many cases the heart of a dispute was commercial, where one or both parties were carrying on activities or exploiting resources in a manner which affected the other. That motivation of course remains relevant today, but these long-established principles give those with the locus the opportunity to use their rights to protect the environment.

A potential plaintiff in a common law claim must have some relationship with the act of the defendant that he complains of. Common law has determined that, with the exception of trespass:

(a) a plaintiff must have suffered some damage to himself or his property; and/or

(b) he must have an interest in the land by way of occupation or possession; or

(c) if the damage is to the person or chattels, there is a reasonably foreseeable link between the act of the defendant and damage suffered by the plaintiff.

It is not therefore open to a person to bring an action for environmental damage purely *pro bono publico*, nor for a person to bring an action on behalf of a class of people unless each member of that class has a good cause of action individually.

Common law environmental claims are of three distinct types:

(a) claims concerning damage to land or an interest in land, eg an oil spill;

(b) claims arising from the use and enjoyment of land, eg noise pollution, which may collectively be termed 'quality of life' claims;

(c) claims for personal injury arising from environmental pollution, eg the *Camelford* case.

This book is primarily concerned with the first two categories, and the following discussion will focus on the applicability of tortious remedies to those categories. Nevertheless many of the areas covered in this book (particularly in this chapter and Chapter 7) are also applicable to personal injury claims. This book does not focus in detail on issues of evidence in toxic tort cases, such as epidemiological evidence, although Chapter 9 touches on this issue.

Before considering who can bring actions in tort it is worth identifying what rights exist in the environmental media as incidents of ownership of land or an interest in land.

ENVIRONMENTAL MEDIA

2.2   The common law rights in the three environmental media that will give rise to a cause of action if those rights are infringed are as follows.

AIR

2.3   The proprietor of land owns the airspace above that land '*usque ad coelum*' (as high as the sky). Any person with a sufficient interest in land can complain about airborne pollution which affects use and enjoyment of land such as noise, smell, smoke, fumes or dust.

WATER

2.4   There is no ownership of water but the proprietor of land abutting water enjoys rights known as riparian rights. Water in this context is a river, a stream, a pool, a pond or a lake. Ownership of a bank of a river or other body of water also gives ownership of the bed of the river to the halfway point if the other bank is in different ownership. Additionally the owner enjoys a number of consequent rights, such as the right to fish, the right of navigation, and the right to use the water within limits defined by common law for domestic, agricultural or industrial purposes.

Underpinning these rights is the further right to receive water from a higher riparian owner without sensible diminution in quantity or quality. A proprietor must guard against infringing the rights of a lower owner as well as protecting his own. In addition to rights arising by virtue of ownership of land, rights in water can also be enjoyed by those who are granted rights by a riparian owner. An example is a lease of fishing rights.

In short, therefore, the owner of land abutting water has a right to take action where there is damage caused to the quantity or quality of that water or where the enjoyment of rights in that water is otherwise interfered with.

Property rights only attach to water flowing in defined channels, eg rivers, or to defined masses of water, eg ponds or lakes. This is so whether the water is surface water or underground water. No rights attach to water that percolates in no defined channel.

Tidal and coastal waters are vested in the Crown. However, rights of fishery can be acquired. Also, a claim of negligence may be available if a public right of fishing or bathing is interfered with in coastal waters by reason of pollution.

LAND

2.5   Subject to the qualification below, the owner of land owns not just the surface of that land and the airspace above it but also what lies underneath, technically down to the centre of the earth. In law the word 'land' also extends to buildings erected on land and objects attached to the buildings. Whatever is attached to the land becomes part of it. Land therefore includes the soil, the building and objects attached to it, trees, shrubs, hedges, plants and flowers growing on it. Minerals and other inorganic substances in the ground are also annexed to the land although ownership of coal, oil and natural gas is vested in the state.

In law, land also includes what are known as incorporeal hereditaments. These are generally rights which exist in land which cannot be seen or handled, as opposed to land and its attachments which are corporeal hereditaments. These may include easements such as rights of way over land and profits *à prendre* such as the right of fishing. Interference with an interest in land is just as actionable as interference with the land itself.

WHO CAN SUE?

2.6   A distinction must be made between torts of strict liability, where the right to sue derives from the ownership or occupation of land, and negligence, where it derives from the breach of the duty of care.

TORTS OF STRICT LIABILITY

2.7 In order to establish liability in the three torts of strict liability—trespass, nuisance and under the rule in *Rylands v Fletcher*—it is necessary to establish a right of occupation or to possession of the land, although the rules are slightly different in each case.

Trespass

2.8 The right to sue in trespass rests with the person in possession of the land in question, possession meaning the occupation or physical control of the land. For the purposes of environmental claims this definition would include any kind of tenant of residential property but not a lodger in a house of another or a guest at a hotel.

Nuisance

2.9 In nuisance it is necessary for the plaintiff to prove damage. The test is more difficult to satisfy than that in the case of trespass, in that the wrong is to the land itself or to an interest in the land or to the enjoyment of the land or interest. The basis of the right is, though, very similar. The right to sue lies with the person having possession or occupation of the land affected. The recent judgment of Havery, R, QC in the case of *Hunter and Others* v *Canary Wharf Limited* (September 1993 unreported) contains a useful review of the issues of title. In this case the plaintiffs are claiming damages for interference with television reception as a result of the construction of the Canary Wharf Tower. The plaintiffs include not only owners of affected premises, but also other occupiers. The Judge considered in particular another recent case of *Khorasandijan v Bush* [1993] All ER 669. In that case the court held that the plaintiff was entitled to an injunction to restrain the defendant from making unwanted phone calls to her home as a licencee of her mother. In the *Canary Wharf* case the judge concluded that the plaintiffs who were mere licencees could not sustain an action in nuisance. He distinguished the *Khorasandijan* case by deciding that it was limited in its scope to harassment cases, and did not extend to the full range of nuisance cases.

Rylands v Fletcher

2.10 Under the rule in *Rylands v Fletcher* the right to sue is not in theory linked to occupation of land. In the case of *British Celanese Ltd v (A H) Hunt* [1969] 2 All ER 1252, it was stated: 'Once there has been an escape . . . those damnified may claim. They do not need to be the occupiers of adjoining or indeed of any land.'

From the environmental point of view in practice a claim under the rule is likely to be of benefit only to a person having an interest in land since damage has to be proved, and environmental damage from an escape of dangerous material will entail damage to land or to an interest in land belonging to the plaintiff.

It is therefore a common element of claims for torts of strict liability that an interest in land or right of occupation is enjoyed and affected.

NEGLIGENCE

2.11 The situation in negligence is different. The test in negligence is whether the defendant owes a duty of care to the plaintiff and whether there has been a breach of that duty. Although property interests are often at the heart of environmental claims in negligence, there are situations where a party who has no legal interest in land that has been damaged may seek a remedy for environmental damage, particularly in cases involving personal injury.

It is beyond the scope of this book to set out in detail the principles of the duty of care. Examples are given below (paras 2.20–2.25) where negligence might be used as an environmental remedy, when the torts of strict liability are not available.

BREACH OF STATUTORY DUTY

2.12 An action for breach of statutory duty may exist, either where an Act of Parliament specifically provides that such a remedy shall lie, or where the Act does not prohibit such a remedy and certain common law requirements are met:

    (1) As with negligence, a plaintiff must show that there has been a breach of the duty complained of and that the plaintiff has suffered damage as a consequence. Liability for the breach is strict.

(2) A potential plaintiff must also show that the injury suffered is within the ambit of the statute. This test has to be applied to the specific wording of the duty under scrutiny, but in simple terms the courts will not entertain a claim for damage suffered which the statutory provision was not intended to protect against.

(3) In cases where the statute is silent as to the availability of the remedy, a plaintiff must show that he is an individual or one of a class of individuals which the duty in question was intended to benefit or protect.

APPLICABILITY OF TORTS

2.13 The torts which can be used in environmental cases are torts of strict liability and negligence. We have seen above that different classes of people are entitled to sue for different torts. However, a potential plaintiff may be able to sue in more than one tort, so it is worth comparing briefly the benefits of bringing a claim as a strict liability claim and/or in negligence.

BENEFITS OF STRICT LIABILITY ACTIONS

2.14 There are two immediate and substantial benefits of a claim in a tort of strict liability, where the locus of the plaintiff is not in question.

Injunctive relief

2.15 The remedy of an injunction (*see* Chapter 7) is available for torts of strict liability but not for negligence. Injunctive relief is a highly important part of environmental claims where there is a continuing discharge causing damage or a continuing activity which interferes with the quality of life.

No need to prove fault

2.16 The second eponymous benefit is the fact that liability can be established without the need to prove fault on the part of the defendant. The judgment of the House of Lords in the *Cambridge Water*

Company case ([1994] 1 All ER 53) has clarified considerably the availability of strict liability in relation to environmental damage and identifying what a plaintiff has to prove. The facts of the case were that the defendants operated a tanning business which involved the use of chemicals for the degreasing of pelts. Over a considerable period quantities of these chemicals escaped from the area of the factory where they were delivered and stored. The chemicals leached into the ground and passed through the chalk lying underneath the factory. Eventually the chemicals hit a layer of clay which caused a pool to form, and facilitated the lateral movement of the chemicals. In turn the chemicals polluted the groundwater which was being abstracted by the plaintiffs from their borehole.

It was accepted that at the time when the escapes occurred the defendants could not have known that the chemicals would escape or that they could cause the damage that they did. The House of Lords concluded that all forms of environmental liability at common law require that the plaintiff establishes that the damage complained of was foreseeable. However, the judgment also confirms that where the requisite elements of the various torts of strict liability are established and foreseeability of damage is shown then the defendant will be liable for the consequences of his act without proof of any fault.

As discussed in paras 2.36ff below, a plaintiff in a strict liability action also has to deal with the 'neighbour test'. The House of Lords judgment has assisted in defining that test, when concluding that the storage of chemicals on a factory site of the type in question was a non-natural use of land in the context of a claim under the rule in *Rylands v Fletcher*. It supports the view that the neighbour test may well become easier to establish in environmental cases as public awareness of the environment and the need to protect it increases.

It is a great advantage to be able to proceed with a claim in the torts of strict liability, obviating the need to prove fault.

Notwithstanding the benefits of proceeding in strict liability a remedy in negligence will often exist in parallel, and if it does, it is highly advisable to plead the case in negligence as well so that if the elements of a strict liability tort are not proved then the back-up is there. If evidence, expert or otherwise, exists of culpable fault, it would be a foolhardy lawyer who failed to prepare a case based on showing evidence of that fault if liability is denied in eg nuisance.

INDIVIDUAL TORTS

TRESPASS

2.17 Trespass to land constitutes a deliberate, or intentional, and unjustified intrusion on the land of another. It is therefore available in principle in any case where a person causes any solid matter to rest on another's land or in any watercourse over which they have rights, or which intrudes into a person's airspace. Therefore trespass will be of particular relevance when the pollution complained of involves the deposition of solid matter on to land by another, or some other permanent physical invasion.

The particular advantage of an action for trespass over other torts of strict liability is that it is not necessary to prove damage to property or person. The mere act of trespass gives rise to liability in damages and, potentially, to an injunction. Where one person causes unwanted matter to rest on another's land then the aggrieved party is entitled to recover damages on the wayleave principle (*see* Chapter 7 on remedies). Finally, an advantage of not having to prove damage is that it makes it simpler to obtain an injunction before pollution occurs, where a defendant threatens to discharge solid matter or allow it to be discharged, in circumstances where the precise effect of the discharge is not known. Trespass will be an important remedy in many environmental cases.

Example 1

One of the leading cases which applies the law of trespass to water pollution is *Jones v Llanwrst Urban Council* [1911] 1 Ch 393. The defendant was the local sewage undertaker. The plaintiff owned the bed of the river downstream of the discharge from the sewage works. The defendants were permitting faecal matter to escape from the works and become deposited on the bed of the river. This rendered the defendants liable to the riparian owner even though there was no fault on the part of the defendant.

Deposition of solid matter may of course take a number of different forms. Discharges of fine material in suspension in the water will equally be actionable. Also of relevance is the discharge of water from abandoned mines containing suspended metal oxides which settle on the bottom of rivers or lakes.

Solid matter may of course also settle on land. A common example of trespass in this regard is dust damage caused by construction works. This has been one limb of the claim referred to above against the developers of Canary Wharf by a large group of plaintiffs for damage to person and to property caused by, among other things, dust.

Other examples may be damage to crops caused by deposits of smuts from factories or power stations. Indeed, there would seem no reason why a claim in trespass should not exist, in principle, in respect of the damage caused by acid rain, which causes significant damage to forests in the United Kingdom. The difficulties with such a claim would lie more with the identification of the wrongdoer than with the application of the principles of trespass. In cases of this sort it is likely that liability also exists in nuisance.

NUISANCE

2.18   Nuisance is an act or omission which results in damage to a person's land or interest in that land or to the enjoyment of that land or interest in land. It is narrower than trespass in that the proprietary requirements are slightly tighter, and, more important, it is necessary for the plaintiff to prove that damage has been suffered. However, the application as regards pollution is much broader, in that it is not necessary to show deposition of solid matter. Therefore nuisance is relevant both where damage is caused by a single incident which leaves no visible trace, such as the pollution of a river, and in cases involving noise and vibration.

As stated, nuisance involves proof either of physical damage to land or interference with the use and enjoyment of land. This latter category also increases the scope of nuisance as an environmental remedy, since it means that activities which are not pollution in the narrower sense of the word, and which do not involve the escape of polluting matter, are still actionable, if enjoyment of the land is interfered with.

This interference with enjoyment has been defined as meaning 'the personal inconvenience and interference with one's enjoyment, one's personal freedom, anything that discomposes or injuriously affects the senses or the nerves' (*St Helens Smelting Co v Tipping* (1865) 11 HLC). Nuisance therefore has an extremely broad application, and will be of particular relevance where quality of life is affected. Decided cases have not only found activities resulting in noise, smell, dust, vibration or smoke to be actionable but also have favoured the plaintiff where the use of neighbouring premises has been such as to cause interference with enjoyment, eg use of premises for prostitution or using a building as a hospital for infectious diseases.

What makes nuisance the most useful of environmental torts is its great flexibility. The set of possible applications is not closed, as the first example below shows.

Example 1

In March 1993 judgment was given in Swindon County Court in favour of an angling syndicate which had complained of damage caused by the escape of rainbow trout into the river Kennet over which they enjoyed fishing rights. (*See* (1993) 4(4) Water Law 127–8 for a full report of the case.)

The nuisance complained of was the effect of some three or four thousand small rainbows which escaped from the defendants' trout farm into the Kennet just before the start of the fishing season. Rainbows are not native to British waters and by the end of that season had either perished or been removed. The real complaint was for the interference with the plaintiffs' right of fishing. Fishing for brown trout that are natural to the river involves skill and experience. The rainbows, which are hand fed, when released into the river will attack anything that looks like food. Therefore the plaintiffs' claim was that the presence of the rainbows ruined their pleasure of fishing for brown trout.

The judge accepted that the rainbows did cause substantial annoyance and interfered with the exercise of a legitimate right and that compensation ought to be paid.

Example 2

The case of *Laws v Florinplace* [1981] 1 All ER 659 illustrates the scope of nuisance as an environmental remedy dealing with damage to quality of life in a person's immediate environment. It also illustrates how common law can provide a remedy where the planning and authorisation process may fail to prevent a particular activity being carried on.

The named plaintiff was one of a group of individuals who owned or occupied properties in a street in Pimlico. The defendants had acquired shop premises in the street and had started to operate them as a sex shop. The shop owners had first erected an illuminated sign to the effect that a 'sex centre and cinema club' was to open shortly. Later signs were placed in the window to the effect that uncensored adult videos were for sale. The plaintiffs issued proceedings for an injunction in nuisance and the case came before the High Court on the hearing of an application for an interlocutory injunction. The court found that the defendant should be injuncted from operating the shop.

This case illustrates the fact that in a nuisance claim the court has to arrive at a view as to the standard of the duty imposed on people to avoid activities which affect those who occupy adjoining land. This issue is dealt with below.

It should not be overlooked, however, that nuisance is also of value in dealing with actual physical damage to land by either a single or persistent escape of deleterious matter from another's land.

Example 3

In the case of *Manchester Corporation v Farnworth* [1930] AC 171 a farmer brought an action against Manchester Corporation for damage to his land caused by emissions from the corporation's nearby power station. The deposits made the grass on the farmer's land unpalatable to cattle and useless for pasture. The House of Lords granted an injunction against the corporation and awarded damages.

Finally, in relation to the applicability of the tort of nuisance, it will be apparent from the case of *Laws v Florinplace* above that nuisance claims, especially where injunctive relief is sought, involve an argument as to whether a particular activity by a defendant is a legitimate use of land or a reasonable activity to pursue on the land. In all such cases the court has to make a judgment as to the standard of the duty which one person owes to another. The fact that a plaintiff can prove that the activity has interfered with enjoyment of property does not automatically render the defendant liable if the court decides that the activity in question is a reasonable use of the defendant's property in all the circumstances.

RYLANDS v FLETCHER

2.19   The nature of this tort was summarised by Lord Blackburn in the original judgment as follows:

> *We think that the true rule of law is, that the person who for his own purposes brings on his land anything likely to do mischief if it escapes must keep it at his peril, and, if he does not do so, is prima facie answerable for all the damage which is the natural consequence of its escape.*

There is no sharp line to distinguish it from other torts in particular nuisance, but it has a number of specific features. The *Cambridge Water Company* judgment supports the view that *Rylands v Fletcher* can be seen as a species of nuisance. It involves the presence on land of something not natural to it, and concerns the consequences of the escape of that non-natural thing. The tort is therefore concerned with single incidents rather than persistent problems.

There are two apparent advantages to *Rylands v Fletcher*, although both have corresponding drawbacks in remedying environmental torts. The first is that it represents the last bastion of strict liability and has been less prone to the introduction of any element of culpability. The problem, however, is that the courts have made it clear that the plaintiff must show that the use of the land from which the offending thing escapes is non-natural. During the last 50 years the courts have been increasingly reluctant to treat use of land for normal commercial purposes as non-natural.

In particular it seems that where a business is perceived as benefiting the community the courts will be reluctant to find defendants liable under the rule, because the use of the land is deemed natural. Thus, in one of the leading cases on this issue, *Read v Lyons and Co Ltd* [1947] AC 156, it was found that building and operating a munitions factory on land in time of war would not constitute a non-natural use of land.

Of direct environmental relevance is the case of *Pride of Derby Angling Association v British Celanese Ltd* [1953] 1 All ER 179. Although the issue of liability in *Rylands v Fletcher* was not directly adjudicated Lord Denning indicated that he did not consider that the provision of sewage disposal facilities could constitute a non-natural use of land. The *Cambridge Water Company* case has given some hope for the continuing relevance of *Rylands v Fletcher* as an environmental tort, suggesting as it does that a tanning operation such as that carried out by those defendants and the storage of chemicals connected with that business may be a non-natural use of land.

The second apparent advantage of the rule in *Rylands v Fletcher* is the fact that a plaintiff does not have to show an interest in land to bring a claim in the tort. This feature, though, as indicated above, is of less relevance to environmental torts, given their concern with damage to land or interference with the quality of life, in that damage of this sort will be linked to the occupation of land in some way.

NEGLIGENCE

2.20   It has been pointed out above that a cause of action in negligence often exists in parallel with remedies in strict liability. However, there are a number of situations where negligence is the only common law remedy.

Insufficient interest in land

2.21   The first situation is where a potential plaintiff does not have a sufficient interest in land to bring a strict liability claim. For example an angling club may have only a licence to fish a stretch of river. It is clear law that a licensee is simply permitted to do something which would otherwise be unlawful, and therefore does not enjoy a possessory title sufficient to bring an action in a tort of strict liability. However, it may well still be the case that a common law duty of care is owed to that licensee. To pursue the example of the angling club, if a pollution of their fishing waters occurs then the polluter is likely to owe a duty of care to the anglers and therefore be liable in damages for a breach of that duty.

This principle could well be capable of broader application to situations where groups of individuals exercise public or private rights which do not amount to interests in land, but where the enjoyment of those rights is affected by pollution, and where the polluter should reasonably have foreseen that those people would be affected. An example of that would be surfers, who suffer from sewage pollution when exercising the public right to bathe, bringing an action against the relevant sewerage undertaker. Other situations might be the interference with the enjoyment of the use of public rights of way by noise pollution or smell.

Public bodies suing

2.22 The need to use negligence as a remedy might also be of benefit to a public body which is concerned with environmental protection but does not necessarily have an interest in land. Regulatory bodies including local authorities have an interest in protection of the environment both in the sense of having a duty moral and legal to those whom they represent, and also where pollution results in cost to that body.

Thus where, for example, the NRA is faced with interference with the clean supply of water, it may well have a remedy if that interference is likely to result in damage too.

The ability of public bodies to bring claims in negligence is of more than academic interest, since it may well be that a cause of action is available to a public or statutory body where no private individual can bring an action through a lack of either locus or funding. The public body would, however, have to show that it had suffered damage and this requirement is likely to limit the applicability of the use of negligence. (*See also* Chapter 1 for public bodies and statutory clean-up costs.)

Failure of a public body to protect the environment

2.23 A third category of cases where torts of strict liability would not apply is where an individual or group seek to bring proceedings against a public body for failure to exercise powers to protect the environment. This category of case interrelates with the remedy of judicial review and also with the final tort to consider, breach of statutory duty.

Cases where liability in nuisance is removed

2.24 A fourth category of cases where proof of negligence is essential is where statute has provided that liability in nuisance should be removed in certain circumstances. An example of this is s 48 of the WRA, which provides that where a person has been granted a licence to abstract water by the NRA, no action in nuisance will lie for damage caused by the lawful operation of that licence.

Paras 2.55–2.59 below on defences provide some examples of statutory defences in environmental claims.

Personal injury cases

2.25 Negligence is of obvious relevance in personal injury claims where no interest in land is affected.

BREACH OF STATUTORY DUTY

2.26 Because of the broad nature of the tort, it is not practicable to provide a definitive list of statutory duties which may give rise to liability. Some statutes specifically create a scheme of tortious liability, such as the Occupiers Liability Act 1957. Others, however, give rise to common law liability enforceable by the courts. These enable an individual to claim compensation for damages suffered as a result of another breaking the provisions of that statute although it does not specifically provide for a remedy in tort.

The most familiar instance of this is in the area of industrial safety legislation which imposes criminal sanctions on employers who breach its provisions but does not specifically provide a remedy to an employee injured as a result of those breaches. As Parliament is constantly passing statutes with the potential to create common law liability, new statutory duties are always arising, and some may never have been tested in the courts.

One area where environmental claims for breach of statutory duty may succeed is that of services supplied by public bodies acting in performance of their statutory duties (eg water companies or local authorities). The courts' approach has been to ask whether Parliament intended to confer rights enforceable at law on a defined class of individuals. This has resulted in the exclusion of the great majority of statutory duties because they are regarded as protecting the interests of the public as a whole rather than those of a defined class of individuals. It may be that where a remedy does not exist for a breach of statutory duty, one may exist for judicial review. (*See* Chapter 7.)

PUBLIC NUISANCE

2.27   Public nuisance is distinguishable from the other torts we have considered by reason of the fact that it is concerned with situations where an act causes damage to a class of people rather than interferes with the private rights of one or more individuals.

Public nuisance is a criminal offence, but is traditionally considered with civil remedies in view of the characteristics it has in common with private nuisance. In particular public nuisance claims are generally more concerned with stopping a continuing problem by way of injunctive relief than with mere punishment. However, the *Camelford* case, considered below, was brought in respect of a single incident of pollution.

Where an individual can show that he or she has suffered over and above the inconvenience suffered by the general public then it is also a civil wrong and can give rise to a cause of action. The *Canary Wharf* case includes a claim in public nuisance. On the trial of preliminary issues, the judge held that he was unable to reach a conclusion, on the evidence before him, whether the plaintiffs had suffered inconvenience over and above the general public.

CLASS ACTION

2.28   The use of public nuisance as an environmental remedy has the attraction that it opens up the possibility of a class action on behalf of a group of people who are all affected by a particular activity, but who would not have the qualifying features to bring a common law action in nuisance or other tort. It also gives some scope for public bodies representing the environmental interest to bring actions on behalf of the public whose interests they are charged with protecting.

PROCEEDINGS IN PUBLIC NUISANCE

2.29   Proceedings in public nuisance are generally brought by the Attorney-General either at his own initiative or acting on the information of a member of the public, and bringing a relator action on their behalf.

Local authorities are also empowered to initiate proceedings in public nuisance, under the powers granted by s 222 of the Local

Government Act 1972. This power has been used on a number of occasions. For a recent example *see Gillingham Borough Council v Medway (Chatham) Dock Ltd* [1992] 3 All ER 923, where a claim was brought in respect of atmospheric pollution.

FURTHER USE OF PUBLIC NUISANCE ACTIONS

2.30   A number of public nuisance actions of an environmental nature have been brought in the past, and it is easy to see situations where activities affecting the environment or the quality of life in a particular locality might form the basis of a public nuisance action.

Given the ability of members of the public to persuade the Attorney-General to bring an action and the role of local authorities to initiate their own proceedings the remedy of public nuisance is perhaps underutilised, since it opens up an area of legal remedy different in kind to the normal common law remedy, and is particularly well suited to environmental problems which more often than not will affect a class of people, not all of whom will necessarily have an individual remedy. Chapter 8 deals with procedures for lobbying local authorities.

Examples

Two recent public nuisance actions concerning the use of the environment were the prosecution of the former South West Water Authority following the pollution of the water supply with aluminium sulphate and the litigation between riparian owners and canoeists on the River Derwent in Yorkshire to determine whether a public right of navigation existed on that river.

R v South West Water Authority, which was heard at Exeter Crown Court in late 1990 and early 1991 arose from the Camelford incident. It concerned the entry into the public water supply of a quantity of aluminium sulphate which had been introduced into the wrong tank at the water treatment works at Lowermoor near Camelford in Cornwall. It was some time before the problem was identified. In the meantime the water supply to the public had become unwholesome. Once the problem was identified the contaminated water was flushed into the river Camel, causing a major fishkill. South

West Water were convicted of an offence of public nuisance, in that their acts endangered the comfort of a class of the public while the unwholesome water was in the public supply. They were also found guilty of polluting the river Camel. The company was fined £10,000.

The River Derwent case was brought by the Attorney-General on behalf of canoeists and the local district council. The defendants were a number of riparian owners who had denied that a public right of navigation existed on the parts of the river over which they had riparian rights. The case eventually went to the House of Lords. The main point at issue was whether the provisions relating to the acquisition of a right of way in the Right of Way Act 1932 applied to watercourses in the same way as they did on land. This case was of particular interest in that it was at heart a dispute between recreational interests (canoeing) and conservation interests (anglers and owners).

COMMON LAW AND COMMUNITY LAW

2.31   EC law is increasingly having a bearing on the prosecution of common law actions in British courts. This influence is felt in two ways:

(a) European legislation and directives can have direct effect in British law so that a breach can form the basis of an action for an injunction or damages in a home court;

(b) Environmental standards which are set by virtue of Community directives will have relevance in determining acceptable standards in cases, particularly in negligence where a breach of the duty of care is being alleged.

Chapter 6 deals with Community law in relation to the environment, and sets out what Community legislation will have direct effect in common law actions brought in this jurisdiction, and the manner in which the courts will be bound by that legislation. That chapter also sets out the various environmental directives.

IDENTIFYING DEFENDANTS

2.32   It is usually not difficult to identify the correct party to sue in an environmental action but in some single pollution incidents it is much easier to identify the effect of the pollution than the cause.

Also there are occasions when more than one party is responsible for an incident of pollution or a series of events has occurred leading to pollution with the result that a number of parties are involved.

INFORMATION FROM STATUTORY AUTHORITIES

2.33   As most one-off pollution incidents involve some potential criminal liability it is likely that the body primarily responsible for prosecuting offenders will have made some investigation of the incident (in the case of water pollution—the NRA; in the case of land or air pollution—the relevant local authority or HMIP). (Chapter 1 provides an outline of the responsibilities of each of those bodies.)

Generally statutory bodies will assist in identifying the circumstances of an incident. However, where a criminal prosecution is pending or a decision whether to prosecute has yet to be made then, understandably, information will not be released that may be prejudicial to a fair criminal trial. Also problems can arise where Acts of Parliament impose criminal sanctions on public bodies not to disclose confidential information which has come into their possession. This duty has to be balanced against the duties now imposed for the release of environmental information. (*See* Chapter 9 for a more detailed consideration of the availability of environmental information.)

LIABILITY FOR POLLUTION

2.34   Liability for pollution is joint and several. *See* eg *Wood v Waud* (1849) 3 ExCh 748 which provides that it is no defence to show that a river has also been polluted by other parties. The effect of this is that all parties responsible for causing a pollution, no matter how small the contribution, will be liable to the aggrieved party. Thus where a number of different contributors to a pollution problem would not necessarily have caused sufficient damage to give rise to a cause of action on their own they will nonetheless be liable jointly. It is no defence for one defendant to point to a co-defendant and say that his acts alone would give rise to a cause of action. The consequence of the principle of joint liability is that if only one party is found liable he will be liable for the whole of the damage that has been caused. This may seem harsh but it must be remembered that ample protection is offered to defendants by way of contribution proceedings, by which one defendant can join another to share liability.

From the plaintiff's point of view the apportionment of liability between defendants is a matter of indifference, and therefore can and should be ignored in prosecuting the action. If one defendant does join other parties as third parties, then, if the third party notice discloses a cause of action, the third party can be joined as a defendant.

CHAIN OF INCIDENTS

2.35 A further problem can arise where a chain of events leads to a pollution incident. To take an example, A Co agrees to supply chemicals to B Co and employs C Co to deliver the chemicals. When the delivery vehicle arrives at A Co part of the load discharges and causes damage to adjacent land. The one certain feature of a situation of this sort is that all the potential defendants will blame the damage on one of the others. A plaintiff will often face the difficulty in the early stages of a claim of not having sufficient information to allocate responsibilities.

Multi-party incidents often involve torts of strict liability. The law provides that the ability of defendants to delegate liability in strict liability torts is much more limited. For example, the general rule in negligence is that an employer can delegate liability to an independent contractor, whereas in nuisance he cannot. Tactically, therefore, commencing proceedings against the owner of the land from where the pollution escaped or the employer of a contractor or series of contractors is the best course of action. Where the first defendant joins third parties in the action, they can be joined as co-defendants if a cause of action is shown to exist in negligence as more information is released during the course of proceedings. It is desirable to amass as much information as possible before commencing an action. The reader is referred to Chapter 9 on information and to the discovery section in Chapter 7.

BOUNDARIES AND DEFENCES

INTRODUCTION

2.36 This section looks first at the boundaries of liability in environmental torts and then at defences which can legitimately be raised in proceedings.

Two principal tests are applied in determining liability: the first, and now necessary, test is one of foreseeability; the second is less well defined but is ultimately just as pervasive as the foreseeability test: it may loosely be described as the neighbour or neighbourhood test. It arises in the Donoghue and Stevenson 'Who is my neighbour?' question; in the question of non-natural use by *Rylands v Fletcher*; in the determination of the standard of duty owed by one party to another in nuisance; in the issue of what is appropriate to a given neighbourhood.

This issue is crucial to the determination of liability but the concept of what is reasonable between neighbours is not fixed. As society's attitudes change, so do the judgments of the courts which inevitably reflect public opinion, albeit often in delayed form.

While matters of public policy are ultimately the domain of legislators, considerable discretion rests with the judges to decide how a reasonable neighbour should or should not behave. The exercise of that discretion is dependent on the evidence presented to the court. Citizens' expectations and awareness of environmental issues and their consequences have overturned the earlier tacit assumption that the operation of industry and commerce was of greater importance than quality of life. That charge might be reflected in future judicial decisions if environmental lawyers can present good quality evidence and cogent argument before the courts.

THE FORESEEABILITY TEST

2.37 The *Cambridge Water* judgment has cleared away much uncertainty on the issue of foreseeability. To establish liability in an environmental tort a plaintiff must be able to show that the damage complained of was foreseeable at the time of the act or omission complained of.

Sometimes evidence of foreseeability is a matter of common sense, and can be brought out at trial in cross-examination. Alternatively or additionally, it may be a matter of expert evidence. It is very important therefore when working with an expert to ensure that he gives an opinion on whether the defendant, taking into account the prevailing scientific standards, knew or ought to have known at the relevant time that his activities were such that they would be likely to interfere with the rights of another, or, in the case of physical damage to land, should have foreseen that damage would be caused if the offending matter escaped. *See* Chapters 7 and 9 for more detailed discussion of working with experts.

It should be reiterated that foreseeability and fault are separate issues. In nuisance, if the damage is foreseeable then the defendant will be liable without fault on his part.

THE NEIGHBOUR TEST

2.38   The neighbour test addresses the issue of what conduct is and is not acceptable as between neighbours who are affected by adjacent activities. This issue arises not only in the classic test in negligence claims, but also, as we have seen, in the standard of the duty imposed in nuisance, and the issue of non-natural use of land in cases based on the rule in *Rylands v Fletcher*. This test is highly relevant in environmental cases which often centre on the competing rights of neighbours. It is also responsive to social change.

The section on statutory defences below (paras 2.55–2.59) illustrates that in some situations Parliament has intervened to provide that certain activities will be protected from action in tort, usually where a statutory authority has been given for that activity to be carried out. The present section looks at the courts' guidance, to date, on where the boundaries are to be drawn at common law, and decisions made in relation to each of the environmental media are considered. First, however, the following general comments should be noted.

(1) The class of potential actions in nuisance, negligence and other torts of a strict liability is never closed (see eg the escaped trout case above). What matters is the proof that a particular activity interferes with a legitimate use and enjoyment of land by another.

(2) The decided cases have highlighted the difficulties in enunciating the general principles as to the application of this test. Each case must be judged on its own merits, and then the test of the reasonable man should be applied. 'Reasonable men' (and women) tend to change their attitudes with the passage of time, which makes clear principles still more difficult to enunciate.

Application of the test

2.39   The leading case to set out this general principle is *Sedleigh-Denfield v O'Callagan* [1940] All ER 349. Lord Wright said in that judgment that:

> *A balance has to be maintained between the right of the occupier to do what he likes with his own and the right of his neighbour not to be interfered with. It is impossible to give any precise or universal formula, but it may broadly be said that a useful test is perhaps, what is reasonable according to the ordinary usages of mankind living in society, or, more correctly in a particular society.*

Definitions of this sort are by their nature so broad as to be difficult to absorb without application to particular facts. However, in some types of environmental claim, eg construction works, the courts have decided that some activities are legitimate even though they interfere with enjoyment of property. Where the courts or Parliament have defined specific boundaries these are considered below and in the later section on defences.

Standard of duty in nuisance

2.40   There are two sides in determining the standard of the duty in nuisance:
   (a) whether the activity complained of is within the reasonable use of land; and
   (b) whether the complaint about an activity of a neighbour is one that a reasonable person would make.

To take an example, everyone would accept that it is reasonable for a person to play music in the home. Equally everyone would accept that music played too loud may become an unacceptable irritation to neighbours. How to strike the balance between the two does not admit of a simple solution. Each case has to be considered on its own merits.

It is to be hoped, however, that increasing public awareness of environmental issues will result in the 'reasonable man' accepting that the right of a person to be protected from interference with the quality of his life or damage to his proprietary interests is paramount no matter how necessary the activities of the wrongdoer may be. The *Cambridge Water* case made it clear that the storage of chemicals at a factory does not constitute a natural use of land. In more general terms it acknowledges the increasing awareness of protection of the environment.

There has always been in nuisance cases involving interference with use and enjoyment of property a principle that the character of the neighbourhood should be taken into account in determining liability. This is summed up in that well-known judicial comment: 'what would be a nuisance in Belgravia would not necessarily be so in Bermondsey' (*Sturges v Bridgman* (1879) 11 ChD). One assumes that the 'reasonable man' of the late twentieth century will have moved on from that view, but there is no doubt that in determining liability in nuisance the court must consider the overall circumstances of the parties and their locality.

Example

In *Gillingham BC v Medway (Chatham) Dock Ltd* [1992] 3 All ER 923, currently subject to appeal, the judge held that planning consent (in that case to convert the former Royal Chatham dockyard into a commercial dock) has an impact on the nature of the neighbourhood and therefore on whether a matter which is not causing physical harm is or is not a nuisance. The judge held that both by development plans and grants of planning consent a local authority can alter the character of a neighbourhood thus rendering activities, which previously would have been actionable nuisance, lawful. In the *Gillingham* case traffic noise from multiple movements of HGV lorries through a predominantly residential neighbourhood which had not been subject to any substantial prior disturbance from traffic was held not to amount to nuisance. The judge argued that the local people had had an opportunity to object and challenge the planning proposals under the Town and Country Planning Act 1990. The judge said that the planning permission could not render lawful a nuisance if the activity could be operated without causing the damage or disturbance.

It may be important to consider the extent to which this principle will apply to nuisance caused by temporary uses authorised under the Town and Country Planning (General Development) Order 1988—where no application for planning permission is necessary and it is not possible to oppose the grant of permission. This might apply to eg clay pigeon shooting.

The *Gillingham* case also leaves uncertain the extent to which authorised pollution (say air pollution emitted under and in accordance with an authorisation granted eg under s6 of the Environmental Protection Act 1990) may be exempt from liability under the common law. The issue has not been determined with any certainty with regard to air pollution but *see also Budden v BP Oil Ltd* (1980) 124 SJ 376. It is reasonable, however, to put forward a general proposition that compliance with an authorisation or permission will not operate as a defence to a common law action unless the relevant statute specifically makes it so.

Some consideration must be given to how these principles apply to the individual environmental media.

WATER

2.41   A person with riparian rights is entitled to enjoy their water without sensible interference from adjacent occupiers. The neighbour test in the case of water is a stiff one where only a small alteration in quality has to be shown to give rise to a claim in nuisance. For trespass it is not even necessary to show damage.

Example

One of the leading water pollution cases is *Pride of Derby Angling Association v British Celanese* [1953] 1 All ER 179 which is a good example of the application of common law remedies in a water pollution claim and illustrates how the neighbour test was applied.

The plaintiffs claimed an injunction to restrain pollution of the River Derwent in Derbyshire. The water was polluted by three defendants in different ways—by harmful industrial effluent, by sewage effluent, and by heated discharges. The claim was made in nuisance, and an injunction was granted restraining the defendants from discharging effluent into the river so as to alter the quality of the water (including temperature) such that it interfered with the plaintiffs' fishing rights. It was suspended for a period to allow the defendants to improve the operation of their plants. One of the defences relied on by the local authority was that they did not create the nuisance. They merely took over the operation of the sewage system. This was rejected on the basis that a person may adopt a nuisance by continuing it. Denning LJ said: 'but their treatment of it was not successful in rendering it harmless; it was still noxious. Their act of pouring a polluting effluent into the river makes them guilty of nuisance.' He also dismissed the defence of statutory authority, remarking that 'They had no authority to pour into the river an effluent that was noxious or polluting'.

Defences

2.42 The defendants in the *Pride of Derby* action put forward a number of defences which relate to the determination of the neighbour test. It is very common in water pollution claims for a defence to be structured round the fact that the activity complained of is being carried on pursuant to consents to discharge effluent issued by the NRA, and/or in accordance with guidelines issued by various bodies as to the acceptability of emissions into the water environment. As will be seen below, the grant of an abstraction licence provides a statutory defence to a claim for diminution in the quantity of water received from a higher owner. However, this is not the case with a consent to discharge or, indeed, a planning consent. Moreover, while compliance with industry standards is perhaps more relevant to a claim in negligence, as Lord Denning's remarks affirm, it will have little effect in a claim in nuisance where the activity has been shown to cause demonstrable harm.

Rights of both parties

2.43 However apart from the issue of statutory authority a balance has to be struck between the rights of the two parties. For example if action is taken against a factory a court would have to weigh the consequences of imposing an injunction that might close down that factory, with resulting loss of employment, against the interests of the riparian owner. In the case of any discharge to the water environment account is likely to be taken of the need for businesses to continue, particularly if they are conducting some socially necessary function such as sewage disposal. In striking a balance between the interests of the two parties, the courts may well find that the levels of given pollutants set by the NRA as acceptable are reasonable. However those standards can change, and there may be pollutants in the effluent which are not specifically authorised by consent.

Location

2.44   In water-related claims, one also has to consider the location and quality of the relevant water. Clearly, if a river or lake has for centuries been of a low standard of purity and has never contained the less pollution-tolerant species, such as trout, this will be relevant in a court action. The NRA maintains a national water quality classification system which grades all waters and is due to be developed under the WRA into a more comprehensive system of water quality objectives for all river catchments (*see* Chapter 1 for more details). This, though, is only likely to be persuasive. It is most certainly not the case that, because a stretch of river has been graded as lifeless for many years, a common law action will not exist to prevent pollution.

First imposition of standards

2.45   Often defendants try to argue that because no-one else is subject to particular treatment standards they should not be the first. Such an argument has no intrinsic merit, and a claim for water pollution should not be avoided simply because it would impose on the defendants an obligation that they have hitherto managed to avoid.

Disputes between owners

2.46   In connection with protection of water rights, one has to consider the position in disputes between riparian owners as well as the impact of the activities of outsiders. In these cases common law has established its own neighbour principles, in particular the right of one riparian owner to use water for ordinary purposes, even though this may exhaust water supply to the detriment of a lower owner.

AIR

2.47 Air includes noise, vibration and smell, as well as other emissions into airspace which interfere with enjoyment of land. The neighbour test is not so clearcut as with water pollution and the question of the correct balance to strike between the competing interests of two parties is more complex. An example of an injunction for noise nuisance which attracted media attention in 1993 was the banishment of Corky the cockerel for over-enthusiastic crowing.

Example

The major reported case on smell, noise and vibration and the application of the neighbour test was *Halsey v Esso Petroleum Co Ltd* [1961] 2 All ER 145. The plaintiff lived in Fulham and Esso operated an oil storage depot opposite his house. Smuts were emitted from the defendants' chimneys which landed on the plaintiff's car and laundry. In addition, a nauseating smell sometimes came from the depot and noise during the night caused the plaintiff's windows to vibrate. Large tankers passed by at night. All of these were found to cause a nuisance and an injunction and damages were granted. The application of this case is considered below.

The decided cases provide some principles regarding liability in atmospheric cases.

Smell

2.48 The facts of *Halsey* have been considered above. Another case where an injunction was granted was *Bone v Seale* [1974] 1 All ER 787. In this case the Court of Appeal upheld the injunction granted by the judge at first instance in respect of smell suffered from pig-farming operations, over a long period. The argument that the farmer had complied with local authority requirements did not impress the court. The wording of the injunction was broad, restraining the defendant 'from . . . carrying on or permitting to be carried on . . . the business of farming so as or in such a manner as by the discharge of noxious or offensive vapours or smells or otherwise to cause a nuisance or injury to the plaintiffs . . .'.

From these two cases it is clear that one does not have to prove that there has been any damage to health or property. The key factors in determining whether a smell amounted to nuisance or not are the character of the neighbourhood and the intensity and frequency of the smell, and thus the impact on the enjoyment of the property.

Noise and vibration

2.49 With noise there is an accepted scale for representing levels of noise—decibels or dB. The most common form of measuring equipment uses a filter which approximates to the human ear and provides a measurement expressed as dB(A).

A number of points can be determined from noise nuisance cases. The frequency, timing (ie day or night) and intensity are key factors. The nature of the neighbourhood is also relevant.

In the *Halsey* case the noise complaints concerned both noise within Esso's site and also that of up to 15 lorries a night arriving at the site, which resulted in a maximum decibel reading of 84 dB. The judge decided that this was sufficient to disturb an ordinary man. To complain about such levels was more than mere delicacy or fastidiousness. Both the *Halsey* and the *Gillingham BC* case confirm the fact that a defendant can be held liable for noise nuisance caused by vehicles even where those vehicles are on a public highway when making the offending noise.

Smoke, fumes and dust

2.50 Any of these matters gives rise to civil liability, typically in public or private nuisance or negligence. Negligence may be of importance where the harm suffered by the plaintiff is as a result of being unusually sensitive (which will prevent the establishment of liability in nuisance—*see Robinson v Kilvert* (1889) 41 ChD 88). Where personal injury is alleged it is often difficult to prove causation between the illness suffered and the emission, particularly where the illness is not uncommon. This will be a matter for expert evidence. In addition, where the pollutant may have come from any one of a number of sources pinpointing the source can be crucial. The gathering of expert evidence at an early stage is important— particularly where the source is transient, eg where it arises from construction sites. This is currently the subject of litigation by local residents in the Docklands area of London against the London Docklands Development Corporation.

Physical damage may be easier to prove (eg dust deposits on washing or cars) and the establishment of liability in nuisance is easier as neighbourhood is not such a relevant factor (*see* eg *Wood v Conway Corporation* [1914] 2 Ch 47 where liability was imposed for a coating of soot deposits on the plaintiff's trees).

Where physical damage and personal injury are not alleged it may nevertheless be possible to seek damages or injunction in nuisance on the basis of interference with enjoyment of the plaintiff's property.

Other reported cases in which dust, smoke or fumes have been considered include the *Halsey* case where liability was imposed for acid smut emissions which damaged clothing and car paint and *Mantania v National Provincial Bank Ltd* [1936] 2 All ER 633.

Miscellaneous sources: radioactivity and electromagnetism

2.51 Damage caused by radioactivity is governed by its own special rules in respect of sites licensed under the Nuclear Installation Act 1965 which governs all nuclear energy and pro- cessing plants but does not apply to Crown sites (eg Ministry of Defence sites). Section 12 of the 1965 Act covers nuclear incidents (defined as an occurrence involving nuclear matter) which arise:

   (a) in the course of transporting nuclear substances in connec- tion with a licensed installation; or

   (b) at or in connection with a licensed site.

Liability will arise if the licensee has failed in its absolute duty (s 7) to ensure that no such incident causes injury to persons or damage to property. The injury or damage must arise out of irradiation or a combination of the radioactive and toxic or explosive or hazardous properties of the nuclear matter. Liability may also arise if the licensee fails in the absolute duty to prevent the emission of radia- tion from waste discharges from the site or from non-nuclear matter (eg contaminated clothing).

Once it can be shown that the breach of duty caused the damage then liability is established without further proof of fault. Proving causation is not easy. For example, if a plaintiff develops leukaemia how can it be proved that the cancer has been caused by radioactive emissions? It might be simply part of the naturally occurring pattern of the disease. Epidemiological evidence will need to be called. It was the reflection by the High Court of this epidemiological evidence which resulted in the failure of the cases against British Nuclear Fuels (1993) 9 SJ 137 (45) 1184.

The only defence to liability is that the breach of duty is due to armed conflict. There is notably no exemption in the case of an unforeseeable natural disaster, eg an earthquake.

In *Merlin v British Nuclear Fuels plc* ([1991] Jnl of Env Law 3 (1) 122) Mr and Mrs Merlin who lived some six miles away from the nuclear fuel reprocessing plant at Sellafield claimed under s 12 of the Act that the value of their house had been diminished by breach of the duties imposed. It was held that damage to 'property' did not include diminution in value, only damage to tangible property. Their claim failed.

The provisions of s 12 do apply to government sites if they would have required a site licence but for the exemption of the Crown from the provisions of the 1965 Act.

Recently it has been suggested that certain illnesses, including leukaemia, are related to the electromagnetic field created by high voltage power lines. Litigation may be anticipated on the normal nuisance or negligence principles about this matter following the grant of legal aid for the investigation of this possible new source of liability.

A final point is that it is clear that the use of a best practicable means defence is not a good one. In *Bone v Seale* the defendants argued that they had done everything possible to prevent the smell nuisance arising and could not do any more. The Court of Appeal held that that did not prevent liability arising.

LAND

2.52   As with water, the neighbour test will be relevant in cases of land pollution where one landowner carries out operations on his land that interfere with another's enjoyment of his land. Most examples concern waste disposal sites where harm is caused beyond its boundaries. This may take the form of fires on the site, gases or leachate escaping from the site or from the movement of waste itself. In *Priest v Manchester Corporation* (1915) 84 LJKB 1934, rain falling on a waste tip caused a gulley to be eroded in a nearby street. In this case, the land was used for tipping in such a way that it caused a nuisance to adjoining landowners. Similarly in *Ballard v Tomlinson* (1885) 29 ChD 115, the plaintiff's water supply which he used for his brewing business was contaminated by his neighbour's use of his well for the disposal of sewage. The two parties' water supplies were connected underground and this allowed the transmission of the pollution to the plaintiff's land.

OTHER ENVIRONMENTAL CLAIMS

2.53   We have seen that the relevance of common law to the environment is apparent not only in cases of pollution of the environmental media but also where human activity interferes with the quality of life to such a degree that the activity becomes actionable in nuisance and/or negligence. (*See* the case of *Laws v Florinplace*.) Once again it is not easy to define useful principles regarding the neighbour test that may be applied in determining whether a particular activity will be actionable or not. However, *Laws v Florinplace* illustrates that a court is likely to look carefully at the historical use of a location, and is likely to control new activities which are inconsistent with that use and cause interference.

CAUSATION

2.54   In many cases the causal link between the defendant and the damage will be obvious. However, there will be occasions when the link is not so clear as was discussed above. There are others, such as where the act of another intervenes (*see* para 2.71) or where responsibility may not be clear although no third party is involved. The classic definitions of the torts relevant to environmental damage presuppose some act of the defendant to do or not to do something. Generally that act will directly result in the damage complained of. Various words are used to describe the defendant's actions such as 'cause', 'allow' or 'permit'. There does not seem to have been a direct decision on this issue, but there are obvious parallels to the long line of criminal cases of which *Alphacell v Woodward* [1974]

AC 824 is the best known. It is likely that, in cases of strict liability, similar principles will be applied to determine responsibility.

The current issue of minewater discharges illustrates the point. It is likely that a court in a civil claim would find liability if a causal event could be identified even if that event was not the immediate cause of the damage. Thus in a case such as *Wheal Jane,* it was nature that caused the pollution. However, it was the owners of the mine who turned off the pumps which allowed nature to take its course.

STATUTORY DEFENCES

2.55   Subject to the specific exceptions set out below the general rule is that the grant of a statutory consent or authorisation does not operate as a defence to a common law action. Those authorisations may go to assist the defendant in an argument as to how the neighbour test should be applied, on the basis that the granting authority is satisfied that the discharge or activity is acceptable in accordance with the statutory criteria established for the relevant operation. The criteria for liability will, however, be different, and therefore the existence of authorisations will not determine liability.

There is inevitably an interface between the planning system and the effect of the authorised activities on the local community. This was well illustrated in the *Gillingham BC* case. The decision of Buckley J is currently subject to appeal, see above.

Water

2.56   There is one significant statutory defence in water cases. Section 48 of the WRA provides that where a person has been granted an abstraction licence then that licence shall be a defence in any common law action in nuisance provided that its conditions have been observed. The defence will not apply where the defendant has been negligent.

A similar exemption exists where an impoundment licence has been granted under s 36. Section 70 of the Act confirms that an abstraction/impounding licence shall not operate to derogate from any civil right of action other than as set out in the Act.

Air

2.57 In general statutes concerning air pollution do not include any provisions which bring about the statutory regulation of common law actions. An exception to this is s 78 of the Civil Aviation Act 1982 which will prevent common law actions in respect of most aircraft noise.

Land

2.58 A waste management licence granted under the EPA is statutory authority to operate a site in accordance with the conditions of the licence. A duly licensed operator would escape liability in nuisance if he could show that he used all reasonable care and skill to prevent it (cf *Manchester Corporation v Farnworth* above). Indeed, he may even escape liability if he can show that the nuisance was inevitable given the conditions of the licence. Similarly with negligence, a site operator may not be liable if he can show that he conducted his operation in accordance with site conditions and with any codes of practice issued under s 34(7).

Radiation

2.59 The Nuclear Installations Act 1965 negates the normal common law rights in respect of radioactive discharges, and imposes in their stead a system of statutory compensation.

LIMITATION

2.60 Environmental torts causing physical damage to property or affecting quality of life are subject to the Limitation Act 1980. Under s 33 the plaintiff in personal injury actions must issue proceedings within three years of the date on which he was injured.

Latent damage: personal injury

2.61 Limitation of actions is most likely to cause hardship where damage occurs but fails to show itself in a discernible form until after the primary limitation period has expired. To take this into account, the Act provides that time begins to run (ie the three-year period starts) either from where the cause of action accrues or from the date of the plaintiff's knowledge (ie when the injury appeared).

The courts also have a wide discretionary power to override a time limit and allow the action to proceed even though the three-year period has ended.

Negligence, nuisance or breach of statutory duty

2.62   In an action for damages for negligence, nuisance or breach of statutory duty the period is six years from the accrual of the cause of action. However, a plaintiff may not become aware of the damage until after the end of the six-year period. The severity of the rule in these cases of latent damage has been eased by the Latent Damage Act 1986, which added a new section (14A) to the Limitation Act 1980. This provides that in cases other than personal injury the six-year period will run from when the damage occurred. However, where the damage only becomes discoverable after the end of the six-year period a plaintiff has a further three years from the date of his discovery of the damage to claim.

Section 14B, however, inserts an absolute long-stop provision, in that claims will be statute-barred 15 years after the occurrence of the original act which gave rise to the damage, irrespective of when the damage occurred. No discretion is given to the court, as it is with personal injury actions.

This second category not only covers damages concerning defective buildings, which originally gave rise to the Latent Damage Act. It also applies to pollution cases where, for instance, a landowner finds out more than six years after the pollution occurred that his land has been damaged.

Continuing damage

2.63   The issue of limitation is also relevant in cases of continuing damage. Where a plaintiff claims an injunction and damages for a continuing nuisance, the claim for damages will be limited to the period of six years immediately preceding the issue of the writ and damages will not be recoverable prior to that date.

STATUTORY AUTHORITY

2.64   The defence of statutory authority relates to situations where the defendant is carrying on an activity pursuant to statutory authority. It is distinguishable from the specific statutory defences referred to above in that it concerns the activity of the defendant as a whole rather than the statutory authorisation of a particular process by an environmental or other agency. Despite its appellation' it is really a doctrine which has been built up by common law decisions.

There has been a line of cases dealing with the issue of liability in nuisance and negligence where the defendant claims the statutory right to do the act which the plaintiff claims is causing damage, the most recent being *Rowling v Takaro Properties* [1988] 1 All ER 163. From these certain principles have been established.

If a defendant can establish that the activity complained of has been specifically authorised by an Act of Parliament then the courts will not find the defendant liable in nuisance for the consequences of the exercise of those powers. Furthermore the courts will be reluctant to find the defendant liable in negligence where the acts complained of are within the powers granted by the Act. The onus is on the defendant to prove whether the activity is indeed authorised by statute. Often the success of this defence relies on detailed consideration of the statute concerned.

Express or implied authority

2.65 Sometimes the statute will give express authority for a particular activity, sometimes it will be implied. As a general rule the defence will be more likely to succeed when the authority is express. However, in some cases the activity will be protected even though not specifically authorised. For example, in the leading case of *Allen v Gulf Oil Refining Ltd* [1979] 3 All ER 1008, where an Act authorised the acquisition of a site for development of an oil refinery, it was accepted that the subsequent operation of the refinery ought to be protected although it was not specifically authorised by statute.

It should be emphasised that where an Act specifically provides for the continuation of liability in nuisance then the defence does not avail. It only arises where the Act is silent.

Acts of statutory bodies

2.66 The defence of statutory authority is likely to be quite important in the field of environmental law. Many common law actions for environmental damage, including 'quality of life' claims, will involve the activities of statutory undertakers, local authorities or large industrial concerns, where some statutory authority will be claimed. Often the defence seems insurmountable.

However, detailed analysis of the statute can reveal weaknesses in the argument. Use of expert evidence may also assist in proving whether the activity is being carried on within the statutory authority or not, and if the exercise is within the statute, whether the defendant is taking reasonable steps to minimise the effect of its activities. Where the court is persuaded to allow liability in negligence, a crucial question will be whether there is reasonable use of the authority enjoyed by the defendant.

The scope of the defence of statutory authority has very recently been considered in the *Canary Wharf* case (see para 2.9 above). There what the statutory authority relied on was that the development of Canada Tower was authorised by Parliament through the approval of a statutory instrument and by virtue of consents issued by the London Docklands Development Corporation. The judge held that neither the statutory instrument nor the consents negatived the right to sue in nuisance, and that the right to construct buildings did not necessarily entail that television reception would be interfered with. The judge distinguished this case from the *Gillingham* case by pointing out that in that case the planning permission to operate the dock could not have been exercised without 24 hour access to the site. It was the effect on the community of that access that was the nuisance complained of.

MISFEASANCE AND NON-FEASANCE

2.67   The case of *Dear v Thames Water* (unreported but *see* Water Law July 1993) deals at some length with the issue of where the line should be drawn between acts and omissions which are susceptible to common law action and those which are issues of policy—which are more suitable for judicial review proceedings. It also deals with the distinction between a positive wrongdoing, by act or omission, as against non-feasance or failure to make a choice to act or omit.

The facts were that the plaintiff's house suffered from regular flooding in times of storm when a stream at the bottom of his garden flooded. The cause of the flooding was that the watercourse received far greater flows as a result of surface water drainage from substantial housing developments that had been constructed over a number of years. Thames Water had no control over this development, although it did have a power to devise a drainage scheme that would alleviate the flooding problem. There was no act or omission on the part of Thames Water that caused the flooding of the plaintiff's property. Any failure to determine and act upon a policy to alleviate the flooding was a non-feasance and challengeable, if at all, by judicial review of their failure to decide on a scheme. The non-feasance was not negligent nor was it a nuisance. This decision should be compared with the *Pride of Derby* case (*see* above).

OTHER DEFENCES

2.68   There are a number of other general tortious defences which may have application in environmental actions.

Act of God

2.69   This defence is sometimes used as a convenient excuse for a defendant's acts or omissions, but may be rebutted by factual evidence. Where weather is concerned, the Meteorological Office keeps accurate records and its officers can be called to give evidence. It is equally important to obtain statements from lay witnesses as to weather conditions at the time.

Act of trespasser

2.70   It is a defence in an environmental tort action to prove that the cause of the discharge or other event was the result of vandalism or other non-consensual act. The onus of proof lies on the defendant. It should be borne in mind that even if the immediate fault lies with the trespasser it may be that it was as a result of negligence that the trespasser gained access to the site in question.

Novus actus/causa interveniens

2.71   This defence applies where some act of a third party or some event arises between the act of the defendant and the damaging act complained of. A possible example of this might be where the fire service attend to put out a fire, and their actions result in polluting matter being discharged on to adjoining land causing damage. It is unlikely that the defence would avail in this case since the fire service were responding to an emergency, and if the original fire started as a result of the defendant's negligence then liability would rest with that defendant. In essence the defendant has to prove that what was an innocent non-harmful act has been turned into a harmful one by a third party, or that his act was not the effective cause of the damage.

Grant of rights

2.72 In environmental damage cases there is often a dispute between physical neighbours. There are situations where a person has been granted a lawful right to do an act which causes environmental damage. For example, a deed may grant the right to divert water from a stream in such a manner that it affects the flow downstream. A successor in title will be bound by the grant of his predecessor notwithstanding the damage to his interests.

Prescription

2.73 Almost any activity which can give rise to environmental liability, whether direct physical damage or affecting the quality of life, may form the basis of a prescriptive right. There is some authority for the view that one cannot acquire the right to do something which is unlawful. However, there are a number of cases which show this is not an immutable principle. The prescriptive right acquired is in the nature of an easement, and therefore all the usual requirements of an easement have to be satisfied before it can be used as a defence. The case of *Cargill v Gotts* [1981] 1 WLR 441 concerned a claim by the plaintiff that the defendant had wrongfully abstracted water from a pond in breach of the plaintiff's riparian rights. Among the issues considered was whether the plaintiff had acquired prescriptive rights to abstract the water. The court decided that the plaintiff had acquired such rights. It is clear from the case, however, that the easement alleged must have been exercised evenly over the period in question. Thus if an easement to pollute has been claimed then the amount of pollution must be even over the period in question.

CHAPTER 3

PLANNING AND THE ENVIRONMENT

INTRODUCTION

3.1　Planning law provides the framework for regulating land and building development and the uses to which they are put.

It covers development of green fields as well as the reconstruction of existing neighbourhoods, buildings in being and their usage. In short, it deals with the very essence of the subject-matter of this book, namely the environment in which we live.

When the statutory planning structure and its implementation is wrongly used or imperfectly framed it can result in misguided disfigurement of towns or the landscape, ecological disruption and disintegration, exposure of communities to harmful pollutants, and long-term economic and social damage. When planning law is properly enforced and monitored constantly it can be constructive, imaginative and of long-term benefit, and can have immediate advantages in the way of improved services, amenities and general quality of life.

A BRIEF HISTORY OF PLANNING LAW

3.2　Indeed, it is the positive aspect of the first tentative steps towards regulating building works in the nineteenth century that established the more comprehensive approaches of the twentieth century. Inevitably, most legislation has appeared by way of reaction to social change, principally as a consequence of industrial development, combining growth in urbanisation, in turn producing conditions harmful to health principally from the inadequacy of housing, water supply and sanitation. Charles Dickens in *Hard Times* vividly describes Coketown, pride of the Gradgrind family, as 'a town of machinery and tall chimneys', reading in part like a Royal Commission on the poverty of urban living.

A series of Royal Commissions in the early part of the nineteenth century triggered the Public Health Act of 1848. Parliamentary concern, at first reluctant but urged on by social reformers, began the process of imposing standards in health and housing. The advent of such regulatory intervention was part of the process whereby the state limited property owners' total freedom to do as they wished with their own land. The first of the Town Planning Acts appeared in 1909 with increasing statutory powers running through the first half of the twentieth century. In 1943 the Ministry of Town and Country Planning was established and in the aftermath of World War II the planning system first appeared in a form in which it substantially survives today. The environmental aspect was not visible until around 1970, when, by a rather convoluted process, the Department of the Environment was created, principally as an administrative step. Indeed, some thoroughly reputable and authoritative text books on planning law, published as recently as the early 1980s, made little or no reference to the protection of the environment and in many you will search in vain for even a mention in the index! Professor David Hughes' book *Environmental Law*, the first of its kind, emerged in 1987.

Whatever the historical perspective, planning law and environmental law are now seen as being interwoven. Many distinguished environmental lawyers in fact started their professional lives as planning lawyers.

THE PLANNING LAWYER'S ROLE

3.3   The use to which land is put and the site and type of developments permitted are of enormous importance in environmental terms. The character of a locality and its implications for the population, the natural habitat, health and well-being, economic security, standard of living and quality of life are affected deeply by the application of the planning system.

At a practical level, planning lawyers have a central role in environmental protection. Developers will seek advice and guidance from them when applying for planning permission. They enable local residents to be heard and their concerns to be given appropriate recognition. Their orchestration and presentation of issues, whether contentious or not, can maximise the value and weight of expert evidence. Also, in selecting experts and the areas of expertise presented, they can determine the completeness of information that is made available for consideration in the decision-making process.

Where a project is viewed locally as controversial, it is clear that local experience and local preferences will only be adequately presented if local people are organised, sustained, supported and represented. It did not need the advent of ELF to demonstrate this, although that inevitably has been its own findings. Local authorities are frequently placed in positions of conflict because of the mixed powers they wield and the differing interests they represent. Not always as a result, but certainly in many instances the economic argument is frequently presented by such authorities as justifying a course even though it may be disadvantageous to all or parts of the local community in the longer term. It would be unrealistic to expect a local authority, which carries responsibility for finance, as well as protection of local amenities and provision of services and for determining what development should be permitted, to present all factors of the argument in a fully balanced way. As a consequence it is likely to be the local citizenry who are best placed, reinforced by expert evidence and professional representation, to argue such matters, even though the responsibility should not be theirs. They should therefore be heard, and a place provided for them as prime parties and not left on the fringes or even regarded as an extraneous nuisance.

Although there is a statutory basis for access to the judicial and administrative process of the planning system, practical difficulties frequently impede the working of this system. Costs, the entitlement to be heard and often the decision-making process itself need to be reformed. What is available should nevertheless be fully utilised, and can be used to advantage.

Example

A case illustrating intervention in the planning process by objectors involved residents in Nottinghamshire opposing a proposal by British Coal to develop a 420-acre open-cast mine near their village. With assistance from ELF solicitors, representations were made to the County Council (the planning authority), and in spite of considerable pressure from British Coal, its planning application was refused. It is possible that there will be an appeal, which will mean a public inquiry. This is an excellent example of local residents heading off a scheme and being well placed if an inquiry should result. It also means the planning authority will take over the functions that would otherwise be carried by the objectors.

Example

A case which demonstrates co-operation between two NGOs utilising the system to protect local interests concerned intervention to prevent the demolition of a footbridge.

ELF solicitors participated in an application to the magistrates' court by Friends of the Earth and another pressure group, ADAPT, to oppose a proposal by Luton Borough Council seeking an Order that would authorise the stopping up and diversion of a highway under s 116 of the Highways Act 1980 and involve the demolition of a footbridge. By co-ordination of such concerned and knowledgeable persons making themselves heard in the locality there was sufficient demonstration of local need and opinion for the magistrates to refuse the Order.

CONCEPT OF DEVELOPMENT

3.4   The town and country planning system in England and Wales regulates the development of land. Development is defined as the carrying out of building, engineering, mining or other operations or the making of any material change in the use of any buildings or other land (s 55 of the Town and Country Planning Act 1990, referred to as 'the 1990 Act' in this chapter). This definition, as can be seen, broadly provides for two types of development: operational development, which comprises activities that result in some physical alteration to land, and material changes of use, which comprises activities that are done in, alongside, on or over land but which do not interfere with the physical characteristics of land (*see Parkes v Secretary of State for the Environment* [1979] 1 All ER 211 at 213).

Before carrying out an activity which would amount to 'development' a developer must obtain the consent of the local planning authority in the form of planning permission (s 57 of the 1990 Act). To carry out development without planning permission is not a criminal offence but may give rise to what is known as 'enforcement action' (for further details of which *see* below).

ACTIVITIES NOT INVOLVING DEVELOPMENT

3.5   If a particular operation or change of use does not involve 'development' as defined above then planning permission will not be required. It follows that such an activity would be beyond the planning system's regulatory control, but may nevertheless be the subject of other controls (*see* Chapter 4).

There has been considerable litigation as to the meaning of 'development' within the 1990 Act, and it is beyond the scope of this book to examine the matter in great detail. However, the following may provide a useful illustration of a few of the issues.

Operational development

3.6   The erection of a block of flats, is clearly a 'building operation'; 'Engineering operations' are defined in the Act to include the formation or laying out of any means of access whether private or public, for vehicles or for foot passengers, including a street.

On the other hand, the erection of fairground swing boats, which could be carried away by six men or dismantled in about an hour, would not amount to a building operation. The courts have taken the view that the structure did not have sufficient permanence to be considered a 'building' (*see James v Brecon County Council* (1963) 15 P&CR 20).

Change of use

3.7 With change in the use of land the key to whether or not development is involved lies in whether the change is 'material' in planning terms. This test involves an assessment of the effect of that change upon the interests of the public as a whole as opposed to the private interests of any particular individual. For example, the change in use of land from use as a field to use as a car park would be considered a material change of use with planning consequences. The introduction of hard surfacing and cars onto the land has an impact on visual amenity, the attraction of cars to the car park has an impact on the surrounding highway network, and there may be some question as to whether vehicular access to and egress from the car park can be carried out safely.

In contrast, a change in the use of a field by Mr X to use by Mr Y does not have any planning consequences. The field remains a field notwithstanding the change in the user (*see Lewis v Secretary of State for the Environment* (1971) 23 P&CR 125).

PERMITTED DEVELOPMENT

SCOPE

3.8 The range of activities which constitute development is very wide. Planning permission is, of course, needed in order to carry out an activity which constitutes development. It follows that the ability to carry out activities on land would be extremely restricted, due to the need to obtain planning permission, if the strict letter of the planning system were not relaxed in some way. Without such flexibility the planning system would be onerous in its effect, in that planning permission would be needed to do almost anything on land from laying crazy paving in your garden to holding a summer fête in a farmer's field.

The legislation provides for planning permission to be deemed granted by the Secretary of State for the Environment by development order for broad categories of development. Thus an application for planning permission does not have to be made for these categories of development as permission is automatically granted.

The categories of development, known as 'permitted development', are set out in the Town and Country Planning (General Development) Order 1988 (the GDO 1988) and include, for example, extension of the roof to a dwelling house subject to limits on volume, the use of land temporarily for markets and banger-racing, development by various utility undertakers and many others.

Permitted development can enable developers to circumvent the normal requirement to obtain planning permission. This could prove a matter of concern to those monitoring environmental issues because, as the standard planning procedures are not used, there is no opportunity to challenge the development proposal.

REMOVAL OF PERMITTED DEVELOPMENT RIGHTS

3.9 The local planning authority or the Secretary of State may remove permitted development rights (*see* Art 4 of the GDO 1988) by means of an 'Article 4 Direction'. These directions can remove permitted development rights of a particular sort either in relation to a specific piece of land within the local authority's area or in relation to the local authority's area generally. The withdrawal of permitted development rights in this fashion may, however, give rise to a liability to pay compensation if a subsequent application for planning permission is refused or granted subject to conditions.

The power to make an Art 4 direction is discretionary. Local planning authorities can exercise this power where they consider it 'expedient' to do so. Local objectors cannot take court action to force the local planning authority to make a direction. If they wish to take action against the local planning authority for a failure to exercise the power they would have to apply for judicial review (see Chapter 7).

Objectors who are faced with unacceptable permitted development have therefore to take a political route, by applying pressure upon local council members. It is generally only where there has been an effective political campaign, with a groundswell of public support coupled with substantial environmental harm either occurring or anticipated, that a direction will be made. *See* Chapter 8 for extra-legal methods.

APPLYING FOR PLANNING PERMISSION

3.10   A person wishing to carry out development must apply to the local authority in whose area the land is situated for planning permission. There is a set procedure for making an application.

OUTLINE APPLICATIONS

3.11   The planning system permits 'outline applications' as distinct from those seeking full detailed planning permissions in respect of development consisting of the erection of buildings. These are permissions which accept the principle of development on a particular site but which reserve certain issues, for example the siting, design and external appearance of buildings, means of access and landscaping, for subsequent approval.

Where outline applications are made it is often difficult for local planning authorities to assess fully the likely environmental effect because the details of the development are unknown. This difficulty is compounded by the fact that once permission is granted the local planning authority cannot deny the principle of development and refuse approval of the reserved matters on the basis that there should be no development at all.

Many developers are well aware of these difficulties and therefore choose to make outline applications. Local planning authorities may only refuse to determine such planning applications where a developer repeatedly submits very similar applications (see s 70A of the 1990 Act). In addition, a local planning authority cannot require a developer to submit an application for full planning permission instead of an outline application. The developer has a free choice. Local planning authorities do, however, have the power to request further information, and if they feel that they do not have sufficient information (eg in order to assess the environmental impact of an outline proposal) they may refuse planning permission.

Objectors faced with an outline application may wish to ensure that the local authority obtains as much information as possible on the anticipated environmental impact of outline proposals prior to determining whether or not to grant permission. This can only be achieved by applying political pressure upon officers and councillors (*see* below).

3.12 Once an application has been lodged with a local planning authority, the authority may direct the applicant to supply further information (eg plans and drawings and evidence to verify the details of any information supplied). As noted above, this power is very important in cases where outline permission is being sought.

Objectors interested in a particular application who are not satisfied with the amount of information provided to the local planning authority ought to express their views to the authority which may then attempt to obtain further information. The local authority's power to obtain further information is, however, discretionary, and objectors cannot use the legal system to force the local authority to act but may find political pressure effective.

PUBLICITY

3.13 Many environmental and community groups have great difficulty in discovering whether applications for planning permission have been made. In the past such groups frequently became aware of developments only when construction began, by which time, of course, permission had long since been granted.

Planning applications are not confidential. On the contrary, they are public documents to which members of the public have a right of access. But very few people have the time or the inclination to peruse the local council's planning files. However, the requirements of public notification at various stages of a planning application provide a means whereby a person interested in participating in the planning processes of a community can become aware of applications when they are made:

(1) All applications must be accompanied by a certificate that either the applicant is sole owner of the land to which the application relates, or the applicant has notified (or attempted to notify) the freehold owner of the land, or the applicant has notified tenants with more than seven years of their terms remaining unexpired, or the applicant has notified all tenants of agricultural holdings on the land.

(2) Where the application is for planning permission for development which either is the subject of an environmental

statement pursuant to the Town and Country Planning (Assessment of Environmental Effects) Regulations 1988; or does not accord with the provisions of the statutory development plan for the area; or would affect certain types of rights of way, a site notice must be displayed for at least 21 days and an advertisement must be placed in a local newspaper.

(3) Certain other specific types of development require notice of the application to be published in the local press and a site notice to be posted. Such developments include those which, in the opinion of the local planning authority, would affect the character or appearance of a conservation area or the setting of a listed building.

(4) Although it can be difficult to find out about applications, short of stumbling upon a site notice, a newspaper notice or knowing the owner or tenant of a particular site, those with an interest in planning matters and applications can maintain personal contact with local councillors and the planning officers of the local authority. They often inform interested third parties that an application has been made, particularly where larger developments are concerned.

(5) Local planning authorities are required to keep a register of all applications (*see* Chapter 9). Part I contains all the applications currently under consideration. An entry of an application is required to be made within 14 days of receipt of the application. This can also provide a useful reference source for objectors.

(6) Under the provisions of the Local Government Act 1972, most local authority documentation is open to public inspection; the Planning Register certainly is. Objectors have the right to examine any application and to take copies (although local authorities may charge for this).

ENVIRONMENTAL ASSESSMENT

3.14   Formal environmental assessment procedures were introduced by the Town and Country Planning (Assessment of Environmental Effects) Regulations 1988 in order to incorporate the provisions of EC Directive 85/337 (Assessment of the Effects of

Certain Public and Private Projects upon the Environment) into English law. This requires what is known as an environmental impact assessment to be carried out and the submission of a document referred to as an environmental statement with the application for planning permission for certain prescribed types of development with significant environmental impacts (known as Schedule 1 developments). It also requires the local planning authority to have the power to require assessment and submission of a statement for certain other prescribed types of development which may have significant environmental impact (these are Schedule 2 developments).

Schedule 1 developments include oil refineries, power stations, radioactive waste-disposal installations, iron and steel works, motorways, long-distance railway lines and certain aerodromes.

Schedule 2 developments include salmon hatcheries, quarries, shipyards, glass factories, breweries, marinas, and water waste treatment plants.

ENVIRONMENTAL STATEMENT

3.15   Once an environmental impact assessment has been carried out it is submitted to the local planning authority in the form of an environmental statement. This provides the following detailed information:

(a) a description of the proposed development, its site, design, size and scale;

(b) the data necessary to identify and assess the main effects the development is likely to have on the environment;

(c) a description of the likely significant effects, direct and indirect, on the environment explained by reference to its possible impact on various targets;

(d) a description of the measures envisaged as necessary to avoid, reduce or remedy identified significant adverse effects; and

(e) a summary in non-technical language of this information.

This procedure provides local planning authorities with a considerable amount of information upon which to base the decision whether or not to grant planning permission. Similarly, it can give objectors an opportunity to obtain detailed information about the content of an application and consequently an opportunity to put forward evidence in opposition to or at variance with it as may be appropriate.

ABSENCE OF ASSESSMENT

3.16   If a developer fails to provide an assessment for a Schedule 1 development, the local authority ought to request him to provide one. If this does not happen and the local planning authority grants planning permission an objector may well have good grounds for seeking judicial review of the decision to grant planning permission.

If a developer fails to submit an assessment for a Schedule 2 development, the local authority may request one. If it does not, then, just as in the case of an Article 4 Direction, objectors will not be able to use judicial review to force the local authority to request an assessment but must mount an effective political campaign aimed at local councillors.

Similarly, where an assessment is provided but is felt to be inadequate, the local authority can request that further information is forthcoming so that a proper assessment is made. Objectors who feel that an assessment is inadequate will, therefore, need to press the local authority officers and councillors to seek further information. The power to seek such further information is, however, discretionary. Again, objectors cannot use the legal process to force the local authority to obtain further information. A political campaign is the only choice.

CALL-IN BY THE SECRETARY OF STATE FOR THE ENVIRONMENT

3.17   The 1990 Act empowers the Secretary of State to 'call in' applications for his own decision. This results in the application being determined not by the local authority at first instance but by the Secretary of State. Generally, he will only exercise this power where the issues surrounding the application for permission are of more than local importance.

The exercise of this power can lead to the holding of an inquiry, at which the local planning authority supports the application. Where such an inquiry is held, it is particularly important for objectors to be prepared and to present a coherent case as the local planning authority will not be cross-examining the developer's witnesses.

DEVELOPMENT PLAN

3.18 The concept of the development plan is fundamental to the present planning system in England and Wales. Local authorities are responsible, on a continuing basis, for providing development plans to guide or influence development in their areas. Plans set out the policies, aims, objectives and goals for an area rather than definite development schemes, but nonetheless they have become more and more important to the decision whether or not to grant planning permission.

The existing development plan system provides for two tiers of plan: the structure plan at county level and the local plan at district level. Together these plans are referred to as the development plan. In metropolitan areas, there is a single plan known as a unitary development plan. For development in national parks there are also Park Plans.

STRUCTURE PLAN

3.19 Structure plans deal with the major planning issues for an area, and set out broad policies and proposals. They are open to public consultation, although recent legislation has sought to streamline this consultative process. Local authorities are free to determine the planning policy for their area, but nonetheless there is a requirement for all structure plans to be approved by the Secretary of State for the Environment. He has the power to approve, reject or return a plan for resubmission giving brief reasons for his decision, if he feels that it does not properly reflect national government planning policy. This means, of course, that central government has the determining role as regards the scope and content of a structure plan and its policies.

The planning Acts provide for structure plans to include policies in respect of the conservation of the natural beauty and amenity of land, the improvement of the physical environment and the management of traffic. Recently local planning authorities have been required to have regard to 'environmental considerations'.

Local planning authorities are urged to pursue policies which encourage the use of public transport, as it is recognised that the need to travel and the choice of mode of transport have an impact upon carbon-dioxide emissions which might be reduced if patterns of development could take such considerations into account. Accordingly, policies should seek to:

(a) relate development closely with public transport (ie it should be located near to railway stations which have spare passenger capacity);

(b) locate development within existing urban areas, but not so as to result in urban 'cramming';

(c) locate development in town centres or near to the public transport network if the proposed use is a high trip generator (eg offices, shopping centre, leisure centre or place of higher education);

(d) locate housing development so as to minimise car use (ie near the workplace, school and other local service facilities);

(e) seek to discourage town centre parking as long as this does not result in increased pressure for development in more energy-inefficient locations elsewhere;

(f) seek to encourage walking and cycling.

LOCAL PLAN

3.20   The structure plan is supplemented by a number of local plans which form the second tier of development plan planning. These elaborate in more detail the broad policies and framework proposals set out in the structure plan. Local plans form the operational policy for an area.

Formerly local plans were not required by the planning Acts, but were discretionary. Consequently many areas of England and Wales were not covered by a local plan. The government has recently introduced legislation to require local planning authorities to produce local plans in their areas.

Local plans also deal with a large number of other detailed matters including policies which seek to restrain development in sensitive areas such as green belt policy designed to check the sprawl of urban areas, or those which specify the locations designated for future housing or retail development, or those which provide standards for the quality of the design and form of development.

3.21 Government policy has been formulated to give guidance on particular environmental problems in the context of the development plan in relation to a large number of matters:

(1) *Noise.* Circular 10/73 on planning and noise envisages that development plan planning will have a role in the prevention and amelioration of noise pollution. Local planning authorities are expected to adopt policies to ensure that noise-generating development (such as factories) and noise-sensitive development such as houses, schools and hospitals are kept separated. This solution is, of course, one that is uniquely capable of implementation via development plan planning.

(2) *Waste disposal.* Waste disposal is a subject to be addressed in the development plan both at structure plan level and, since the recent Planning and Compensation Act 1991, in waste local plans. Para 5.9 of Planning Policy Guidance Note (PPG) 12 emphasises that waste treatment and disposal should be considered at structure plan level.

(3) *Hazardous substances.* Specific controls exist in the UK regulating the presence of certain classified hazardous substances on land. Para 6.21 of PPG 12 provides that:

Development Plans should take account of the location of hazardous installations within, or in the vicinity of, the plan area and the need for new, or the relocation of existing, hazardous development. Structure Plans may indicate general locations where further hazardous development may be acceptable and detailed development plans should set out the criteria for the control of hazardous development and for development within the vicinity of hazardous installations. . .

(4) *Water.* PPG 12 also addresses the need to protect groundwater resources:

Particular attention should be paid to the protection of groundwater resources which are susceptible to a wide range of threats arising from land-use policies. Once groundwater has been contaminated, it is difficult if not impossible to rehabilitate it. Changes in land use may also affect the availability of groundwater resources by restricting recharge or diverting flows. . .

(5) *Minerals.* The use of land for the working of minerals brings many difficulties to the town planner. Minerals can only be worked where they occur, and the mining operations associated with such working, by reason of their scale, duration and location, may have considerable impact upon the environment.

Accordingly, in the past, many local planning authorities have addressed the issues raised by mineral workings in specific minerals plans. The Planning and Compensation Act 1991 has recently given statutory force to such plans.

National policy as to minerals planning within the development plan can be found in Minerals Planning Guidance Note 1. Para 21 provides that:

The policies and proposals in structure plans should express in general terms the mineral planning authority's strategy for mineral working and related development, taking into account national and regional policies. This strategy should indicate the provision for mineral working which the authority proposes to make, proposals to safeguard deposits, proposals to secure the extraction of the mineral whilst minimising the harm to the environment and proposals to ensure the reclamation and beneficial after-use of old mineral excavations.

ADOPTION OF DEVELOPMENT PLANS

3.22   The development plan is, therefore, obviously an important tool for both environmentalist and developer. The ability to influence the content of the policies in the development plan of an area is an important consideration for all, as its contents broadly define the types and locations of development to be permitted in the locality. Environmentalists must recognise that participation in the adoption process of the development plan can give them added ammunition in the fight to head-off unwanted development in their area. Development plan policy is the starting-point for the assessment as to whether or not to grant planning permission. If policies are formulated in such a way that specific development proposals will be contrary to those policies, the environmentalists will have helped the case against granting permission for such proposals considerably (*see* paras 3.23ff below). Consequently, objectors who are aware of development proposals in their area ought to consider becoming involved in the development plan process as a tactical means of strengthening their case when the planning application is made.

The planning system at present invites public participation in the formulation of development plan policy, particularly at local plan level.

Structure plans are in force for every non-metropolitan area in England and Wales. County councils are required to keep under constant review matters which may be expected to affect the development of the county area or the planning of its development. Where circumstances change the county can prepare draft alterations to the structure plan or even a replacement plan. In such cases they must adopt the following procedure:

(1) Following publication of the draft alterations or draft replacement plan the county council must undertake a consultation exercise, which they must take into account before they finally determine which matters are to be placed on deposit for public inspection.

(2) Once on deposit the proposals for the structure plan are open to objection by the public.

(3) An examination-in-public of some or all of the objections will be held. This is rather like an inquiry. The Secretary of State will appoint a panel to report upon the examination of the objections to the proposed alterations or replacement plan.

(4) After consideration of the panel's report the council may then determine whether to modify the proposals; if they do so they will then be required to take into account any objections to these modifications.

(5) The authority will consider whether to adopt the alterations or the replacement plan with or without these modifications.

Similar procedures apply to the adoption of local plans, with the exception that there is no examination-in-public. Instead, the local planning authority must hold a public inquiry before an inspector who again prepares a report.

DETERMINATION OF APPLICATIONS

INTRODUCTION

3.23 The basis for deciding whether or not to grant planning permission is the same for both the local planning authority and the

Secretary of State on appeal (*see* para 3.40). The 1990 Act requires the decision-maker to have regard to the development plan and to any other material considerations (*see* s 70(2) of the 1990 Act).

By virtue of a recent amendment to the legislation, however, the Act now emphasises the importance of the development plan by providing that where a decision requires the development plan to be taken into account the determination shall be made in accordance with the plan unless material considerations indicate otherwise (*see* s 54A of the 1990 Act). This effectively introduces a presumption in favour of granting planning permission for development proposals which comply with the requirements of the development plan.

PROPOSAL AND DEVELOPMENT PLAN

3.24   The starting-point for any planning decision must, therefore, be to assess the proposal against the development plan, and to answer the question: 'Does the development accord with the provisions of the development plan?' There are three possible outcomes:

(1) Proposals which are not in accordance with the policies in the development plan are only to be granted planning permission where the developer can point to other material considerations which reveal that there are *convincing reasons* why the development should be permitted.

(2) Proposals which accord with the policies in the development plan are to be granted planning permission *unless* other material considerations indicate that planning permission ought not to be granted.

(3) Proposals which accord with some policies but not with others are to be determined on their merits. That is to say, the positive and negative aspects are to be *balanced* against one another. If the negative aspects outweigh the positive ones permission ought not to be granted. If not, permission ought to be granted.

Objectors should purchase a copy of the development plan(s) from the local planning authority and study this well. Objectors who can point to specific policies in a development plan and establish that a development proposal does not accord with those policies are likely to be taken very seriously. It is for this reason that participation in the formulation of a development plan can be important (*see above*, para 3.22).

OTHER MATERIAL CONSIDERATIONS

3.25 An application to a local planning authority for planning permission must not only be in accord with the development plan, but must satisfy other material considerations. This has been defined to mean: 'any consideration which relates to the use and development of land is capable of being a planning consideration. Whether a particular consideration falling within that broad class is material in any given case will depend upon the circumstances' (*see Stringer v Minister of Housing and Local Government* [1971] 1 All ER 65 at 77). The factors which arise for consideration are very broad indeed and it is not possible therefore to set out a definitive list of 'material considerations'. Instead, those considerations which most commonly arise will be discussed.

Need

3.26 Developers often argue that a particular development is needed on a particular site to meet a national, regional or local need. An example might be the building of a hospital in a town which does not have one.

Alternative sites

3.27 A related consideration is whether there are other more appropriate sites for the development to be located. A development might be needed in an area, a region or even nationally but good planning requires consideration of whether the location the developer has chosen is the best.

For example, if a developer were proposing to locate a hospital next to a large industrial manufacturing plant which operated 24 hours a day seven days a week, it might be arguable that a more appropriate site existed on the other side of our fictitious town, say next to rolling meadows and parkland, where disturbance of patients would be minimal. The developer's proposed site might pose traffic difficulties which would not exist elsewhere.

Enabling development

3.28 It can be argued that permission ought to be granted for a development because the financial profits from that development will be used to bring about some planning advantage that is in the public interest. This is known as 'enabling development'.

Generally, this argument arises in connection with a listed building which is falling into disrepair. A developer will ask for planning permission to carry out some development, say to build two or three houses in the grounds of the listed building. He will then use the profits to restore the listed building. It is clearly in the public interest that buildings of sufficient quality to be listed are preserved for the future.

Financial considerations

3.29   The financial viability of a development is clearly material to any decision whether or not to grant planning permission. Objectors can sometimes use this argument against a proposed development, but it is extremely technical and requires expert valuation evidence. For example, in a property market which has a surplus of empty office space, it would not be sensible to grant planning permission to build more offices if the likelihood is that they will remain empty once built.

Personal circumstances

3.30   The personal circumstances of a particular developer can be relevant to the decision as to whether or not to grant planning permission, but only in exceptional circumstances.

For example, a home owner might wish to build an extension to his house in his garden to be used by his spouse who was injured in a road accident, is confined to a wheelchair and thus unable to use the upstairs of the property. This is an extreme example but it emphasises the fact that it is only exceptionally that personal circumstances can be relevant.

Policy

3.31   Policies which do not form part of the development plan have been adopted by both the Secretary of State (in the form of national planning policy) and local authorities (in the form of non-statutory policy).

(1) National guidance usually takes the form of planning policy

guidance notes (PPGs) (*see* above). These can be obtained from HMSO or planning officers at a local planning authority. They cover a wide number of planning issues from housing to archaeology.

(2) Local authority non-statutory guidance is issued by the local planning authorities, but not all authorities issue such guidance. Objectors need to check whether such guidance exists and if so whether it is relevant to the particular development proposal.

THE BALANCING EXERCISE

3.32 The decision whether to grant planning permission is, effectively, a question of balance. The decision-maker has to identify the relevant issues by having regard first to the development plan and then to any other material considerations and then attribute weight to these issues. It is this weighing exercise that determines whether planning permission will be granted.

It is therefore vital that objectors:

(a) frame their objection by reference to the development plan and other material considerations. They must ensure that the decision-maker identifies all the relevant considerations;

(b) emphasise the weight to be given to those factors which support a refusal of permission and explain why little weight ought to be given to the factors which might support a grant of planning permission.

Cost benefit analysis is also relevant to any planning proposal. This is considered in Chapter 10.

CONDITIONS

3.33 The planning system also provides mechanisms which can be used to mitigate against the adverse environmental effects of development. This is achieved through the use of conditions and planning obligations, both of which impose restrictions on how development may be carried out and/or how the land use may continue in the future.

Planning permission can be made subject to conditions upon which the use of land will be contingent. Breach of the terms of a condition may lead a local authority to issue a breach of condition notice requiring adherence to the terms of the condition. There are criminal sanctions for continued breach of the condition. The mechanism for continuing control of land use thus exists within the planning system.

Planning legislation leaves considerable discretion in the imposition of planning conditions to the local planning authority. The main restrictions upon the scope and extent of planning conditions have been imposed by the courts, which have held that they must be imposed for planning purposes and must fairly and reasonably relate to the proposed development (*Newbury District Council v Secretary of State for the Environment* [1981] AC 578). In addition, national policy guidance on the imposition of conditions suggests that they should be both necessary and reasonable, enforceable, precise and relevant both to planning and to the development permitted.

Planning conditions must not only comply with legal requirements but also adhere to government policy. This policy is set out in Circular 1/85, which discusses in great detail the various criteria to apply and includes examples of model conditions. For example, conditions can be imposed requiring deliveries to retail developments to be made between certain hours, or requiring specific building materials to be used.

Planning agreements and planning obligations

3.34   Planning agreements are entered into between a developer and a local planning authority. Such an agreement may regulate the use of land by reference to planning purposes. It is an enforceable contract which can be enforced by injunction and against the developer's successors in title. It can therefore provide limitations and restrictions in the use of land along similar lines to planning conditions.

Section 106 of the 1990 Act as amended provides that planning obligations may:

(a) restrict the development or use of land;

(b) require specified operations or activities to be carried out in relation to the land;

(c) require the land to be used in any specified way;

(d) require the payment of a sum or sums of money either in a lump sum or periodically either indefinitely or for a specified period.

This means that local authorities and developers can agree restrictions to apply to a development to mitigate against the environmental impact which might otherwise arise.

COMMUNITY BENEFITS

3.35 Furthermore, planning obligations enable the developer to offer community benefits which do not necessarily relate to the particular development for which planning permission is sought (eg providing a nursery school or a park or to build flats). This is known as planning gain.

Government policy states (Circular 16/91 at para B3):

The term planning gain has no statutory significance and is not found in the Planning Acts . . . [It] has come to be used very loosely to apply both to the normal and legitimate operation of the planning system and also to attempts to extract from developers payments in cash or in kind for purposes that are not directly related to the development proposed but are sought as 'the price of planning permission'. Equally, the term 'planning gain' has been used to describe offers from developers to a local authority that are not related to their development proposal. The Planning Acts do not envisage the planning powers should be used for such purposes; and in this sense 'planning gain' is outside the scope of the planning process.

Developers anxious to share in the housing and development booms of the 1970s and 1980s were willing to provide facilities which normally would have been the responsibility of the public sector, rather than wait for them to be provided by local or central government. It is common today for developers to contribute to what are known as off-site infrastructure costs. The fact that they do so is likely to influence the views of a planning authority and objectors must be prepared to respond to this.

The problem remains of determining when a particular community benefit should be provided by the public sector and when it should be provided by the private sector. Where the limits of responsibility of the public sector and the private sector are unclear, there will inevitably be disagreement between developer and local planning authority. This used to cause particular difficulty at the planning appeal stage where the Inspector or the Secretary of State found themselves confronted by a development permission for which ought only to have been granted if the development met some requirement that could be controlled by a planning obligation. Thus they could not permit the development in the absence of the local authority's agreement.

Unilateral undertakings

3.36   Recent legislative changes have permitted developers to offer unilateral undertakings. This raises some interesting tactical opportunities for developers and their advisers to consider. It will always be in the developer's interest to obtain planning permission while incurring as little expenditure on extraneous community benefits as possible. The unilateral obligation allows him to take a chance on the appropriate extent of such community benefit required to overcome any planning objections to his development. For example, he can decide on the type or amount of community benefit he will offer, and the length of time a particular restriction should be imposed on his land. He chooses which undertakings to submit to the Secretary of State and takes the risk of obtaining the permission or not.

It is always in the developer's interest to ensure that any negotiation as to community benefit which occurs before an inquiry remains 'without prejudice', for obvious reasons.

Objectors need to be aware that local planning authorities may negotiate for some community benefit with developers. However, it can be difficult to discover whether such discussions are taking place. It is important for objectors to maintain a good relationship with the local planning authority officers and local councillors. If such discussions are taking place objectors must ensure that they are made aware of the purport of them and must either seek to persuade the local planning authority that no planning gain will outweigh the environmental impact of the development or must list their own demands for consideration by the local planning authority in the negotiations.

Again, because the power to enter into a planning obligation is discretionary the courts will be very unlikely to act to prevent a local planning authority from exercising that power.

REGISTRATION

3.37 Under present legislation (as under the former system of control) planning agreements have to be registered as local land charges.

Many environmental groups are concerned that planning agreements are entered into subsequent to secret negotiations which do not involve the public. For this reason, some have argued, planning obligations should be registered, not just as local land charges, but also in the planning register maintained under the provisions of s 69 of the 1990 Act. It was felt that it was easier to obtain information from the planning register than from the local land charges register. However, the government resisted this change, arguing that administrative inefficiency would result if planning agreements had to be placed on both registers.

Modification or discharge

3.38 Planning obligations will not necessarily restrict a development for all time; they can be modified or discharged in limited circumstances.

A developer may achieve modification or discharge of an s 106 agreement most conveniently by entering into a second s 106 agreement modifying or extinguishing the terms of the first. Objectors can influence this by bringing pressure to bear upon local planning authorities.

In addition, a person against whom a planning obligation is enforceable may apply to the local planning authority for its modification or discharge. He also has a right to appeal to the Secretary of State for a failure to determine the application within specified time limits or against a determination in any event. The lands tribunal no longer has jurisdiction over planning obligations.

Such an application may be made only after the expiry of the 'relevant period'. This is defined as five years from the date of the obligation or such other period as may be prescribed by regulations. A planning obligation will be capable of modification or discharge if it 'no longer serves a useful purpose'.

OBJECTIONS TO APPLICATIONS FOR DEVELOPMENT

3.39   The following outlines the steps involved in objecting to a development proposal which is before a local authority for consideration:

(1) Objectors need to have an effective means of becoming aware of proposals in that area by establishing good working relationships with the local planning authority, and by searching for notices on site and in local newspapers.

(2) Objectors must have a copy of the development plan for their area.

(3) They must obtain all possible information about the development proposed and the planning history of the site. If objectors believe that insufficient information has been given, they must make their views known to the local planning authority in writing and contact the local councillors. Such pressure may cause the planning authority to ask the developer for more information.

(4) They must obtain any relevant national policy guidance and/or local non-statutory guidance.

(5) They must ascertain whether the development is of a type for which environmental assessment has to be carried out. If such assessment is necessary but has not been provided, objectors must make their views known to the local planning authority in writing and to the local councillors. If the development is of a sort for which environmental assessment may be required, and one has not been carried out, objectors may wish to attempt to persuade the local planning authority that one ought to be conducted. They should also inform the local planning authority and local councillors if they believe an assessment to be inadequate.

(6) Objectors need to assess the proposal against the development plan and decide whether there are other material considerations.

(7) Objectors must determine whether they need to seek expert advice in understanding the technical evidence produced by the developer or in formulating their objection. It is much easier to conduct a case on appeal if experts have been involved from an early stage.

(8) An objection must be submitted in writing. Objectors must emphasise the policies with which they believe the proposal conflicts and the material considerations which indicate that planning permission ought not to be granted. They need to explain why the positive factors to which the developer will point are not to be given great weight.

(9) Objectors ought to be cautious about using petitions or sending one letter representing a large group of people. Individual letters have much more impact, but must not be pro-forma letters. Each person concerned should explain their views in their own words. Objectors should put forward positive planning objections.

(10) Objectors should ensure that they are informed of the local planning authority's decision. If planning permission has been granted objectors may wish to consider seeking judicial review of the decision, and the time limits for making an application are very tight.

(11) Where possible objectors should carry out a costs analysis.

Objectors have no right of appeal against a grant of planning permission by a local planning authority. This means that it is extremely important that objectors make their views known, and in a clear and reasoned way, prior to any decision. Those who have sought ELF intervention have tended to fare better.

The only option for objectors who wish to challenge the grant of planning permission by a local planning authority is judicial review which can help in some cases but is expensive and risky. The burden of showing that local authority behaviour is unreasonable (ie that it is such that no reasonable authority would have acted that way) is very high and can be difficult to discharge. It is much better for objectors to persuade a local authority round to their view, and then the developer can appeal to the Secretary of State if he wishes, and the issues can then be debated at an inquiry.

Objectors who take an active role early in the course of an application may thereby establish themselves as major players for any future inquiry, with the result that inspectors will treat them as if they were a statutory party (*see* below). See also the recommendations in Chapter 8.

APPEALS AND INQUIRIES

3.40   A developer has a right of appeal to the Secretary of State in the following circumstances:
   (a) where the local planning authority has refused to grant planning permission for the development or has granted permission subject to conditions; or
   (b) where the local planning authority has failed to issue a decision within eight weeks of the application or such other longer period as may have been agreed.

THE PARTIES

3.41   The various regulations which apply to appeals provide that the statutory parties to an appeal are the developer, the local planning authority and any person with a legal interest in the land which forms the subject of the application. Third party objectors who do not have a legal interest in the land are not recognised as parties in the appeal. This can cause difficulties for objectors, particularly with regard to obtaining sight of evidence and other documentation prior to the appeal. However, objectors who have taken an active interest in a case, who represent a large number of people or who intend to give detailed evidence at an appeal themselves generally find that the inspectorate will treat them as if they were statutory parties. In these circumstances when an application is going to go to appeal it is best for objectors to ask the planning inspectorate whether they would treat the objector(s) as if they were a statutory party in so far as procedure is concerned, but particularly with regard to obtaining the evidence prior to the appeal, and whether they would require the other parties to do the same.

   In the unlikely event that the inspectorate decline to treat objectors as if they were a statutory party, little can be done, except in so far as a breach of natural justice occurs in which case an application for judicial review could be made. A local planning authority may provide objectors with copies of the relevant documentation if the inspectorate do not.

   Third parties (ie environmental groups and other objectors) do not have a right of appeal to the Secretary of State where a local planning authority has granted permission for a particular development. They may, however, attempt to challenge such a decision in the High Court by making an application for judicial review.

Third party groups who wish to become involved in the appellate process always have major financial constraints. It is therefore important for objectors to liaise closely with the local planning authority so that together they present a cogent and co-ordinated objection against the development proposals and keep costs to a minimum by avoiding duplication, particularly as regards the evidence presented by witnesses. In any event there may be issues which a local planning authority might feel unable to raise (eg because they were rejected as reasons of refusal) but which objectors could raise.

If objectors are concerned with only a small number of issues it is perfectly proper for them to limit their evidence to these issues, thereby also possibly keeping their costs low.

On an appeal the Secretary of State has the power to consider an application as if it had been made to him in the first instance. He is free to refuse permission, grant permission or grant it subject to conditions, and is not bound by the views of the local planning authority. Appeals are conducted by three different methods:

(a) by written representations;

(b) by hearing; and

(c) by inquiry.

See also Chapter 10 where tactics for objectors are covered.

WRITTEN REPRESENTATIONS

3.42 The most popular procedure by which appeals under s 78 of the Town and Country Planning Act 1990 (referred to hereafter as s 78 appeals) are determined is written representations. It can only be used by the agreement of both the appellant and the local planning authority. It is used mostly in relation to the smaller types of development which do not have a substantial impact upon a local community. Where there is organised and vociferous local objection to a development proposal this procedure is generally not followed.

Using this procedure, the parties make their submissions in the form of a written statement to the Secretary of State (or more usually to one of his inspectors) setting out their arguments on the appeal. The developer then has 17 days in which to respond to the local planning authority's statement.

The inspector then arranges for a site visit to take place. No submission on the arguments will be heard at that visit.

Third parties, who made representations to the local planning authority when the application was first heard, are notified that this procedure is to be adopted and are invited to make submissions themselves. The failure to notify third parties can have serious consequences, as it deprives them of their right to be heard and may be taken to offend against the rules of natural justice. In *Wilson v Secretary of State for the Environment* [1988] JPL 540 a decision of the Secretary of State was quashed for this reason.

The advantages of this procedure are clear. It provides for a quick and cheap method of dispute resolution. However, it also suffers from certain disadvantages and most environmental lawyers advise against using it unless the issues are very straightforward. The fact that there is no detailed cross-examination of the evidence means that the issues are not necessarily fully explored. This can lead to difficulties, particularly for local planning authorities and local objectors who have no right to reply to the appellant's statement. On the other hand, a shrewd developer may deliberately choose this procedure precisely because the objectors have no method of putting in rebuttal evidence. Consequently, local planning authorities need to consider the circumstances and issues very carefully before agreeing to a hearing by written representations.

Local objectors need to bear in mind the possibility that written representations may be called, particularly as the appellant and the local planning authority might agree to adopt this procedure before local objectors have been informed that it is even being considered. Again, objectors need to foster good contacts with the local authority in order to be informed of this possibility before it occurs. If local objectors are well organised, and they feel that the written representations procedure is inappropriate, they have at least the prospect of persuading a local planning authority which is leaning towards using this procedure to ask for a hearing or an inquiry instead.

THE HEARING

3.43 It is a common misconception that the parties to an appeal have a statutory right to a public inquiry. In fact, the 1990 Act provides a developer with the right to be heard by a person appointed by the Secretary of State for the Environment. This right can be satisfied by having either a public inquiry or what is known as a hearing. The decision as to which type of forum ought to be used in a particular case is at the discretion of the Secretary of State. However, he has indicated in Annex 2 of Circular 10/88 that hearings will only be used where both parties consent. If he were to decide to hold a hearing where one party did not consent, the expression of policy in that Circular might give rise to a successful claim in the High Court on an application for judicial review of breach of legitimate expectation.

The informal hearing is generally used, with the agreement of the parties, in cases involving smaller-scale development which do not involve complex issues and which have not given rise to substantial third-party interest. A hearing amounts to an informal inquiry where the inspector leads a general discussion on the matters at issue. It is a far more relaxed and informal forum than the planning inquiry and generally the parties will not have legal representation. There is no cross-examination.

The advantages of this procedure over an inquiry are speed and cost. The time-scale for the exchange of documents is shorter than that for inquiries, and the fact that lawyers and expert witnesses are generally not in attendance may reduce cost.

The criticisms of this procedure, however, are similar to those set out above for the written representations procedure, and local planning authorities and local objectors need to bear similar considerations in mind.

Public local inquiries

3.44 Public local inquiries provide the most formal forum for the resolution of s 78 planning appeals. They are, however, much more informal than the courts. Inquiries are held by inspectors appointed by the Secretary of State. Generally, the inspector who holds the inquiry also determines the appeal. However, in cases involving large-scale development or development which has attracted considerable local interest, the Secretary of State himself will determine the appeal after receiving a report from the inspector who holds the inquiry. The details of the procedure to be adopted depends upon who is to determine the appeal.

At some inquiries an assessor may be appointed to help the inspector to address issues which are normally of a technical nature, for example hydrology, or which call for some particular expertise (such as the assessment of risk of bird-strikes at an airport or particular horticultural issues). If an assessor is appointed he will prepare a report for the inspector.

3.45   The aim of pre-inquiry procedure is to ensure that all parties participating in an inquiry have prior knowledge of all matters to be raised there. (*See* Circular 10/88.) Procedure runs from the 'relevant date', which will be the date of the Secretary of State's letter to the parties giving notice of the inquiry date. There are a number of stages, not all of which are relevant in every case.

Outline statement

3.46   In the case of a major public inquiry (eg in relation to an airport or some other development of national significance) the first procedural stage is the preparation of an 'Outline Statement' by each of the parties. This is intended to set out the main submission that each of the parties will make at the inquiry. It provides the inspector with a framework of the issues so that he may organise the efficient running of the inquiry. Very often, however, this document is not required.

Pre-inquiry meeting

3.47   One or more meetings may be held to enable the parties and the inspector to discuss the organisation of the inquiry with the aim of ensuring that it is conducted quickly and efficiently. Such meetings are generally only held where there will be a number of third parties involved in addition to the appellant and the local planning authority, as in major public inquiries of national or regional interest and/or for inquiries which involve particularly technical issues.

Statement of case

3.48   The parties are required to submit a 'Statement of case', to clarify the main issues in advance of the inquiry, and to hold the parties to them as far as possible. The statement must contain full particulars of the case which a person proposes to put forward at an inquiry and a list of any documents which that person intends to refer to or to put in evidence. In the jargon of the planning world this document is often referred to as a 'Rule 6 Statement' and is required pursuant to s 78 of the Town and Country Planning Act 1990.

Generally this document must be submitted by the local planning authority within six weeks of the relevant date and it must be served upon the other parties. The appellant has nine weeks from the relevant date to submit his. In any event, however, this document should be served no later than four weeks before the date of the inquiry.

The problem with drafting any pre-inquiry document is that most parties will not want to commit themselves in detail to a particular line of argument. Consequently, drafting these documents is quite difficult. It requires enough detail to be put in, but not so much that the opposing party can anticipate the full detail of the argument.

Proofs of evidence

3.49   Proofs of evidence (and a summary if the proof is longer than 1,500 words) must be sent to the inspector not later than three weeks before the date fixed for an inquiry. These documents set out the detailed evidence that each of a party's witnesses will speak to. They generally begin with a brief explanation of the witness's name, qualifications and experience and the subjects to be addressed in the evidence. Planning witnesses then generally set out a description of the site, the planning history of the site, the proposed development, the relevant planning policies, an assessment of the proposals against those policies and a conclusion. The objectives in a proof (as in advocacy generally) are twofold: to advance the party's own case and to undermine the other party's case.

Date and place of inquiry

3.50   The inspectorate fixes the date and location for the inquiry, which must be held within 20 weeks of the relevant date, and will inform the parties.

INQUIRY PROCEDURE

3.51   The procedure of an inquiry is at the inspector's discretion. Consequently, the procedures adopted can only be challenged by way of an application for judicial review on the basis that an inspector has exercised that discretion unreasonably and/or has acted in breach of natural justice. For example, if on the first day of an inquiry a developer produces some evidence of which he has not given prior notice, the local planning authority and/or objectors in these circumstances might well ask for an adjournment in order to have an opportunity to properly consider this new evidence. An inspector who did not grant an adjournment in these circumstances might be open to judicial review, although the circumstances do have to be quite extreme. An objector alone is unlikely to obtain an adjournment in similar circumstances.

A standard procedure for inquiries has, however, developed. Generally, planning inquiries take place at the offices of the local planning authority involved. The inspector sits in the middle at a table with the parties on either side. (The side for each is not fixed.) Third-party objectors usually sit among the general public, although in certain cases where they are likely to play a significant role in the inquiry the inspector will ask them to sit beside the local planning authority. The procedure generally adopted is as follows:

(1) Inspector

    (a) *Introduction.* The inspector begins by introducing himself/herself by name and explaining his/her qualifications. The inspector explains whether he is to determine the appeal or whether he is merely to make recommendation to the Secretary of State for his decision. The inspector ensures that an attendance sheet is passed around and all those present (including advocates) must sign.

    (b) *Taking appearances.* The inspector goes on to take the appearances of those who intend to address him. He starts with the appellant. The advocate for the appellant stands and gives his or her name and professional status (eg barrister, solicitor or consultant). The advocate should then explain the number, names and professional qualifications of the witnesses he intends to call (although the latter part is usually taken very briefly).

The advocate usually also takes the opportunity at this point to check that the inspector has the proofs and appendices (which should have been sent previously), and may indicate the order in which the witnesses are intended to be called. The appearances of the other parties are taken in the same way. Third parties are asked whether they are supporters or objectors.

(c) *Explanation of procedure.* The inspector explains the procedure he intends to adopt, and usually asks whether a list of proposed conditions has been drawn up. He always indicates that the fact that he is asking for conditions does not mean that he has any views on the merits of the appeal at that stage. The inspector reminds the parties that any application for costs must be made before the close of the inquiry and cannot be made at a later time. The inspector generally checks that he has the correct application plans before him and asks for confirmation as to which plans form part of the application and which are purely illustrative.

(2) The appellant's case
  (a) appellant's opening address;
  (b) appellant's witnesses in turn;
  (c) evidence in chief;
  (d) cross-examination;
  (e) inspector's questions;
  (f) re-examination.

(3) The local planning authority's case. There is no opening speech, but apart from that the procedure is the same as for the appellant.

(4) The local planning authority's closing speech.

(5) The case for other interested parties. Again, there is no opening speech but procedure is otherwise the same.

(6) The interested parties' closing speech.

(7) The appellant's closing speech.

OPENING SPEECH

3.52 The opening speech provides the developer with the opportunity to set the scene for the inspector. It should be a brief outline of the appellant's case. Generally an opening speech:

  (a) gives a brief description of the development and the planning history of the site;
  (b) identifies the relevant planning policies against which the application falls to be determined;
  (c) states the environmental impact of the development;
  (d) gives the positive arguments as to why the development ought to be permitted;
  (e) summarises why the objections are not such as to outweigh the positive case for the grant of planning permission;
  (f) summarises any relevant points of law.

Opening also enables the developer to pre-empt the anticipated objections of the objectors. Pre-empting the objectors' points is a very effective way of reducing the impact that objectors might otherwise have. A developer's witness can explain in questioning that he has answered that question already or that it was dealt with in opening. It is a defensive technique often used by advocates and objectors ought to watch out for it.

EXAMINATION-IN-CHIEF

3.53   The developer then calls his first witness. The witness goes to a table set aside specially for witnesses from where he/she will give their evidence.

Evidence is generally given by reading out the proof (or if the proof is greater than 1,500 words, the summary). It is therefore important to ensure that a sufficient number of copies of the documents to be referred to are available for all parties (and there should also be some for the general public).

The developer's advocate may well ask supplementary questions (often trying to pre-empt the objectors' questions in cross-examination, as discussed above).

An advocate may not ask his own witness on matters central to the issues of the case. In practice, however, it is very difficult not to 'lead' a witness. Most professional planning advocates do it (and indeed are often not aware of doing so). Thus, while it is something to be guarded against, it is not to be over-emphasised in practice.

CROSS-EXAMINATION

3.54   After the witness has finished giving his evidence, the local planning authority and the other objectors are then entitled to cross-examine. Supporters are generally not entitled to ask questions of the appellant's witnesses (ie those appearing for the developer), although in rare instances the inspector may permit clarificatory questions.

The objectives of cross-examination are to advance one's own case and to undermine the other party's case.

Advancing one's own case

3.55 Cross-examination provides the opportunity to advance one's case by attempting to elicit favourable testimony from the other party's witness. Tactically it is better to elicit favourable evidence from a witness before attempting to undermine his/her evidence or credibility. It is often difficult if not impossible to ensure that a witness for the other party agrees with one's own case, for obvious reasons! Nonetheless there are a number of ways this can be attempted. It is beyond the scope of this book to give detailed advice on the art of advocacy but the following may prove useful.

Many advocates begin their cross-examination by asking a series of general questions, apparently unrelated to the specifics of the issues at the inquiry but which are actually relevant. Witnesses sometimes give an answer to a general question without thinking the consequences through. When the advocate has obtained a favourable answer to a general question, he stores this and will come back to the point later in the cross-examination to spring the trap upon the unsuspecting witness in relation to the specific.

Undermining the other party's case

3.56 Undermining the other party's case can be achieved by discrediting a witness's evidence and by reducing his/her credibility.

  (1) One of the most effective techniques, if executed properly, is to examine all the evidence for inconsistencies in the other party's case. Witnesses often have difficulty in explaining such inconsistencies and indeed sometimes alter their evidence to get out of a tight spot.

  (2) Another effective technique can be to ask a witness (particularly a technical expert witness) to define the terms he uses. Some expert witnesses can find this difficult. This technique is especially impressive if used by a third-party

objector, who will generally not be expected to have the technical knowledge to know the meaning of the phrases. A professional advocate using this technique risks looking as if he does not know his subject.

(3) It can also be an advantage to establish that the other party's witness has had less involvement with the case or the site in question than one's own witness. This can be particularly important in enforcement cases (*see* paras 3.63ff below) which turn on the factual use of the site in the past. Some local planning authorities do not have the financial resources to ensure that their officers visit sites as often as would be liked. This can give rise to problems for them, if, say, they have not visited the site in question or have visited it only once, some time in the past.

There are many techniques to be used in advocacy of which the above are just a few. The most effective techniques may be learned from observation of experienced advocates and analysis of their approach, as well as personal experience.

RE-EXAMINATION

3.57 The purpose of re-examination is to clarify, develop or explain matters which have been dealt with in cross-examination. Questions in re-examination may only relate to matters already raised in cross-examination. An advocate is not entitled to omit matters from the evidence-in-chief and then produce them with a flourish in re-examination, even though techniques like this may be seen in media portrayals of advocates everywhere.

OTHER MATTERS

3.58 When all the evidence has been heard the inspector usually asks for a discussion to take place concerning any conditions and/or planning obligations proposed. This discussion usually involves argument on drafting, but from time to time can involve debate on the principle of imposing a particular condition on a development should planning permission be granted. These matters are dealt with below.

Objectors need to ensure that they take every point open to them at an inquiry. Saving a point up for the High Court is not advisable as there is no appeal on a point of fact to the High Court and there are authorities to the effect that no new point of law may be raised before the High Court either.

3.59 The advocates give closing speeches, summarising the case. A closing speech should:
(a) provide a summary of the issues;
(b) explain the relevant parts of the development plan; and
(c) indicate how the development proposals relate to it.

Supporters of the proposals should provide a summary of the points in favour and the benefits arising from the development and provide a reasoned response to the objectors' case. Objectors should refer to the points against the development and the disadvantages arising from it. They should explain why the positive points made by the developer are not to outweigh these negative aspects.

Inspectors frequently ask for closing speeches to be given in writing. This means that the advocate writes out (usually in note form) the substance of his closing speech for submission to the inspector and reads from this at the inquiry.

Costs

3.60 The costs incurred in conducting a planning appeal are not generally recoverable, whether a party wins or loses. This is to be contrasted with the courts, where the winner of a legal action will have his costs paid by the loser.

This factor can be a severe limitation upon appellant (ie the developer) and objector alike. It means that prior to presenting a case at inquiry a party has to ensure that he has sufficient funds to cover the costs, whatever the outcome. Whether or not to appear and present a case becomes a question of balancing the likely cost with the likely outcome and determining whether it is worth committing that cost. For environmental groups this can prove to be particularly difficult as funding and resources are often extremely limited. Funding is discussed in Chapter 10.

A party can apply to have his costs met by another party but must make this application before the close of the inquiry. Costs may be awarded for unreasonable behaviour by the opposing party which has caused unnecessary expense. To demonstrate that a party has behaved unreasonably is in practice quite difficult. For example it is not sufficient merely that they take a different view on the issues. It may be perfectly reasonable to hold such a view.

Costs may be awarded against a local planning authority which has refused planning permission with no reasonable grounds for doing so or which was unable to support its refusal of planning permission with evidence at the inquiry. Costs may also be awarded against an appellant who has appealed with no reasonable prospect of success (eg where planning policy is clearly against the development).

Site visit

3.61   The inspector always makes an accompanied site visit to the appeal site either during the course of the inquiry or, more usually, after its close. Most inspectors will also make an unaccompanied 'drive-by' visit before the start of the inquiry.

The inspector invites each party to send a representative on the site visit. Both the appellant and the local planning authority must be present at all times. There is nothing to prevent advocates from attending the site visit, although in practice they rarely do so. This is because the inspector will not discuss the details of the case further, neither will he accept further evidence, although any questions he asks will obviously be answered. Objectors may also ask to be present.

The decision

3.62   The decision is given by letter (a decision letter). If the decision was to be taken by the inspector the letter will set out the argument and the decision. If the decision was to be taken by the Secretary of State it will be accompanied by the inspector's report and will explain the decision by reference to that report.

Called-in decisions (ie those taken by the Secretary of State) take much longer than decisions by inspectors. As a result it can take anything from two weeks to 18 months for a decision to be reached. The length of time is obviously determined by the complexity of the issues involved.

ENFORCEMENT PROCEDURES

3.63 In addition to the continuing control offered by conditions and planning obligations the town and country planning system has a statutory system of enforcement which enables local planning authorities to take action against those who carry out development without obtaining planning permission.

Where a local planning authority believes that a breach of planning control has occurred, ie development without planning permission or a breach of a condition imposed on the grant of planning permission, it may serve an enforcement notice. Local authority enforcement officers are employed specifically to investigate whether breaches of planning control are occurring in their area. Indeed local authorities have the power to serve a notice upon any occupier of land asking specific questions about their use of the land (*see* s 171C of the 1990 Act). A refusal to answer, a late response or a false response may result in prosecution.

The service of an enforcement notice is discretionary. Consequently, as discussed above, the High Court is unlikely to force a local planning authority to serve an enforcement notice. Judicial review could only require an authority to consider whether or not to serve a notice. The councillors take the decision whether or not to enforce. As a result, political pressure by environmental groups can often cause local authorities to examine particularly carefully whether or not enforcement action is justified (*see* Chapter 8).

ENFORCEMENT NOTICE

3.64 An enforcement notice:
  (a) sets out the matters which the local planning authority believes constitute a breach of planning control;
  (b) must specify the steps the local authority requires to be taken to remedy that breach; and
  (c) must be served upon the owner and occupier of the land in question.
A local planning authority has the power:
  (a) to require any material change in the use of land which has occurred without planning permission to cease;

   (b) to require the removal of any operational development which has occurred without planning permission; or

   (c) to require any lesser step as is necessary to remedy any injury to local amenity.

A local authority may not, however, affect operational development or uses of land which are lawful and/or time barred. Any attempt to affect such rights is not permissible and on any appeal (*see* paras 3.66–3.73 below) the Secretary of State or his inspector would have to amend the enforcement notice to preserve these rights.

The time limits after which enforcement action cannot be taken are:

   (a) in respect of operational development, four years from the date on which the operations were substantially complete;

   (b) in respect of a material change of use, 10 years from the date of the breach for planning control (save for changes in use of buildings to a dwelling house where the period is four years); and

   (c) in respect of a breach of condition, 10 years from the date of the breach.

Enforcement notices do not come into effect immediately. They must specify a date on which they are to come into effect and that date must not be less than 28 days after service. Once in effect, the notice will set out a period (or periods) within which the steps required must be taken (the compliance period). If the compliance period expires and the works have not been carried out then a criminal offence is committed and the local planning authority may institute a criminal prosecution.

APPEAL AGAINST AN ENFORCEMENT NOTICE

3.65   A person upon whom an enforcement notice has been served has right of appeal to the Secretary of State. An appeal must be instituted before the enforcement notice takes effect. Any appeal made after this date will be invalid as the enforcement notice will be in force. It is extremely important, therefore, that the appellant adheres to the time limits.

The local planning authority should enclose a copy of the appropriate appeal form with the enforcement notice. If an appeal is to be instituted this must be filled out and sent to the Department of the Environment.

Once an appeal has been lodged the enforcement notice is suspended pending the determination of that appeal. As a result the appellant can continue the matters alleged to be a breach of planning control.

In certain cases, however, where local planning authorities are particularly concerned by the effects of activities, they may serve a stop notice. This requires a person to stop any particular activity notwithstanding that the compliance period in the enforcement notice has not expired. They cannot be served against the use of a building as a dwelling house. If an enforcement notice appeal is upheld (other than on ground (a) below) compensation may be payable to the appellant by the local planning authority. Stop notices are used very cautiously indeed.

GROUNDS OF APPEAL

3.66   The appeal form sets out a number of grounds of appeal and asks the appellant to tick those grounds he/she intends to pursue. It then requires a brief explanation of these grounds. These grounds are set out in the 1990 Act and are referred to by reference to their paragraph letters as grounds (a) to (g). Briefly, these are:

Ground (a)

3.67   Planning permission ought to be granted for the development alleged to be a breach of planning control in the enforcement notice.

Ground (b)

3.68   The matters alleged in the enforcement notice have not occurred as a matter of fact.

Ground (c)

3.69   Although the matters alleged in the enforcement notice have occurred as a matter of fact, they do not constitute a breach of planning control.

Ground (d)

3.70   The matters alleged to constitute a breach of planning control are immune from enforcement.

Ground (e)

3.71   The enforcement notice has been improperly served.

Ground (f)

3.72   The enforcement notice is excessive in its requirements.

Ground (g)

3.73   The time for compliance in the enforcement notice falls short of what should reasonably be allowed.

ENFORCEMENT PROCEEDINGS

3.74   The three methods of conducting an appeal set out above (para 3.41) are available in enforcement appeals. The procedures are not significantly different.

The procedures for a local inquiry in an enforcement notice case are the same as for an inquiry in relation to a planning appeal, with the exception that, where witnesses are giving evidence on fact, some inspectors prefer to have the evidence given on oath and witnesses may be sworn in.

CRIMINAL SANCTIONS

3.75   Once an enforcement notice has come into force, a failure to comply with it is a criminal offence. A defendant can choose to be tried either in the Crown court with a jury or before the magistrates.

If convicted in the magistrates' court the maximum fine is £20,000, in the Crown court there is no limit to the fine.

INJUNCTIONS

3.76 Local planning authorities also have the power to seek an injunction to restrain an actual or an apprehended breach of planning control. This power is only to be used in extreme cases (in particular where both enforcement action and criminal prosecution have failed).

APPEALS TO THE HIGH COURT

3.77 Recourse from a decision on a planning appeal under s 78 or an enforcement appeal can be had to the High Court. All applications for judicial review have to be made in the High Court. At present only the litigant in person or Counsel may appear.

It is important to distinguish between statutory review and general judicial review because the High Court will not normally entertain an application made under the general judicial review proceedings which ought to have been made or could be made in the future pursuant to particular statutory review provisions (*see R v SSE ex p Royal Borough of Kensington and Chelsea* [1987] JPL 567 and Chapter 7 for a discussion of judicial review).

STATUTORY REVIEW

3.78 The High Court has both general powers of judicial review and specific jurisdiction to review the decisions of particular bodies. This power, conferred by statute, is usually referred to as 'Statutory Review'.

The Town and Country Planning Act 1990 provides for the review of certain decisions of the Secretary of State for the Environment (usually acting by his inspector) and of local planning authorities:

(1) Section 287 of the 1990 Act provides jurisdiction to the High

Court to hear applications which challenge the validity of a
development plan.

(2) Section 288 of the 1990 Act provides jurisdiction to the High
Court to hear applications which challenge the validity of a
number of orders listed in s 284(2) and (3), including most
importantly decisions made by the Secretary of State on an
s 78 planning appeal.

(3) Section 289 of the 1990 Act provides jurisdiction to the High
Court to hear applications which challenge the decision of
the Secretary of State in enforcement cases.

Section 287: challenges to the development plan

3.79   Section 54A of the 1990 Act has made it even more important that both developers and objectors ensure that the development
plan contains policies which reflect their interests. Challenges to
plans may therefore become more common than they have been in
the past.

The right to make an application under this section arises at
the date of the publication of the first notice of the approval
or adoption, alteration or replacement of the plan. The application must be made by notice of motion entered at the Crown
office and served within six weeks of that date. This type of challenge cannot be made earlier—when, for example, the inspector's
report is received or when modifications are proposed. The challenge can be made by any 'person aggrieved' by the plan (*see* para
3.82).

Section 288: challenges to decisions on a section 78 planning appeal

3.80   The right to make an application under this section arises at
the date of the decision letter of the Secretary of State (or the inspector, as the case may be). The application must be made by notice of
motion entered and served within six weeks of that date, irrespective
of when the decision letter is received. The time limit is strictly
applied as it is set by statute. The application can be made by any
'person aggrieved' by the decision (see below).

Section 289: challenges to decisions on a section 174 enforcement appeal

3.81 The procedure under this section is somewhat different to that outlined above in relation to ss 287 and 288. The section confers a right to 'appeal', as opposed to making an application.

The right to appeal arises at the date on which notice of the decision letter of the Secretary of State (or the inspector, as the case may be) was given to the parties. The appeal is made to the court by way of an application for leave to appeal within 28 days from that date. Only with very good excuse can this period be extended. This time limit is set by the rules of court and there is a discretion under Ord 3, r 5 to extend time.

The appeal can only be made by the person who appealed under s 174, by any other person having an interest in the land or by the local planning authority. An objector cannot appeal under this section and must consider an application for judicial review under the court's general jurisdiction.

The application must be filed together with the decision letter, a draft originating notice of motion and an affidavit verifying any facts relied upon (*see* Ord 94, rr 12 and 13). Before filing, these documents must be served upon the other parties.

At the application for leave it is for the appellant to establish that there is an 'arguable' case which ought to be heard by the court. If leave is granted the notice of motion must then be served upon the other parties within seven days of the grant of leave. If leave is refused there is no right of appeal. This is in contrast with the procedures under the general jurisdiction for judicial review which allow for a re-hearing before the Court of Appeal.

Person aggrieved

3.82 The courts have given a certain amount of attention to who is a 'person aggrieved', and the category has been interpreted quite widely. It certainly includes third parties who have made representations to the Secretary of State at planning inquiries (*see Turner v SSE* (1973) 28 P&CR 123 and *Times v SSE* (1990) *The Times*, 21 June). In addition to s 289, certain other provisions provide for a more restricted qualification.

Objectors can only challenge a decision to grant planning permission or the adoption of a development plan by way of statutory review pursuant to s 288 of the 1990 Act. In an enforcement notice case objectors can only appeal against a decision by way of judicial review (as the s 289 procedure is only available to developers and local planning authorities).

A High Court appeal may be started by a developer or a local planning authority without including objectors. There is a procedure available by which objectors can apply to the court to be 'joined' in the appeal. However, the court is unlikely to allow this unless the objectors can show that they have a particular interest to defend or a particular point to make which cannot be made by one of the existing parties.

Grounds for review

3.83   The grounds by which the court can exercise its review function are generally the same for both statutory and general judicial review jurisdictions. These are discussed in Chapter 7.

Power and discretion of the court

3.84   In a statutory review the terms of the statute define the nature of the remedy. Planning decisions are quashed, enforcement notices are remitted. In a general judicial review the remedies are the prerogative orders referred to in Chapter 7. In each case the court has a discretion whether or not to exercise its powers.

Bolton v SSE (1990) 61 P&CR 343 defined the criteria for a court to consider when deciding whether or not to exercise its powers where a decision-maker has failed to take into account a relevant consideration. In brief, the court need not exercise its powers if the matter is trivial or of small importance and, even if it were taken into account, it would be unlikely to affect the decision. If the matter is larger and might make a difference to the decision, the court ought to exercise its powers.

Even if a ground for review can be substantiated, the court, in the exercise of its discretion, may still refuse to grant relief.

The danger with challenging decisions is that all the authority has to do is to redetermine properly. Thus even a victory in the High Court does not guarantee a successful conclusion, and more likely than not High Court proceedings will be pre-emptive.

THE TRANSPORT AND WORKS ACT 1992

3.85   Major infrastructure developments such as marina development or railway construction raise environmental issues; for example, compulsory acquisition may be the only method of acquiring the land for such developments; a marina may interfere with navigation rights; or the construction of a railway might give rise to actions in private nuisance unless the right to sue for nuisance is removed. Because of this, Parliamentary permission for these projects has traditionally been sought in the form of a private Bill.

CRITICISMS

3.86   In recent years, however, the private Bill procedure has been criticised on several grounds. The number of private Bills being sought has increased, and with the general growth of interest in environmental issues, they have become more controversial. As a result, the time taken for Bills to pass through Parliament has increased. Many are unhappy that a significant amount of time has to be spent debating issues of only local or regional concern. This argument, of course, has to be placed in the context of a Parliament already under considerable time pressure in dealing with issues of national significance. Environmentalists have often regarded the private Bill procedure as providing developers with a means of bypassing the normal planning process, replacing the detailed investigation of a public inquiry with a semi-judicial hearing into the petitions by a select committee.

STATUTORY PROVISIONS

3.87   The result has been legislation in the form of the Transport and Works Act 1992. It provides an extra-Parliamentary procedure for obtaining consent for specified classes of development which formerly required a private Bill. It relates only to the following:
   (a) the construction and/or operation of transport systems (ie a railway, a tramway, a trolley vehicle system and guided transport systems such as aerial cableways, monorails and magnetic levitation trains);
   (b) the construction or operation of an inland waterway or

works which interfere with rights of navigation in territorial
waters (ie the construction of a barrage, bridge, pier, pipeline
or tunnel and the like).

PROCEDURE

3.88   Applications for consent are made to the Secretary of State
for the Environment. The developer must produce an environmental
statement and notify and consult persons with an interest in the
land, the local authority and other statutory bodies. Applications
must be advertised in the *London Gazette* and a local newspaper.
Objections may be made, and if they are not withdrawn a public
inquiry will be held. The Secretary of State has a discretion to give
a person who has made an objection an opportunity to be heard at
such an inquiry before an inspector. Third-party objectors who have
lodged an objection to a particular application under the 1992 Act
are likely to be given such an opportunity.

The Secretary will then determine, on consideration of the inspector's report, whether to confirm the draft orders. He publishes his
decision in the form of a notice.

A person aggrieved by this decision may challenge it by an
application to the High Court. The application must be made within
42 days of the date of the notice of the decision. The High Court's
jurisdiction is only a review jurisdiction. The right to make an
application is a form of statutory review (*see* para 3.78).

This relatively new procedure is directly comparable to the procedures and considerations of the planning system. The comments
and considerations set out above apply equally to applications for
consents under the 1992 Act.

HIGHWAYS AND FOOTPATHS

3.89   There is much public concern at the environmental impact of
the increased demands of transportation and the construction of
new roads to service this demand. It is beyond the scope of this work
to examine the law and procedures relating to highways. However,
a brief summary of these procedures is set out to provide the reader
with a basic understanding of the system.

The Secretary of State for Transport is responsible for the national network of 'trunk roads'. He is under a continuing duty to keep the trunk road network under review. Where he is satisfied, after taking into account the requirements of national and local planning, that it is expedient for the purpose of extending, improving or reorganising the network, he can seek an order to construct a new highway or order that an existing highway should become a trunk road.

PROCEDURE

3.90 The procedure is similar to that of the planning system. The Secretary of State must publish a draft order and publish a notice in a local newspaper giving details of the order and indicating a period of not less than six weeks in which objections to it may be made. He is also required to consult with various local authorities and statutory bodies. An environmental assessment must also be provided.

Objections may then be made. If an objection is made by any of the consultees or any other person who appears to the Secretary of State to be affected by the proposals, and is not withdrawn then a local inquiry will be held. The inquiry procedure is similar to that at a planning inquiry. An inspector will be appointed to conduct the inquiry and report to the Secretary of State.

Objections

3.91 The considerations for objectors at highways inquiries are very similar to those at planning inquiries. In particular, objectors attempt to undermine the Department of Transport's assessment of the need for the particular proposal (ie reduce the weight to be given to the positive arguments for the scheme), and to increase awareness of the environmental impact of the scheme (ie increase the weight to be given to the arguments against the scheme). Objectors might wish an inspector to consider whether the need for a scheme is such as to outweigh its environmental impact, or indeed whether there is a need for the scheme at all. *See also* Chapter 8 on this point.

The Secretary of State decides whether to confirm the order. There is again a right to statutory review of the order, by way of application to the High Court to quash the order. Application must be made within six weeks of the date on which notice of the Secretary of State's decision was first published.

Procedures relating to consent for the construction or improvement of motorways or 'special roads' as they are known are very similar.

STOPPING UP AND DIVERSION

3.92 In addition to the powers to construct new highways statute also provides powers to extinguish highways, known as 'stopping up' a highway, and powers to divert the route of highways. These powers are contained in a number of different statutes, the most important provisions of which are s 116 of the Highways Act 1980 and s 247 of the Town and Country Planning Act 1990.

Section 116 of the Highways Act 1980 empowers a highway authority to apply to the magistrates' court for an order to stop up or divert a highway where the highway is unnecessary, or can be diverted so as to make it nearer or more commodious to the public.

In some instances a development proposal for which planning permission is being sought under the provisions of the Town and Country Planning Act 1990 may affect the existing highway network and necessitate the stopping up or diversion of an existing highway. Section 247 of the Town and Country Planning Act 1990 empowers the Secretary of State (or his inspector) to order that a highway be stopped up or diverted where he is satisfied that it is necessary to do so in order to enable the development to be carried out.

PUBLIC PATHS

3.93 There is little point in preserving and protecting the environment if there is no access to enjoy it. The network of public footpaths and bridleways in England and Wales has become increasingly important in environmental terms in order to afford public access to and enjoyment of the countryside. Of course, with this there is a consequent danger that increased access to the countryside will increase damage to it. As a result of the tension between these factors, matters surrounding the existence and routing of footpaths and bridleways are increasingly giving rise to controversy and even litigation.

Creation of footpaths or bridleways

3.94 Footpaths and bridleways are rights of way and they can be created by statute or at common law. Local authorities have the power to make public path creation orders under s 26 of the Highways Act 1980. The procedures relating to the confirmation of such orders is similar to that set out above in relation to the construction of highways.

At common law there are two criteria which must be satisfied in order for a footpath or bridleway to be created; first, there must have been a dedication by the landowner of a public right of way across his land, and secondly, there must have been acceptance by the public of that right of way.

(1) *Dedication*. Dedication may be made by express act or by words. It may also be implied from evidence of user by the public and from acquiescence to that user by the landowner, in the absence of any clear express intention to dedicate. Section 31 of the Highways Act 1980 provides that a presumption that a way has been dedicated as a right of way arises where a way has been enjoyed by the public as of right and without interruption for a full period of 20 years. However this presumption may be rebutted by evidence to the contrary.

(2) *Acceptance*. Acceptance of the way by the public is usually to be established through evidence of user.

Maps

3.95 Local authorities are required to keep a definitive map and statement for their area which shows public paths. If a footpath or bridleway appears on the definitive map, the map shall be taken as conclusive evidence of its existence (*see* s 56 of the Wildlife and Countryside Act 1981).

Objections to maps

3.96 There are two ways in which the definitive map may be objected to; first, when the local authority modifies the map pursuant to the statutory duty to keep the map under review an objection may be lodged against any modification; secondly, any person can apply to the local authority for an order modifying the definitive map.

In either case the procedures are similar to those used in the planning system set out above, in that objections to either the modification or the application may be lodged and if not withdrawn an inquiry will be held before an inspector.

Issues commonly considered at inquiries relate to:

(a) factual evidence of user: who used the way and when;

(b) whether that user was user as of right. This means that the public must have openly asserted their right to use the way as opposed to using it under the cloak of any licence or permission from the landowner. Thus the belief of users of the way that they were using the way pursuant to a public right is particularly important;

(c) whether that user was without interruption, ie without actual physical stopping of the enjoyment of the way;

(d) the intention of the landowner.

Any parties to inquiries need to gather evidence that relates to these and other issues.

There are statutory provisions similar to those which exist in relation to highways which provide powers to stop up or divert existing footpaths and bridleways.

Again, there is provision for statutory review of confirmation of the map or order by means of an application to the High Court to quash the order.

NATURE CONSERVATION

3.97   The protection and conservation of plants, animals and birds is obviously a matter of importance to environmentalists. There is no comprehensive statutory code for conservation. The Wildlife and Countryside Act 1981 is probably the single most important piece of legislation.

The 1981 Act lists the wildlife to which it applies. The Act makes it an offence to interfere with this wildlife, although there are a number of defences and exceptions, eg where the interference could not have reasonably been avoided or it was necessary for crop protection, disease prevention or the protection of public health and safety.

There are, of course, times when wildlife has to be interfered with, sometimes for its own sake (eg for veterinary care) or sometimes in order to carry out development on land. If developers discover protected species on land which they wish to develop, they cannot carry out this development without committing the offence of interfering with protected wildlife. The Act provides for a mechanism whereby a licence may be obtained (usually subject to conditions) to permit interference with protected wildlife in limited circumstances.

A licence is usually to be obtained from the Nature Conservancy Council (NCC) (the watchdog body set up to regulate the statutory system) or in limited cases from the Secretary of State.

Objectors can object to the body considering granting a licence.

COMPULSORY ACQUISITION

3.98 Large construction projects such as constructing highways, large town centre redevelopment or marina development necessarily involve problems of land assembly. The statutory systems relating to such projects (the Town and Country Planning Act 1990, the Highways Act 1980 and the Transport and Works Act 1992) provide powers, usually to public authorities, to acquire land compulsorily.

PROCEDURE

3.99 Procedure is as follows. A draft Compulsory Purchase Order (CPO) is published by the party seeking to acquire the land compulsorily. Objections may then be made. If those objections are not withdrawn an inquiry will be held, although generally CPO objections are entertained with the planning/highway objections and there is no separate inquiry. A decision is then published and there is scope for a statutory review of that decision in the High Court.

An order will only be confirmed where a decisive case for acquiring the land in the public interest has been made. The compulsory acquisition of land has the effect of forcing a person to be dispossessed of their land. It is a Draconian measure and is recognised as such.

As a result, objectors to CPOs need to attempt to undermine the argument that the particular development is needed in the public interest. Valuable argument can be found in proposing alternative sites (ie arguing that if the development is needed, it is not needed in the particular locations proposed). Viability arguments may also be used.

Once an order is confirmed the acquiring body serves landowners with a 'notice to treat'. Once this notice has been received the procedures relating to the assessment of compensation take effect (*see* below). Following the issue of a notice to treat, the acquiring body will serve a notice of entry which specifies a date from which they will take possession of the land.

COMPENSATION

3.100   Compensation is payable in a number of circumstances:
  (a) upon compulsory acquisition of land;
  (b) under the planning system, when an Article 4 direction is made or when a stop notice is served but the enforcement notice is quashed on appeal;
  (c) for injury sustained due to the exercise of land drainage functions by a public body (*see* s 14(5) of the Land Drainage Act 1991);
  (d) for damage caused by the NRA in the exercise of its powers under ss 159 to 157 of the Water Resources Act 1991.

Local amenity and community groups may find land that they own becomes subject to an order for compulsory purchase, and consequently, that compensation issues become relevant to them.

The basis of compensation is different in each case and it is beyond the scope of this text to examine the matter in detail.

Lands tribunal

3.101   The forum for resolution of all disputes on compensation is the lands tribunal, a special administrative tribunal established by the Lands Tribunal Act 1949. Its staff consist of a lawyer as chairman and professionally qualified members (such as surveyors and planners). It is based in London but does hold sittings outside the capital. Proceedings in the lands tribunal are similar to those in a court and appeal lies directly from the tribunal to the Court of Appeal and from there, with leave to the House of Lords.

The lands tribunal also has jurisdiction to deal with applications to discharge or modify restrictive covenants on land and with valuation matters arising from non-domestic rating.

Application to the lands tribunal is made by filing a notice of reference together with an appropriate fee. If the application relates to a dispute over compensation payable on compulsory acquisition of land then a copy of the notice to treat must accompany the notice of reference. Parties may call expert evidence to support their cases but this must be exchanged before the hearing date. Interlocutory applications to determine the manner in which matters are to progress can be made (eg whether a preliminary point of law ought to be determined prior to the main hearing).

Parties are given not less than 14 days' notice of the time and place for the main hearing by the Registrar of the lands tribunal. Counsel, solicitor or any party in person has a right of audience before the tribunal. Evidence is usually given orally but there is scope for affidavit evidence. Only one expert may be called by each side unless the tribunal directs otherwise. The decision and the reasons for that decision must be given at the same time. Costs are at the discretion of the tribunal and may be taxed if they are not agreed. The decision of the lands tribunal may be enforced in the same way as a decision of the High Court, although leave to enforce from the High Court must be obtained first.

THE LOCAL GOVERNMENT OMBUDSMAN

3.102 The Local Government Act 1974 created the Commission for Local Administration for England and the Commission for Local Administration for Wales. Their function is to provide guidance to local authorities on good administrative practice.

Under the auspices of the commissions local commissioners (ombudsmen) are appointed to investigate complaints from members of the public who allege that they have sustained injustice in consequence of maladministration by a local authority. Complaints may be made directly to the ombudsman or through a councillor of the local authority concerned. The complaint must specify the action which it is alleged amounts to maladministration.

An ombudsman cannot investigate any action in which the person making the complaint has a right of appeal to a statutory tribunal, a minister or another remedy in law. The ombudsman procedure is, therefore, particularly useful where a local authority has a discretionary power to act but fails to do so, notwithstanding requests from local objectors. (Examples are failures to serve enforcement notices, stop notices or Article 4 directions.)

The local authority concerned is given an opportunity to investigate the allegation and to respond to the ombudsman, who will then begin his investigation. Investigations are conducted in private and procedure is at the discretion of the ombudsman. He has extensive powers to require disclosure of documents. The ombudsman's report does not usually name any person involved except where a member of a council has acted in breach of the National Code of Local Government Conduct. If the report concludes that injustice has been caused by maladministration, the council then has a duty to consider it and notify him within three months of any action which has or will be taken. If the local authority does not give this notification or the commissioner is not satisfied with the action taken he is to write a further report setting out his recommendations for the action which he thinks the authority ought to take to prevent similar injustice in the future. If the local authority still does not respond, the commissioner can require the local authority to set out its position in a statement in a local newspaper.

Maladministration is not defined in the 1974 Act, but it has been usefully defined by Richard Crossman as including 'bias, neglect, inattention, delay, incompetence, ineptitude, perversity, turpitude, arbitrariness and so on'. The Commission has published a booklet, 'Complaint about the Council?' which states that:

> *If a council do something the wrong way, do something they should not have done, or fail to do something they should have done, that is maladministration. Some examples of maladministration are: neglect and unjustified delay, failure to follow a council's agreed policies, rules or procedures, failure to have proper procedure, malice, bias or unfair discrimination, failure to tell people of their rights, failure to provide proper advice or information when reasonably requested, providing inaccurate or misleading advice.*

Objectors, who are pushing for a local authority to take action which is discretionary, sometimes find the threat of a complaint to the ombudsman very useful. However, care needs to be taken as some local authorities do not take kindly to such threats.

CONCLUSION

3.103 Inevitably, this has been a brief exposition on the wide ranging aspects of the town and country planning system and related matters which serve to protect the environment. As was discussed, the systems do not readily acknowledge a role for third parties. This can be seen in the ways in which it is difficult for objectors to obtain information and become 'officially' involved in appeals and inquiries. If the provisions of the Fifth Action Programme are implemented (see Chapters 6.11 and 10.49) it is hoped that the position of objectors will improve in the future.

What has been demonstrated is the need for those concerned with the shaping of our environment to take and maintain an active interest in planning and related issues.

CHAPTER 4

AUTHORISATION

INTRODUCTION

4.1 Chapter 1 considered the statutory framework for environmental protection. In particular, attention was paid to the institutions that have responsibility for protecting the environment. It was explained that one of the main functions of these regulatory bodies is to oversee the regulation of discharges into the environment and other activities having an impact on the environment by the determination of general standards and the issue of consents for specific discharges. This chapter looks in detail at these functions.

Knowledge of how the authorisation system operates benefits those concerned with the effect of discharges into the environment in two particular ways:

(1) It enables them to influence regulators in exercising their powers. This is of relevance not only in respect of determination of existing applications but also to the regulators' statutory powers to vary or revoke existing consents, in order to reflect changing environmental or technological standards. (*See* Chapter 8.)

(2) It permits them to make direct contributions to the decision-making process by means of objections to applications for authorisations and involvement in appeals.

This chapter should be read in conjunction with the part of Chapter 8 which deals with influencing regulators.

As with planning applications, it is difficult for objectors to know when an application for an authorisation to discharge has been made. The obligations on regulators or applicants to advertise specific applications are considered below. All too often potential objectors learn too late, if at all, of the existence of applications. Regulators are reluctant to commit themselves to notify objectors of applications made even where they are fully aware of the genuine interest of the objectors in the outcome of the application. While it is understandable that to set a precedent of obligation to notify on regulators would create a very difficult administrative burden, there surely ought to be some way to improve the publicity of applications. One way might be to impose an obligation to notify all known interests within a given geographical radius of the location of the proposed discharge point.

The authorisation process, although analogous to town and country planning, tends to be more informal, and in general it is probably easier to secure the release of information relevant to the application from regulators. In any event much of this information will be available on public registers or by virtue of the Environmental Information Regulations (*see* Chapter 9).

Whether objectors try to persuade a regulator to exercise powers to vary or revoke consents or wish to object to an application, they must generally make written submissions, although there may be an inquiry which they can attend. Written submissions should be as concise as possible. Objectors should avoid trying to cover too much ground, particularly if they lack information or expertise to comment on specific issues. It is often better to focus on the specific ways in which the application, if granted, will affect the objector.

Obviously on many occasions objectors will find it necessary to involve experts in preparing submissions. Invariably evidence as to the impact of the authorisation on the environment will be relevant to the determination. Indeed there are occasions when technical issues are the only key ones and, if resources are limited instructing an expert will be more important than instructing a lawyer.

WATER

4.2 The statutory controls over discharges into or operations affecting the water environment are contained in the Water Resources Act 1991 (WRA) and the Land Drainage Act 1991 (LDA).

This section will look in some detail at consents to discharge effluent, and more briefly at abstraction and land drainage authorisations which have many procedural elements in common.

Application procedure

4.3   As a preliminary it should be borne in mind that a WRA consent may not be the only consent required for the discharge in question. The relevance of IPC consents, waste management or disposal licences or licences under the Food and Environmental Protection Act 1985, in relation to discharges into the water environment, are considered below.

Section 88(1) of the WRA provides that an offence under s 85 (pollution of controlled waters) shall not be committed in respect of a discharge of trade or sewage effluent where the NRA has given consent to the making of that discharge. For the definitions of 'effluent', 'trade effluent', and 'sewage effluent', *see* s 221 of the WRA.

Schedule 10 to the WRA sets out the procedure for consent applications. Applications are made to the NRA, by completion of a form supplied by it. Paragraph 1(4) and (5) contains provisions for publicity of applications. It provides that all applications shall be advertised by the NRA in the *London Gazette*, and for two consecutive weeks in a local newspaper. However the person seeking the consent may apply to have the requirement waived if the NRA is satisfied that the discharge will have no 'appreciable effect' on the receiving waters. This exception rather begs the question of what is appreciable. The views of the NRA and those with an interest in the receiving waters often do not coincide. The advertisement system leaves a good deal to be desired, in that those most affected may easily miss an application.

If an application is pending it is sensible for concerned individuals to watch the local press. Some representative bodies monitor applications in the *London Gazette*, and concerned individuals may find that a blanket objection has already been submitted, to which supplementary observations can be added. The NRA is, unfortunately, reluctant to advise potentially affected persons even where it knows that an application is pending and that a genuine objection exists.

Paragraph 2 of Sched 10 provides that the NRA must consider all objections received within six weeks of advertisement of the application; decide whether or not to grant the application; and if so whether to impose any conditions. If an application has not been determined within four months then it will be deemed to have been refused.

Consent conditions

4.4 Paragraph 2(5) sets out a broad range of conditions which the NRA is entitled to impose when granting a consent. Briefly these are:

(a) the place of any discharge and the construction of any outfall;

(b) the nature, origin, composition, temperature, volume and rate of discharge, and the periods when it can be made;

(c) the treatment of the effluent prior to discharge;

(d) the provision of facilities for sampling purposes;

(e) the provision of monitoring devices;

(f) the keeping of records;

(g) the provision of information.

Over a number of years consents have become much more sophisticated, and the above list shows just how much scope there is to regulate the discharge, if consent is given. Those objecting to an application will find it worth bearing these powers in mind as a fall-back position. Sometimes expert advice may be helpful in arguing for the imposition of particular conditions which will minimise the effect of the discharge.

Calling-in of applications

4.5 Paragraphs 3 and 4 contain provisions for the calling-in of applications by the Department of Environment (DoE). Paragraph 3 imposes an obligation on the NRA to notify all parties who made objections or representations of its intention to grant an application. Those parties then have the option to request the DoE to call the application in. The DoE has the choice of either upholding the preliminary decision or causing a local inquiry to be held. The DoE also has inherent powers to call in applications.

Variation and revocation

4.6 Paragraphs 6 and 7 set out the procedure for variation and revocation of consents once granted. The NRA must specify in the consent the period before the consent can next be reviewed. The minimum period is two years.

Paragraph 6 imposes a duty on the authority to review consents from time to time, and gives it the power after such a review to vary or revoke that consent. This duty is an important one to bear in mind, as it imposes, in effect, an obligation on the NRA to consider third party representations as to the detrimental effect of a discharge. An example where this worked in practice was the response of the NRA to expert evidence submitted by the Anglers Conservation Association regarding the problem of deposition of silt in river beds when cress beds are cleaned out. As a result of these representations conditions controlling the levels of suspended solids to be present in discharges were imposed throughout the relevant region in cress farm consents for the first time.

Paragraph 6 also enables the DoE to exercise the powers of variation and revocation itself:

(a) to give effect to community obligations; or

(b) for the protection of public health or of the flora or fauna dependent on the aquatic environment; or

(c) in consequence of any representations or objections made to it.

It is worth emphasising at this point that there is no restriction on who is permitted to make representations or objections. In relation to individual applications, it is inevitable that objectors who have a proprietary interest are likely to receive greater weight than those who do not. However in the case of major discharges or of the presence of offending matter in a large number of discharges, greater weight ought to be given to objectors with a general brief for the water environment. Needless to state, if the NRA or the DoE fails to act properly in response to representations or objections then they are potentially open to a judicial review of their decision. *See* Chapter 8 on influencing regulators.

Appeals

4.7 The applicant has the right under s 91 of the Act to appeal to the DoE against the decision of the NRA to refuse, impose conditions, vary or revoke a discharge consent. No right of appeal exists for objectors. However the DoE is under a duty to notify all objectors to the original application, so that they can maintain objections in the appeal.

The procedure for appeals is set out in the Control of Pollution (Consents for Discharges) (Secretary of State Functions) Regulations 1989.

Effect of a consent

4.8 The grant of a consent to discharge effluent does not operate as a defence to a common law action. Compliance with a consent may be seen as evidence against a breach of duty of care in a negligence claim. However the test for determining liability in a pollution claim is not necessarily compliance with consent standards.

CONSENTS FOR ABSTRACTION AND ASSOCIATED MATTERS

4.9 The problem with an abstraction application, perhaps even more than with discharge consents, may not be so much the impact of the individual application but its effect on the relevant water catchment in concert with other existing licences. The drought years of 1989–91 brought into sharp focus the devastating environmental impact that low flows can have, in that the toxicity of pollutants and the ability of life systems to flourish in rivers are both highly dependent on the flow rate and temperature of the water.

Licensing conditions

4.10 Subject to a number of exceptions set out in ss 26–9 of the Act, abstraction or impoundment without a licence is an offence (*see* Chapter 5). Sections 34–63 provide the framework for obtaining consents. This framework is very similar to that described above for discharge consents as regards the method of application and determination, advertisement, rights of objection, and procedure on appeal. It is not proposed therefore to consider these areas again, but rather to look at features of the licensing system that are specific to abstraction licences.

  (1) An application can only be made by the occupier of the land adjacent to overground water or above underground strata.

(2) By virtue of s 39 of the WRA the NRA must have regard to the rights and privileges of those who would be affected by the grant of a licence. This is because the grant of a licence protects the grantee from a civil action in nuisance arising from the exercise of the licence (*see* s 48).

(3) The NRA is under a duty to take into account all matters that it would take into account if determining a Minimum Acceptable Flow (*see* Chapter 1). Broadly speaking this means, *inter alia*, that it must have regard to the level of flows in inland waters, and to the environmental and recreational duties imposed on the NRA in ss 16 and 17 of the WRA. Section 51ff set out the procedure for modification of licences. Again this procedure has much in common with that for discharge consents.

(4) There is also, as we have seen above (*see* Chapter 1), an authorisation procedure for the carrying out of works to a watercourse or to dams and weirs and to secure the free flow of watercourses. These are contained in s 109 of the WRA and ss 23, 25 and 28 of the LDA. These sections require anyone wishing to carry out such works to obtain consent from the NRA or an Internal Drainage Board as the case may be. Works carried out without consent are deemed to be a nuisance and the statutory body may require their removal and secure the payment of a daily fine until they are removed.

LAND

WASTE LICENSING

4.11   The regulation of the disposal of waste on land is at present the subject of substantial reorganisation as the relevant parts of the EPA come into effect.

Example

An illustration of this is the case referred to ELF by the Hadzar, Shemal Green and Hanbury Action Group. This related to a proposed waste disposal site near Droitwich. Representations made by the Group assisted in persuading the county council to refuse the application.

As stated in Chapter 1, the waste management licensing system of Part II of the EPA was implemented by the Waste Management Licensing Regulations 1994 ('the Regulations'). These came into force on 1 May 1994 and implemented EC Directive 75/442/EC as amended by Directives 91/156 and 91/692. The new licensing provisions of the EPA are explained in para 4.14ff below. Sections 35 to 44 establish the new waste management licensing system. A Waste Regulation Authority (WRA) grants a waste management licence which authorises the treatment, keeping or disposal of controlled waste in or on land or the treatment or disposal of controlled waste by a mobile plant (s 35(1) of the EPA).

Controlled waste

4.12   Controlled waste is waste that is controlled by the EPA. It is defined as 'household, industrial and commercial waste or any such waste' by s 75(4) of the EPA. A more detailed definition of household, industrial and commercial waste is given in s 75(5), (6) and (7) respectively. This has now been amended by reg 24(8) of the Regulations in order to bring the UK into line with Dir 75/442. The above definitions have been altered so that waste which is not 'Directive Waste' as defined by reg 1(1) is no longer household, industrial or commercial waste. 'Directive Waste' is any substance or object in the categories set out in Part II of Sched 4 to the Regulation which the producer or the person in possession of it discards or intends or is required to discard. These are:

1. *Production or consumption residues.*
2. *Off-specification products.*
3. *Products whose date for appropriate use has expired.*
4. *Materials spilled, lost or having undergone other mishap, including any materials, equipment, etc., contaminated as a result of the mishap.*
5. *Materials contaminated or soiled as a result of planned actions (e.g. residues from cleaning operations, packing materials, containers, etc.).*
6. *Unusable parts (e.g. reject batteries, exhausted catalysts, etc.).*
7. *Substances which no longer perform satisfactorily (e.g. contaminated acids, contaminated solvents, exhausted tempering salts, etc.).*

8. *Residues of industrial processes (e.g. slags, still bottoms, etc.).*
9. *Residues from pollution abatement processes (e.g. scrubber sludges, baghouse dusts, spent filters, etc.).*
10. *Machining or finishing residues (e.g. lathe turnings, mill scales, etc.).*
11. *Residues from raw materials extraction and processings (e.g. mining residues, oil field slops, etc.).*
12. *Adulterated materials (e.g. oils contaminated with PCBs, etc.).*
13. *Any materials, substances or products whose use has been banned by law.*
14. *Products for which the holder has no further use (e.g. agricultural, household, office, commercial and shop discards, etc.).*
15. *Contaminated materials, substances or products resulting from remedial action with respect to land.*
16. *Any materials, substances or products which are not contained in the above categories.*

Inclusion in this list does not in itself mean that the substance is waste. The DoE's Circular 11/94 gives guidance on this definition and provides a test to determine whether a substance or object has been discarded: 'Has the substance or object been discarded so that it is no longer part of the normal commercial cycle or chain of utility?' An answer of 'No' to this question should provide a reasonable indication that the substance or object is not waste. The circular then goes on to provide guidance:

*A substance or object should **not** be regarded as waste:*

(a) solely on the grounds that it falls into one of the categories listed in Part II of Schedule 4 to the Regulations;

(b) solely on the grounds that it has been consigned to a recovery operation listed in Part IV of Schedule 4 to the Regulations;

(c) if it is sold or given away and can be used in its present form (albeit after repair) or in the same way as any other raw material without being subjected to a specialised recovery operation;

(d) if its producer puts it to beneficial use; or

(e) *solely on the grounds that its producer would be unlikely to seek a substitute for it if it ceased to become available to him as, say, a by-product.*

A substance or object **should be** *regarded as waste if it falls into one of the categories listed in Part II of Schedule 4 to the Regulations and:*

(a) *it is consigned to a disposal operation listed in Part III of Schedule 4 to the Regulations;*

(b) *it can be used only after it has been consigned to a specialised recovery operation;*

(c) *the holder pays someone to provide him with a service and that service is the collection [and taking away] of a substance or object which the holder does not want and wishes to get rid of;*

(d) *the purpose of any [beneficial] use is wholly or mainly to relieve the holder of the burden of disposing of it and the user would be unlikely to seek a substitute for it if it ceased to become available to him as, say, a by-product;*

(e) *it is discarded or otherwise dealt with as if it were waste; or*

(f) *it is abandoned or dumped.*

Site licences

4.13   Section 35(2) provides that 'site licences' are granted to the occupier of the land which authorises the treatment, keeping or disposal of waste in or on land and 'mobile plant licences' to those treating or disposing of waste by means of mobile plant.

Under the Act the WRAs will need to have regard to any Waste Management Papers (WMP) issued by the Secretary of State (s 35(8) of the EPA). Such papers have been issued since 1976 and used to be merely advisory. Section 35 of the EPA now imposes a duty upon WRAs to have regard to WMPs and any other guidance issued by the Secretary of State. Examples of WMPs advising on site regulation and imposition of conditions are No 4 (WMP4) (Licensing of Waste Management Facilities) and No 26 (WMP26) (Land Filling Waste).

In 1994 the DoE produced an updated third edition of WMP4. This provides the formal guidance under ss 35(8) and 74(5) of the

EPA (governing the meaning of a 'fit and proper person'). In its introduction, it states that it should be read in connection with the Act and the Regulations.

Further guidance is provided by Annex 4 to the DoE's Circular 11/94, 'Environmental Protection Act 1990: Part II Waste Management Licensing: The Framework Directive on Waste'.

OBTAINING A LICENCE

Application

4.14   An application is made to the appropriate WRA with the appropriate fee. Paragraph 2.9 of WMP4 details the information that the application should contain, such as the location of the facility, ownership of the site, the planning permission, established use certificate or other such planning document, any relevant convictions, an assessment of the physical environment of the site and the working plan. Generally the working plan is the document explaining how the site will be operated, restored and completed. More specifically, it sets out the infrastructure of the site, the waste management processes to be carried out on site, the pollution control measures, the monitoring arrangements; plans for landfill sites provide details of the management of gas and leachate.

The WRA will determine whether the applicant is a 'fit and proper person' to hold a licence (s 74 of the EPA). Chapter 3 of WMP4 provides guidance on this term. Essentially, a person is not fit and proper if under s 74(3)(a) he has been convicted of a relevant offence (reg 3 of the Regulations lists all relevant offences) or if under s 74(3)(b) he is not technically competent (reg 4 of the Regulations sets out the certificates awarded by the Waste Management Training and Advisory Board that the applicant must hold to be a technically competent person).

Technical competence of applicant

4.15   Technical competence is not a final determination since if the development of the operation outstrips the licensee's technical competence he will cease to be a fit and proper person. Similarly, conviction of a relevant offence is not absolute and the WRA may exercise its discretion. Thus, the WRA cannot take into account a conviction that has been overturned on appeal or, where it is subject to an appeal, the WRA must await the outcome of the appeal. It is, however, the responsibility of the licensee to show that when he was convicted there were mitigating circumstances or that he has taken all appropriate measures to ensure there is no repetition. WMP4 sets out the relevant factors that the WRA must consider: whether it was the applicant or another relevant person that was convicted, the number of offences committed and the nature and gravity of the offence.

WMP4 stresses that the technically competent person has to be in a position to control the day-to-day activities authorised by the licence and carried out at the licence site. However, it will be the responsibility of the licensee to demonstrate to the WRA how the management structure of his organisation and the control mechanisms meet the WRA's requirements.

Financial requirements

4.16   In addition, under s 74(3)(c), the licensee must have made financial provision adequate to discharge the obligations arising under the licence. Paragraph 3.70 of WMP4 emphasises that this obligation should be read in the light of the conditions of the licence. Thus, financial provision depends on the site's capabilities for pollution and harm and must reflect whether the licence conditions are designed to prevent pollution or harm to human health. It should not be used to attempt to provide unlimited cover. Licensees must have clearcut plans for the provisions for the full costs of their operations including environmental precautions. The WRA will require a business plan showing how the licensee will be financing the requirements of the operations. WMP4 at para 3.90 advises that the licensee obtain an audit certificate to show he has fulfilled the tests set out in the WMP. This would certify that adequate provision has been made to comply with liabilities defined by the WRA. The WRA may require the insertion of a licence condition that remedial action must be taken in the event of a specified occurrence such as failure to contain pollution of watercourses. WMP4 suggests three ways to cover the costs of these measures: insurance, self-insurance and an overdraft facility. Of course, the licensee may wish to avoid this by showing that he has made adequate practical provisions for this eventuality and so avoid making financial provision.

Consultation on applications

4.17   Under s 36(4)(a) of the EPA the WRA must consult with the NRA, the Health and Safety Executive (HSE) and, under s 36(7), if the site is located in an SSSI, the NCC in England or the CCW in Wales. If there is any disagreement between the NRA and the WRA then the matter must be referred to the Secretary of State for the Environment under s 36(9). If the WRA has not made a decision within four months of the date it received the application then the application is deemed to have been rejected. Consultees have 21 days in which to make representations (s 36(10) of the EPA).

Conditions on licences

4.18   The WRA may impose such conditions as it thinks fit on waste management licences (s 35 of the EPA). Under s 35(3) these must relate to the activities that the licences authorise and the precautions and works to be undertaken as a result of these activities. The EPA does not provide a list. Conditions may relate to the period after the activities have ceased and under s 35(4) some may be imposed that give the licensee rights to ensure that the licence is observed. This may enable the licensee to enter a neighbour's land with monitoring equipment. In effect, a licensee may be granted permanent access to adjoining land. Under reg 13 of the Regulations no conditions may be imposed only to secure the health of persons at work.

Paragraph 2.17 of WMP4 details the types of conditions that may be imposed:

(a) those setting absolute but simple requirements, eg what is to be displayed on notice boards;

(b) those setting absolute environmental performance standards but which give the operator discretion on meeting those standards, eg standards for control of gas, odour or litter;

(c) conditions which require the operator to carry out an activity in the way his working plan has described it.

The WRA must decide what measures are necessary to achieve the primary obligations of the licence and should incorporate them as enforceable licence conditions. Appendix A to WMP4 gives a checklist of the key matters to be considered by WRAs when drafting licences to ensure the working plan and licence conditions provide effective control.

Provision for discharges into groundwater

4.19   Specific provision is made in the Regulations for dealing with applications for activities which may lead to the discharge into groundwater of substances in Lists I and II in Dir 80/68/EEC. Regulation 15 stipulates that such activities will be subject to prior investigation and if the WRA is not satisfied that the groundwater will not be affected it may impose conditions to prevent contamination of the groundwater. The investigations will include the examination of the hydrological conditions of the site, the possible purifying powers of the soil and the sub-soil, and the risk of pollution and alteration of the quality of the groundwater from the discharge. There must also be appropriate monitoring and guidance, as specified in Appendix C to WMP4.

Exclusions

4.20   Various activities are excluded from the waste licensing system. Regulation 16 provides for the exemption of certain activities from the waste licensing system which are controlled by other systems such as recovery of waste under Part I of the EPA (all those processes subject to the IPC system) or disposal of liquid under Parts II or III of the Water Resources Act 1991.

Regulation 17 also exempts from s 33(1)(a) and (b) (*see* para 5.32 of Chapter 5) of the EPA those activities set out in Sched 3 to the Regulations. Forty-three such activities are listed. Regulation 18 provides for a system of registration for those activities.

Finally, Annex 5 of the Circular 11/95 gives extensive guidance on the activities excluded under regs 16 and 17.

4.21   A WRA may vary (s 37 of the EPA), suspend (s 38) or revoke (s 38) a licence.

Variation and modification

4.22   Under s 37(1)(a) a WRA may vary a licence if it believes that it is necessary to ensure that the licensee's activities do not cause pollution of the environment or danger to public health or do not become seriously detrimental to the amenities of the locality affected by his activities. The licensee may apply to modify the licence under s 37(1)(b) but he must pay a fee in accordance with the Waste Management Licensing (Fees and Charges) Scheme 1994. Paragraphs 2.25 to 2.29 of WMP4 provide guidance on the need for modifications if changes at the site will affect 'the primary objectives of licensing'. If the changes (which may include controls of gas, leachate, litter and odour) affect the achievement of performance standards then modifications will be necessary. Minor modifications such as changes to the day-to-day development of the site can be effected through changes to the working plan. WMP4, therefore, makes a distinction between modifications which may be made through the working plan and those which affect licence conditions. The test is whether the changes to the operation of the site will compromise the prime objectives of licensing. It cites the example of an improved lining technique for landfills as a change which, since it will demonstrably improve the site's standards, can be dealt with by changing the working plan.

Revocation

4.23   The WRA may partially or wholly revoke a licence under s 38(3) and (4) respectively on the bases that:

(a) the licensee is no longer a 'fit and proper person' because he has been convicted of a relevant offence (s 38(1)(a));

(b) continuation will result in environmental pollution or harm to health (s 38(1)(b));

(c) pollution cannot be avoided by modifying the licence (s 38(1)(c)).

Under s 38(5) the licence ceases as authorisation for the licensee's activities but the WRA may, in revoking the licence, specify requirements which continue to bind the licensee.

Suspension

4.24   Suspension of a licence is governed by s 38(6). The grounds for suspension are:

(a) the licensee has ceased to be a fit and proper person if he is no longer technically competent (s 38(6)(a));

(b) serious pollution of the environment or serious harm to

human health has or is about to be caused by the licensee's activities (s 38(6)(b));

(c) that the continuation of the activities will continue to cause serious pollution of the environment or serious harm to human health (s 38(6)(c)).

A suspension means the licence has no effect (s 38(8)). The WRA is also given the power by s 38(9) to direct the licensee to take measures to deal with or avert the pollution or harm. If the licence holder fails to comply with such a direction he will be liable to a fine, imprisonment or both (s 38(9)).

Revocation and suspension must be made in writing and state the time from which the revocation or suspension is to take effect (s 38(12)).

SURRENDER OF LICENCES

4.25   The Act empowers a licensee to surrender his licence but the WRA must accept the surrender (s 39 of the Act). Under s 39(2) the licensee makes the application with the appropriate fee. The WRA must inspect the land to ensure that it will not cause environmental pollution or harm human health. If it will not, the WRA must accept the surrender. The WRA must consult with the NRA. If the NRA rejects the surrender then the matter is referred to the Secretary of State for his decision (s 39(7)). However, if the WRA does not determine the application within three months then it is deemed to have been rejected (s 39(10)).

Chapter 7 of WMP4 provides guidance on the surrender of licences. It defines harm to human health as direct and indirect: direct if somebody can gain access to the site and indirect if contaminants are released from the site. Harm to the environment will be through emissions, discharges or migration of contaminants. If the WRA accepts the surrender it must issue a certificate to the licensee.

Certificate of surrender

4.26   Paragraph 7.8 lists five conditions for the grant of a certificate. The site must be:

(a) physically stable, ie contaminants should not be able to move from the site or from the collapse of unstable ground;

(b) largely free of contamination by waste materials;

(c)   clear of deposited residues or discarded waste materials;
(d)   free of residues;
(e)   free of continuing discharges.

Regulation 2 of the Regulations states that the application must be made in writing and include the information set out in Sched 1 such as full name, address, map and a description of the activities. There may be further requirements depending on whether it is a landfill site or not.

4.27   WMP4 states that the information should be contained in a completion report which should also cover the history of the site and the kind of contaminants likely to be present on the site.

TRANSFER OF LICENCES

4.28   The procedure on transfer of licences has been changed by s 40 of the Act. The holder and the proposed transferee must make a joint application with the appropriate fee to the WRA (s 40(2)). The WRA need only satisfy itself that the transferee is a 'fit and proper person' (s 40(4)). The WRA must decide the application within two months. If it does not, it lapses although the transferee may appeal (s 40(6)).

As with the surrender of licences, reg 2 of the Regulations stipulates that the application must be made in writing but must include all the information set out in Sched 2, ie full name and address, the number of the licence, full name and address of the transferee or if a company its registered office and number together with the full names and addresses of each director, manager or secretary, details of any conviction relevant to s 74(3)(a) of the EPA, sufficient information to establish that the person who is to manage the site is a technically competent person and details of the financial provision the proposed transferee will make to meet his obligations under the licence.

APPEALS

4.29   A right of appeal under s 43(1) of the EPA to the Secretary of State for the Environment is available if an application for a licence is rejected or a modification of conditions is rejected. The same applies to a licence granted subject to conditions, modification to licences and conditions, revocation and suspension of a licence and rejection of an application to surrender or transfer a licence.

Procedural provisions are contained in regs 6 to 9 of the Regulations. The notice of appeal must be made within six months after the decision is made or the date the application is deemed rejected (reg 7) and must be accompanied by a statement of the grounds, a copy of any application and supporting documentation, a copy of any waste management licence, relevant correspondence, any other relevant document such as a planning permission and whether the appeal should be heard or determined by written representations. A report must be prepared by the person hearing the appeal and the notification of the outcome must be made in writing.

A right of appeal is also available under s 66(5) if a WRA decides that information is not commercially confidential and should, therefore, be included on the public register (*see* Chapter 9). In this instance, the time limit is 21 days.

SUPERVISION

4.30 Section 42(1) places a duty on the WRA which granted the licence to ensure that the licensee complies with the licence conditions and that the activities licensed do not cause pollution of the environment, harm to human health or become seriously detrimental to the amenities of the locality. Circular 11/94 states that this, in effect, places a duty on the WRA to supervise and monitor licensed activities in its area. A short chapter in WMP4 sets out guidelines. This places the responsibility of monitoring on the licensee but the WRA must periodically undertake its own sampling and cross-checking of records compiled by the licensee.

THE FOOD AND ENVIRONMENTAL PROTECTION ACT 1985

4.31 Provision for the deposit of waste at sea is covered in Part II of the Food and Environmental Protection Act 1985. Under this Act the Minister for Agriculture, Fisheries and Food (MAFF) is the licensing authority. Section 5 requires a licence for the deposit of substances and articles either in the sea or under the seabed from a vehicle, vessel, aircraft, hovercraft, marine structure, floating container or a structure on land constructed or adapted wholly or

mainly for the purpose of depositing solids at sea. The sea is
defined by s 24(1) as: 'any area submerged at mean high water
springs and also includes so far as the tide flows at mean high
water springs, an estuary or arm of the sea and waters of any
channel, creek, bay or river'. Regulation 16(1)(d) of the
Regulations exempts such operations from the new waste management licensing system. Essentially, all disposal and recovery of
operations taking place below the high water mark are not caught
by Part II of the EPA. The following is an example of ELF involvement in a waste disposal problem.

Example

A site in Scabba Wood, east of Doncaster, South Yorkshire,
was in operation pursuant to a regulatory licence, and
appropriate planning permission had been granted.
Concerned local residents were referred to an ELF environmental consultant who came to the view that the site was
intrinsically unsafe, with the real prospect of explosive gas or
leachate passing through the landfill containment, which
comprised a one-metre thick layer of clay, with potentially
devastating local consequences.

Representations were made to the regulatory authority,
Doncaster Metropolitan Borough Council as well as to the site
operators. It was clear that the potential risk had not been
fully considered but the report of the consultants raised sufficient concern, and the operators of the site have ceased further
activity there.

This case demonstrates the value of local vigilance and
shows that, even if a licence is granted, where the facts are such
as to cause concern (and are supported by evidence), an intrinsically unsafe operation can be stopped.

Air

4.32 It is convenient to consider the authorisation systems for
IPC and APC together. Although they form different systems of
control and are regulated by different bodies—HMIP in the case
of IPC and local authorities in the case of APC—the systems are

very similar and arise from the same statutory provisions in EPA Part I. The Act refers to enforcing authorities, a term which embodies both HMIP and local authorities according to whether IPC or APC authorisation is needed. The same terms are used in this text.

Application

4.33 An application for an authorisation must be made to the appropriate enforcing authority. The regulations which set out the procedures to be followed in such an application are the Environmental Protection (Applications, Appeals and Registers) Regulations 1991. The procedure normally has three key stages:
 (a) information gathering from the applicant;
 (b) information collection from other sources (such as advertisements, consideration of public representations and consultation with specified statutory bodies);
 (c) determination by the enforcing authority in the light of the data obtained.
In exceptional cases the Secretary of State has power either to direct the enforcing authority to grant or refuse an application (s 6(5) of the EPA) or to call in an application to be dealt with by himself (EPA, Sched 1, para 3). If the call-in procedure is instigated by the Secretary of State then either a local inquiry or informal hearings may be held. The Secretary of State will direct the enforcing authority to decide the application in a particular way.
 The regulations set down the information which the applicant must provide. This should include:
 (a) a full description of the process, including details of how the applicant intends to or is using BATNEEC (*see* below) to prevent or minimise releases into the environment or to render such releases harmless;
 (b) details of the amount, content and monitoring of any releases of prescribed substances;
 (c) a detailed environmental assessment of the implications of the process or substances released;
 (d) IPC applications must include information on how the applicant intends to achieve BPEO (*see* below).

Further information

4.34 If the enforcing authority requires further information to determine the application, it may request this. If the applicant fails to provide it the enforcing authority may refuse to determine the application: EPA, Sched 1, para 1.

Advertising of application

4.35 The applicant must advertise the application (reg 5) between 14 and 42 days after the application was made in a newspaper circulating in the area in which the process is to be carried on. The advertisement must contain details of the process, the availability of full information on the public registers (*see* Chapter 9 below), the location of the register and an invitation to make representations within 28 days to the enforcing authority.

Consultation on applications

4.36 Regulation 4 provides for mandatory consultation by the enforcing authority in all cases with the HSE (concerning the health and safety of people at work in connection with the process). In addition in all IPC applications the MAFF must be consulted and in IPC applications which concern release of substances into water, the NRA. If there may be a discharge to a sewer the sewage undertaker must be consulted and if a site of special scientific interest may be affected then English Nature or the CCW should be contacted. In all cases the enforcing authority must contact the consultee within 14 days of the application being made and give it 28 days to make representations.

Any representations made as a result of consultation or advertisement must be considered when the application is determined: EPA, Sched 1, para 2.

Fees

4.37 Fees are payable in respect of a number of matters under s 8 of the EPA, including applications for authorisations. If the fee is not submitted with the application, the application will be refused: s 6(2) of the EPA.

ROLE OF OBJECTORS

4.38 The role of objectors in the application process may be three-fold:

(a) to make individual representations on the proposal;

(b) to lobby the consultees in order to see if they will take up any of the objections;

(c) to ensure that the statutory procedures set out in the regulations are complied with.

Lobbying and representations may relate both to whether an authorisation should be granted at all and to the conditions which should be imposed. In considering conditions regard should be had to the sections on BATNEEC and BPEO below and to the relevant guidance notes.

Where the statutory procedures are not followed judicial review may be possible (*see* Chapter 7).

It is also important to bear in mind in making representations and objections in relation to IPC and APC applications that the UK is committed both by the Treaty of Rome as amended by the Maastricht Treaty and in DoE policy to a precautionary approach to pollution control (*see* Chapter 6).

DETERMINATION OF APPLICATIONS

4.39 The Environmental Protection (Authorisation of Processes) (Determination Periods) Order 1991 sets out the periods in which applications should be decided. The enforcing authority usually has four months in which to determine an application unless a longer period is agreed with the applicant. If an applicant wishes to appeal then at the end of the period it may contact the enforcing authority stating that it elects to treat the failure to determine as a refusal: EPA, Sched 1, para 5. Applications to local authorities normally have to be determined within 12 months.

The enforcing authority must (within the period laid down) either grant the application subject to the conditions required or allowed by the EPA or refuse it: s 6(3) of the EPA. In the case of refusals there is an obligation to refuse if the enforcing authority considers that the applicant would be unable to carry on the process in compliance with the contemplated conditions: s 6(4) of the EPA. DoE guidance ('Integrated Pollution Control—A Practical Guide' and, in respect of APC, General Guidance Note 1) also indicates that a refusal is likely if the process is to involve a release which constitutes a recognised health hazard either in the short or long term. These matters are of importance to objectors.

CONDITIONS

4.40   Under s 7 of the EPA the enforcing authority has wide powers to impose conditions:

(1) It has to include conditions which the Secretary of State directs should be included (under s 7(3) of the EPA) in all authorisations, authorisations of a particular description or a particular authorisation.

(2) It should bear in mind a number of statutory objectives in setting other conditions and set those which it considers appropriate to achieve those objectives.

(3) There is a further power to impose such conditions as appear to the authority to be appropriate.

Conditions may not be imposed, however, for the sole purpose of protecting the health of persons at work. This is to avoid an overlap with the provisions of the Health and Safety at Work Act 1974.

Some guidance as to what the conditions might include is set out in s 7(8) which (without prejudice to the generality of the powers set out above) says that conditions may:

(a) impose limits on amounts of emissions or substances used in a process;

(b) require advance notification of any proposal to change the way in which the process is carried on.

STATUTORY OBJECTIVES

4.41   The statutory objectives to be taken into account in setting authorisation conditions are in s 7(2) of the EPA:

(1) They must ensure compliance with any directions given by the Secretary of State for the implementation of any EC or international obligations.

(2) They must ensure that any limits or requirements as to environmental quality standards or objectives made under relevant enactments are met. This will include water quality objectives made under the WRA and environmental quality

objectives under s 3 of the EPA. This section permits a number of alternative mechanisms to be used. Standard limits for emissions of any substance into any environmental medium may be set either generally or concerning particular processes or localities. Uniform requirements for measurement of substances in respect of which standard limits have been established may also be laid down. Standards or requirements for any process may be established. Quality objectives or standards for the whole of the country or different parts of it may be set in relation to any substance or environmental medium. They may be set so that gradually they become tougher on polluters. The UK has obligations under EC directives to meet standards in respect of sulphur dioxide, nitrogen dioxide and lead. These obligations are now incorporated into the Air Quality Standards Regulations 1989.

(3) They must achieve compliance with any requirements of any plan which has been made by the Secretary of State under s 3(5) of the EPA. This subsection allows a statutory plan to be made establishing limits for the total amount of emissions of certain substances in the country or any part of it and allocating quotas to persons carrying on processes for the release of substances covered by the plan. The limits may be set so as to improve progressively the quality of the environment. No plans have yet been made under EPA Part I.

(4) They must ensure that in the carrying on of a process BATNEEC will be used for:

    (a) preventing the release of prescribed substances or, where that is not practicable, minimising the release and in any event for rendering harmless any prescribed substances which are so released;

    (b) rendering harmless any other substances which might cause harm if released.

    Prescribed substances are set out in a table and are prescribed in relation to a particular medium rather than generally. Harm (and therefore, indirectly, 'harmless') is defined broadly in s 1 of the EPA as harm to the health of living organisms or other interference with ecological systems and in the case of man includes offence caused to any of his senses or harm to his property. BATNEEC applies to both Part A and B processes but is to be applied in respect of APC only in respect of emissions to air: s 7(5) of the EPA.

(5) In respect of IPC only, where the process will involve the release of substances into more than one environmental medium (eg air and water), the objective of BATNEEC shall relate to minimising the pollution which may be caused to the environment as a whole, having regard to the BPEO for the substances which may be released: BPEO pollution of the environment is defined in s 1 as the release into any environmental medium of a substance capable of causing harm to man or any other living organisms supported by the environment.

In addition, in all authorisations, to the extent that express conditions do not deal with BATNEEC, there is an implied condition that BATNEEC will be used to achieve the objectives set out in (4) above.

According to DoE guidance ('Integrated Pollution Control—A Practical Guide' and, in respect of APC, General Guidance Note 1), conditions should only be imposed if they are:

(a) precise and clear so as to be enforceable;
(b) relevant to pollution control (not eg concerned with general amenity considerations which might be dealt with by means of planning conditions);
(c) workable.

Clearly the two key concepts of BATNEEC and BPEO are central to the controls imposed and need to be examined in more detail.

BATNEEC

Meaning and general guidance

4.42   The Act offers some guidance on the meaning of BATNEEC in s 7(10), which states that it includes reference to technical means and technology and also number, qualifications, training and supervision of employees and the design, construction, layout and maintenance of the site where the process is carried on. The relevant EC Directives refer to the use of the best technical means available—a wider scope of matters would appear to fall within 'techniques'. Section 7(11) requires enforcing authorities to have regard to any guidance issued to them by the Secretary of State concerning

BATNEEC (or indeed BPEO). The DoE has issued general guidance on the meaning of BATNEEC in its guide, 'Integrated Pollution Control—A Practical Guide'. Similar guidance appears in General Guidance Note 1 in respect of APC. These notes break BATNEEC down into two constituent parts:

(1) 'Best Available Techniques' are considered first. For a technique to be classed as 'available' it needs to be accessible generally; if there were a monopoly supplier or a technique were only available outside the UK this would not prevent it from being 'available'. A technique regarded as 'best' is one that is the most effective at achieving the BATNEEC objectives. More than one set of techniques may be 'best' if they are equally effective.

(2) 'Not Entailing Excessive Cost' is to be applied differently depending on whether authorisation is sought for a new process or for an existing process:

(a) for new processes the 'best' must be used unless it can be shown that the best techniques involve excessive costs when weighed against the environmental protection benefits and compared with the environmental and economic consequences of the next best techniques;

(b) existing processes receive more favourable treatment. The guidance says that they should be allowed to adapt gradually. Enforcing authorities in applying the NEEC test to existing plants should have regard to the technical characteristics of the process, its rate of utilisation and life expectancy, the nature and volume of the emissions and the desirability of not entailing excessive costs for the factory concerned, having regard to the economic situation of undertakings in the same category.

In general terms the guidance explains that BATNEEC may be expressed in terms of either technical means or emission standards. It recommends that emission standards should normally be used, to leave the operator free to adopt even cleaner technology and the choice of means to reach the standard.

On the other hand recent guidance issued to local authorities concerning APC recommends the use of specific conditions to make plain to the operator the standards expected and uses the example of a condition specifying training for those operating a waste incinerator: *see* General Guidance Note 2. It will become clearer as IPC and APC are introduced how the balance between express conditions and reliance on the implied BATNEEC condition will develop and the use of emission standard express conditions and technique description conditions.

Specific guidance

4.43   In addition to the general guidance, there are specific notes concerning fuel and power, metals, minerals, chemicals and waste disposal, and others are being prepared gradually for each process to give coherence and consistency to the system. These notes will explain the standards which are regarded as achievable within BATNEEC and the ways in which those standards can be achieved technically by that particular process.

As an implied condition BATNEEC is dynamic. The operator of a process must continue to comply with the condition as technology and techniques develop. Unlike most conditions attached to consents or authorisations in environmental law BATNEEC is not 'cast in stone' at the time the authorisation is granted. It develops as techniques develop. Should an operator fall behind technical developments there are ways under the EPA Part I in which these new developments can be enforced: *see* below.

Enforcement

4.44   Finally it should be noted that the BATNEEC condition, whether express or implied, is enforced primarily by criminal sanctions (*see* below) and in any criminal proceedings concerning compliance with BATNEEC the operator of a process is faced by two additional evidential problems:

  (a) the burden of proof is placed on the defendant to show that there were no better available techniques than that adopted;

  (b) if the condition in the authorisation required the keeping of records to establish compliance with that condition (typically one setting maximum permissible emission levels of a prescribed substance), then the fact that the records have not been properly kept is evidence (though not conclusive evidence) that the condition has been breached.

BPEO

4.45 The objective of achieving the 'best practicable environmental option' applies to IPC and not to APC. The latter is only concerned with emissions to one environmental medium and thus there is no need for the delicate balancing of environmental consequences envisaged by BPEO. The underlying purpose of BPEO is to ensure that when an authorisation concerning emissions to more than one environmental medium is granted the techniques used offer the best option for the environment when taken as a whole. For example, a decision to reduce air emissions in favour of placing the waste in a landfill might well be desirable for the atmosphere but not be the best overall environmental option because of the risk of the substance escaping from the landfill and entering groundwater supplies.

BPEO has developed through the reports of the Royal Commission on Environmental Pollution—in particular the Eleventh Report. Unlike BATNEEC it is not the subject of detailed guidance. The Eleventh Report gives some idea of how it may be applied. In general terms BPEO is the option (or options, as there may not be one 'best' option) which provides most benefit or least damage to the environment as a whole at acceptable cost in the long and short term. The Report stresses the need for a proper assessment of the options. In relation to IPC these should be contained in the information provided on an application for an authorisation. Local derogations should not be permitted for social or political reasons, the Report concludes. The words 'best practicable' have received some judicial attention in relation to the term 'best practicable means', which was the test previously imposed for minimising and controlling pollution, under the Alkali etc. Works Act 1906. It has been held that they include questions both of cost (both to the operator and to the wider community) and risk of pollution: *see Adsett v K and L Steelfounders and Engineers* [1953] 2 All ER 320.

BPEO and BATNEEC provide considerable technical challenges for industry and for enforcing authorities. These are in part met by the guidance notes and also by the statutory duty on enforcing authorities to keep abreast of developments in pollution control technology: s 4(9) of the EPA.

4.46   Not only is there general guidance on IPC and APC in the form of the IPC Practical Guide and APC General Guidance Notes 1–5 but also much more specific guidance is available in respect of particular industries and processes. It is crucial that any person making an application for authorisation or opposing an authorisation or seeking to influence the conditions attached to an authorisation use the relevant guidance notes. HMIP regional offices should be able to assist in providing information about the available and most up-to-date guidance notes. Expert input will invariably be essential if effective opposition is to be prepared.

APC Notes are particularly important on the question of upgrading existing plants as they provide standard timetables for such upgrading.

AUTHORISATION MODIFICATIONS AND REVOCATIONS AND THE ROLE OF OBJECTORS

4.47   Sometimes objections are not brought before an authorisation is granted or objections are unsuccessful, but the wide powers to vary and revoke authorisations mean that objection to and monitoring of an undesirable prescribed process is a continuing matter. If fresh evidence of pollution or harm comes to light revocation or variation of the authorisation might be sought. The powers to revoke are vested solely in the enforcing authority but nevertheless effective lobbying may be successful.

Variation

4.48   Variation of authorisations may arise because of an operator's desire to develop or change a process or an enforcing authority's decision to impose more (or conceivably less) stringent controls. There is a statutory duty to review authorisation conditions at least once every four years: s 6(6) of the EPA.

Section 10 permits an enforcing authority to vary an authorisation at any time and obliges it to do so if the objectives of s 7 require new or different conditions to be included. The variation is effected by a 'variation notice' served on the operator of the process. This must state the proposed variation, the date on which it is to take effect, the fee payable and a requirement that the operator should inform the enforcing authority of the action it proposes to take in response to the notice. If the variation involves a substantial change in the manner in which the process is being carried on, then the advertisement and consultation requirements for an application for an authorisation are triggered: EPA, Sched 1, Part II (*see* above). A substantial change is defined as a substantial change in the substances released from the process or in the amount or any other characteristic of any substance to be released. The Secretary of State may give directions as to what constitutes a substantial change and may also direct enforcing authorities to exercise or refrain from exercising their powers under s 10: s 10(6) and (7) of the EPA.

Operators of processes may seek variations in some circumstances:

(1) The holder of an authorisation may wish to transfer it and may do so provided that he informs the enforcing authority within 21 days of the transfer: s 9 of the EPA.

(2) The operator of a process may wish to make a 'relevant change' to the process, ie one which is capable of altering the substances released from the process or the amount or characteristic of the substances: s 11(11) of the EPA. An operator proposing this may first seek a determination from the enforcing authority as to whether this would involve any breach of condition, and—if it would not—whether the enforcing authority would be likely to exercise its powers under s 10; if it would involve a breach, whether the authority would consider varying the condition.

In any event an application may be made at any time for a variation of conditions contained in any authorisation, whether this would involve a relevant change or not: s 11(3)–(6). If the variation would involve a substantial change (for meaning of which, *see* above) then there must be publicity and consultation in the way in which the application is dealt with. A fee is payable: s 11(9) of the EPA.

These powers offer considerable flexibility for operators to 'test the water' and, in the case of minor changes, to obtain a variation with the minimum of delay and administration. More important changes remain liable to full public and internal scrutiny.

Revocation

4.49   The ultimate control is the removal of an authorisation altogether. Section 12 of the EPA permits an enforcing authority to revoke an authorisation at any time, by the service of a revocation notice which must take effect at least 28 days after its service to give the holder of the authorisation time to appeal.

Without prejudice to the general power to revoke, s 12(2) allows an enforcing authority to revoke an authorisation where it has reason to believe the process has not been carried on or not carried on for a period of 12 months—presumably the 12 months preceding the revocation notice.

ENFORCEMENT OF AUTHORISATION

Criminal liabilities

4.50   Criminal liabilities in respect of IPC and APC are considered in Chapter 5 and are a key part of the enforcement of the controls. However there is a wide range of other possible enforcement mechanisms.

Non-criminal enforcement powers

4.51   Although the non-criminal enforcement mechanisms are the exclusive preserve of enforcing authorities, effective lobbying—particularly that making use of the monitoring information on public registers (*see* Chapter 9)—may persuade an enforcing authority to act. This is especially the case in respect of prohibition notices where a duty to enforce is imposed on the enforcing authority.

The powers of variation and revocation may be regarded as indirect enforcement powers. In addition there is an impressive array of enforcement mechanisms. If an enforcing authority considers that a process operator has or is likely to contravene any condition of an authorisation then it may serve an enforcement notice under s 13 of the EPA. The notice must specify the breach or anticipated breach, the steps which the enforcing authority requires to be taken to remedy or avoid the breach and a time within which those steps must be taken. The Secretary of State again has retained powers to direct enforcing authorities as to whether and how to exercise their powers under s 13 of the EPA.

Prohibition notices

4.52 Where there is an imminent risk of serious pollution of the environment the appropriate procedure is a prohibition notice: s 14 of the EPA. The Act does not define the terms 'imminent' and 'serious'. If an enforcing authority concludes that there is such an urgent risk then it must serve a prohibition notice, whether or not the cause of the risk is a contravention of the conditions of the authorisation. The notice may relate to parts of the process not previously regulated by the conditions contained in the authorisation. Prohibition notices must include details of the risk, the steps to be taken to remove the risk and the period for compliance, and a direction that the authorisation in the meantime is suspended in whole or part or is subject to further conditions. Powers of direction as to the use of the powers under s 14 are retained by the Secretary of State: s 14(4) of the EPA.

Both prohibition notices and enforcement notices are enforced by criminal sanctions. If an enforcing authority considers that prosecution would be an ineffectual remedy then High Court proceedings, presumably for an appropriate mandatory or prohibitory injunction, may be instituted: s 24 of the EPA.

Powers of enforcing authorities

4.53 The extensive enforcement powers are only of use if the enforcing authority has adequate ancillary powers to acquire information and data which allow it to assess whether enforcement, variation or revocation procedures should be instituted. The powers are contained in s 17 and include:

(a) entry to premises where a prescribed process has been or is being carried on and, in respect of premises where the process is no longer being carried on, only to enter if there is reasonably believed to be a risk of serious pollution to the environment—although the process need not have been prescribed when it was in operation (ie it started before the introduction of the EPA Part I). These powers are exercisable at any reasonable time and, where there is an immediate risk of serious pollution, at any time without warrant. On entry there may be such examination as is necessary, a power to direct that all or any part of the premises be left undisturbed pending investigation and a power to take photographs, samples etc;

(b) to require the production of records and information whether or not it is a condition of the authorisation that those records be maintained;

(c) to require any person whom the authority has reasonable grounds to believe is able to give information relevant to the investigation to answer such questions as may be asked;

(d) to require any person to co-operate and provide assistance to the authority in the investigation;

(e) to seize, test and if necessary dismantle or destroy any article or substance which has caused or is likely to cause pollution of the environment. There are further powers to deal with the cause of imminent danger of serious pollution under s 18 of the EPA.

The exercise of these powers is not subject to judicial control or approval.

APPEALS

4.54   In view of the extensive powers of enforcing authorities to refuse authorisations or impose stringent conditions and to vary or revoke authorisations it is not surprising that the exercise of these powers is subject to review by appeal.

Grounds for appeal

4.55   Section 15 of the EPA provides for appeals to the Secretary of State against:

(a) a refusal to grant an authorisation;

(b) the conditions attached to an authorisation;

(c) a refusal of a variation sought by the holder of an authorisation;

(d) a variation notice;

(e) a revocation notice;

(f) an enforcement notice;

(g) a prohibition notice.

The appeal rights are limited to the holder of the authorisation or the applicant or the person served with a notice. The public are not given rights of appeal. No doubt the public might seek judicial review of a decision of an enforcing authority or the Secretary of State provided they could show sufficient interest in the decision. There is no statutory basis for a further appeal against the Secretary of State's decision to the High Court but judicial review might be sought.

Appeal procedures

4.56 Appeal procedures are set out in the Environmental Protection (Applications, Appeals and Registers) Regulations 1991. There is a six-month time limit for appealing against a refusal or deemed refusal of an application for an authorisation. In respect of appeals against enforcement, prohibition or variation notices the time limit is two months from the date of the notice. A revocation notice appeal must be made before the notice comes into effect.

With one exceptional case appeals do not suspend the operation of the notice pending the outcome of the appeal. The exception is for revocation notices. In this case presumably if the suspension is going to lead to serious environmental problems then the enforcing authority should consider a variation notice and/or enforcement or prohibition notice.

The appeal may be dealt with by way of written representations or hearing (not a formal inquiry). Public participation is assured to some extent at least by the need for appeals to be entered onto the public register and by the need for enforcing authorities to inform any interested person or persons who made representations on the grant (or variation) of the appeal. In the case of appeals proceeding by way of hearing (so long as at least part of the hearing is to be in public) a newspaper advertisement giving details of the hearing must be placed in a local newspaper: *see* regs 11–13 of the Environmental Protection (Applications, Appeals and Registers) Regulations 1991.

OTHER AUTHORISATIONS

Exemption from requirement to fit dust or grit arresting apparatus to furnaces

4.57 This exemption is considered in detail in Chapter 5. There is no prescribed form for applying for such exemption. Application is made to the relevant local authority and if the local authority fails to determine the application within eight weeks a deemed exemption is granted. If there is an adverse determination an appeal may be made to the Secretary of State: s 9.

Chimney height approvals

4.58 New buildings that have chimneys requiring building regulation approvals are dealt with under the Building Act 1984 by local authorities. The complexities of the building regulation approval systems are beyond the scope of this book. Approvals under s 14 of the 1993 Clean Air Act (*see* Chapter 5) for the height of chimneys attached to the more substantial furnaces are obtained following application to the relevant local authority. If the local authority fails to determine an application within four weeks an unconditional approval is deemed to have been granted. An appeal may be made to the Secretary of State against an adverse determination by a local authority.

Clean Air Act authorisations: inquiries and objections

4.59 The provisions of the Clean Air Act 1993 allow for the Secretary of State to convene a local inquiry in connection with any matter to be determined by him under the Act. Section 250 of the Local Government Act 1972 on local inquiries generally applies to such inquiries.

There is no obligation on local authorities to keep specific registers or to advertise applications made to them under the Clean Air Act and it may therefore be difficult for objectors to become involved in the process of granting authorisations under the Act. An application under the Act is, of course, often connected to an application for planning approval (*see* Chapter 3) which will be subject to publicity requirements allowing objectors to become involved in objecting to all approvals sought.

Construction site noise consents

4.60 A person intending to carry out construction works may seek consents from the local authority for site noise.

Noise abatement zones: consent to increase registered noise level

4.61 Where a noise abatement zone has been designated by a local authority, a maximum noise level is registered for buildings of the classes specified in the zone designation and this level may not be exceeded. It is possible to seek to increase the registered level by application to the local authority. This is considered in detail in Chapter 1.

OTHER ATMOSPHERIC POLLUTION CONTROLS: THE STATUTORY FRAMEWORK

Statutory nuisance and the atmosphere

4.62 Statutory nuisance controls are very important in respect of atmospheric pollution, particularly noise. The procedures and offences in relation to statutory nuisance are described elsewhere (Chapter 5). They are generally quick and effective. Local authorities are under a duty to act in relation to statutory nuisances and even if they fail to act individuals may make use of the statutory nuisance provisions (*see* Chapter 5). A number of statutory nuisances relevant to the atmosphere exist, each of which is defined in relation to the words 'so as to be a nuisance or prejudicial to health'. The relevant heads of statutory nuisance from s 79 of the EPA include:

(1) *Smoke emitted from premises* so as to be prejudicial to health or a nuisance. Smoke is defined in s 79(7) of the EPA as including soot, ash, grit and gritty particles emitted in smoke.

This seemingly wide ranging head of statutory nuisance is in fact restricted by legislation avoiding overlap between the statutory nuisance powers and the Clean Air Act 1993. The restrictions are set out in s 79(3) of the EPA and exclude:

(a) smoke from eg a chimney of a private dwelling within a smoke control area;

(b) dark smoke (for the meaning of which *see* Chapter 5, para 5.48) emitted from a chimney of a building or a chimney serving the furnace of a boiler or industrial plant attached to a building or fixed or installed on land;

(c) dark smoke otherwise emitted from trade or industrial premises.

This leaves the emission of something less than dark smoke other than in a smoke control area (but it may be difficult to argue that it amounts to a nuisance if the smoke is not dark) or the emission of dark smoke other than from a chimney and in any event not from industrial or trade premises.

(2) *Fumes or gases* emitted from premises so as to be prejudicial to health or a nuisance. Fumes and gases are defined in s 79(7) of the EPA respectively as airborne solid matter smaller than dust and as including vapour and moisture precipitated from vapour.

Section 79(4) restricts the operation of this head of statutory nuisance to emissions from private dwellings.

(3) *Any dust, steam, smell or other effluvia* arising on trade or industrial premises and being prejudicial to health or a nuisance. Dust is defined to exclude dust emitted as an ingredient of smoke. Industrial and trade premises are defined in s 79(7) of the EPA and include manufacturing premises and premises used for any other treatment or process. In addition, premises not used for any industrial trade or business purpose, if used for burning matter in connection with any like purpose, are included in the definition.

(4) *Noise* emitted from premises so as to be prejudicial to health or a nuisance. Noise is stated in s 79(7) of the EPA to include vibration.

The Noise and Statutory Nuisance Act 1993 amends EPA Part III by introducing a further ground of statutory nuisance in respect of noise—where noise is prejudicial to health or a nuisance and is emitted from or caused by a vehicle, machinery or equipment (which may include a musical instrument) in a street. Street includes highways, roads, squares or courts or footways open to the public. The amendments to s 79 of the EPA provide that the new noise ground cannot apply to noise arising from traffic or the armed forces or from a political or other demonstration.

The amendments include special provisions concerning the responsibility for noise arising from vehicles or machinery or equipment. These make the registered keeper and driver of a vehicle from which the noise is emanating liable to be served with an abatement notice even though he is not the cause of the noise. (He may seek to appeal against the notice.) Similarly, in relation to machinery or equipment the operator of the machinery or equipment may be served with an abatement notice whether or not he causes the nuisance.

The best practicable means defence (*see* 4.45) is available in respect of the street noise nuisance ground, as is the defence that a consent was properly given under s 60 or s 61 of the Control of Pollution Act 1974 (*see* Chapter 5, para 5.57).

There are special provisions concerning the service of abatement notices in respect of street noise nuisances in s 80A of the EPA. Section 82 of the EPA is amended to allow individuals to take action in respect of street noise nuisances. Local authorities are given additional powers to enter and in certain circumstances remove unattended vehicles, machinery or equipment which is a cause of a street noise nuisance.

CHAPTER 5

CRIMINAL LAW AND STATUTORY NUISANCE

INTRODUCTION

5.1 Chapter 1 shows that the principal Acts concerned with regulation of the environment contain criminal sanctions for use against those who pollute the environment or operate outside consents. This chapter will look at those criminal offences which exist in respect of each of the environmental media. Before doing so it will look at the role of the regulators in bringing prosecutions; the opportunity for private prosecutions; who has the right to bring a private prosecution; who can be prosecuted; and common law defences which apply to all environmental offences.

THE ROLE OF THE REGULATORS

5.2 Criminal sanctions are the teeth of the regulatory system and the implementation of an effective prosecution policy by the regulators is central to protection of the environment. This is so both in the sense of how sharp the teeth are and also how effectively they are used. Some of the offences are easier to prove than others, as we shall see below. However, what is also important is the prosecution policy adopted by the environmental agencies. There has been a good deal of criticism over the years of how few prosecutions are brought in relation to the number of pollution offences that are committed. For instance Greenpeace discovered that in 1986 the old water authorities initiated only 254 prosecutions in response to over 20,000 recorded pollution incidents. The position of water authorities was even more questionable when one took into account the fact that those authorities were themselves responsible for about 20 per cent of those incidents by way of sewage discharges.

There is no doubt that the position has improved, so far as water pollution prosecutions is concerned, since the NRA was formed. The significant number of successful prosecutions against the privatised water undertakers alone shows the shortcomings of the old system. The fact remains that still only a very small proportion of pollution incidents result in prosecution. In the case of HMIP only six prosecutions were brought in the period 1987–91 to deal with 118 'serious' air pollution incidents.

Funding

5.3   Part of the problem is one of funding. Defended prosecutions can be extremely expensive and consume large amounts of staff time which is diverted from other pollution control work. However the problem can also be perceived as one of philosophy. Regulatory bodies, as will be apparent from the above statistics, use the threat of prosecution much more often than the reality. One of the factors which undoubtedly influences the regulators is the degree of public disquiet generated by a particular incident. There is considerable stigma attached to a criminal prosecution, whether of a small farmer or of a large corporation. This stigma can result in subsequent improvements, whether by way of investment or improved practices, which make further pollution from the same source less likely.

Persuading regulators

5.4   Although, as will be seen, there is considerable scope for private prosecutions, the regulators are generally in the best position to bring prosecutions. It is therefore often a good tactic for individuals or groups who are affected by a pollution incident to make their feelings known to the regulators, and urge them to bring a prosecution if they are wavering. (*See* Chapter 8 on influencing regulators.)

Judicial review

5.5   As well as the approach of persuading regulators there is also the question of whether a decision to prosecute or not is capable of challenge by judicial review. Decided cases concern enforcement of criminal law generally but are of relevance to environmental regulators.

This issue has been the subject of a useful article by Christopher Hilson in the Criminal Law Review: (1993) CLR 739. A distinction has to be made between the ability to review a prosecution policy on the one hand and an individual prosecution on the other.

The current state of the law is as follows:

(1) The courts will review a policy not to prosecute in given circumstances, but only on *Wednesbury* unreasonable grounds (ie that it was a policy that no reasonable prosecuting authority could have arrived at, *see* Chapter 7 for more detail).

(2) The courts will review an individual decision not to prosecute, or an individual decision to prosecute or to prefer a less serious charge than is believed to be appropriate.

In this category the decision can be reviewed either on Wednesbury unreasonable grounds or on the ground that a stated prosecution policy gave rise to a legitimate expectation that the prosecution would or would not be taken, as the case may be.

A case based on legitimate expectation generally stands a better chance of success than one on *Wednesbury* grounds. The problem is that prosecution policies are not in the public domain. It is known that the NRA has such a policy, but has resisted disclosure of it for the very reason that it is not keen for prosecution decisions to come under public glare.

The position with HMIP is that it follows the Crown Prosecution Service code of practice, applying those principles to the issues that it has to consider. The two basic tests are:

(a) is it in the public interest to prosecute? (This will take into account such matters as the extent of the breach; the attitude of the polluter; and whether the breach can be dealt with in another manner, eg by serving a notice under the EPA);

(b) is there a sufficiency of evidence?

The position with local authorities and other enforcement agencies cannot be stated here but the question should be put to the relevant body if the issue arises.

There is an argument that any such policies ought to be disclosable under the Environmental Information Regulations (*see* Chapter 9). In any event where the matter is an issue the regulator should be asked to disclose the policy upon which a given decision to prosecute or not was made.

THE ROLE OF PRIVATE PROSECUTIONS

5.6   The discretion vested in the regulatory bodies as to whether to prosecute or not reinforces the importance of mobilising public opinion to press the regulators to bring prosecutions. It also illustrates the fact that not every incident will be prosecuted even though a good case exists. In turn, this brings into issue the relevance of private prosecutions as an environmental remedy.

Later sections of this chapter consider the ability to bring private prosecutions in respect of the various media, while Chapter 7 deals with the procedural and evidential aspects of private prosecutions. At this point it is worth mentioning some tactical considerations that may arise when deciding whether to initiate a private prosecution.

(1)   First it is worth reiterating the point made above that where possible a regulatory body should be persuaded to bring the prosecution itself. That body will invariably have better access to evidence and resources to bring a case.

(2)   If the regulatory body cannot be so persuaded, then an aggrieved party's motivation in bringing a private prosecution is likely to be either:

(a)   the pollution complained of affects the aggrieved party over and above what is perceived as the interest of the public whom the regulatory body represents; or

(b)   an issue of public importance is at stake which, for political or other reasons, the regulator does not wish to take on.

Example 1

In 1986 a successful private prosecution was brought under the now repealed Control of Pollution Act 1974 against Thames Water Authority for breach of discharge consents for sewage effluent discharged from the Aylesbury sewage treatment works. The case was initiated by the Anglers Conservation Association on behalf of a local angling club. That case was of itself important as the first known private prosecution of an environmental offence. It was also brought to highlight a pollution problem specific to the angling club that issued the summons, which the regulators had failed to deal with, unsurprisingly, as they were also responsible for the pollution!

Example 2

A further prosecution brought against British Coal by the Anglers Conservation Association in 1993 on behalf of local angling clubs illustrates the second point. It alleged an offence under s 85 of the Water Resources Act 1991. The charge was that British Coal caused pollution by turning off minewater pumps, thus causing the underground water table to rise and discharge water containing rust into a river. Although the prosecution failed on a point of law, the case attracted widespread interest and contributed to the wider consideration of the pollution of waters by minewater following cessation of mining operations.

(3) A criminal prosecution undoubtedly has greater publicity value than many civil cases (though it is, of course, subject to the *sub judice* restrictions on publicity during the currency of the case, *see* Chapter 8). This factor is one to be considered when making a decision on a potential private prosecution. Publicity can be a negative as well as a positive tool and a prosecution brought for one of the two reasons set out at (2) above is more likely to have a positive impact than one which serves no obvious purpose and might be perceived as purely political or possibly vindictive.

(4) It is explained below that, subject to any statutory provision, there is no restriction on who can initiate a prosecution. No locus needs to be shown. Where evidence of an offence exists, prosecution is the most broadly available environmental remedy. For both individuals and groups private prosecutions can offer a good opportunity to address an environmental problem which may affect a large body of people.

(5) The question of costs should also be mentioned. Detailed consideration is given to costs and private prosecutions in Chapter 10. Briefly, criminal prosecutions are seen, quite correctly, as being taken in the interests of the public at large and therefore—as a very general but not universal principle—the prosecutor's costs will be paid out of central funds.

WHO MAY PROSECUTE AND BE PROSECUTED

5.7 As pointed out above, there is no legal restriction on who can initiate a prosecution. The general rule is that any natural or legal person may prosecute an offence, unless a specific restriction is made by statute. Thus the problem of locus is less significant in this field than in any of the others that we consider. There are, however, some bars to commencement of private prosecutions.

Later sections of this chapter set out the individual offences relating to each of the environmental media, and consideration is given there and in Chapter 7 to the evidence that is required to prove these offences.

Evidence

5.8 In all cases careful thought has to be given to the practicalities of obtaining evidence. A private prosecutor enjoys none of the rights of entry for the purpose of taking samples, or the powers to compel the supply of information that are vested in the regulators (*see* Chapter 1). The defendant in criminal proceedings is under no obligation to disclose any documents or other information during the course of proceedings.

Statutory restrictions

5.9 Some statutes restrict the ability to bring private prosecutions or require the prosecutor to obtain the consent of the Attorney-General or other body before the prosecution is commenced.

Intervention by the Director of Public Prosecutions

5.10 It should also be borne in mind that once a prosecution has been started the Director of Public Prosecutions (DPP) has the statutory right to take over a prosecution, and to continue or discontinue that prosecution without reference to the original prosecutor, *see* s 6 of the Prosecution of Offences Act 1985. This power was exercised in the *Camelford* case where a water pollution prosecution was initiated by a local angling club but taken over by the Crown. Where this power is exercised the original prosecutor is entitled to recover costs from central funds.

So far as defendants are concerned the appropriate party to be charged will be the person, company or other body that caused the pollution. The principal Acts generally contain a provision allowing individual officers of an organisation to be charged where there is evidence that the offence has been committed with the consent or connivance of, or is attributable to any neglect of, such an officer. *See* eg s 210 of the Water Industry Act 1991, s 217 of the Water Resources Act 1991, and s 111 of the EPA.

COMMON LAW DEFENCES

5.11   There are some general common law defences applicable to all criminal charges which are worth mentioning in the context of environmental offences.

Necessity

5.12   The defence of necessity is available where a discharge is made in order to avoid danger to life or health. This defence was in issue in the prosecution of South West Water following the Camelford incident where the question was whether the sequence of events which led to the discharge of the contaminated water into the River Camel was an emergency or not. The test is whether the origin of the sequence is avoidable and foreseeable. If it is then the defence will not be available.

Third party action

5.13   It will be a defence if the accused can show that the pollution was caused by the act of a third party such as a trespasser. Thus where a vandal gets access to a site and fractures a pipe which results in a pollution then the site owner will have a defence. This will also be relevant to proof in any case involving a 'causing' offence where the prosecution has to show that a particular act or omission was the effective cause in a sequence of events, and that some intervening event did not occur which relieves the defendant of responsibility.

Act of God

5.14 As with common law claims, Act of God will be a defence. *See* Chapter 2.

OFFENCES RELATING TO WATER

INTRODUCTION

5.15 This section will look primarily at the two principal water pollution offences, the first under s 85 of the Water Resources Act 1991, and the second under s 4 of the Salmon and Freshwater Fisheries Act 1975. More briefly it will consider other pollution, abstraction and land drainage offences.

It is worth quoting the relevant part of the two principal offences in full, since they have a number of elements, which will be considered in turn.

WATER RESOURCES ACT OFFENCE

Section 85 of the Water Resources Act 1991

5.16 Subsection (1) states:

A person contravenes this section if he causes or knowingly permits any poisonous, noxious or polluting matter or any solid waste matter to enter any controlled waters.

Subsection (3) states:

A person contravenes this section if he causes or knowingly permits any trade effluent or sewage effluent to be discharged—
(a) into any controlled waters . . .

'Causing' pollution

5.17 A person for the purposes of this section is any legal person including a company. The distinction between causing and knowingly permitting is one that has been the subject of a good deal of judicial discussion. Most important the 'causing' part of the offence indicates an offence of strict liability, *see Alphacell v Woodward* [1972] AC 824. This means that once the prosecution has proved that a causal link exists between the act or omission of the defendant and the pollution incident, then liability is established. It is irrelevant that the defendant could not have foreseen that the pollution would occur and irrelevant that he had not acted negligently. The word 'cause' has been interpreted very broadly, to include any positive or negative act by the defendant which can be linked to the pollution incident.

'Knowingly permitting' pollution

5.18 The phrase 'knowingly permitting' covers a situation where the defendant has not been causally involved in the chain of events leading to a pollution, but was aware of those events and allowed them to occur. An example might be if a person allows polluting matter to pass across his land from a neighbour, and fails to take steps to prevent that matter from entering a watercourse, or in the case of a continuing pollution, if the polluter was not responsible for the original pollution he fails to remedy the pollution once it has started.

What is pollution?

5.19 Each of the words 'poisonous, noxious or polluting' has its own separate meaning, but the broadest, and consequently the most applicable, is the word 'polluting'. This word has had many definitions, none of them entirely satisfactory. For common law civil claims, the test is whether the discharge results in sensible alteration to the quantity or quality of water. This is probably a reasonable test for criminal liability, in that it will be necessary to show some noticeable alteration to the quality of the receiving water, but it is not essential to prove immediate or even long-term damage to flora and fauna. In truth the dividing line between what is pollution and what is not is better informed by common sense than technical definitions.

Solid waste matter

5.20 The final words of subs (1) refer to solid waste matter. This expression is intended to cover the placing of rubbish which may not be polluting in a river or watercourse.

Discharges of sewage or trade effluent

5.21   Subs (3) has been included as this covers a significant category of potential discharges into the water environment, those which are made by a sewage undertaker or in the course of a trade or business. *See* s 221 of the Water Resources Act for a definition of these two phrases. Section 85(3) makes all such discharges an offence unless the accused can show that the discharge was in accordance with an authorisation. Unless pursuant to an IPC consent these authorisations are under Sched 6 to the Water Resources Act.

Evidence required

5.22   The difference between these two subsections is particularly important when it comes to collecting evidence. For the subs (1) offence it is not essential to proceed on the basis of a water sample where there is other evidence of the pollution. In the case of the subs (3) offence a sample is essential as proof will need to be given that the discharge in question did not comply with an authorisation. *See* Chapter 7 for a detailed consideration of evidence required in prosecutions.

In earlier water pollution Acts the offence covered in subs (1) and (3) formed two entirely separate offences. Now the discharge of any polluting matter, whether trade/sewage effluent or not, is *prima facie* an offence, subject to the authorisation defence. It is this principle which lends support to the argument that if a consent to discharge does not list a particular substance and it can be proved that a person has caused that substance to enter a watercourse and pollute then that must be an offence.

Example

The recent prosecution of ReChem lends support to this proposition (*see* ENDS No 224). This prosecution was brought by Welsh Water plc. In addition to the consents required to discharge into watercourses, consents are also required to discharge trade effluent into sewers connected to sewage treatment works (*see* Chapter 3). In this case the prosecution argued that hexachlorobenzenes were present in samples of the effluent analysed for which consent had not been given and that as such an offence had been committed where polluting matter was discharged which was not specified in the consent. The judge in his ruling upheld this view, and found that any discharge of matter present in the effluent, arising from the trade in question for which no consent existed, was an offence.

DEFENCES TO SECTION 85 OFFENCES AND MODE OF TRIAL

5.23 Before looking at the offence under s 4 of the Salmon and Freshwater Fisheries Act, mention should be made of the statutory defences to the s 85 offence.

Emergency

5.24 It is a defence for a defendant to show that the entry in question was caused or permitted in an emergency in order to avoid danger to life or health. The defendant must have taken all reasonable steps to have minimised the effect of the discharge, and also have reported the incident to the NRA as soon as reasonably practicable after the incident occurred. This defence is comparable to the common law defence of necessity. As we have seen above the merit of this defence is questionable where the origin of the sequence of events that led to the discharge was the defendant's negligence.

Authorised discharge

5.25 A defence is available where the discharge is of trade or sewage effluent and it is made in accordance with an authorisation. Normally this will be an NRA consent to discharge, but it must comply with any other relevant authorisation, eg an IPC consent.

Minewater

5.26 There is also a statutory defence where a mine owner permits water from an abandoned mine to enter controlled waters. This defence will not apply if the mine owner had caused the discharge by some conscious act or omission.

Section 85 is triable either summarily by magistrates or on indictment by the Crown court. In the former case the maximum fine is £20,000, and/or up to three months imprisonment. In the latter the court has power to imprison for up to two years and levy an unlimited fine.

5.27   Section 4 of the Salmon and Freshwater Fisheries Act 1975 makes it an offence to:

> *cause or knowingly permit to be released into any waters or the tributaries of waters containing fish any liquid or solid matter that causes the water to become poisonous or injurious to fish, spawning grounds, spawn or the food of fish.*

A private prosecution under this section may only be brought if the person bringing the prosecution has obtained a certificate from the MAFF pursuant to s 4(3). This requires the person to show that he has a material interest in the waters in question.

In most cases this offence is likely to have been committed in addition to the s 85 offence. It is, though, of obvious interest to those seeking to deal with incidents which cause palpable harm to the aquatic environment.

Defence

5.28   It will be a defence to a charge under this section to show that the discharge was pursuant to a consent to discharge under the Water Resources Act 1991. The other two defences available for the s 85 offence are not available in the case of s 4. However the common law defence of necessity is available (*see* para 5.12 above).

The penalties for this offence are, on summary conviction, a sum not exceeding the prescribed sum, and £40 for each day the offence continues, and, on indictment, an unlimited fine or up to two months' imprisonment.

5.29   Section 90 of the Water Resources Act contains two minor offences in relation to rivers. Subsection (1) makes it an offence to remove any part of the bed of a river adjacent to a sluice, weir, or dam. Subsection (2) makes it an offence to cut or uproot vegetation from a river so that it falls into the river or to fail to remove it from the river.

Abstraction and impoundment

5.30   Sections 24 and 25 of the Water Resources Act 1991 provide that it shall be an offence to abstract or to impound water unless in accordance with a licence granted by the NRA. Abstraction is from 'any source of supply' which in effect means any water, overground or underground.

Impoundment relates to the diversion or holding up of water from any source which is not discrete, ie unconnected with any other watercourse. This offence therefore covers such matters as the construction or alteration of weirs or dams.

The penalty for both offences is a fine, up to the statutory maximum if tried summarily, and an unlimited fine if tried on indictment.

In the case of abstraction it will be a defence if the abstraction is of a small quantity of not more than five cubic metres, and not forming a continuous operation.

Controls on structures that impede flow

5.31   Section 109 of the Water Resources Act 1991 and ss 24 and 25 of the Land Drainage Act set out statutory controls on the construction and alteration of structures which affect or impede the flow of, in practical terms, any watercourse. These sections provide a machinery for obtaining consents, and penalties for failure to observe that machinery.

Offences relating to the pollution of land

5.32   The new waste management regime introduced by the Environmental Protection Act 1990 ('EPA') and the Waste Management Licensing Regulations 1994 (SI No 1056) ('the Regulations') has been given force by s 33(1) of the EPA.

Controlled waste

Subsection (1)(a) provides that it is an offence for any person to:

deposit controlled waste, or knowingly cause or knowingly permit controlled waste to be deposited in or on any land unless a waste management licence authorising the deposit is in force and the deposit is in accordance with the licence.

Section 33(1)(b) forbids anyone:

to treat, keep or dispose of controlled waste, or knowingly cause or knowingly permit it to be done, in or on any land or by means of any mobile plant except under or in accordance with a waste management licence.

Causing and permitting

5.33 The DoE Circular 11/94 gives guidance on the term 'knowingly cause or knowingly permit'. It uses the example of a landfill operator who allows controlled waste to be deposited on his site rather than doing it himself. He is equally responsible with the depositor for ensuring that the deposit is properly carried out. Persons included are any producer or holder of waste who knowingly permits waste to be treated, kept or disposed of in or on land which is not covered by a waste management licence. It also refers to s 33(5), which makes the deposit of controlled waste from a motor vehicle an offence under s 33(1)(a). It advises that this places the onus on the owner or manager of vehicles used to transport controlled waste to ensure that his employees do not fly-tip waste. The discussion above (paras 5.17 and 5.18) relating to the definition of 'cause' and 'knowingly permit' is relevant here.

The activities relating to controlled waste are, therefore, deposit, treating, keeping or disposing of.

Treating, keeping or disposing of waste

5.34 Section 29(6) of the EPA provides that waste is 'treated' when it is subjected to any process including making it reusable or reclaiming substances from it.

The DoE Circular 11/94 states that 'keeping' of waste covers a range of situations where, whether or not it can be argued that the waste has been deposited, it nonetheless is retained in the hands of the holders.

'Disposal' is defined in reg 1(3) as any of the operations listed in Part III of Sched 4 to the Regulations:

1. *Tipping of waste above or underground (eg landfill, etc).*
2. *Land treatment of waste (eg biodegradation of liquid or sludge discards in soils, etc).*
3. *Deep injection of waste (eg injection of pumpable discards into wells, salt domes or naturally occurring repositories, etc).*
4. *Surface impoundment of waste (eg placement of waste into lined discrete cells which are capped and isolated from one another and the environment, etc).*
5. *Specially engineered landfill of waste (eg placement of waste into lined discrete cells which are capped and isolated from one another and the environment, etc).*
6. *Release of solid waste into a water body except seas or oceans.*
7. *Release of waste into seas or oceans including seabed insertion.*
8. *Biological treatment of waste not listed elsewhere in this Part of this Schedule which results in final compounds or mixtures which are disposed of by means of any of the operations listed in this Part of this Schedule.*
9. *Physio-chemical treatment of waste not listed elsewhere in this Part of this Schedule which results in final compounds or mixtures which are disposed of by means of any of the operations listed in this Part of this Schedule (eg evaporation, drying, calcination, etc).*
10. *Incineration of waste on land.*
11. *Incineration of waste at sea.*
12. *Permanent storage of waste (eg emplacement of containers in a mine, etc).*
13. *Blending or mixture of waste prior to the waste being submitted to any of the operations listed in this Part of this Schedule.*
14. *Repackaging of waste prior to the waste being submitted to any of the operations listed in this Part of this Schedule.*
15. *Storage of waste pending any of the operations listed in this Part of this Schedule, but excluding temporary storage, pending collection, on the site where the waste is produced.*

Part IV of Sched 4 also lists the following operations which amount to recovery:

1. *Reclamation or regeneration of solvents.*
2. *Recycling or reclamation of organic substances which are not used as solvents.*
3. *Recycling or reclamation of metals and metal compounds.*
4. *Recycling or reclamation of other inorganic materials.*
5. *Regeneration of acids to bases.*
6. *Recovery of components used for pollution abatement.*
7. *Recovery of components from catalysts.*
8. *Rerefining, or other reuses, of oil which is waste.*
9. *Use of waste principally as a fuel or for other means of generating energy.*
10. *Spreading of waste on land resulting in benefit to agriculture or ecological improvement, including composting and other biological transformation processes, except in the case of waste excluded under Article 2(1)(b)(iii) of the Directive.*
11. *Uses of wastes obtained from any of their operations listed in paragraphs 1 to 10 of this Part of this Schedule.*
12. *Exchange of wastes for submission to any of the operations listed in paragraphs 1 to 11 of this Part of this Schedule.*
13. *Storage of waste consisting of materials intended for submission to any operation listed in this Part of this Schedule, but excluding temporary storage, pending collection, on the site where it is produced.*

Paragraph 9 of Sched 4 to the Regulations then applies the lists in Parts II and IV to the offences under s 33(1)(a) and (b).

Section 33(1)(c) of the Act prohibits anyone from treating, keeping or disposing of controlled waste in a manner likely to cause pollution of the environment or harm to human health.

Depositing waste

5.35 Problems have occurred over the meaning of 'deposit'. In *Leigh Land Reclamation Limited v Walsall MBC* [1991] JPL 876 it was held that waste was only deposited when it reached its final resting place. This has been resolved by the decision of *Berkshire CC v Scott* (1993) *The Times*, 14 January. The court decided that *Leigh*

Land had been wrongly decided and that deposit does not mean final deposit and can include a temporary deposit.

Section 33(1)(c), referred to in Circular 11/94 as 'a wide ranging offence provision', is not dependent on the existence of a licence. Again the Circular provides guidance. Pollution of the environment occurs where substances or articles constituting or resulting from the waste and capable of causing harm to man or other living organisms supported by the environment are released or escape into an environmental medium. The release may occur from land where controlled waste is treated or kept or on land where controlled waste is deposited.

A person committing an offence will be liable to imprisonment for up to six months and a fine of up to £20,000.

STATUTORY DEFENCES

5.36   Three defences are available to all three offences under s 33(1) (s 33(7) of the EPA).

Exercising due diligence

5.37   If the accused took care to find out from persons who were in a position to provide the information whether the deposit or use of the waste to which the charge relates would be an offence, and he had no reason to suppose he was being given false information, he will not be liable. Essentially, this means that he must show he took all reasonable precautions and exercised due diligence.

Acting in the course of employment

5.38   It is a defence for a person to show that he acted under instructions from his employer and neither knew nor had reason to suppose that he was committing an offence under s 33.

Emergency

5.39   The accused may show that he acted in an emergency to avoid danger to the public and that as soon as possible after the act was done details were given to the relevant WRA. This defence will not be available if the accused acted negligently in creating or permitting the emergency to occur.

5.40 There are exemptions to the main offence (s 33(1) of the Act). Section 33(2) exempts household waste from domestic property which is kept, treated or disposed of within the curtilage of the dwelling by or with the permission of the occupier of the dwelling. Further exemptions are listed in regs 16 and 17 of the Regulations and these are discussed in Chapter 4, para 4.20.

WASTE AND THE DUTY OF CARE

5.41 One of the most innovative provisions of the EPA is s 34, which imposes a duty of care on anyone who imports, produces, carries, keeps or treats controlled wastes. A code of practice entitled 'Waste Management, The Duty of Care: A Code of Practice' has been issued by the Secretary of State clarifying this duty. Section 34 requires the holder of the waste to take all such measures applicable to him in that capacity as are reasonable in the circumstances:

- (a) to prevent anybody committing an offence under s 33 of the Act;
- (b) to prevent the escape of the waste from his control or that of any other person;
- (c) if he transfers the waste to ensure that it is transferred to an authorised person with the proper documentation and that a written description of the waste is given to avoid a contravention of s 33 or the duty of care itself.

It is, therefore, a threefold duty.

- (1) The holder must ensure that the waste is exempt from licensing controls such that it falls outside the duty of care or that it will be taken to a disposal or intermediate facility authorised to take that waste. It is incumbent upon the holder to know the proper description of the waste, whether it is controlled waste, whether the facility is licensed and whether any conditions are imposed. The duty goes further in imposing duties upon the holder to take checks after the waste has been transferred. A holder must report suspicious handling to the WRA.
- (2) The waste must be properly packaged, handled and secured to prevent any spill or leak. This arm of the duty continues during transportation to its final destination. In practice it

means storage to prevent damage by vandals, waste containers adequate for their purpose, adequate labelling, skips
covered to prevent waste falling out and packaging resistant
to wind and rain.

(3) The holder must continue to take care when transferring
waste. Authorised persons are WCAs, holders of a waste
management or disposal licence, any exempt person by
virtue of regulations made under s 33(3) of the Act and a
carrier registered under s 2 of the Control of Pollution
(Amendment) Act 1989. Appropriate documentation is an
adequate written description to enable others to avoid
harmful or unauthorised deposit of the waste or to prevent
it from escaping.

Documentation of waste

5.42   Regulations have been made dealing with the making and
retention of documents. The Environmental Protection (Duty of
Care) Regulations 1991 (SI No 2839) require the transferee of waste
to ensure that a transfer note is completed and signed. This must
identify the waste to which it relates, and its quantity, time and place
of transfer, if it is in a container and, if so, the kind of container,
name and address of transferee, if the transferor is an importer of
waste and whether either the transferor or transferee is the holder
of a waste management licence or falls into any other category set
out in the regulations.

If a holder fails to comply with these duties then he will be liable
to a fine and/or conviction (s 34(6)). An individual may bring proceedings under these regulations, but they will probably be more
widely used by WRAs. Prosecutions have been taken in a wide
variety of circumstances.

Example

In May 1992 a Yorkshire tyre company consigned 15 waste
tyres to a company in Middlesborough. The latter gave a fictitious licence number and the tyre company was prosecuted
on the basis that it did not make the further checks to see that
the wastes were transferred to an 'authorised person' such as
a licence holder. Another company was fined £250 after failing

to raise a s 34 transfer note following the deposit of over 1,000 tonnes of rubble at an unlicensed site. In another case, an individual was prosecuted for failing to raise a transfer note and to ensure the waste was passed to an authorised person. He was fined £200.

(*See* 5.41)

FLY-TIPPING

5.43 Fly-tipping is the unauthorised disposal of waste. This offence is governed by s 6 of the Control of Pollution (Amendment) Act 1989 and the Controlled Waste (Registration of Carriers and Seizure of Vehicles) Regulations 1991 (SI No 1624). In the past, the major problem in stopping fly-tipping was the inability to trace the operator of vehicles depositing waste. Under the regulations the WRA should try to find the name and address of the vehicle's registered keeper and user from the registration number allocated to it by the country where it is registered. If this fails, then s 6 allows a WRA to apply to a justice of the peace for a warrant to seize the vehicle. The justice must be satisfied that there are reasonable grounds to believe that an offence involving the unlicensed deposit, treatment or disposal of waste has occurred and that the vehicle was used to commit that offence. Once issued, the warrant allows any constable or authorised officer to stop the vehicle and seize it and its contents. The vehicle and its contents are kept by the WRA until returned to someone who produces satisfactory evidence that he is entitled to them. If no such evidence is produced, the WRA disposes of them. Before disposing of them, the WRA must publish a notice in a local newspaper identifying the vehicle, its contents, where it was seized, where it may be claimed and giving 28 days for its retrieval.

LITTER

5.44 To enforce the clearance of litter, a district or London borough may serve a litter abatement notice. The notice may be served by a litter authority, a Crown authority with control over Crown land, on a statutory undertaker, a designated educational institute or on the occupier of land subject to a litter control order. It is designed to enforce the duties of the authority such that the land is cleared within a certain time or prohibiting the land from becoming defaced with litter. A person has 21 days to appeal against the notice but if he fails to comply with the notice then he will be subject to a fine if the land is not cleared.

In addition, a private individual may make a complaint to a magistrates' court or summary application to a sheriff on the ground that land is defaced by litter. This covers the same categories of land as above. A person affected may be the owner of a house overlooking the land or one who drives by a littered roadside. The Act itself does not define an aggrieved individual. The person making the complaint must give the person whose duty it is to keep the land clean five days' notice of his intention to apply to a magistrates' court. It is within the court's discretion whether to issue an abatement notice. In both the cases it will be a defence to show compliance with the duties imposed by the Act.

AIR

IPC AND APC OFFENCES

5.45   The same enforcement mechanisms and offences apply to both IPC and APC, with enforcement in respect of IPC offences being centrally administered by HMIP and that for APC offences being local authority controlled (*see* Chapter 2).

The principal offence in the EPA Part I is set out in s 23 and is carrying on a prescribed process without authorisation or in breach of the conditions of an authorisation contrary to s 6. The offence is triable either summarily before the magistrates or on indictment in the Crown court and is subject to a maximum £20,000 fine on summary conviction. On conviction on indictment an unlimited fine and/or up to two years' imprisonment may be imposed. Where the allegation is that there was failure to comply with the implied authorisation condition that BATNEEC be employed then the burden of proving that there was no better technique falls on the accused (s 25). (*See* Chapter 4 for discussion of BATNEEC.)

Other offences (which are also set out in s 23 and carry the same penalties as above) are failing to comply with or breaching any requirement of a prohibition notice or enforcement notice (*see* Chapter 4) and failing to comply with a court order made under s 26 of the EPA. Section 26 allows a court to make an order following conviction for breach of s 6 or an enforcement or prohibition notice either instead of or in addition to any punishment for the offence. The order may require the defendant to take specified steps to remedy the breaches of the legislation within a fixed time period. During that time period there can be no further criminal liability.

There are a number of other less significant criminal offences under the EPA Part I, all set out in s 23 and including:

(a) failing to give notice of transfer of authorisation when the person carrying on the prescribed process changes;

(b) failing to comply with a requirement imposed under s 17 (*see* Chapter 4 above);

(c) obstructing an inspector in the exercise of his powers or duties;

(d) making a false entry in any records required to be maintained under the terms of an authorisation.

There are no restrictions on the bringing of private prosecutions under the EPA Part I. Extensive information is available from public registers (*see* Chapter 9) which may be of use in collating evidence.

APC before EPA Part I is fully implemented

5.46 In respect of those factories still regulated under the Alkali etc Works Regulation Act 1906 or s 5 of the Health and Safety at Work Act 1974 pending the full implementation of the EPA Part I (*see* Chapter 2 above) the key criminal offences are as follows:

(a) it is an offence to breach ss 1, 2 or 9 of the 1906 Act;

(b) it is an offence to breach s 5 of the 1974 Act.

In each case the penalties are identical and are governed by s 33 of the 1974 Act. The offences are triable either way and on summary conviction the maximum fine is £20,000. On indictment an unlimited fine may be imposed.

Prosecutions under these provisions may only be brought by HMIP unless the consent of the DPP is obtained.

5.47   There are three offences under the Clean Air Act 1993 ('the 1993 Act'):
 (a) emission of dark smoke from a chimney;
 (b) emission of dark smoke from industrial premises, other than from a chimney;
 (c) emission of dust and grit from non-domestic furnaces.

Emission of dark smoke from a chimney

5.48   Section 1 of the 1993 Act makes it a criminal offence to emit dark smoke from a chimney. Dark smoke is defined in s 3 of the Act as being smoke (which includes soot, ash, grit and gritty particles) which, if compared with a chart known as a Ringelmann Chart, would appear to be as dark as Shade 2 or darker. It is not necessary for the prosecution to prove that there was comparison with a Ringelmann Chart—this will often be unnecessary where evidence is given by an experienced local authority environmental health officer. Photographs are often important pieces of evidence, particularly if a private prosecution is contemplated.

The person at risk of conviction is the occupier of the building to which the chimney is attached. Chimneys which are not part of a building but which serve a fixed boiler or industrial plant are covered by s 1(2) which permits the prosecution of the person having possession of the plant or boiler if dark smoke is emitted.

Defences

5.49   There is a wide range of available statutory defences to prosecution for an offence under s 1 of the 1993 Act. Dark smoke may be emitted:
 (a) if it is due to the lighting of a cold furnace, provided that all practicable steps are taken to prevent or minimise the emission;
 (b) where it is due to the failure of the furnace or other apparatus which was either unforeseeable or if foreseeable, unavoidable. To rely on this defence it must also be proved that the smoke release could not have been prevented after the failure of the equipment;

(c) where the dark smoke was due to the use of unsuitable fuel because suitable fuel was unavailable (to rely on this defence it must be shown that all practicable steps to prevent or minimise the emission were taken including the use of the least unsuitable fuel);

(d) if there is a failure to inform the defendant of the belief that an offence has been committed in accordance with s 51. Section 51 requires that if an authorised officer believes an offence to have been committed under s 1 then that person shall 'as soon as may be' notify the occupier of the premises and shall confirm the notification in writing (if it was not in writing originally) within four days of the day after that person became aware of the offence.

Exemptions

5.50 Section 42 exempts smoke, dust or grit from control under the 1993 Act if it comes from the combustion of mine or quarry refuse (s 42(2)). There are separate provisions relating to mine and quarry emissions in the 1993 Act.

Crown premises are currently exempt from the Clean Air Act although breaches of the Act are to be reported to the responsible minister (s 46).

There are special provisions in relation to smoke emitted from railway engines and vessels (ss 43 and 44).

Permitted periods of emission of dark smoke are exempted from control under s 1 by s 1(3) of the 1993 Act. The permitted periods are set out in the Dark Smoke (Permitted Periods) Regulations 1958.

Emissions other than from chimneys

5.51 The Act provides for a separate offence of emitting dark smoke from any industrial or trade premises other than from a chimney (which is controlled under s 1). Industrial or trade premises are those used for any industrial or trade purposes or premises not used for those purposes but on which matter is burnt in connection with any industrial or trade process (s 2(6)).

The occupier or any person who caused or permitted the emission is liable to conviction.

Example

In *Sheffield City Council v ADH Demolition Ltd* (1984) 82
LGR 177 it was argued that a bonfire of site rubbish on a
demolition site which released dark smoke was not emitted
from industrial or trade premises. It was held that there was
an emission in connection with an industrial or trade process
and the conviction was upheld.

The burden of proving that the emission was dark shifts to the
defence (who then have to prove it was not dark) when material is
burned on trade or industrial premises and in the circumstances that
the burning would have been likely to give rise to the emission of
dark smoke. If the prosecution can prove those two matters the
occupier or any person who caused or permitted the burning must
prove that no dark smoke was emitted.

As for s 1 a number of statutory defences exist. Emission is permitted where the defendant can prove that he took all practicable
steps to prevent or minimise the emission and that the emission was
inadvertent.

In addition regulations can exempt certain processes from
control. The Clean Air (Emission of Dark Smoke) (Exemption)
Regulations 1969 exempt from control (subject to strict conditions
being met) the burning of certain substances.

Emissions of dust and grit

5.52   Finally in relation to dust and grit emissions from non-
domestic furnaces which contravene s 5 (*see* Chapter 1) (unless the
defendant can prove that the best practicable means were employed
to minimise the emission) the occupier of the building in which the
furnace is located is guilty of an offence and liable to a fine of up to
£5,000.

Penalties

5.53   All of the offences under ss 1 and 2 are strict liability
offences—the prosecution need not prove that the defendant
intended to cause the emission or, indeed, even knew of the emission
provided that he is the occupier etc of the source of the dark smoke.

All the offences are summary only. Commission of any of the three offences leads to a maximum fine of £5,000 except in the case of s 1(1) in respect of domestic premises where £1,000 is the maximum.

CLEAN AIR ACT 1993: DESIGN AND INSTALLATION OF FURNACES AND CHIMNEYS

5.54   Offences relating to furnaces are contained in ss 4 and 6–8 of the 1993 Act. The main offences are as follows:

(1) It is a criminal offence under s 111 to fail to give notice to a local authority of the installation of a furnace covered by s 4 (*see* Chapter 1). This is a summary only offence punishable with a fine of up to level 3 (currently £1,000).

(2) It is an offence under s 4 to install a furnace which is not capable of being operated continuously with the fuel for which it was designed without emitting smoke. This offence is punishable with a fine of up to level 5—currently £5,000.

(3) Section 6 requires that certain more major furnaces are fitted with grit and dust arresting apparatus. The apparatus must have been approved by the local authority or have been installed in accordance with approved plans and be properly maintained and used. To operate a furnace other than in accordance with all of these requirements is an offence punishable with a fine of up to £5,000.

(4) A similar offence applies (with equal penalties) to major domestic furnaces under s 8.

(5) Section 7 allows local authorities or the Secretary of State to exempt certain furnaces from s 6. If the exemption is limited to use for a particular purpose then, if the furnace is used for another purpose, an offence is committed under s 7(6).

Chimney design offences are contained in s 14 which requires that the occupier of a building shall not cause or knowingly permit the installation of a substantial furnace as defined in s 14(2) unless the chimney height has been approved and if approved conditionally that any conditions are being complied with. There is a similar offence in s 14(4) relating to fixed boilers or industrial plant. In both cases the offence is punishable by a fine of up to level 5—£5,000.

CLEAN AIR ACT 1993: SMOKE CONTROL AREAS

5.55   The principal offence in respect of smoke control areas is contained in s 20 of the 1993 Act. This provides that the occupier of a building within a smoke control area from whose chimney smoke is emitted shall be guilty of an offence. A similar offence is included in s 20(2) in respect of smoke emitted from chimneys which serve the furnaces of any fixed boiler or industrial plant. In both cases the offence is subject to any exemptions contained in the smoke control area order (or imposed by the Secretary of State under ss 21 or 22) and to the duty in s 51 (*see* Chapter 1). It is a defence to prove that the emission was not caused by the use of any fuel other than an authorised fuel. Fuels may be authorised by the Secretary of State by regulations made under s 20(6). Numerous sets of regulations have been issued since this provision was introduced in the 1956 Act. The offences are punishable by a fine of up to level 3—currently £1,000.

Section 23 provides for further less important offences concerning the acquisition or sale of fuel other than authorised fuel for use in a smoke control area.

CLEAN AIR ACT 1993: INFORMATION PROVISIONS

5.56   The 1993 Act includes a number of provisions relating to the acquisition of information to assist local authorities in their enforcement of the legislation. These powers are backed by criminal sanctions. The information powers are not open to use by the public or an interest group—although the information acquired by local authorities in the exercise of their powers may be available to public inspection. *See* discussion of the Environmental Information Regulations in Chapter 9.

Section 12 permits local authorities to serve a notice on the occupier of any premises requiring details of the matters burned in a furnace to which ss 5–11 may apply. To fail to comply with the notice within the time specified (not less than 14 days) is an offence, as is providing false information knowingly. In both cases the offence is punishable with a fine of up to level 5 (currently £5,000).

Much broader information acquisition powers are provided for in ss 36–38. These provisions allow a local authority to serve a notice under s 36 requiring information concerning the emission of pollutants and other substances into the air from the premises. The range of information which may be requested is restricted by the Control of Atmospheric Emission (Research and Publicity) Regulations 1977. It is the duty of the occupier of the premises to respond. A right of appeal to the Secretary of State is provided for in s 37. A failure to comply with the notice within the time specified (not less than six weeks) or to knowingly or recklessly provide false information is an offence punishable by a fine of up to level 5—currently £5,000.

Information may also be sought under s 58 of the 1993 Act in respect of Parts IV (miscellaneous atmospheric pollution controls—*see* below) and V (which includes the information acquisition provisions in ss 36–38) of the Act. The offences are similar to those outlined above.

CONTROL OF POLLUTION ACT 1974 AND NOISE

5.57 It is an offence under s 61(1) and (5) to exceed the registered noise level emitted from a building in a noise abatement zone established under the 1974 Act. The offence carries a maximum fine of £5,000 on first conviction and on subsequent conviction carries a maximum fine as if the person were convicted under s 80(4) of the EPA (statutory nuisance offence—*see* Chapter 4, para 4.62) and up to £50 per day for each day the offence continues.

MISCELLANEOUS ATMOSPHERIC POLLUTION OFFENCES

5.58 There are a number of miscellaneous criminal offences relating to atmospheric pollution including:

(a) cable burning under s 33 of the Clean Air Act 1993. This is a summary only offence and does not apply where the cable is a prescribed process under the EPA Part I. The offence is punishable with a maximum £5,000 fine;

(b) breaches of regulations concerning the contents of fuel for motor vehicles and furnaces made under ss 75 and 76 of the Control of Pollution Act 1974 (now consolidated into s 32 of the Clean Air Act 1993). The offence is triable either way and punishable by fine;

(c) crop residue burning, subject to very limited exceptions (and even then subject to stringent conditions), is now prohibited by the Crop Residue (Burning) Regulations 1993. It is a crime punishable by a maximum £5,000 fine to breach the regulations;

(d) fires on or which affect highways are subject to control under the Highways Act 1980, ss 161 and 161A. In outline these provisions make it an offence to light a fire on a highway or on other land which causes injury or danger or interruption to a highway user. The maximum fine in all cases is £5,000.

STATUTORY NUISANCE

OFFENCES

5.59   Part II of the Environmental Protection Act 1990 ('the EPA') consolidated the law of statutory nuisances. Section 79 lists activities which are statutory nuisances but all must be in such a state as to be prejudicial to health or a nuisance: premises; smoke, fumes or gases emitted from premises; dust, steam, smell or other effluvia arriving on industrial, trade or business premises; any accumulation or deposit; any animal noise; any other matter declared by any enactment to be a statutory nuisance. It is the duty of all local authorities to inspect their area for statutory nuisances and to investigate complaints made by the inhabitants of their area. See Chapter 4.62 *et seq* for more detailed discussion of s 79 nuisances.

Abatement notices

5.60   If a local authority discovers a statutory nuisance then it must serve an abatement notice. This prohibits the nuisance or restricts its occurrence or recurrence. It may also require works to be carried out to ensure that the nuisance is stopped or that its occurrence is restricted. The notice is served on the person responsible for the nuisance, on the owner of the premises where it arises from a structural defect or on the owner of the premises if the person responsible for the nuisance cannot be found. This person has 21 days in which to appeal against the abatement notice. If he does not, and fails to comply with the notice, then he will be guilty of an offence and liable to a fine of up to £20,000.

Defences

5.61 The defence of best practical means is available. If the person served with an abatement notice can show that he has used the best practical means to prevent or counter the effects of the nuisance then he will not be liable. This defence cannot be used in respect of:
(a) nuisance from fumes or gas emitted from premises;
(b) smoke unless emitted from a chimney;
(c) dust, steam, smell or effluvia, accumulation and deposits, arrivals and noise from premises, with the exceptions of trade, industrial or business premises.

Complaints by individuals

5.62 If an individual makes a complaint, a local authority is not under a duty to prosecute the offender. It may take steps to remedy the nuisance and recover the expenses of doing so but the decision still remains with the local authority. The Act for the first time allows private individuals to take action to abate statutory nuisances. An individual can make a complaint to a magistrates' court. The court can order that the defendant abate the nuisance and carry out such works as are necessary to prohibit its recurrence.

The aggrieved individual must, before commencing proceedings, give three days' notice of intention to commence proceedings to the defendant for a noise nuisance and 21 days for all other cases. The defence of best practical means is available to the defendant. However, the individual can only take such action where the nuisance already exists and not, as the local authority may do, where a nuisance is threatened. Despite this, it is an effective weapon for a private individual. Therefore, anyone whose health has been injured or threatened by a nuisance, or whose premises have been adversely affected, may apply to a magistrates' court without the necessity of complaining to his local authority. See Chapter 7 on procedure.

CHAPTER 6

EUROPEAN COMMUNITY LAW

INTRODUCTION

6.1 The influence of the European Community ('EC') on the development of environmental law in the United Kingdom is substantial and increasing.

INFLUENCE OF THE EC

Regulations and directives

6.2 There are two ways in which this influence is felt. First and most significantly, EC environmental policy is expressed by way of EC legislation in the form of regulations and directives which the Member States are bound to implement in national legislation. This EC legislation does not apply to all aspects of the environment, in the way that, say, the EPA did. Rather, directives and regulations deal with environmental issues in piecemeal fashion, and their effect becomes more pervasive as the number of them increases, and the impact on national environmental legislation deepens. Appendix 5 lists the principal EC environmental directives and the corresponding national legislation that has implemented them. This appendix amply illustrates how extensive the influence of EC legislation has already been on UK environmental regulation.

Some EC regulations and directives will have direct effect, ie will be binding on national courts without the need to be incorporated in national legislation. The effect of all this is twofold. First the impact of EC legislation, whether by direct effect or through implementation in national legislation, governs the whole range of

214

regulation of the environment as discussed in Chapters 3 and 4 above. Secondly it affects the way in which decision-makers, whether regulators or judges, arrive at those decisions and exercise their discretion.

European Court of Justice

6.3 The second way in which the influence of the EC is felt is in offering a direct remedy in the European Court of Justice (ECJ). The EC can bring infringement proceedings against a Member State for failure to implement legislation or breach of a directive under art 169 (*see* para 6.39). National courts are entitled to refer any question as to the applicability and meaning of EC legislation to the ECJ for interpretation, pursuant to art 177 (*see* para 6.40).

EC LAW AS A DIRECT REMEDY

6.4 Given the way in which EC environmental policy impinges on UK environmental law, European law is less readily available to individuals or groups as a direct remedy than some of the other remedies discussed in this book. However it is extremely important that practitioners are aware of EC environmental legislation which may be relevant to any of the areas of the environmental law discussed in Chapters 2–5 and the application of those remedies identified within those chapters or within Chapter 7.

The possibility of proceedings under arts 169 or 177 is also important, whether in terms of persuading the Commission to commence infringement proceedings or as a reference on a point of law under art 177.

This chapter will start by reviewing the development of environmental policy in the EC. A discussion of regulations and directives and their effect on national legislation follows; the chapter then considers the individual and the EC and looks at the use of art 169 and art 177 proceedings; finally, there is an analysis of the institutional framework of the EC.

DEVELOPMENT OF EC ENVIRONMENTAL POLICY

6.5 The EC consists of three treaties:

(a) the European Coal and Steel Community (ECSC) formed by the Treaty of Paris 1951;
(b) the European Economic Community (EEC), formed by the Treaty of Rome 1957 (the Treaty);
(c) the European Atomic Energy Community (EURATOM), also formed by the Treaty of Rome.

The institutions and procedures of all three treaties are largely the same and throughout this chapter they will be referred to as the EC. Reference to treaty articles will be to the Treaty. Nowadays, the EC is more often referred to in the media as the European Union since the Maastricht Treaty was known as the Treaty of European Union. This treaty also changed the term 'European Economic Community' to 'European Community'.

EC COMPETENCE ON ENVIRONMENTAL MATTERS

6.6   The EC was originally designed as an economic community, as its name suggests. The Treaty set out those areas in which it had competence, ie those matters upon which it could legislate and act. Therefore, if the Treaty did not refer to a specific subject then the EC had no resulting competence. No reference was made in the Treaty to the environment. The founding Member States wanted to establish an economic not an environmental community. Essentially, they wanted to create a 'common market' by eliminating barriers to trade such as duties and tariffs. The environment was not considered relevant since they wished to establish a body of law (competition law) to regulate the free trade of the EC. Upon a strict interpretation of the Treaty the EC did not have competence to legislate in the environmental field. Despite this seeming insurmountable obstacle the EC has not avoided involvement in environmental affairs. Nevertheless, it was not until the Single European Act of 1986 (SEA) that the EC gave itself the power to legislate specifically on environmental matters.

Environmental matters and free trade

6.7   During the mid-1960s it became obvious that national environmental laws could hinder free trade and that environmental co-operation between Member States was a natural progression from the principles of free trade. The EC found that differences in national environmental law could distort free trade. For example, more stringent anti-pollution legislation in one Member State would mean higher production costs and a higher price for the consumer. If the same industry in another Member State did not adopt similar measures then its prices would be lower and it would have an unfair advantage. Free trade would suffer.

As stated above, the EC is unlike the Member States in that it can only legislate on a matter if the Treaties give it specific competence in that area. This competence is given to the EC by a Treaty article— the so-called legal basis (which is explained in more detail below). One of the ways in which the validity of a piece of EC legislation may be challenged is by a claim that it has an improper legal basis, ie that the article upon which a piece of legislation is based does not give the EC the power to legislate in that area, thereby rendering it invalid. Regulations and directives have to state the article in the Treaty upon which the competence of the EC is based.

Although the Treaty did not mention the environment the EC gave itself the power to act in environmental affairs by using two of the more general articles in the Treaty—arts 100 and 235. The former gave the EC Council broad powers to harmonise national legislation 'as directly affect the establishment or functioning of the common market'. The latter is very wide and is essentially a 'catch-all' which allows the EC competence where the Treaty has not given it the necessary powers:

If action by the Community should prove necessary to attain, in the course of the operation of the common market, one of the objectives of the Community and this Treaty has not provided the necessary powers the Council shall, acting unanimously on a proposal from the Commission and after consulting the European Parliament, take the appropriate measures.

Article 235 was mainly used for directives that were essentially environmental such as the Wild Birds Directive, 79/409/EEC (OJ L103 25.04.70). Pollution control directives were mainly the province of art 100. Eventually, however, Member States decided to challenge the legal basis of such directives and art 169 proceedings (*see* below) were used in *Commission v Italy* [1981] 1 CMLR 331. In this instance Italy argued that the Directive 73/404/EEC (OJ L347 17.12.73) on the biodegradability of detergents was invalidly based on art 100. The ECJ rejected this argument stating that:

Provisions which are made necessary by considerations relating to the environment and health may be a burden on the undertakings to which they apply and if there is no harmonisation of national provisions on the matter, competition may be appreciably distorted.

ACTION PROGRAMMES

6.8   The EC therefore used these two articles to pass measures protecting the environment. It was not until the passing of the First Action Programme in the early 1970s that a more formal environmental policy was developed.

In October 1972 it was decided in a declaration by the Heads of Government that the EC should have an environmental policy on the basis that improvement in living standards should not exclude quality of life. This, in turn, led to the adoption of action programmes.

An action programme is not legislation. It is more a statement of policy detailing legislation to be adopted. The action programmes have therefore underpinned EC environmental legislation since the First Action Programme which covered the period 1973–76.

First Action Programme

6.9   The First Action Programme sets out a series of principles defining the objectives of EC environmental policy which have been repeated in subsequent programmes. In addition, it also sets out three categories of action:
(a)   the reduction and prevention of pollution and nuisances;
(b)   action to improve the quality of the environment; and
(c)   co-operation with international bodies, particularly the Organisation of Economic Co-operation and Development (OECD), the Council of Europe and the United Nations.

Further action programmes

6.10   Since then there have been four further action programmes covering the years 1977–81, 1983–86, 1987–92 respectively and most recently, in March 1992, the Fifth Action Programme, entitled 'Towards Sustainability' for the period 1992–2000+ (OJ 1993, C138/1).

Fifth Action Programme

6.11   This latest action programme marks a change in EC environmental policy away from a media-based approach (ie air, land and water) to a more integrated approach looking at implications of industrial activities on all areas of the economy. It focuses on what needs to be done for five key economic sections, industry, energy, transport, agriculture and tourism. Its focus is not only the protection of public health and the environment in each sector but also the sustainability of those sectors.

Another way in which it differs from the previous action programmes is that it considers alternative instruments as well as purely legislative measures. It considers market-based instruments designed to encourage the responsible use of natural resources and the avoidance of pollution and waste. It also highlights financial support mechanisms such as the Cohesion Fund as means whereby projects to improve the environment can be financed. Finally, it recommends improved data systems, scientific development and technological development and improved access to information.

THE SINGLE EUROPEAN ACT 1986 (SEA)

6.12   It was the arguments that raged over the legal basis for environmental legislation that eventually led the EC to formalise the position. As will be seen later the legislative procedure prior to the SEA was cumbersome (*see* the discussion of qualified majority voting at para 6.55 below). Essentially, it allowed any one Member State to block a measure even where all other 11 Member States had decided to adopt it. While resolution of this problem (the national veto) was the main purpose behind the SEA the EC also took the opportunity of including provisions to cover environmental policy.

Principles of EC environmental policy

6.13   Article 130R sets out the basic principles of EC environmental policy:

> (1) *Action by the Community relating to the environment shall have the following objectives:*
> > (i) *to preserve, protect and improve the quality of the environment;*

> (ii) to contribute towards protecting human health; and
>
> (iii) to ensure prudent and rational utilization of natural resources.
>
> (2) Action by the Community relating to the environment shall be based on the principles that preventative action should be taken, that environmental damage should as a priority be rectified at source, and that the polluter should pay. Environmental protection requirements shall be a component of the Community's other policies.
>
> (3) In preparing its action relating to the environment, the Community shall take account of:
>
> (i) available scientific and technical data;
>
> (ii) environmental conditions in the various regions of the Community;
>
> (iii) the potential benefits and costs of action or the lack of action;
>
> (iv) the economic and social development of the Community as a whole and the balanced development of its regions.
>
> (4) The Community shall take action relating to the environment to the extent to which the objectives referred to in paragraph 1 can be attained better at Community level than at the level of the individual Member States. Without prejudice to certain measures of a Community nature, the Member States shall finance and implement the other measures.

Thus, the EC decided to place priority upon the protection of the environment and quality of life. It also formally introduced the 'polluter pays' principle into the SEA. It did temper this by acknowledging that implementation of environmental policy must take into account 'the economic and social development of the Community as a whole'.

Definition of pollution

6.14   Although art 130R(2) introduced the concept of 'polluter pays', it did not define pollution. When therefore does someone become a polluter? The section below (para 6.27ff) on the formulation of directives sets out the categories of directives passed by the

EC—one of which is the setting of limit values and minimum concentrations. These set the level of emissions on the basis, presumably, that to exceed those values would lead to environmental damage or pollution. Following this through, pollution occurs when values or limits presented in directives are exceeded. Therefore while the EC does not define pollution it can be argued that not every emission constitutes pollution but only those which cause environmental damage.

Other procedural matters

6.15 Further articles were introduced setting out the procedure for the adoption of environmental legislation. Article 130S sets out the procedure for the adoption of such legislation (*see* the discussion of qualified majority voting at para 6.55 below). Article 130T states Member States' rights to deviate. The latter recognised that some Member States had higher environmental standards and were concerned that they might be weakened by EC legislation. It therefore allows for stricter standards to be adopted than those agreed under art 130S as long as trade is not distorted.

Member States also included an article (art 100A) specifically allowing for environmental legislation within the single market process. This article refers at 100A(3) to environmental measures but only so long as such measures are designed to establish a single market:

> *The Commission, in its proposals envisaged in [art 100A, para 1] concerning health, safety, environmental protection and consumer protection, will take as a base a high level of protection.*

THE MAASTRICHT TREATY

6.16 The Treaty on European Union was signed on 7 February 1992 and continued with the introduction of further enabling provisions. The following changes were made:
(1) Article 2 was amended to include the promotion of 'sustainable and non inflationary growth respecting the environment'.
(2) EC environmental policy must aim for 'a high level of

protection'. This previously only applied to environmental legislation adopted under art 100A.

(3) The 'precautionary' principle requiring action to be taken before a link has even been established between pollution and the environment was added to art 130R(2).

(4) A new formulation of the principle of subsidiarity was introduced. Essentially, it allows for action to be taken at the lowest possible level and in its new formulation, it emphasises that the Community will only act if the proposed action cannot be taken by the Member States. In other words, if the Member States cannot effectively protect the environment then it is the EC's responsibility to do so.

(5) Article 130S gave the Council the power to allow for temporary derogations for a Member State where a provision agreed under this article will leave it open to disproportionate costs. This acknowledged that some Member States have a less highly developed system of environmental protection and that to be forced to bring their processes up to date could involve them in excessive cost. In addition, financial support may be made available from the Cohesion Fund.

(6) Article 3131, which has relevance beyond the environmental sphere, added the requirement that laws should be made at their most appropriate level, whether this is at national or EC level.

Subsidiarity

6.17 There has been debate over the meaning of subsidiarity. There was much debate over its definition in the period before the signing of the Treaty and ratification did not conclude it. Essentially, it means that the EC should only legislate to the extent necessary. This could lead to a situation in which the EC passed more framework directives (*see* para 6.23 below), leaving Member States to implement more detailed provisions. Subsidiarity may even be used to repeal existing legislation which is best left to Member States. At present, this has not happened but this topic has the potential to be used by Member States to halt the more pervasive influences of the EC. At the Edinburgh summit in December 1993 broad guidelines were laid down for the application of the subsidiarity principle. These include:

(a) the Commission when making proposals will have to show the objectives cannot be achieved by action by Member States;

(b) framework directives should be preferred to detailed measures and directives themselves to regulations;

(c) whether the issue has transnational aspects which cannot be addressed satisfactorily by Member States;

(d) action at EC level will have to be justified in terms of 'clear benefits by reason of its scale to effects compared with action at the level of Member States'.

SOURCES OF EC LAW

6.18 Mention has already been made of the three treaties. The Treaty, together with the amending acts such as the SEA and the Maastricht Treaty, may be regarded as the EC's constitution since it created the various institutions and their procedures, sets the limits of the EC's jurisdiction and defined its objectives.

However, the actual legislative acts of the institutions can be seen as secondary sources of EC law. These, in turn, are divided into regulations, directives, decisions, recommendations and opinions (the latter three, not being as significant to environmental matters, will not be considered in detail). Article 189 of the Treaty empowers the Council and the Commission to make regulations and directives, take decisions, make recommendations and deliver opinions. The hierarchy of these various types of legislation is important when considering whether they have direct effect—a concept of great importance to the Member States which will be considered in more detail later in this chapter.

REGULATIONS

Legal effect of regulations

6.19 A regulation has general legal effect since, under art 189, 'It shall be binding in its entirety and directly applicable in all Member States'. The Member States have no discretion in the implementation of regulations and they enter into effect on the date specified (within the text of the regulation) or 20 days after they are published in the Official Journal of the European Communities (OJ). Regulations, like directives and decisions, must state the reasons upon which they are based. This is an aid to their interpretation and they start with a preamble setting out these reasons and their legal basis.

Regulations are directly effective in Member States and there is usually no need for the enactment of national legislation to give effect to them. Indeed, the ECJ has ruled that national implementing measures are not proper. Several reasons lie behind this:

(1) Regulations take effect on the date they were enacted and uncertainty over interpretation may arise if Member States pass laws to implement them.

(2) Subtle changes may be made if regulations are implemented in national law.

(3) Member States may refer interpretation of regulations to the ECJ under art 177 of the Treaty, as will be seen later. If regulations were implemented by national law a national court might decide not to refer cases. This could adversely affect the uniform interpretation of EC law such that a regulation could acquire a different interpretation in Member States.

Implementation by regulations

6.20   Regulations have not often been used as a vehicle for environmental measures but have recently been used to implement new administrative procedures. Thus, Reg 880/92/EC (OJ L99 11.04.92) established a voluntary scheme for the award of ecolabels to products which reduced environmental impact; the European Environment Agency (EEA) was introduced by Reg 90/1210/EEC (OJ L120 11.05.90) and Reg 2455/92/EC (OJ L251 29.08.92) set up a system of notification of exports to, and imports from, a third country. They have also been used to implement international treaties concluded by the EC for its Member States. Regulation 3626/82/EEC (OJ L384 31.12.78) implemented the Convention on International Trade in Endangered Species of Wild Flora and Fauna (CITES) and Reg 594/91/EEC (OJ L67 14.03.91) the Montreal Protocol to the Vienna Convention for the Protection of the Ozone Layer.

DIRECTIVES

6.21 The EC has built up a considerable body of legislation addressing environmental problems and it consists almost exclusively of directives. It is the directive, therefore, that has been the principal tool in the environment field.

Implementation of directives

6.22 A directive is binding only 'as to the result to be achieved' but leaves 'the choice of form and methods' of implementation to the individual Member State—art 189. The directive sets out the objective but leaves to the Member State the manner in which it achieves that objective. It therefore anticipates that Member States will use their own legislative procedures and forms to implement the directives but that the result will be the same in each country. However, explicit reference to the directive must be made in national implementing measures to identify its origin. Directives also appear in the OJ but, unlike regulations, they set a date by which they must be implemented—usually one or two years.

Framework directives

6.23 Directives can be subdivided into 'framework' and 'daughter' directives. The framework directives set out regimes to be implemented to control pollution. For example, Dir 75/442/EEC (OJ L194 25.07.75) provides the framework of EC action in the field of waste management. Similarly, Part I of the EPA, under which the system of IPC was introduced in England and Wales, implemented the Air Framework Directive, 84/360/EEC (OJ L188 16.07.84).

Daughter directives

6.24 Framework directives are followed by daughter directives which are more detailed and specify the targets, such as quality objectives or limits, to be achieved. The framework directive on dangerous substances in water, Dir 76/464/EEC (OJ L129 18.05.76), has spawned several daughter directives dealing with specific substances such as, among others, mercury, cadmium, DDT and chloroform. The Commission also specified a list of substances to be the subject of the next daughter directives (Com (90)9, 08.02.90).

Others deal with specific problems such as the freedom of access to information (*see* Chapter 9) on the environment or nature conservation, such as Dir 79/409/EEC which provides a system of protection for all species of wild birds in Europe.

As far as the individual is concerned, he may have a say in how the directive is implemented in that the government may issue a consultation paper requesting representations from interested parties.

See Appendix 5 for a list of significant environmental directives and of the resultant national legislation that puts them into effect.

DIRECT EFFECT

PRINCIPLES

6.25   It was initially thought that only regulations would have direct effect. However, the ECJ eventually extended the concept to directives as long as certain criteria were met. To put matters simply, a provision has direct effect if it grants rights to individuals which must be upheld by the national courts. To be directly effective two requirements must be met:

(1)   The provision must be part of the law of the land in that the national courts must recognise it as valid and binding law.

(2)   It must be appropriate to confer rights on individuals:

   (a)   the provision must be clear and unambiguous;

   (b)   the provision must be unconditional;

   (c)   the operation of the provision must not be dependent on further action being taken by Community or national authorities.

The ECJ developed the doctrine in order to protect the rights of individuals and to ensure that Member States implement directives properly and on time. An individual may wish to rely on a directive if his rights have been infringed—eg by using it as a defence in a criminal case or pleading it in a civil case. All that is required is for the date by which the directive should have been implemented to pass. It does not matter if the Member State has implemented it or not.

Vertical and horizontal direct effect

6.26 However, it is important to note that the doctrine does not apply as between private individuals but only arises in actions against the state. This is the distinction between vertical and horizontal direct effect. The former applies between the individual and the state and the latter between individuals. In essence, directives can, therefore, only be invoked against the state and not against private individuals. This, at first sight, would appear to be a major obstacle in the path of an individual wishing to rely upon direct effect. To overcome this, the ECJ has, over the years, defined 'state' more and more widely. Thus, all administrative bodies such as the NRA, the HSE or the Drinking Water Inspectorate would fall into this category following the ECJ's decision in *Foster v British Gas* [1990] ECR I-3313 in which it ruled that British Gas was an emanation of the state. The recent case of *Griffin v South West Water Services Ltd* (unreported) concluded finally that water companies fell within the definition of emanations of the state as set out in *Foster v British Gas*.

Whether an environmental directive falls within the direct effect doctrine is a matter of interpretation for each directive. All of the criteria set out have to be met. The nature of environmental directives lends itself to the doctrine of direct effect. They are usually clear and precise in setting maximum values for certain discharges or prohibited acts such as the harmful disposal of waste.

FORMULATION OF DIRECTIVES

6.27 Environmental directives can generally be categorised into three types: those setting maximum values, minimum concentrations and limit values; those prohibiting the use of certain substances or their discharge; and those requiring Member States to perform certain acts.

Directives setting specific limits

6.28 The first category sets out values that are usually specific, unconditional and do not depend on any further action by the EC or Member States. Directive 80/779/EEC (OJ L229 30.08.80) sets limit values for the ground level concentration of sulphur dioxide and suspended particulates (smoke). The values are given in microgrammes per cubic metre using prescribed methods to measure both sulphur dioxide and smoke and must be met during specific periods. Thus, during the winter (1 October to 31 March) smoke must not exceed 130mg and sulphur dioxide 180mg if smoke is less than 60mg or 130mg if smoke is more than 60mg. These limit values are unconditional, state precisely that they must not be exceeded and Member States are given no discretion for future action.

Other directives, such as 76/464/EEC (OJ L129 18.05.76) on pollution of water by dangerous substances, set both limit values and quality objectives. Thus, limit values are set for different types of processes or industrial activities while quality objectives are given for various waters such as, among others, estuaries, coastal waters and water abstracted for drinking. The competent authority has to select from the quality objectives those most appropriate to the water. Emission standards will then be set by the authority to see that the objective is achieved. The quality objectives are precise and unconditional and while the competent authority has to select the appropriate objective the water has to comply with all objectives since more than one may apply.

Directives setting prohibitions

6.29   Similarly, directives of the second category are usually phrased in absolute terms and are, therefore, directly effective. A prime example is Dir 78/319/EEC (OJ L84 31.03.78) on toxic and dangerous waste which requires such waste to be disposed of without risk to man and the environment. No qualification is imposed allowing certain waste which does pose such a risk. It is clear and precise and does not allow the Member States any discretion in its implementation. Directive 79/409/EEC (*see* para 6.24 above) on the conservation of wild birds is similar in its absolute prohibition of the deliberate destruction of wild birds, their nests and eggs; the hunting of birds except for the purposes listed in Annex II; the sale of live birds except those listed in Annex III. None of these depend on the implementation of any condition or further action by Member States.

Directives requiring performance

6.30   However, the last category does not fall neatly into this analysis. For example Directive 85/339/EEC (OJ L176 06.07.85) requires Member States to draw up programmes to reduce waste arising from drinks packaging. While the provisions of this directive are clear and unconditional it leaves to the Member State the actual contents of the programme. The circumstances of any particular Member State will vary. Member States may prohibit a type of packaging, impose a tax upon it or specify methods of collection to achieve the objects of the directive and is not, therefore, directly effective. It is also a good example of the definition of a directive in that it leaves the 'choice of form and methods of implementation' as defined in art 189 to the Member State.

Environmental Impact Assessment Directive

6.31   The Environmental Impact Assessment Directive 85/337/EEC (OJ L175 05.07.85) lists in Annex I the projects which must be made subject to an environmental impact assessment (EIA). This directive requires Member States to perform an act in setting up a scheme. However, Annex II lists projects which shall only be subject to an assessment if Member States consider that they require one. The provisions relating to both annexes are clear and precise but Annex I does not allow Member States any discretion whereas Annex II does. Some of the directive's provisions are, therefore, directly effective while others are not. This third category very much depends on the interpretation of the directive whether it is directly effective or not. *See* Chapter 3 for a discussion of EIA.

THE INDIVIDUAL AND EC LAW

6.32   In a book of this nature it is unrealistic to detail every single environmental directive that the EC has adopted conferring on individuals a right of action. From the early days when it had to contrive a legal basis for its environmental legislation the EC has introduced a substantial body of over 200 environmental measures. To set out in detail the provisions of the directives imposing noise limits on lawnmowers, regulating the deliberate release of genetically modified organisms or reducing the tonnage and volume of containers in waste for disposal is beyond the scope of this book. For a more comprehensive list of regulations, directives and decisions reference should be made to other works, such as Nigel

Haigh's *Manual of Environmental Policy: the EC and Britain.* The texts of regulations and directives can be found in the OJ, although Appendix 5 sets out some of the key environmental directives and the relevant national implementing legislation.

The ECJ has recognised the importance of the role of the individual in upholding EC law before national courts in its decision in *Van Gend & Loos* (Case 26/62, [1993] ECR 1):

> *the vigilance of private individuals to protect their rights amounts to an effective supervision in addition to the supervision entrusted by Articles 169 and 170 to the diligence of the Commission and the Member States.*

How can the individual use the institutions of the ECJ to his advantage?

6.33   This question can best be answered by illustration, showing how a particular directive (Dir 80/778/EEC (OJ L229 30.08.80)) has passed into UK legislation and how an individual may invoke its provisions for his/her benefit.

Example

The directive covers all water for human consumption, including public and private water supplies, and lays down standards for water used for drinking or for food and drink manufacture. It is intended to protect the health and life of individuals. It also states that regular water quality monitoring must be carried out and samples taken at the point where water is made available to the user. More specifically, the directive sets out 62 water quality standards and guidelines for water quality monitoring. It has three annexes. Annex I lists the water quality standards; Annex II deals with water quality monitoring and Annex III the methods of analysis. Member States have to set values for the Maximum Admissible Concentration (MAC) and the Minimum Required Concentration (MRC) of water and have to ensure that water meets these standards. The third type of standard is the Guide Level (GL) and, in this instance, the Member State is given a discretion whether to set a standard or not.

The directive was implemented by the Water Act 1989, which has now been consolidated into other Acts such as the Water Resources Act 1991 and the Water Industry Act 1991. Initially the directive was implemented by administrative means and the Commission brought infringement proceedings referred to at para 6.39 below—Case C-337/89. As a result the Water Act 1989 set detailed statutory standards for the quality of drinking water. Full legal effect was given to these standards by the Water Supply (Water Quality) Regulations (*see* para 6.39 below). This was the first time that a system of statutory water quality objectives and standards for drinking water had been introduced in England and Wales.

Directly effective directives: water quality

6.34 With all these problems concerning implementation, of what use is the directive to the UK citizen? The doctrine of direct effect, explained earlier, gives an individual rights which must be upheld in national courts. Therefore, if it can be shown that the directive on drinking water is directly effective then it will confer rights upon the individual. Certain directives were examined above (paras 6.27ff) to decide whether they were directly effective. It is submitted that the terms of the directive on drinking water are clear and unambiguous—it sets definite water quality standards, no conditions are placed on its implementation and no further action is required by EC or national authorities. If an individual drank water supplied by a water company and suffered injury as a result of the water company's non-compliance with the directive then he should be able to sue the water company for damages, relying on the terms of the directive. Similarly, if a community suffered health problems arising from poor quality drinking water then it also would have the right to sue the water company supplying the water. The directive has been implemented into the UK law but this does not stop the individual relying upon it before national courts.

Directly effective directives: air quality

6.35 The same analysis can be applied to other directives. Directive 80/779/EEC (OJ L229 30.08.80) sets limit values for air quality. As stated above, this directive would have direct effect. The terms of the directive state that, 'in order to protect human health in particular, it is necessary to set for these two pollutants [sulphur dioxide and suspended particles] limit values which must not be exceeded in the territory of Member States'. Likewise, Dir 82/884/EEC (OJ L378 31.12.82) sets a limit value for lead in the air and Dir 85/203/EEC (OJ L87 27.3.85) does the same for nitrogen dioxide; both of these directives are directly effective. The citizen has therefore been granted a right for the protection not only of water quality but also of air quality.

Other directives

6.36 Action by individuals need not be confined to directives designed to prevent pollution. If an organisation refused to divulge environmental information contrary to the terms of the directive on the freedom of access of information on the environment (*see* Chapter 9) then an individual could use the directive to assert his right to the information. Similarly, the directive on environmental impact assessment ensures that the interests of the parties are taken into account in the consent procedure necessary for development of land. If the individual is not permitted to be consulted during the consent procedure he can enforce this right through the courts.

Action to enforce EC standards

6.37 The discussion above deals with the situation where an individual has suffered harm. However, what is the position if an individual has not suffered injury (eg from drinking polluted water or breathing contaminated air) and the Member State is still not observing EC law? It makes a nonsense of the fact that these directives are designed to protect the health of individuals if one cannot invoke them against the competent authority in his Member State. The individual may take action through the courts to enforce EC standards.

Locus

6.38 One important qualification must be made. An individual must have the necessary *locus standi* to sue. The individual or association must have been directly affected. If an individual's neighbour has drunk contaminated water then he cannot sue on his behalf in the courts using the drinking water directive. More obviously, an individual cannot have a right of action on behalf of a seal harmed in contravention of Dir 83/129/EEC (OJ L91 09.04.83) on the import of seal skins. Even more important in respect of action to enforce EC standards, where individuals have not been harmed, is the rule that standing is governed by national law and this varies from Member State to Member State. Reference should be made to the section in Chapter 7 on judicial review.

TYPES OF ACTION IN EUROPEAN COURTS

ARTICLE 169 PROCEEDINGS

6.39 If a Member State does not implement a directive properly or applies its laws contrary to EC law then under art 169 the Commission has the power to bring a Member State before the ECJ. Before taking these infringement proceedings the Commission will try to resolve matters by writing to the Member State asking for an explanation and if it is not satisfied then by issuing a Reasoned Opinion setting out the grounds of non-compliance. Before the Maastricht Treaty, if the ECJ decided that the Member State was in breach of EC law it could not enforce the ruling. It relied on Member States doing so as a matter of political necessity. Article 171 merely required a Member State to take measures to comply with the judgment of the ECJ. The ECJ could not impose any sanctions and the Commission would have had to commence fresh art 169 proceedings for failure to fulfil obligations under art 171—a somewhat circular process.

However, the Maastricht Treaty introduced a new art 171. Now, if the Member State does not comply, the Commission may bring the case back before the ECJ for the court to impose a penalty.

Under the old procedure the UK was found liable for non-implementation of Dir 80/778/EEC (OJ L229 30.08.80) on the quality of drinking water in Case C-337/89, *Commission v United Kingdom*, the first such case ever brought against the UK. Under this directive the UK government had to ensure that all relevant water supplies would contain less than 50 parts per million (ppm) of nitrates by 1985. Upon investigation by the Commission it was found that nitrate levels were between 50 and 100 ppm in areas of the country. The requirements of the directive were eventually implemented by the Water Supply (Water Quality) Regulations 1989 (SI 1989 No 1147 as amended).

The need to comply with EC directives can place great financial burdens on industry. The Bathing Water Directive 76/160/EEC (OJ L31 05.02.76), designed to protect fresh or seawater bathing, and the Urban Waste Water Directive 91/271/EEC (OJ L135 30.05.91), designed to reduce the pollution of freshwater, estuarial and coastal waters by domestic sewage, industrial waste water and rainwater runoff, have required the 10 water companies to undertake expensive capital investment programmes. This will entail expenditure of over £26 billion over the next 10 years, of which around £12 billion relates to improvement of sewage services.

A similar procedure is available to Member States under art 170 to take proceedings against another Member State for non-implementation of a directive but this has only been used once.

REFERENCE UNDER ARTICLE 177

6.40   Any court or tribunal in a Member State may refer, under art 177, any legislation including the Treaty to the ECJ for interpretation. This is usually done when there is doubt over the meaning of EC law and its compatibility with domestic law. The reason behind this procedure is to ensure the uniform interpretation of EC law across the EC. It is the national court's responsibility to refer a matter to the ECJ but, due to the adversarial nature of proceedings in the UK, it is usually done on the application of one of the parties to a case.

For example, the ECJ reached its decision in *Foster v British Gas* [1990] 3 All ER 897 upon a preliminary ruling. The ECJ stated:

> *it followed that a body, whatever its legal form, which has been made responsible, pursuant to a measure adopted by the State, for providing a public service under the control of the State and had for that purpose special powers beyond those which resulted from the normal rules applicable in relations between individuals, was included in any event among the bodies against which the provisions of a Directive capable of having direct effect might be relied on.*

One of the major tools at the ECJ's disposal to develop EC law has been the preliminary reference procedure.

When a point of EC law is raised before the English High Court the procedure is governed by Ord 114 of the Rules of the Supreme Court (RSC). The English court will make an order setting out the request for a preliminary ruling in a schedule and the proceedings are stayed unless the court orders otherwise. The schedule sets out a precise statement of the case so that the ECJ can understand the issues raised. This enables Member States and other interested parties to submit their observations.

It is in the discretion of the English court whether to refer the case to the ECJ or not. It may decide that the law is so obvious that no reference is needed. The court may, when giving judgment, leave it open to the parties to appeal and so avoid making a decision on whether to refer or not. However, it is with respect to those courts against whose decision there is no judicial remedy (ie no appeal) that the question becomes most important—the House of Lords in this country. The courts will try to rely on the *acte clair* doctrine by which if the law is so clear as to admit of no reasonable doubt the Member States' courts must interpret EC law for themselves. This is a very broad statement of a complicated doctrine. It is inappropriate in a work of this type to discuss this doctrine in more detail. All that can be done is to state that a referral remains in the discretion of the national court.

ECJ CASE LAW

DOCTRINE OF DIRECT EFFECT

6.41 Reference has already been made to the doctrine of direct effect. The ECJ has gone further in protecting individuals' rights by insisting that when Member States implement legislation they must do so in a clear and precise legal framework which allows individuals to uphold their rights before national courts. For example, in *Commission v Federal Republic of Germany* (Case 131/88) it was found that Germany had not properly implemented Dir 80/68/EEC (OJ 1980 L20/43) concerning the protection of groundwater from pollution caused by dangerous substances. The ECJ found that this directive sought to create rights and obligations for individuals and that it had not been implemented specifically enough to allow individuals to uphold these rights.

DOCTRINE OF INDIRECT EFFECT

6.42 The ECJ has widened the doctrine of direct effect to avoid the problem of horizontal direct effect as in *Foster v British Gas.* Under its policy of increasing the scope of EC law it has developed the doctrine of indirect effect under which national courts are under an obligation to interpret their national laws in the light of the objectives and wording of EC directives. It does not matter if the national provision pre- or post-dated the EC directive. In effect, this is a retrospective doctrine since all national legislation must take into account any relevant EC legislation.

LIABILITY FOR FAILURE TO IMPLEMENT A DIRECTIVE

6.43 The progressive approach of the ECJ is further highlighted by *Francovich v Italy* (Case C-6/90) where it laid down the principle that a Member State may be liable to an individual for harm caused by a failure to implement a directive. Two Italian firms had gone bankrupt leaving employees with substantially unpaid salaries. Italy had not implemented a directive establishing an EC-wide system providing minimum protection of employees in case of insolvency of their employer. The Italian court submitted the case to the ECJ under the preliminary ruling procedure asking whether an individual may claim damages suffered as a result of a Member State's failure to implement a directive. The Treaty does not refer to the non-contractual (ie tortious) liability of the Member State arising out of a breach of an EC obligation. The ECJ decided that such a liability can arise as long as it meets the following criteria:

(1) The result pursued by the directive involved the conferring of rights in individuals.

(2) The content of those rights can be determined by reference to the directive.

(3) There must be a causal link between the failure by the Member State to implement the directive and the harm caused to the individual.

PREDOMINANCE OF EC LAW

6.44 One of the most significant judgments of the ECJ occurred in the English case of *R v Secretary of State for Transport, ex parte Factortame* [1991] 1 All ER 70 and [1990] ECR I-2433. The ECJ decided that national courts must set aside national laws that are an obstacle to the implementation of EC law. An action was brought by Spanish owners of British trawlers who sought judicial review of the Merchant Shipping Act 1988 which they alleged breached principles of EC law since it excluded the trawlers from using British waters. There was a doubt whether the Act was compatible with EC law. However, it would take two years to be referred to the ECJ in which time the plaintiffs would be ruined. They asked for interim relief restraining the Secretary of State from enforcing it against them. The House of Lords referred the matter to the ECJ. The question at issue was whether a national court, having before it a case concerning EC law, and considering that a rule of national law was the sole obstacle precluding it from granting interim relief, must disapply that rule. The ECJ replied that the national court must set aside the national legislative provisions which might prevent EC law having full force and effect. It relied on art 5 of the Treaty which ensures the legal protection afforded to individuals by directly effective provisions.

ENVIRONMENTAL PROTECTION VERSUS FREE TRADE

6.45 The ECJ has been proactive not only in the field of individuals' rights. The founder Member States wanted to create a common market. However, such economic expansion through free trade does not always sit easily with environmental protection. In the *Danish Bottles* case (Case 302/86 [1989] 1 CMLR 619) the ECJ effectively ruled in favour of the environment over free trade. Denmark introduced a law which restricted the types of container permitted to market drinks to ensure that they were all returnable. Obviously, other Member States would have had to alter their production processes to comply and the Danish law, effectively discriminated against them. The ECJ upheld the Danish law stating that such national laws were permissible provided that they applied to domestic and imported goods without distinction and were necessary to satisfy national environmental objectives. Environmental protection therefore can be used as a basis upon which to derogate from the common market as long as it is proportionate to the end to be achieved.

Similarly, in the *Wallonian Waste* case (Case C-2/90), the ECJ upheld a Belgian trade-distorting measure. Belgium introduced a law banning the import of non-hazardous waste even though it restricted the free movement of goods. The ECJ decided, however, that the ban was justified on environmental grounds. It referred to art 130R(2), that environmental damage should be rectified at source and, therefore, waste should be disposed of as near as possible to its place of origin.

THE INSTITUTIONS OF THE EC

6.46   The EC comprises four major institutions: the European Commission (the Commission), the Council of the European Communities (the Council), the European Parliament (the Parliament) and the European Court of Justice (ECJ). The addresses of these bodies are given in Appendix 6. There are other lesser institutions such as the Court of Auditors, the European Social and Economic Committee and the European Investment Bank but their significance in environmental matters is not sufficient to warrant detailed consideration here.

THE COMMISSION

Composition

6.47   The Commission consists of 17 people appointed by the governments of the Member States for renewable periods of five years (the period was four years before the European elections in June 1994). At present, the five largest countries, United Kingdom, France, Germany, Italy and Spain, appoint two commissioners and the other countries, one. The commissioners' terms expire simultaneously so the whole of the Commission retires together. (The ECJ can compel a commissioner to retire on the grounds of serious misconduct or if he or she no longer fulfils the conditions required for the performance of his or her duties.)

Representation

6.48 While the commissioners may be appointed by their Member States, it is the Commission that represents the supranational aspects of the EC. The commissioners do not represent their country and they perform their duties independently of any instructions from their respective Member State. However, political pressure may be exerted by the Member States on the Commission as a whole. The Commission cannot ignore the representations of Member States because its role is to reconcile national interests. Although it is an independent body it must pay particular regard to national issues to avoid antagonising any particular Member State.

It meets in private and takes decisions by a majority vote. It has a written procedure whereby draft decisions are submitted to the commissioners and if no objection is received then the proposal is adopted.

Functions

6.49 One of its major functions is the proposal of legislation. In this role it acts as the initiator of legislation. One of its more far-reaching proposals is the proposal on Integrated Pollution Prevention and Control (IPPC) (Com (93)423 Final).

Organisation

6.50 The Commission is organised into Directorates-General (D-G) of which there are 23 headed by a Director-General who is responsible to a particular commissioner. Some commissioners may be responsible for more than one D-G.

Each commissioner is assisted by his cabinet. This is a group of individuals personally appointed by the commissioner to help him in the administration of a D-G. Each cabinet formulates the proposals for legislation which it distributes to other D-Gs asking for their views. When agreement has been reached the proposal will be put to the Commission which may adopt it by simple majority or via the written procedure.

The D-G responsible for the environment is D-G XI which is subdivided into three Directorates:

(a) Directorate A: responsible for nuclear safety, industry and the environment and civil protection;
(b) Directorate B: responsible for the quality of the environment and natural resources;
(c) Directorate C: responsible for environmental instruments and international affairs.

Each of these, in turn, is subdivided into further departments.

The complaints procedure

6.51   Under art 155 the Commission is responsible for ensuring that the Treaty and measures taken by the EC institutions are applied. This allows it to take action to satisfy itself that EC law is being applied in the Member States. Therefore, if it discovers that a Member State has disregarded EC law it has a duty to investigate the matter and take steps to prevent the breach. Formal action as described under art 169 is available, although the Commission may prefer to negotiate with the Member State in order to reach an agreed solution. However, with over 200 environmental measures to supervise, it is unlikely that the Commission can effectively carry out this task. It has neither the staff nor the resources to monitor every breach of eg a limit value in the water directives or the destruction of birds covered by the Wild Birds Directive.

The Commission has therefore developed a complaints procedure. Where there has been a breach of EC law an individual may notify the Commission of this in writing. A special form has been designed for this purpose and each complaint is entered into a central register kept by the Commission and given a number. It is not essential that the form be used, merely that the complaint be in writing. No formal requirement such as prior action, whether legal or otherwise, by the complainant is required. It does not matter, therefore, that he has been directly affected or that it took place in his Member State.

The Commission will gather the necessary information in order to come to a decision and may make a study or send its officials to investigate. Generally, it will arrive at a decision within one year of the complaint being made. The Commission may then institute art 169 proceedings or otherwise but there is no procedure either to compel art 169 proceedings or to complain about the Commission's decision. The proceedings are private, in that the Commission does not publish any detailed information, although the individual can bring the matter to public attention.

The use of the complaints procedure has increased considerably, from 10 in 1982 to 480 in 1990, of which the UK made the greatest number—125.

Examples of breaches where this procedure may be used are:

(a) under Dir 85/337/EEC (OJ L175 27.06.85) on environmental impact assessments: if the public is not consulted when details of the development are submitted by the developer of the project;

(b) under Dir 76/160/EEC (OJ L31/1 08.12.75) on the quality of bathing water: if a beach/river comes under the directive the Commission must check whether the quality of the water is monitored and meets the requirements of the directive. An individual may bring this to the attention of the Commission;

(c) under Dir 78/319/EEC (OJ L84/43 30.03.78) on the disposal of dangerous waste: if waste is disposed of in such a way that the environment is not damaged. An individual may choose to complain if waste is disposed of contrary to the directive.

These examples are, of course, not meant to be exhaustive but give a flavour of how the procedure may be used.

THE COUNCIL

Functions

6.52 Unlike the Commission, the Council is not independent of the Member States, and it is the forum where national interests are represented most directly. In effect, it is the legislature of the EC since it is the principal decision-taking body. It also concludes agreements with foreign countries and, together with the Parliament, decides on the EC budget. The Council may delegate its power to enact legislation to the Commission. However it can only pass Acts on a proposal from the Commission.

Composition

6.53 The Council consists of a delegate from each Member State who is usually a Minister of State. If general matters are being discussed, the delegate will be the Foreign Minister but if more specific matters, such as the environment, are under consideration, the relevant minister, in this case the Secretary of State for the Environment, will be the delegate.

The presidency of the Council rotates at six-monthly intervals between the Member States. The UK will next occupy the presidency in January–June 1998.

Organisation

6.54   The Committee of Personal Representatives (COREPER) assists the Council in the day-to-day running of the Council since ministers can only be present in Brussels for short periods.

Qualified majority voting

6.55   Under arts 100 and 235 unanimity is required in the Council for environmental legislation to be passed. Both of these articles state that unless all members of the Council vote in favour of a measure then it will not be adopted. One member of the Council could therefore effectively block the legislative procedure—the national veto. In order to ensure a speedy completion of the single market, the SEA increased the number of measures which required qualified majority voting. Under this procedure the votes of the Member States as represented are weighted. This means that the larger Member States such as the UK have 10 votes and the smaller Member States have decreasingly fewer votes with Luxembourg having only two. A qualified majority is 54 out of a total of 76— effectively a two-thirds majority. This means that one of the smaller Member States cannot block a measure and only an alliance of Member States can now do so. Under art 100A(1) a qualified majority is required but under art 130S unanimity is usually required, except where the Council unanimously votes that voting may take place by qualified majority.

However, the Maastricht Treaty amended art 130S so that most environmental legislation can be adopted using qualified majority voting and the 'co-decision procedure'. Measures may still be adopted under art 100A as this also increases the use of the 'co-decision procedure' (as opposed to the 'co-operation procedure' in art 130S—*see* para 6.57 below for an explanation of these procedures). The changes introduced by the Maastricht Treaty will probably lead to most EC environmental legislation being adopted under art 130S which will mean a speeding-up of the legislative procedure.

THE EUROPEAN PARLIAMENT

Function and composition

6.56 The European Parliament is not the legislature of the EC. It is the Council that fulfils that role, with the Commission proposing the legislation. The Parliament is essentially an advisory and consultative body. At present it consists of 518 MEPs elected every five years. The number of members elected is in proportion to the population of each Member State. Its official seat is in Strasbourg with the committees of the Parliament meeting in Brussels and the General Secretariat in Luxembourg. The first election by direct universal suffrage took place in 1979 and the most recent was in June 1994.

Powers

6.57 It was the SEA which increased the Parliament's powers over legislation. Previously, consultation had always been mandatory. The general legislative procedure is for the Commission to make a proposal to the Council. Under the consultation procedure the Council consulted the Parliament but was not obliged to take up any amendments made by the Parliament. However, under the 'co-operation procedure' set out in art 149 the Parliament is empowered to reject or propose amendments to legislation. Under this, the Council adopts a 'common position' based on the Commission's proposals but if Parliament rejects this common position then the Council may only adopt the measure if it does so unanimously. The Parliament may also propose amendments. If the Commission adopts those amendments the Council can agree to the amended proposal by qualified majority, or agree another unanimously, or allow the proposal to lapse.

The Maastricht Treaty has replaced art 189 with a similar procedure in art 189C. By art 189B this treaty has also introduced a new 'co-decision procedure' under which a Conciliation Committee has been set up to resolve disputes. This committee consists of representatives from the Council and Parliament. For the first time it gives the Parliament the power to veto legislation. The procedure is similar to the 'co-operative procedure' except that the Commission must submit the proposal to both the Council and the Parliament. If the Parliament votes to reject the common position then the Conciliation Committee must meet to agree on a joint text by a qualified majority (*see* below). Following this, the Parliament may confirm its rejection of the common position in which case the legislation is not adopted.

Democratic deficit

6.58 One of the major criticisms of the EC's institutions has been the lack of democratic accountability or the so-called 'democratic deficit'. This has focused on the secrecy of the EC's legislative procedures; the 'co-decision procedure' was designed to combat this. The voice of the people of the Member States is heard most vigorously in the Parliament through the MEPs, their elected representatives. Therefore, the Parliament had to be given more say in the legislative process.

In the same way that individuals may lobby their MP in the UK so they can make representations to their MEP. This means that their views may be heard in the European Parliament. It has to be said, however, that with the citizens of 11 other Member States wanting their say, lobbying may not be particularly effective.

The European Court of Justice

Composition and functions

6.59 The ECJ sits in Luxembourg and consists of 13 judges appointed by the agreement of the Member States. Overall, its function is described by art 164:

> *The Court of Justice shall ensure that in the interpretation and application of this Treaty the law is observed.*

Its primary function is therefore to interpret the meaning of the Treaty and the legislation made by the other institutions. In addition, it hears disputes between the Member States for infringement of the Treaty, reviews the legitimacy of the actions of the other institutions and interprets EC law on a reference under art 177 from a national court.

The European Environment Agency

6.60   One last body of direct relevance to this work is the European Environment Agency (EEA), set up under Reg 1210/90/EEC (OJ L120 11.05.90). Its headquarters are in Copenhagen. Its primary role is the gathering of information and data on the state of the environment in the EC. Allied to this is its responsibility to create the European Environment Information and Observation Network. Member States must pass their main environmental information networks to the EEA so that it can create the necessary network. In addition, it must produce a report on the state of the environment in the EC every five years and make predictions on the state of the environment and costs of environmental protection.

It does not, therefore, have any policing powers to enforce environmental legislation. Despite this, the regulation specifically requires the EEA's role to be reassessed two years after its establishment. This may potentially lead to it adopting the role of a European Environment Inspectorate.

Chapter 9 deals specifically with the sources of environmental information in the UK and information from the EEA can be used in conjunction with these.

CHAPTER 7

REMEDIES

INTRODUCTION

7.1   The first five chapters of this book looked at environmental law in terms of its statutory framework, common law, planning, authorisation and criminal sanction and at who is able to apply that law.

This chapter examines the remedies through the courts that these various bodies of law offer. It deals with common law; criminal remedies; statutory nuisance claims; and judicial review. The chapter focuses on the procedural requirements of the various remedies and on the preparation of evidence. This chapter should be read in conjunction with those on substantive law and with Chapters 8 and 9 on extra-legal remedies, experts and information. The application of planning and EC law is covered within those chapters of necessity. Much of the material in this chapter is technical and procedural in nature, but it is hoped that the advice it contains is practical and focused on the problems that arise in effecting remedies in environmental cases.

COMMON LAW

7.2   It was pointed out in Chapter 2 that common law offers a very effective remedy provided the aggrieved person can satisfy   the requirements as to who can sue. This section looks at problems arising when commencing common law actions in environmental cases.

7.3 Chapter 2 discussed the entitlement to sue and the problems with identifying defendants. This section looks at the particular problems of multiple plaintiffs.

Multiple plaintiffs

7.4 The starting point is that English law does not recognise class actions, ie actions where one person sues on behalf of a class of people who have suffered damage from a single source but who have not suffered in an identical manner. However, in practical terms the problem has been substantially resolved by flexible developments in procedure. English law does recognise representative actions where one plaintiff represents a number of individuals whose interests are identical, eg all members of a club suing for an injunction to restrain someone from continuing a nuisance.

Where representative proceedings are not available, once proceedings are issued there are other procedural devices to enable multiple-plaintiff litigation to be conducted with greater economy. In particular there is the option of one affected person bringing a test case the outcome of which will be binding in relation to some or all of the issues that fall to be decided.

A useful document which deals with the issue of multiple-party litigation is the 'Guide for use in Group Actions' which has been prepared by a working party of the judiciary and practitioners and issued by the Supreme Court Procedure Committee in August 1991.

The following areas which are raised in detail in that guide may be relevant to environmental litigation:

(1) The mechanism for dealing with multiple plaintiffs, and the use of co-ordinating committees to reduce overall costs, particularly where numerous firms of solicitors are involved.

(2) The use of alternative forms of procedure. A representative action, as mentioned above, is one possibility but has the drawback that it is only applicable where the interest of all those represented is identical in a claim for damages or an injunction. Where there is no such identity of interest then the alternatives are:

(a) to issue one set of proceedings involving all the parties; or

      (b) to issue one set of proceedings for each plaintiff which
          are run concurrently but with one of those actions as a
          test or lead case.

  (3) The assignment of a judge. On application to the relevant
      division a single judge can be assigned to deal with a multi-
      plaintiff action from its commencement. This means that
      that judge then deals with interlocutory matters in the same
      way, for example, as a case started in the official referee's
      court.

FORUM

7.5   In the absence of any forum specifically designed for environmental claims (*see* Chapter 10), common law actions will start
either in the county court or the High Court. The usual rules apply
as to jurisdiction: cases involving damages claims of less than
£25,000 must be started in the county court. Those having a value
above that can be issued in either, but claims having a value of above
£75,000 will normally be issued in the High Court.

    Where High Court proceedings are an option, then consideration
might be given to commencing proceedings in the Official Referee's
court which has particular experience in dealing with complex
expert evidence such as may often be in issue in environmental
claims. It is now possible to issue a writ directly in the Official
Referee's court, rather than transferring from other divisions. A
further advantage of the Official Referee's court is the involvement
of the trial judge from the first directions hearing. This involvement
is likely to result in more robust interlocutory orders, and the trial
date is fixed on that first hearing rather than much later in the proceedings as in other courts. Order 36 of the Rules of the Supreme
Court (RSC) deals with practice.

    Where the initial primary objective of the action is to try and
obtain interim injunctive relief there is much to be said for using
the motion procedure in the High Court, as this permits almost
immediate access to the court and gives the plaintiff control over
the listing of the first hearing. The county court also offers
quick access for interim injunction applications. Tactical
considerations in relation to injunctions are discussed at paras
7.17–7.19 below.

EVIDENCE

Before proceedings are issued

7.6 Before commencing proceedings it is sensible that as much evidence (as possible) should be put together. Expert advice will more often than not be highly relevant to determining liability and preferably at least a preliminary advice should be obtained before proceedings are issued so that a reasonable overall view can be taken of the merits of the case. An expert will have relevant knowledge as to the appropriate standards where there is an issue, for example, as to the duty of care or the application of the 'neighbour test' as discussed in Chapter 2 (*see* Chapter 9 for a discussion of experts and what they can offer).

Experience shows that one is often caught to a greater or lesser extent by the difficulty that it is only as the case proceeds that all the facts come to light, particularly on discovery. Notwithstanding this all available information ought to be collated, and all sources of information from third parties exploited. Chapter 9 considers the availability of environmental information generally.

In particular the Environmental Information Regulations (the EI Regulations) give scope for securing information prior to issuing proceedings. However, these regulations, and the enabling Acts which set up public registers, impose limitations on the disclosure of information that is the subject-matter of proceedings. What is more difficult is that the restriction also applies in relation to prospective proceedings. This restriction begs a very difficult question, namely, when are proceedings first contemplated? It is inevitable that, where the person seeking the information does not know the detail of what is to be revealed, it is only following a review of that information that a clear view can be formed as to the possibility of proceedings.

The Information Directive (90/313/EEC: OJ 158 23.6.90), together with public registers, provides greater scope for securing environmental information prior to the initiation of proceedings than is the case with other forms of litigation. Whether industry and others like it or not, that is the consequence of the directive. The impact of the directive should not be diluted by unduly restrictive qualifications in national regulations. There has, to the writers' knowledge, not been any case which has adjudicated on the class of people included within the definition of 'relevant person' in the EI Regulations or on the scope of the exemptions. It is to be hoped that it will not be too long before the courts have the opportunity to consider these matters.

There is a limited power to obtain pre-action discovery under the RSC. It only applies to personal injury actions (*see* Ord 25). Both the party making the application and the party against whom it is made must be likely to be made a party to the proceedings.

Discovery

7.7   As indicated above it is likely that, even in the best prepared cases, important information will emerge on discovery. No matter what the rules may say, service of a defendant's list of documents is frequently only the first step in this process. More often than not a plaintiff will have, by persuasion or compulsion, to secure further and better discovery from a defendant. It is important therefore for a plaintiff to look carefully at the types of documents that a defendant might be expected to have. In this regard any experts retained ought to be consulted, as they will have a better idea of what documents might exist of a technical nature.

One area of dispute that can arise in the course of discovery in environmental cases is that of confidentiality. This may be of particular relevance in dealing with statutory bodies such as water undertakers who receive information from third parties in the course of their activities. In most cases where there is a restriction on disclosure there is also a substantial list of exemptions, and thus an initial refusal to disclose ought to be carefully considered before it is accepted. One of the most relevant exemptions is disclosure for the purposes of legal proceedings. *See* s 210 of the Water Resources Act 1991 (WRA) and s 66 of the Environmental Protection Act 1990 (EPA).

As is explained in para 7.6 above, there is considerable scope for obtaining relevant documents from third party sources. Given the difficulties that discovery can cause a practitioner should investigate whether any category of documents may be obtained from a different source.

EXPERT EVIDENCE

7.8 Chapter 9 looks at the basic science relating to the environment and the types of expert evidence available as well as the relationship between lawyer and expert. At this point it is necessary to emphasise the crucial importance of expert evidence to the success of most environmental cases. To that end it is very important to establish a good dialogue between lawyer and expert. It is for the lawyer to guide the expert on legal matters such as the burden of proof and to make clear to an expert that an objective opinion is being sought, not just what the client wants to hear. It is for the expert, having been given the legal principles and tests that will be applied, to comment on issues of causation, standards of care and damage.

The early involvement of an expert will assist in pleading the case accurately, and in defining the issues which will be of relevance in the discovery process and the preparation of lay witness statements. Expert advice is specially relevant to the way in which particulars of negligence are pleaded.

Experts will be aware of the latest technology available, and of current technical literature relating to the issue in question.

LAY EVIDENCE

7.9 Preparation of good quality witness statements is of increasing relevance now that all civil courts require pre-trial exchange of statements and also that these statements be lodged at court seven days before a hearing commences. Furthermore, the signed statement of a witness will often stand as evidence-in-chief of that witness.

Much care should therefore be taken to ensure that witness statements cover effectively all elements of the plaintiff's case which have been pleaded and which the defendant has not admitted. Additionally those statements should be prepared in the light of the expert evidence so that if, for example, the expert identifies a particular type of damage then the lay evidence will explain the consequences of this damage in practical terms. The value of expressing in plain language the nature of the interference with property or enjoyment of life should never be underestimated. It will be evident from Chapter 2 that 'quality of life' issues will often be at the root of environmental claims. Convincing evidence given by lay witnesses is often the only way to present these issues.

Thought should be given as to how individual witnesses are likely to come over in court, in particular when cross-examined.

TRIAL

7.10   There will be occasions in more substantial cases where trials of preliminary issues are desirable. This will be particularly relevant where elements of the plaintiff's claim are not in dispute, so that, if the preliminary issue is decided in the plaintiff's favour then the claim can be settled without recourse to further litigation. Order 33 of the RSC gives the court considerable flexibility in making directions for the trial of given issues separately from others.

So far as possible it is desirable to minimise the issues in dispute when the case comes to court. Effort should therefore be made to agree uncontroversial matters which may not have been admitted in initial posturing in the pleadings. Where a defendant is unco-operative a notice to admit facts can be served. This offers some protection to the plaintiff if unnecessary costs are incurred in proving matters that ought to be capable of agreement.

In addition it may prove possible to agree factual matters arising during the course of proceedings. To this end, if the court has not already ordered it, it is often sensible for the two experts to meet in order to try and focus on the significant areas of dispute and eliminate peripheral matters.

It is now standard practice in all civil courts to lodge bundles of relevant documents at court seven days before the trial starts. Although this deadline is frequently difficult to adhere to, it is very much in a plaintiff's interests to present the documentation to the court in advance so that the judge has an opportunity to absorb the gist of the case before the trial starts.

DAMAGES

7.11   Almost all common law claims will involve a claim for damages. Subject to the principles set out below, it is important to set out clearly in lay witness statements the extent of the damage which has been suffered. In assessing general damages rather than quantifiable losses, the court can only arrive at a reasonable figure for compensation on the basis of what it understands as to the extent of the interference suffered by the plaintiff.

A consideration of the principles of assessment of damages is beyond the scope of this work. This section examines only the aspects of damages that are particularly relevant to environmental claims.

Methods of assessment

7.12 A number of cases have identified principles for assessing damages in environmental claims. It will be recalled that in most environmental cases the right to sue is dependent on showing some proprietary interest that has been affected, in that the interest itself or the use and enjoyment of it has been damaged. This is relevant to an important distinction that has been drawn in assessing damages, between damage to the interest itself and damage to its use and enjoyment.

(1) *Damage to the interest.* In the former type of case the principle adopted is to look at the diminution in the value of the asset as a consequence of the act of the defendant. The asset may be a freehold or a leasehold interest in land or a legal right, eg of fishing. Where a permanent or irreversible diminution of value can be shown then that will be used as the basis for assessing damages. Thus if a pollution of water means that a plaintiff has permanently lost the value of the rent paid for fishing, or if a noise nuisance has permanently reduced the value of a property then that loss will be the starting point of an assessment.

Example

This approach was adopted in the lands tribunal case of *Burgess v Gwynedd County Council* [1972] RVR 222. This case concerned the permanent loss of salmon fishing pools as a consequence of roadworks. The compensation was based on the difference between the value of the fishing before and after the works took place.

Example

This principle was accepted as the correct one by the court in the case of escaped rainbow trout mentioned in Chapter 2 above. The court based its award on the cost to the syndicate of the fishing in question, applying a multiplier in respect of the amount of the fishing lost in the relevant season. To this was added a factor of +50 per cent to reflect the fact that the enjoyment of the fishing was worth more than was paid for it. This method of assessing damages for loss of fishing was also accepted in another case brought by the Anglers Conservation Association in Cambridge County Court, when the judge accepted the formula of subscription income × 150 per cent × loss of sport as a correct basis for assessing damages.

(1) It is suggested that the addition of an 'amenity factor' is appropriate in all cases where the plaintiff complains of interference with the use and enjoyment of property as well as physical damage to it.
(2) *Damage to use and enjoyment.* In some cases, however, permanent loss is not suffered, and the courts have adopted a different basis of assessment.

Example

The two leading cases of an environmental nature which resulted in discussion of the correct measure of damages in cases of this sort were *Bone v Seale* [1975] All ER 787, and *Halsey v Esso Petroleum* [1961] 1 WLR 683. The former case concerned problems caused by smell from an adjacent pig farm. The plaintiffs suffered from the smell for 12½ years. In the Court of Appeal the level recovered was reduced from £500 per year to £1,000 for the whole period. Stephenson LJ stated that he had a difficult task to perform since the plaintiffs were unable to prove diminution in the value of the property and awarded the £1,000 'doing the best' he could. He did refer to *Halsey* where the plaintiffs had to put up with more interference in the form of smell, noise and vibration, saying, 'In 1961 the learned Judge gave him, for all that, damages of £200. I do not think that it could be suggested that was a high figure, in those days. . . .'.

Veale J in *Halsey* was at a similar loss to find an appropriate method to calculate damages to Halsey since he said, 'I
must do the best I can to award to him a sum in respect of the
nuisances by noise and smell. . .'. There would not, therefore,
appear to be a defined rationale behind the decisions on
damages concerning 'pure' loss of enjoyment claims.
However, *Bone v Seale* suggested that there may be cases
where parallels could be drawn with personal injury litigation.

Special damages

7.13 In all tortious cases there is an entitlement to recover all
quantifiable expense incurred as a direct result of the incident complained of. The usual principles of collating special damages claims
will apply. Incurred expenditure should be supported by receipts
and/or estimates wherever possible. Loss of profit claims must relate
credibly to profits earned in earlier years. Expert evidence may be
required to validate a loss of profit claim. Claims for future sums to
be incurred should be comprised in estimates from reputable contractors or suppliers.

Economic loss

7.14 No consideration of damages is complete without some
consideration of the complex issue of economic loss. Thankfully the
issue is less applicable to damages in environmental cases than in
other cases. The case of *Murphy v Brentwood DC* [1990] 2 All ER
908 was more concerned with principles of liability in negligence
than with principles of damage. The point established by the case
was that where loss can only be expressed in financial or economic
terms (in the *Murphy* case, reduction in the value of a property)
there can be no liability in negligence for economic loss unless the
plaintiff relied on negligent advice or there is some other special relationship of proximity.

This principle does not apply, however, where there is direct
physical damage to property. Almost invariably environmental torts
will involve direct damage to property or person, so that the
problem will not arise.

Also, as Chapter 2 has shown, in most cases of environmental
damage one of the torts of strict liability will apply. Since *Murphy*

was concerned with issues of liability in negligence, it does not have any relevance to the determination of strict liability claims.

The issue of economic loss is also relevant to the ability of third parties to claim damage consequential on the damage suffered by the plaintiff. The third party will be most unlikely to have a claim. Thus, for example, if the NRA made a claim at common law for the cost of reinstatement of a river it is not a claim for damage to an asset belonging to it and therefore may be consequential and therefore irrecoverable. However, as Chapter 1 makes clear, there are some statutory provisions that specifically permit regulatory bodies to recover the cost of environmental clean-ups.

Wayleave principle

7.15   A further matter of relevance to the issue of damages in environmental cases is the applicability of the wayleave principle. This applies in cases where proceedings have been brought in trespass. It has been seen above that an action in trespass can be brought whenever there is a deposition of solid matter on the plaintiff's land. In such cases the courts have held that the presence of the unlawful deposit is an unauthorised occupation of the plaintiff's land, and the plaintiff ought to be compensated on the basis of the rental value if the occupation had been authorised. Thus if the plaintiff can produce some evidence of the open market value of the land of which he has lost the use, that should form the basis of the assessment of damages. See *Whitwham v Westminster Brymbo Coal Co* [1892] 2 Ch 538.

Aggravated damages and punitive/exemplary damages

7.16   The final area to consider in relation to damages claims is the possible relevance of an award for aggravated damages. Where the plaintiff's feelings have been injured, with resulting mental stress, and the situation is made worse by bad faith or wilful conduct damages will be increased. Aggravated damages are not available in negligence.

This is an extension of the compensatory principle, but punitive or exemplary damages may be awarded to punish the defendant and deter him from similar behaviour in the future. However, in *Rookes v Barnard* [1964] AC 1129, Lord Devlin, finding that such damages confused the civil and criminal functions of the law, limited their application to two cases. First, where there is oppressive, arbitrary or unconstitutional action by servants of the government and secondly where the defendant's conduct is calculated to make a profit for himself which may exceed the compensation payable to the plaintiff. In essence the defendant, knowing that what he is doing is wrong, weighs the advantage he may gain in committing the wrong against the risk of compensating the plaintiff.

Example

An example where such damages may be recoverable is a water company knowingly and persistently polluting water but doing nothing to remedy the situation. In *Gibbons v South West Water Services Limited* (1992) *The Times,* 28 November, which concerned the *Camelford* drinking water pollution case, the plaintiffs claimed exemplary damages on the basis that the defendant had acted in an arrogant and high-handed manner in ignoring customers' complaints after the initial contamination of the water. The Court of Appeal found that the plaintiffs could not claim exemplary damages since the claim fell outside the torts for which they were recoverable as set out in *Rookes v Barnard*. The plaintiffs had claimed in negligence and public nuisance. Despite this finding the court made comments to the effect that not only will compensatory damages cover physical, psychological and mental damage, but 'full account will be taken of the distress and anxiety which such an event necessarily causes'. To the extent that any of these effects was magnified or exacerbated by the defendant's conduct, the ordinary measure of damages will compensate.

INJUNCTIONS

7.17 The injunctive remedy is of considerable relevance in environmental claims where the continuing activity of a defendant is complained of, *see* eg the case facts referred to in the section on nuisance in Chapter 2.

As well as being one of the ultimate remedies of common law proceedings, an interim injunction can be sought at the start of proceedings so as to protect the plaintiff's position until the trial of the action by way of an interlocutory injunction.

Injunctions are a discretionary remedy. It is for the court to decide whether an injunction is appropriate. It is also a general principle that an injunction will not be granted where damages are an adequate remedy. Therefore, even where a continuing nuisance is proved to the court it does not automatically follow that an injunction will be granted. It is important to bear this in mind both in deciding whether to apply for an interlocutory injunction and in preparing evidence for the final hearing.

Interlocutory injunctions

7.18   In all cases where an interlocutory injunction is being considered, a crucial matter to consider will be the fact that if the court grants the application, then the plaintiff will have to give the court an undertaking in damages. The effect of this is that if the court at the main hearing decides that an injunction ought not to have been granted then the plaintiff has to pay damages in respect of all damage suffered by the defendant during the period that the injunction was in force. In many environmental cases those damages could be very substantial if cessation of or interference with a business activity is involved. Furthermore the defendant is entitled to call evidence to satisfy itself that the plaintiff can meet the undertaking for damages. Many plaintiffs in environmental claims are relatively impecunious, and therefore the risk taken by offering the undertaking may well be the determining factor in deciding whether to apply for an interlocutory injunction or not.

If an interlocutory injunction is applied for, then it will be by way of motion in the High Court, or on application to a county court. In cases of extreme urgency the application can be made *ex parte*, ie without notifying the defendant. In many cases it is better practice to serve the relevant paperwork on the defendant and give him the opportunity to appear at the *ex parte* hearing. If an injunction is granted *ex parte* the defendant will, in any event, have the right to apply to the court to have the injunction discharged or varied. Evidence in support of the application will be by way of affidavit. For details of procedure on interim injunction applications *see* Ord 29, RSC.

Although a note of caution has been expressed over the use of the procedure it is a highly effective remedy. Securing an interim injunction is like the salesman getting his foot in the door and can open the way to a negotiated settlement which would not be available if the injunction were simply sought as one of the end-products of the proceedings. Furthermore, even if a final settlement is not reached, the defendant can often be persuaded to offer undertakings pending trial. Finally the application may at least result in an order being made for a speedy trial.

The case of *American Cyanamid Co v Ethicon Ltd* [1975] 1 All ER 961 set out principles that apply in determining whether an interlocutory injunction ought to be granted. Very briefly the court needs to be satisfied that the plaintiff has a good arguable claim to the right that it is sought to protect. Once satisfied of this the court must decide whether to exercise its discretion to grant an interlocutory injunction on the balance of convenience. The relevant factors in determining that balance are numerous, but of particular relevance is whether, ultimately, damages are likely to be an adequate remedy.

Final injunctions

7.19   If it is decided not to seek an interlocutory injunction, then injunctive relief can still be claimed along with damages in the particulars/statement of claim. As the remedy is a discretionary one it is important that the plaintiff brings out the reasons why an injunction is sought in the expert and lay evidence before the court. Thus the nature and extent of the interference caused by the activity complained of should be clearly explained.

The great majority of injunctions are of a restrictive nature, ie to stop a defendant from doing something unlawful. However, in environmental cases both mandatory and *quia timet* or anticipatory injunctions can be of relevance.

(1)   *Mandatory injunction.* In cases where it is sought to restrain a defendant from continuing pollution, the real effect of the relief sought is often mandatory in that the defendant has to carry out some positive act, eg by way of installation of equipment, in order to comply with the restraining part of the order. As a general rule courts are more reluctant to exercise their discretionary powers where mandatory relief is sought. In particular, scrutiny will be given as to the adequacy of damages as a remedy. The cost to the defendant of complying with an injunction will be relevant, and it is advisable for the plaintiff to consider the issue of cost in presenting

evidence, expert if appropriate, as to the practicality and expense to the defendant of remedial works.

(2) *Anticipatory injunction.* Equally there are circumstances where a *quia timet* or anticipatory injunction may be of great importance in environmental cases. The case of *Laws v Florinplace* referred to in Chapter 2 is a good example of stopping a nuisance before it is started. In such cases it is necessary for the plaintiff to demonstrate that the fear of the anticipated act is well founded.

If an injunction has been granted or undertakings given to the court then any breach of it will render the defendant liable to contempt proceedings. Such proceedings are commenced by motion in the High Court or by application in the county court. It is important to bear in mind when framing the original application for the injunction that once granted it must be capable of practical enforcement. Thus the wording ought to be such that evidence of any breach can be adduced in a relatively straightforward way. It may well be that expert advice will be needed on the wording. The wording of an injunction can tend towards the specific or the general. A specific wording can make the injunction easier to enforce but may have the consequence of being insufficiently broad to remedy the whole of the mischief complained of. On the other hand a broadly worded injunction may prove very difficult to enforce in contempt proceedings. *See* the facts of *Bone v Seale* (above) which illustrate this difficulty.

Punishment for contempt is either a fine or imprisonment. Officers of a company or other body are liable to be committed for contempt as well as the body itself. Punishment is in the discretion of the court and if the breach is not considered serious enough no punishment may be administered. Care should therefore be taken to ensure that any contempt proceedings relate to clear breaches, for which good evidence exists, so as to avoid the risk of an adverse order for costs. Contempt proceedings are commenced by originating motion in the High Court. Evidence is by way of affidavit.

Costs

7.20   In many environmental cases, particularly where the issue has gone to trial the costs can be enormous, not unusually exceeding the damages.

The requirement to justify costs incurred on taxation of costs is becoming increasingly exacting. It is standard practice that time spent for which records do not exist will not be allowed, or will be allowed at minimal rates. Paying parties are challenging experts' fees and seeking breakdowns of those fees. Chapter 9 looks at working with experts, and agreeing fees. Given that experts' fees can form a large proportion of a bill, it is essential that those instructing check that the expert maintains accurate time records so that an adequate breakdown can be prepared if needed. *See* Chapter 10 for further comment on experts and cost.

The same crucial importance of recording time accurately applies, of course, to solicitors.

CRIMINAL LAW

7.21 Chapter 5 sets out the framework of criminal enforcement for environmental offences. It examines who is able to bring a prosecution and the circumstances when private prosecutions might be advisable. This chapter deals with the procedural aspects of the criminal remedy and the evidential requirements, first in general terms and then in the context of preparing specific prosecutions.

It is worth emphasising that the role of a prosecutor is somewhat different to that of a plaintiff in civil proceedings, in that the prosecutor has a duty to the court to present the case fully but fairly so that the defence know the whole case that is made against them and are not taken by surprise. Therefore the prosecutor is more an administrator of justice than the advocate of a cause. For this reason there are basic duties imposed on the prosecution for the early and comprehensive disclosure of witness statements and other documents.

STARTING PROCEEDINGS

7.22 All criminal proceedings start life in the magistrates' court. The prosecutor lays an 'information'. This specifies the offence which it is alleged has been committed and what the intended defendant has done to commit that offence. The information should identify both the complainant and the accused. If necessary the court may ask the complainant to attend court to elaborate on the information. Either way, if the court is satisfied, then it will issue a summons which is served either by the court or, if the prosecutor so wishes, by himself. Different courts have different procedures for the issue of the summons, but generally these days the court itself prepares the summons on a computer-generated form.

It has been seen in Chapter 5 that most environmental offences are triable either by the magistrates' court (summarily) or the Crown court (on indictment). The importance of this distinction is that in all cases where the defendant has the option to elect for a Crown court trial there is automatically the right to ask the prosecution for advance information, pursuant to the Magistrates Courts (Advance Information) Rules 1985. Under these rules the prosecution is under a duty to disclose copies of all witness statements or a summary of what they contain. The duty is a continuing one and therefore is equally applicable to evidence which is put together after the proceedings have been started.

In practice this advance information will almost invariably be the supply of copies of the prosecution's witness statements. It is therefore important that those statements are in reasonably advanced preparation when the proceedings are commenced, as the advance information has to be served before the first effective hearing.

THE FIRST HEARING

7.23 The summons specifies the date for the first hearing. Often that date will not be suitable, and the court will be asked to adjourn.

At the first effective hearing the defendant has to plead one way or the other. If there is a guilty plea the case will proceed, with the prosecution giving a brief outline of the facts and the defence entering a plea in mitigation.

If there is a not guilty plea then, if appropriate, the defendant can elect either for a summary or a Crown court trial. It is also open to the prosecution to make representations as to the appropriate mode of trial. Finally the magistrates can on their initiative commit the case to the Crown court.

If the case remains in the magistrates' court then it will be adjourned to a date based on time estimates supplied by the parties.

COMMITTAL AND PROCEDURE IN THE CROWN COURT

Committal

7.24 It is open to the defence either to agree to the committal, in which case there is a shortened procedure, or to elect for an 'old style committal'. In the latter case the prosecution has to call its evidence and the defence has the opportunity to cross-examine that evidence in order to try and establish that there is no case to answer and therefore that it ought to be dismissed.

Procedure

7.25 Once a case has been committed the magistrates' clerk will prepare the committal papers and remit them to the relevant Crown court. The prosecution is required, if it has not already done so, to prepare an indictment which sets out the charges which the defendants have to answer. It is possible to add further charges at the indictment stage but these should only be pursued if the evidence to substantiate the charge was contained in the evidence before the magistrates.

Subject to any interlocutory applications the Crown court will list the case for a trial. The speed with which trial dates come up will vary from court to court. In some cases it can be within two or three months, so it is advisable for the prosecution to have its case in a state of readiness as soon as possible after committal. In some cases the parties will wish to ask the court to deal with interlocutory applications, or to hold a pre-trial review. Such applications are dealt with by the judge in open court.

It will be the prosecution's responsibility to ensure that its witnesses are present at trial. While courts are generally helpful in trying to secure the release of witnesses as quickly as possible, witnesses are often involved in lengthy waits to give evidence. It is advisable therefore to serve witness summonses even on 'friendly' witnesses, in case attendance at court may present problems for that witness. Public bodies often insist on their employees being served with witness summonses for the sake of impartiality. Summonses are simply obtained by supplying the court with the names and addresses of the witnesses to be summonsed. The court then completes a form and returns it for service. As with a subpoena in a civil case the summons must be served personally, and this is generally done through enquiry agents.

7.26 There are two factors that need to be borne in mind at all times, particularly when a prosecution is first commenced:
  (1) The onus is on the prosecution in a criminal case to prove its case beyond reasonable doubt.
  (2) All elements of an offence must be proved directly without the use of hearsay.

A private prosecutor in an environmental case does not enjoy the rights of entry or the power to compel the passing of information that a statutory regulator will have. Although the liability of the defendant may be perfectly clear, it is often quite a different matter to turn the obvious into evidence that will secure a conviction. This section looks at some general issues involved in collecting evidence and then considers particular aspects of prosecuting offences of pollution of the various media.

General matters

7.27 A prosecutor must consider carefully the need to prove by direct evidence all elements of the case. The principal tool is the use of 'section 9' statements. These statements are in a form which complies with the requirements of various Acts and regulations. They can produce exhibits for the purpose of proving documents so produced.

In most cases the bulk of the evidence will have been prepared and served at the committal stage. However, the prosecution is entitled to serve notice of additional evidence at any time, even during the trial itself, although the judge has a discretion as to whether to allow service at such a late stage.

While the defendant can be invited to admit documents or evidence without the need for formal proof, he is under no obligation to do so, and the prosecution must be ready to prove through witnesses the whole of its case.

Exceptions

7.28 There are, however, some provisions which attenuate the full rigour of formal proof.
  (1) *Computer records*. Under s 69 of the Police and Criminal Evidence Act 1984 (PACE), provided that certain procedural

matters are attended to, a print-out from a computer will be admissible evidence of the information it records.

(2) *Public documents.* The prosecution is entitled to apply for documents to be treated as public documents and thus not requiring formal proof. An example of such a document is an Ordnance Survey map.

(3) *Business records.* Under s 24 of the Criminal Justice Act 1988 business records are admissible even though they do not represent direct evidence of the information contained in the record. It is possible that this exception to the hearsay rule may be of help in environmental cases where public register data, comprising records of compliance with consents as well as the consents themselves and applications for them, are used.

Where there is a dispute as to the applicability of these exemptions then application can be made to the court for a ruling.

It should be borne in mind that there is no obligation on the defence to produce any documents nor, if it so chooses, to call any witnesses or evidence at the trial. This underlines the onus on the prosecution to prepare the evidence that is needed to prove the case. The ability to cross-examine defence witnesses on their evidence should be treated as a luxury that may not be available.

Nevertheless, there is no property in a witness, and the prosecution are quite entitled to approach employees of the defendant company to give statements. If they decline to make a statement then the prosecution are able to compel their attendance at court with a witness summons. If this course is adopted it is, of course, advisable to be sure of what that witness will say if examined.

Where a defendant wishes to avail himself of any statutory defence, however, the onus is on the defence to prove the applicability of that defence, and to call evidence to substantiate it.

EXPERT EVIDENCE

7.29 As with civil cases, in many prosecutions expert evidence will be crucial in proving the prosecution case. Experts may be required to prove the analysis of samples, to establish the chain of causation, to prove the pollution complained of, or to determine whether best environmental practices have been used.

Unlike the practice with lay witnesses, it is permissible for the expert to see the remainder of the prosecution's evidence when preparing his report. It is also not only acceptable but desirable for the prosecution lawyers to be in close contact with the expert during preparation of his evidence.

It is permissible for an expert to present a written report to court, and such a document can be before the jury. A report can be mixed opinion and fact. An expert is entitled to give evidence of fact where he has direct knowledge of the facts concerned. While the expert is generally subject to the same rules of evidence as any other witness, an exception is made in relation to reliance of the expert on research of others in his particular field of expertise, which is comprised in academic texts. Additionally, it is open to the prosecution to apply under s 30 of the Criminal Justice Act 1988 for such evidence to be admitted without direct evidence where it would be impracticable for direct evidence to be given.

Where the evidence to be given is particularly complex then it should be borne in mind that those who are to determine liability will be the jury or lay magistrates. Although the prosecutor may, through preparing the case, have acquired considerable expertise on the matter at issue the magistrates or the jury will not have that knowledge. It is well worth considering the merit of preparing a presentation of the particular expertise in general terms before dealing with the case itself. Additionally if the use of aids such as overhead projectors or videos can assist this process then they should be used.

The use of experts is considered in greater depth in Chapter 9.

DOCUMENTS

7.30   As indicated above, unless one of the exemptions to the hearsay rule can be established, then all the documents upon which the prosecution relies must be produced by a witness who is in a position to prove their contents.

At the trial itself a distinction has to be drawn between those documents it is proper for the jury to see and those which it is not. It is a fundamental rule of criminal evidence that a witness must give evidence orally. Therefore statements from witnesses must not be shown to the jury, unless their contents have been admitted by the defence.

However, it is perfectly proper for the jury to see, *inter alia*, admitted documents, public documents (*see* para 7.28 above), and expert reports. Indeed it is desirable for these documents to be before the jury. The normal practice is to prepare one set of documents for every two jury members.

Bundles of evidence should also be prepared for the judge and the defence, together with a bundle of any other non-jury documents.

In the case of an indictable offence there is a duty on the prosecution to disclose all unused material to the prosecution. *See* the Attorney-General's Guidelines at [1982] All ER 734. The effect of this is that all witness statements or expert evidence prepared but not relied on must be disclosed to the defence. In addition, all relevant correspondence or other documents must be disclosed. It is for the defence to decide whether a particular document is relevant to the obligation or not. The best advice therefore is to err on the side of over-disclosure to avoid any risk of documents that have not been disclosed emerging at trial.

EVIDENCE AND WATER PROSECUTIONS

7.31 Chapter 5 looked at the two principal water pollution offences under s 85 of the WRA and s 4 of the Salmon and Freshwater Fisheries Act 1975. In both offences a distinction has to be drawn between polluting discharges of sewage or trade effluent which are in breach of a consent to discharge, and non-consented discharges which cause pollution. For both offences it is necessary to prove that the discharge is polluting. In the case of a consented discharge evidence will also be required by way of sample to show that the discharge was in breach of a consent.

Breaches of consents

7.32 A discharge of trade or sewage effluent does not constitute an offence unless it is in breach of the consent or the conditions attached to it. It is necessary therefore to have in evidence an analysed sample which proves a breach of that consent.

A potential prosecutor has the choice of relying on a sample taken by himself or on one taken by the NRA.

(1) Section 209(1) of the WRA provides that the results of any analysis of a sample taken by the NRA will not be admis-

sible in evidence unless the tripartite sample procedure has been complied with. This procedure requires that the sampler must notify the occupier of the land in question of the intention to have the sample analysed, take the sample and then and there divide it into three parts, give one to the occupier of the land, have one analysed and retain one in case of the need for future analysis. The case of *NRA v Harcros Timber and Building Supplies Ltd* (1992) *The Times,* 3 April established that this obligation relates to *all* samples taken by the NRA pursuant to their powers whether of the effluent or of the watercourse up- or downstream of the discharge. This may well apply to civil as well as criminal proceedings and is, at present, a serious evidential difficulty. It is hoped that amending legislation will attenuate the effects of this position in the relatively near future.

(2) In the case of a sample taken by a private prosecutor there is no such obligation. However, where a 'private' sample is taken, in practice it is highly advisable to use the tripartite sampling procedure if possible. This is to avoid the risk that the defendant might challenge the validity of the analysis of the sample if no opportunity has been given for a second analysis. (*See* comments in Chapter 9 on choice of analyst.)

Whether a prosecutor relies on NRA samples as evidence or takes his own, there are advantages and disadvantages.

(1) *NRA samples*

(a) The NRA automatically takes samples of all consented discharges and has them analysed. The regularity of the sampling depends on the significance of the receiving water. However, because of the relative cost and complexity of taking a formal sample rather than a normal monitoring sample, most NRA samples are not tripartite and therefore are not admissible. How a sample is taken is a matter of discretion for the NRA, and nothing obliges it to take a sample in a tripartite manner.

(b) As explained in Chapter 9 the results of the analysis of all NRA effluent samples are entered on to the public register. With respect to all analyses there is an obligation on the NRA to state whether the sample complied with s 209 or not.

(c) Any private prosecutor intending to rely on NRA samples needs to obtain a printout from the public register setting out the analysis of samples. While those analyses may show breaches of consent, unless the relevant samples were tripartite then they will not be admissible. It is then open to the prosecutor to request the NRA to take the next sample to comply with s 209. As stated above, it is in the NRA's discretion whether to agree to do so or not.

(d) Once the prosecutor has identified a tripartite sample in breach of the consent on the register, it is necessary to consider the consent itself, particularly in the case of consents to discharge sewage effluent. Such consents often permit a discharger to breach the consent on a certain number of occasions in any 12-month period and be exempt from prosecution (known as the percentile condition). Thus to establish a breach it is necessary to look back at all samples taken in the previous 12 months, count the total number of samples and the number in breach, and then compare those numbers with a 'look-up' table attached to the consent which indicates the permissible number of failures in respect of a given total. If the total number of breaches is the same as or less than the number in the 'look-up' table no breach of the consent has occurred. It is also important to point out that the percentile condition relates to the particular parameter which the offending sample breaches, not just any breach. Thus if the offending sample is in breach of an ammonia limit for the purposes of the 'look-up' table, a check should only be made of the analysis of samples for ammonia for the previous 12 months to determine whether the percentile condition has been complied with. The fact that some samples may have been in breach of other parameters in the consent is irrelevant. In some consents there is additionally an upper limit, which, if exceeded, renders the discharger liable to prosecution on the basis of a single sample.

(e) Once a prosecutor has identified on the register a sample which shows a breach of a consent to discharge, and which complies with s 209, then if the NRA is not prosecuting itself, it will be open to a private individual to initiate a prosecution based on that sample. An initial approach should be made to the NRA to establish whether it is willing for the prosecutor to take statements from the relevant officers to prove the taking of the sample, the transfer and storage of the sample, and the analysis of it. It is in the discretion of the NRA whether to make officers available to make statements. It is likely that the NRA legal department will want to vet any statements made by such officers. Generally the NRA will be co-operative. Some charge may be made for officers' time.

(f) Clearly, if the NRA officers do not give statements it will still be possible to summons them to court to give evidence. However, it could be a risky course of action and the lack of evidence may well create difficulties in complying with advance information requirements.

(2) *Prosecutor's samples*

(a) The obvious advantage of self-sampling is that it puts the prosecutor in control of the collection of evidence. There are, however, a number of potential disadvantages. To secure a sample in breach of consent involves potential difficulties of access, expense and chance.

(b) The NRA has statutory powers to enter onto land for the purpose of taking samples. In the case of many trade and sewage discharges the consented point of entry is on private land. Access to take a sample will therefore be practically difficult, and, even if possible, will result in trespass—which may be challenged by the defendant. It is not considered that the trespass would render the sample inadmissible. No such problem exists where the discharge is to a place where the public have access, eg a beach or a publicly navigable river.

(c) If access to the discharge point can be secured then the risk still remains that the sample when analysed will not disclose any breach of the consent conditions. The process of taking a sample in a tripartite manner and having it analysed is a fairly expensive one, and is unlikely to be one which a potential prosecutor can afford to repeat indefinitely. There is no doubt that some discharges will be more likely to result in a breach than others, and a potential prosecutor would be well advised to evaluate the costs and likelihood of a breach emerging before embarking on the sampling.

For prosecutions based on breaches of consent conditions, both self-sampling and reliance on the NRA have drawbacks, but in neither case are they so intimidating that a potential private prosecutor should be frightened off, if good grounds exist for bringing such a prosecution.

Unconsented discharges

7.33 A prosecution may be possible not only for offences of discharging trade or sewage effluent outside consent conditions but also in respect of any discharge into a watercourse for which there is no consent. Most such discharges are one-off incidents. They are therefore likely to have been reported to the NRA, with the result that the NRA will attend the incident and take the necessary samples, and will initiate its own prosecution if the evidence warrants it. In these cases, as the source of the pollution disappears rapidly, it is unlikely that a private individual will have sufficient evidence of his own to initiate a prosecution if the NRA does not.

However, if the pollution complained of is a continuing one then it may be possible to bring a private prosecution. The advantage of proceeding in relation to this sort of incident is that, since compliance with a consent is not a defence, it is not necessary for the prosecution to rely on samples to establish the offence. Straightforward evidence from a lay witness and/or an expert which proves that the defendant is discharging into a watercourse and that the discharge is polluting will be sufficient. (See Chapter 3 for a discussion of the meaning of 'polluting'.) The prosecution of British Coal referred to in Chapter 5 at para 5.6 is an example of such a prosecution.

EVIDENCE AND AIR POLLUTION

7.34 The collation of sufficient evidence is crucial. The very nature of atmospheric pollution is that finding its source may be difficult (particularly if there are a number of sources). In addition, finding a suitable and accepted method of measuring the effect of the pollution may also be problematic. Consistent anecdotal evidence from persons affected can be very useful, particularly if it is collected in a systematic manner—eg by the keeping of a diary. In many cases the early involvement of the local authority environmental health department will be important. Often environmental health officers have more experience of finding sources of various types of atmospheric pollution than a private prosecutor would have. Their evidence may form the basis of expert evidence at trial.

STATUTORY NUISANCE

7.35   The basis of a claim for statutory nuisance is outlined in Chapter 5 and is also referred to in Chapter 4. While the remedy of statutory nuisance has been and remains in frequent use to deal with housing problems, it is a remedy which is well suited to deal with a range of environmental problems. It is a quick and often effective remedy and one that is not complicated to use if self-help is necessary due to lack of funds.

PROCEDURE

7.36   Section 82 of the EPA gives to the magistrates the power to act on a complaint made by a person aggrieved by the existence of a statutory nuisance.

The EPA does not define an 'aggrieved person'. However, the phrase is traditionally broadly defined. In practice, as the complainant has to show that he has suffered prejudice to health or a nuisance, it is likely that showing one or both of those will necessarily demonstrate sufficient proximity of the complainant to the nuisance to bring him within the definition of an 'aggrieved person'.

Prior to making a complaint the aggrieved person must, under subs (6), give notice to the relevant person as defined by subs (4), of his intention to bring proceedings under this section. This notice must specify the matter complained of by reference to the list of nuisances set out in s 79(1). No special form of notice is required.

This notice must be served not less than 21 days before proceedings are commenced, except in the case of a noise nuisance, where at least three days' notice must be given.

Under s 82(2) if the magistrates are satisfied that the alleged nuisance exists, then they should make an order for either or both of the following purposes:

(a) requiring the defendant to abate the nuisance, within a time specified in the order, and to execute any works necessary for that purpose;

(b) prohibiting a recurrence of the nuisance, and requiring the defendant, within a time specified in the order, to execute any works necessary to prevent the recurrence.

The magistrates may also impose a fine not exceeding level 5 on the standard scale. Furthermore the magistrates may exercise their powers under s 35 of the Powers of Criminal Courts Act 1973 to make an award of compensation to the aggrieved person. Finally by virtue of s 82(12) where the nuisance is proved the magistrates must make an award of costs to the aggrieved person of 'such amount as the court considers reasonably sufficient to compensate him for any expenses properly incurred by him in the proceedings'.

By s 82(8) it is an offence to fail to comply with an order made by the magistrates under s 82(1).

Statutory nuisance proceedings commenced under s 82 will be commenced by laying an information before the justices which, if approved, will result in the issue of a summons that will be served on the defendant.

As the proceedings are summary, there is no obligation to disclose evidence by way of advance information. As with any other proceedings, witness statements and, if necessary, experts' reports will be required to prove the elements of the offence. Where abatement of the nuisance is sought, that evidence should direct itself to the steps that need to be taken to abate. *See* further comment on evidence below.

STATUTORY NUISANCE AND EVIDENCE

7.37   The seven categories of statutory nuisance listed at s 79 of the EPA all entail showing that there has been prejudice to health or a nuisance. The definitions of these phrases is considered in Chapter 5.

This section will focus on evidence so far as proof of nuisance is concerned. As is the case with a common law claim for nuisance, it is necessary to show that the matter complained of has caused interference with use and enjoyment of property, or, more broadly, with quality of life. Whether such interference is a nuisance is ultimately a matter of opinion, but any witness statement should set out in as much detail as possible how the act complained of has affected quality of life.

Section 79 of the EPA imposes a duty on every local authority to investigate nuisances in its area. In many cases of statutory nuisance, therefore, it is possible to involve the local authority in preparation of evidence even where the authority does not take action itself.

Local authority environmental health departments have specialist officers able to measure the extent of, eg, noise, smoke or fumes. For a number of problems such as noise there are accepted standards that define the level at which noise becomes prejudicial to health. Even where a local authority is the subject of the nuisance complaint, the duty still remains to investigate complaints.

It is also open to the complainant to employ his own independent expert to investigate and measure the extent of the nuisance. *See* Chapter 9 for discussion of experts and definitions of pollution.

JUDICIAL REVIEW

SCOPE

7.38   Judicial review is the process by which the High Court supervises the proceedings and decisions of inferior courts, tribunals and other bodies or persons who carry out quasi-judicial functions or who are charged with the performance of public acts and duties. The procedure gives the opportunity to those aggrieved by a decision of an administrative body to challenge it.

This function of the High Court to regulate the decision-making process of other bodies, though now regulated by statute, by Ord 53, RSC and s 31 of the Supreme Court Act 1981, has its historical foundation in the common law and was exercised in the name of the Crown through the use of the prerogative writs of mandamus, certiorari and prohibition.

(1)   An order of mandamus is an order whereby the High Court requires a body to exercise its jurisdiction where it has failed to exercise it, but ought to have done so.

(2) An order of certiorari is an order whereby the High Court quashes the decision of a body which has exceeded its jurisdiction.

(3) An order of prohibition is an order whereby the High Court requires a body not to take a particular course of action where it is anticipated that this would exceed that body's jurisdiction.

The High Court also has the power to grant injunctive relief, both interlocutory and final, in judicial review proceedings.

The High Court's powers are limited therefore, in that the court cannot require a body to exercise its jurisdiction in a particular way, but can only review the manner in which that jurisdiction is exercised. Judicial review is concerned not with the merits of a decision but with the manner in which the decision is made.

Relevance to environmental cases

7.39 Judicial review is an area of law that is still growing. It is a remedy of considerable relevance to environmental cases, since locus is more easily established than in the other remedies that have been discussed. Common law and statutory nuisance claims are essentially concerned with the enforcement of private rights. Private prosecutions, although open to all to bring, are of course limited to situations where an act of pollution is criminal in nature.

Quasi-judicial decisions

7.40 This still leaves a range of decisions by public or quasi-public bodies which have an environmental impact, but which are not capable of challenge through common law, criminal law or the planning/authorisation processes. In some cases the decisions are of a quasi-judicial nature where statute or regulations have not provided any statutory right of appeal. A good example of this is the Environmental Information Regulations. If there is an improper refusal to supply information then that decision will be liable to judicial review.

Judicial review is often the only effective point of appeal in relation to the exercise of decision-making functions by local authorities and regulators (discussed in Chapters 3 and 4).

Decisions affecting a class of people

7.41 Judicial review is also a possible remedy in a broader range of cases where a body has made a decision which affects a class of people. Chapter 1 sets out the statutory framework for regulation of the environment in this country. It sets out the powers and the duties which are given to and imposed on regulators. Chapters 3, 4 and 5 refer to the powers and duties of regulators in relation to authorisation and enforcement.

These regulators inevitably make very many decisions which affect the environment and those who are concerned with its protection. All of these decisions are subject to potential review in the manner set out at paras 7.45–7.49 below. Those advising in environmental cases should bear the possibility of judicial review in mind at all times. This extends beyond recognising the possibility of review after the decision has been made. It is just as important to ensure that a decision-maker is aware, before a decision has been made, of the possibility of review. Much can be done to ensure that a fair decision is made by letting the decision-maker know what should be taken into account in arriving at the decision, and in particular pointing out the relevant duties imposed on him.

Chapter 3 looks at the analogous remedy, created by the Town and Country Planning Act 1990, of statutory review of cases by the High Court.

Locus

7.42 Order 53, Rule 7, RSC and s 31(3) of the Supreme Court Act 1981 provide that the court should not grant leave to bring proceedings 'unless it considers that the applicant has sufficient interest in the matter to which the applicant relates'.

This rule obviously begs the question of what amounts to 'sufficient interest'. There is now a lengthening list of cases dealing with the issue of standing where public interest groups are involved. These include the following: *The Rose Theatre Trust Case* [1990] QB 504; *R v Poole Borough Council ex p Beebee and others* [1991] 2 PLR 27; *R v Swale Borough Council ex p RSPB* [1991] PLR 6; and the recent cases brought by Greenpeace in respect of the Thorp reprocessing plant (1993) *The Times*, 30 September and Friends of the Earth in respect of drinking water standards (1994) *The Times*, 4 April.

7.43 It seems clear enough that there is a greater judicial willingness to recognise the standing of public interest groups and their need to show some relationship with the specific issue complained of. There is also undoubtedly recognition of the stature that groups such as Greenpeace and Friends of the Earth have as authoritative voices on environmental issues.

Greenpeace in the Thorp case were able to show a link between their complaints and the concerns of the residents in the locality. In purely environmental cases, this is not so easy. In the Beebee case, for example, snakes the main protagonists don't talk! Even in these cases, however, it is helpful to be able to show a pre-existing interest in the particular site rather than in the protection of sites nationally.

Time limits

7.44 All applications for judicial review have to be initiated within three months of the decision being made and communicated to the aggrieved party. However, this period is subject to the additional requirement that the application should be brought expeditiously. Thus the court has power to refuse leave to bring proceedings even where an application is made within the three-month period if it has not been brought expeditiously. In these circumstances, it is imperative that a view is taken promptly whether or not to apply for leave to bring proceedings. This will be all the more so where prejudice would be suffered as a result of challenging the decision in question in the courts.

Grounds for review

7.45 The grounds by which the court can exercise its review function are generally the same for both statutory and general judicial review jurisdictions. There are three broad categories.

Illegality (abuse of jurisdiction)

7.46 A public body whose powers and duties are set out in statute may not act beyond the limits of those powers. Accordingly, a decision-maker must understand the law that regulates his decision-making power correctly and must give effect to it.

For example, in *Mansi v Elstree RDC* (1964) 16 P&CR 153 the court considered a local authority's powers under s 172 as to what it may require a person to do in an enforcement notice. The court held that the powers provided by the section were limited to the extent that an enforcement notice could not require the cessation of an established use of land. As a result any notice which requires this is illegal. This ground will also relate to the duties imposed on the decision-making body and a failure to take them into account.

Irrationality (abuse of discretion)

7.47   Public bodies must not behave irrationally or 'unreasonably'. An 'unreasonable' decision is one which is so unreasonable that a reasonable authority could not have arrived at it. This is sometimes called 'perversity' or, colloquially, 'Wednesbury unreasonable'. (*See Associated Picture Houses v Wednesbury Corporation* [1948] 1 KB 223.)

It follows from this that a decision-maker must not take into account irrelevant considerations and must not fail to take into account relevant considerations, eg a relevant planning policy on an appeal under s 78.

Again in *Hall & Co v Shoreham UDC* [1964] 1 WLR 240 a condition requiring a developer to construct a public right of way was unrelated to the development and was irrelevant to the considerations before the Secretary of State.

Procedural impropriety

7.48   A public body must also comply with the principles of natural justice in exercising its powers. Thus the procedures set down by statute and in regulations must be followed, together with the general principles of 'fairness'.

In the planning sphere this may mean eg adherence to the Town and Country Planning (Inquiries Procedure) Rules. These rules give rise to the need for a decision-maker to give proper, adequate, clear and intelligible reasons for his decision (*see Save Britain's Heritage*).

More generally it places an onus on any body to abide by its own rules when coming to a decision. If no rules exist then it is essential that those affected by the decision have the opportunity to state their own case, and have access to any documents on which the decision will be based.

However, in addition to a breach of natural justice or the regulations the applicant must establish that he/she has suffered 'prejudice' as a result.

Proportionality

7.49 It is arguable that there is a fourth category for review. The principle of proportionality was developed in Europe. The introduction of European law into the UK has had the result that this principle is slowly gaining ground.

The principle means that an appropriate balance must be maintained between the adverse effects which an administrative authority's decision may have on the rights, liberties or interests of the person concerned and the purpose which the authority is seeking to pursue.

It is arguable, however, that this balance forms part of the assessment of reasonableness, and therefore does not amount to a category on its own.

POWER AND DISCRETION OF THE COURT

7.50 In a judicial review the remedies are those prerogative orders already mentioned. In each case there is a discretion for the court as to whether or not it exercises its powers.

In *Bolton v SSE* the criteria for the court to consider when deciding whether or not to exercise its powers were defined in relation to the situation where the decision-maker has failed to take into account a relevant consideration:

(a) if the matter is trivial or of small importance in relation to a particular decision then it follows that even if it were taken into account there is no real likelihood of it making any difference to the decision, and the court should not exercise its powers;

(b) if, on the other hand, the matter might make a difference to the decision, the court ought to exercise its powers.

Even if a ground for review can be sustained the court in the exercise of its discretion, may refuse to grant relief.

The danger with challenging decisions is that all the authority has to do is to redetermine properly. Thus even a victory in the High Court does not guarantee a successful conclusion, and more likely than not, High Court proceedings will be pre-emptive.

Only about 28 per cent to 35 per cent of applications reach a final hearing, and of them only one in six results in a successful challenge. (It should be pointed out, however, that a large proportion of the cases are homelessness cases and between 31 per cent and 42 per cent of applications are withdrawn.)

PROCEDURE

7.51   The remedy of judicial review is only available in the High Court. The practice is set out in Ord 53, RSC.

Before commencing proceedings consideration ought to be given as to whether alternative remedies exist, eg by way of statutory appeal, or perhaps based on principles of promissory estoppel.

It is also advisable to send a letter before action to protect one's position on costs. Proceedings commence by way of an *ex parte* application for leave to commence proceedings. An application in form 86A is lodged, together with an affidavit. It is then open to the applicant to make a 'table' or an oral application. Papers are placed before a judge who will either grant the application or refuse it. In the case of oral applications, the paperwork is served on the respondent party and a hearing is fixed before the judge.

In the case of a table application, whether by direction of the judge or as a consequence of refusal, an oral application can be made.

Once leave has been granted all the applicant has to do is issue and serve a notice of motion on the respondent, and pay the requisite fee. The respondent has the opportunity to serve evidence in reply. The application will then enter the Crown Office listing system.

Chapter 10 considers the question of costs in relation to judicial review applications.

CHAPTER 8

EXTRA-LEGAL REMEDIES

INTRODUCTION

8.1 This book demonstrates that, imperfect though the law and the legal and administrative systems may be, they can, fully used and properly supported, provide sound and effective environmental protection. There are, however, some situations in which the legal process, as it stands, falls short of the need. It is that condition which this chapter addresses.

Such a topic may be thought to have no place in a work devoted to the practical working of the law save to highlight where deficiencies exist and by so doing advance the cause of law reform. In fact it goes beyond that. The *extra*-legal avenues (as distinct from those *not* legal) identified here, are conducted in a manner aimed at ensuring the utmost publicity for and public debate of issues that might otherwise disappear into the black hole of a legal vacuum. 'Direct action' is one description of this emergent activity which makes, in an orderly fashion, points that the established avenues do not and in a form that can be innovative and attention grabbing. Inevitably such action can attract activity of a non-acceptable form (albeit, at times, understandable), involving confrontation and conflict with the established law and those responsible for its enforcement.

The seeking out of avenues of such rough justice is likely to be prompted by frustration and even despair after all other orthodox means seem to have been exhausted. Deliberate challenge to the law and its upholders, however, frequently fails to produce the desired result and, even more disastrously, often succeeds in diverting attention from the primary point at issue. A protest that degenerates into confrontational violence attracts concentration upon the consequences of that violence and often leads into legal processes totally removed from the purpose of the original action. As such, it becomes counter-productive. The very point at issue is lost to other issues, generally of a civil liberties kind (doubtless important in their own way) but superseding what was always intended as the main point of exposure.

CRIMINAL JUSTICE BILL

8.2   The right to demonstrate one's views in a peaceable manner is fundamental. Provisions in the Criminal Justice Bill provide a worrying opportunity for the curtailment of this right, which is of particular relevance in the case of environmental issues. At the time of writing, it seems likely that this swingeing piece of legislation will become law in November 1994. Its full significance may not have been appreciated when the Bill was first published. The government said that its primary aim was to contain new age travellers and protect landowners from senseless and damaging invasion by itinerant groups. As the Bill progressed through Parliament it became apparent that it could also be used to prevent any gathering on land in the ownership of another even if there for peaceful and hitherto lawful protest. It means that protestors against the construction of a new motorway, simply by congregating on land acquired by the Department of Transport for construction, are breaking the criminal law and are liable to prosecution. By criminalising such activities with the prospect of fines and, worse, a custodial sentence the government can stifle all protest. The Bill ranks as a serious inroad into one of our traditional freedoms.

How this legislation will work in practice, its implications for local residents, campaigners and police, and their relationships with the community has yet to be demonstrated.

THE USE OF EXTRA-LEGAL REMEDIES

8.3   There are many occasions, nevertheless, where activities outside the legal process (but, it must be reiterated, not illegal in themselves) are appropriate, and even to be recommended by the practitioner. It has to be recognised, moreover, that these extra-legal routes have been growing in the past decade.

Leaving aside political and socio-political implications, it is clear that many see recourse to action other than through the judicial process as a step of last resort. In recognising this, it must be asked whether our institutions and those responsible for administering them are *able* to respond to the needs and expectations of modern society, given the increased awareness of the citizenry of 1994. Whatever the reason, whether the result of frustration or disenchantment, or, more dangerously, alienation, this leads to antagonism at best and hostility at worst, with the consequence that many see the available law and its manner of implementation as irrelevant, outdated, and inadequate. Some, of course, are opportunists and prefer the confrontational approach: the concern in the present chapter is limited to those citizens who are looking for an effective approach with a difference, either in tandem with orthodox steps or separately.

CHANGING OPINIONS

8.4   Such people pursue non-legal remedies in an effort to change opinions in some way or other. This can range from persuading a regulator to support an objection to a planning application, right through to major campaigns for change of public attitudes to environmental issues, and to effect this through enlightenment and pressure in which the role and use of the media is of major importance.

Almost by definition the need for such action will arise in the following circumstances:

(a) there is no remedy available to cover a particular situation;
(b) there is a remedy but it is not available to the aggrieved party;
(c) there is a remedy available to the party concerned but there is insufficient admissible evidence to satisfy legal requirements;
(d) there is a remedy but the party entitled has failed to satisfy a procedural requirement such as a time constraint;
(e) all legal processes have been exhausted but to no effect;
(f) the remedy lies with a regulatory authority which chooses not to act;
(g) although steps are available, the party entitled is deterred from taking them by reason of insufficient funds, no or limited entitlement to legal aid or fear of suffering an award of damages and costs.

IMPORTANCE OF PUBLIC AWARENESS

INTRODUCTION

8.5   The most important need is to raise public awareness to the particular issue. Whereas confidentiality and privacy have a proper place in our society, too often these provide cover for undesirable activity as well as inactivity. The focus for this awareness should be at a local level since often the silent majority is unaware, or worse, inaccurately aware, of projected steps affecting the locality and the full consequence of those plans. National issues are frequently more fully ventilated than local ones.

Weighing of benefits

8.6   Certainly a new bypass, as an example, should bring benefit to local residents: there will, however, be broader considerations and these should be identified and their importance suitably weighed.

(1) Would a new road lead to the disappearance of other amenities?

(2) Does the road entail the creation of additional access roads, and even stimulate greater traffic movements, to the detriment of safety measures and the increased generating of pollution?

(3) Is the road of a size and expense disproportionate to local needs and are there a number of seemingly disparate bypass schemes under way that taken together could develop into an unheralded primary motor route attracting much greater flow of heavy traffic with increase of noise and fumes to the detriment of those living in the area?

(4) Is there a complete understanding of what is being given up in the process of seeking to ease congestion or the extent to which the success of such relief measures is dependent upon reliance placed on traffic projections and needs?

(5) Does the 'cut and fill' method of construction to be used for the new roadway have implications upon the outflows of surface water and what are the consequences for the water table given the likely collecting of lead benzene and rubber in the runoff from the new major road?

(6) Is there an alternative that could cause less upheaval while producing similar results?

(7) Has the project been properly costed and how is cost effectiveness being interpreted?

These considerations, limited though they are to the one narrow issue of a new road, indicate the variety of concerns and the extent of knowledge that needs to be available and tested to the full. At local level, the meaning and importance of such considerations to the neighbourhood and its community help explain the significance of *local* involvement and the establishment of specific interest groups. It also illustrates how important it is for such groups to have good professional guidance at the earliest stage possible as well as a consciousness of how to publicise these issues. *See also* Chapter 10 on action groups and self-help.

TWYFORD DOWN AND OXLEAS WOOD

8.7   The two well-publicised extremes in 1993 of Twyford Down, as an example of failure on the part of public opinion, and Oxleas Wood as a success, stand out in stark contrast as illustrations of the importance of getting things right and doing them at the right time. In both cases, the need was to overturn decisions that came about only after the due process of law, both domestic and EC, had been fully exhausted. In both cases, the final arbiter and only hope lay with the Secretary of State. He exercised his power of veto over Oxleas but authorised the terrible scar to the Hampshire landscape at Twyford Down. There were some distinguishing factors between the two cases but one important element in the reprieve of Oxleas Wood is that it came in the aftermath of the enormous publicity generated by the campaign at Twyford Down which had occupied large amounts of media time and space, and it was clear that a similar groundswell of opinion (perhaps, more accurately, 'road show') was taking shape in support of the Wood. In grieving for one, concerned parties must be heartened by the emerging strength of the power of public opinion, particularly where it produces operational delays and impact upon costs. Accordingly such parties should not be deterred from mounting similar objections as the occasion arises. But as previously stressed, the timing, content and co-ordination of the operation is all-important.

GETTING THE MESSAGE ACROSS

8.8   The message in any campaign must be in a form likely to appeal to local people and to the local media as well as the decision-makers whose views are being challenged. Newspapers, regional radio and television are always keen on a story having special significance within their circulation area, particularly if it can be personalised, as in:

The young couple pictured here with their four year old son cannot sell their house because of the blight caused by the proposed motorway extension. 'Tommy's asthma has got worse since all this started,' says his mother. 'There is building work going on just next to our garden wall. We need to move but there are no buyers and the traffic fumes can only make his asthma worse.'

This is followed by interviews with local estate agents, their doctor, their councillor, MP, and so on.

THE CAMPAIGN STRATEGY

ACTION GROUP

8.9   Establishing an identifiable action group with a catchy acronym improves focus and gives the operation a persona significantly separate from the individuals pressing the issue. The campaign must be shown to be for the communal good and not simply to satisfy the needs of the few, while at the same time featuring individual stories as the means of personalising and 'humanising' the problem.

The setting up of a campaign group generally emerges out of a process of self-selection from among those householders most directly concerned. Although 'natural' leaders tend to emerge, it is desirable that there is representation of a broad span of interest within the grouping. This avoids subsequent breakdown in the solidarity of the campaigners in the event that perhaps part of the objectives are satisfied and the debate becomes fragmented and the hitherto common front comes apart.

WRITTEN INFORMATION

8.10   Formulating the primary arguments and setting them out in short written form requires at least some simple printed matter. If professional guidance as to content, design and printing of information sheets is available, that will prove very valuable.

PUBLIC MEETINGS

8.11   Circulation of written material and the holding of public meetings, preferably with sympathetic local councillors present, serves to cement as well as instruct local support. Likewise bringing in the Member of Parliament serves to assist the momentum which, with sufficient energy and commitment, will develop into a rolling campaign.

Campaigners need to be aware of the importance of providing those whom they wish to impress (or convert) with a clear and concise statement of the issues: they should not assume that others (even those in authority) have all the relevant information!

PROFESSIONAL ASSISTANCE

8.12   Access to ELF and its nationwide membership of practitioners at an early stage is of importance. In urging this the authors are mindful of the many occasions where professional consultation has been sought at too late a stage. Receiving guidance on good points that should be concentrated upon, distinguishing the strong arguments and the weak, even the method of presentation, can make all the difference between failure and success. Having the benefit of experienced expert guidance at an early stage can only be an advantage.

INFLUENCING OPINION

8.13   In making their case, campaigners will find it beneficial to involve others not directly affected, particularly if an appeal is made to a well-known personality or personalities who can increase the profile and public awareness of the issues. Local councillors are aware of their responsibilities to their constituents although party politics can cause councillors to face a conflict of interest if the planning or other relevant committee is made up of politicians of a similar hue. If, of course, they are not, campaigners can turn this to their advantage! Petitions are useful tools in convincing a councillor of the importance of the matter and campaigners are advised to enlist the support of one or more such local representatives for the campaign. Care must be taken in the choice of the message that the signatories support and in ensuring that signatures are genuine and the people are local.

Funding and organisational considerations are dealt with in Chapter 10 and the points raised there should be read in conjunction with this chapter.

INFLUENCING LOCAL AUTHORITIES

PLANNING DECISIONS

8.14 Most planning decisions are made by the planning committee of the relevant local authority. The committee is comprised of local councillors advised by the officers of the council.

As well as making objections known to the planning department and its officers, campaigners should find it well worth lobbying the councillors who will be making the decision. Often it is advisable to prepare a dossier of significant documents, including a summary of objections. This is particularly relevant where there is a recommendation from officers for approval of the application. It is important that campaigners ensure that the strength of feeling is conveyed. Therefore they should set out particulars of any petition circulated and of representative bodies that have supported objections.

A further benefit for campaigners of lobbying councillors is the certainty that relevant information has actually reached the committee. Generally, documentation available to the committee is limited to the planning officer's report, the contents of which objectors cannot control. It is therefore all-important for campaigners to get their points home. *See also* the numerous references to lobbying of local councillors in Chapter 3. Those references emphasise the importance of lobbying in determining the attitudes and decisions of officers. The planning system is primarily geared to the argument between applicants and planning departments. The participation of third-party objectors is often limited. Thus influencing councillors and officers can be the most effective contribution campaigners can make to the decision-making process.

OTHER LOCAL AUTHORITY FUNCTIONS

8.15 Chapters 2, 3 and 5 demonstrate the strong involvement of local authorities in the statutory system for the control of pollution of land and air. They have powers of enforcement and are also responsible for determining authorisation applications. Decisions taken by the officers can therefore have a significant impact on the local environment.

The opportunity to scrutinise local authority decisions, unlike those of other environmental agencies, such as the NRA, is guaranteed by the fact that all officers are ultimately answerable to committees of elected councillors. Thus where officers decide to act in a particular way, or, indeed, not to do so, objectors should consider lobbying local councillors as one route to securing the reversal of those decisions.

Local councillors also have a role where a local authority has a discretion whether to designate areas for particular types of protection. For example, there are powers to set up litter control areas or noise abatement zones (covered in Chapter 1). The likelihood of persuading reluctant officers to act should be enhanced if campaigners can apply political pressure through committees as well as making direct representations to officers.

The effectiveness of this course of action is illustrated by one of the ELF referrals.

Example

Residents of the Cuckoo Estate in Ealing banded together to challenge a local authority decision to allow development of a local 'green'. Pressure was put on the authority to reverse their decision and to register the land as a village green. This was linked with an application for judicial review. The combined effect was to achieve a reversal of the decision.

PARLIAMENT

8.16 Political lobbying can form an important measure in trying to resolve environmental problems. Matters on which lobbying may be effective range from parochial issues such as the initiation of a prosecution, through active involvement in seeking amendments to legislation (such as recent attempts to clarify liability for minewater discharges in the coal privatisation legislation) to promoting major campaigns such as the reduction of carbon monoxide emissions into the atmosphere from motor vehicles.

REFERRING INDIVIDUAL CASES

8.17   Sometimes issues arise which do not admit of a local solution. The matter may have been decided by a regulatory body such as the NRA or HMIP which, unlike local authorities, are not subject to direct scrutiny by elected politicians. Alternatively, a local authority decision may have a national perspective, or local politicians may not share the view of an aggrieved party. In any of these cases it can be beneficial to refer the issue to the local MP so that he or she can raise the matter with the regulator or the government department. Sometimes this will be done by way of a parliamentary question, and sometimes by letters written by the MP. Alternatively it may prove possible to arrange a meeting with the relevant minister or one of his officials. While MPs have only limited resources for following through individual complaints, their involvement can be very useful in persuading the regulator or the department to take the issue seriously.

AMENDING LEGISLATION

8.18   Over the last 10 years there has been a steady stream of legislation concerned wholly or in part with the environment or in respect of activities which have an environmental impact. It seems likely that this process will continue.

It is quite often the case that people believe that particular Bills do not deal with environmental protection as firmly as they ought. Where that situation arises, pressure groups frequently seek to secure amendments to the legislation to improve such protection. Regrettably the most sensible of amendments often fail due to government intransigence, but even if the process is not successful in changing the Bill, it will be important in raising awareness of the problem and generating public concern.

If the local MP approached by a particular pressure group is not directly involved in the particular Bill then he/she can refer to the

MP best situated to help. Often a number of pressure groups join together to support a particular amendment. It is normal practice for pressure groups to prepare a briefing note, which supplies the necessary background and can give material for a speech. Pressure groups are also often required to supply a draft amendment.

Obviously pressure groups can seek political support in the House of Lords or the House of Commons or both. For the purpose of raising issues for debate generally, the committee stage in the Commons is perhaps the best forum. When it comes to tabling amendments, the House of Lords is often the better forum, since voting according to party lines is less tightly controlled, and members are more likely to vote through amendments independently of government pressure.

A typical bill where amendments have been sought in the Lords is the Coal Industry Bill, where pressure groups have sought to increase the level of protection from minewater discharges following the abandonment of mines.

Raising environmental awareness

8.19 Parliament can be a good forum for raising environmental issues generally, even when there is no pending legislation, but when there is a public concern over a particular policy issue. In the case of road building for example, the fact that lobbying groups have been able to raise the issue through MPs in Parliament has contributed to the undoubted change in public attitudes that is occurring to major road construction.

As well as the raising of such issues in general debate, specific problems can be addressed by way of private members' Bills. While few such Bills are ever passed, it is an effective way of raising the level of awareness of given issues.

Influencing regulatory authorities

8.20 Campaign groups often need to monitor the activities or, more correctly, the inactivity of the regulatory authorities that control discharges into the environment (as pointed out in Chapter 4). It is surprising how sluggish regulators can be in the use of their powers but equally how responsive they are once publicity, or even the threat of it, appears.

THE POWER OF PUBLIC OPINION

8.21 By such means toxic emissions can be reduced or plants and industrial processes requiring licences and operating in breach of or even without such licences, stopped. The Hillingdon Hospital incinerator problem is an example, *see* Chapter 4. Most such cases go unreported save in the local media and occasionally in the national media. The ELF experience, however, records many instances where pressure brought to bear on regulators, particularly when formalised by way of written complaint, professionally prepared, has produced positive results. *See also* Chapter 10.

Not unnaturally, some regulators prefer to be left in peace and to follow their procedures at their own pace and in line with their own policies. Clearly, a way in which pressure groups can influence the outcome of such decision-making is to make the regulator aware that peace will be in short supply if representations are ignored.

This observation is not intended to be unkind to regulators or to be needlessly critical of their role. All public institutions have a certain sense of autonomy in their operations even though they are there to serve and represent the public interest in preserving and protecting the environment. The strength of public opinion therefore ought to affect regulators' decisions, but that public concern has to be communicated. There are a number of ways in which this can be done. Apart from lobbying the decision-makers (the government ministers), the public may bring political influence to bear on those who administer the regulatory authority. Additionally, the powers of public opinion may be sustained and orchestrated, through the media and otherwise. Beyond that is the proactive line of influencing future policy by contributing to the policy-making process.

RELATIONS BETWEEN REGULATORS AND THE PUBLIC

8.22 Chapter 1 described the bodies that have responsibilities for the protection of the environment as well as those that have obligations and duties by reason of their activities and the potential damage to the environment resulting from them. This section looks at the interrelationship between those experiencing environmental problems and the authorities with environmental responsibilities. It will be evident from Chapters 3, 4 and 5 that these bodies have extensive powers and duties for enforcement, planning and authorisation.

In the main the interests of regulatory bodies and the public are the same, and the regulators take the initiative in dealing with an environmental problem without the need of any intervention or encouragement from the public. There are however circumstances where regulators do have different perceptions and priorities from community groups, so that the latter may perceive a need to influence them.

GETTING THE MESSAGE ACROSS

8.23   The circumstances in which it may be necessary or desirable to take steps to influence regulatory authorities to remedy an environmental problem vary quite widely. For example:

(1) It is likely that one or more of the regulators will be involved with any given problem. Even where a common law remedy exists, statutory bodies are involved as holders of relevant environmental information, and also as the possible agency for resolving the problem. A water pollution problem may be resolved either by an injunction or by the imposition of a sufficiently tight authorisation to control the discharge and hence the pollution.

(2) A private remedy may exist but an aggrieved party may not have the funds to initiate a claim.

(3) An individual group may elect for an issue to be handled by the public's own watchdog.

(4) A problem may be so widespread that individual action could not achieve a sufficiently broad remedy.

Political pressure

8.24   Regulatory bodies are politically influenced, either directly or indirectly. Most of their broader policies are likely to be influenced by the views of those who fund them. While the NRA and other agencies have achieved a considerable independence, the frequency with which individual officers express support for a particular cause privately that they feel they cannot endorse in public, is noticeable and demonstrates that their hands are not entirely free.

It is clearly better for campaigners to have the regulator working on their side than against them. The best way for them to secure the support of a regulator is to put it in such a position in relation to any pollution control or enforcement issue that it will be more awkward for it to maintain an uncommitted posture than to support the course of action proposed. Often the political pressure that imperceptibly forms the attitude of a particular authority is governed by the costs commercial interests would incur if the authority were persuaded to adopt a more interventionist approach. If, however, environmental groups are sufficiently well informed and representative of a body of opinion there will come a point when the weight of their arguments are more persuasive than those of commercial interests.

Tactics

8.25   A number of points need to be made in relation to the question of how best to influence a regulator.

(1) It is important that the regulator is made aware that the aggrieved party knows what the statutory duties of that body are. Chapter 1 looked at the broad duties imposed on all authorities having responsibility for environmental protection. There is no harm in reminding the relevant authority of the manner in which those duties impinge on the problem in question.

(2) A campaigner must be absolutely clear what the authority is being asked to do. It may be that a planning authority is being asked to serve an enforcement notice; or HMIP is being persuaded to bring a prosecution; or the NRA is being requested to vary or revoke a consent. An authority may be asked to take more than one action and, indeed, it may be necessary to secure the support and action of more than one authority. There may be situations where a campaigner, as well as asking a regulator to take executive action itself, will wish to encourage a regulator to support objections being made in relation to the decision of a different regulator, eg for a regulator to object to a planning application on environmental grounds.

(3) If the action that is being promoted carries broad public support campaigners need to make the authority aware of

the strength of the support. This may be done by presenting a petition or individual letters from all or at least a sample of those affected. Where possible third party representative bodies that have some interest in the problem should be encouraged to record their support for the proposed action. Thus, for example, in the case of objections to a planning application support from the local parish council, and from the relevant environmental agency, might be secured. Equally written support should be canvassed from non-statutory bodies involved with the protection of the environment. (*See* below.)

(4) The quality of material submitted is important. Well-argued submissions are more likely to influence an authority to change its position. In particular, if expert evidence is available to support a given course of action then that should be presented. By way of example the Anglers Conservation Association (ACA) was involved with a case where problems were being experienced on a trout stream by silt discharges from a cress farm when cleaning out its beds. The water authority (as it then was) considered the expert's report prepared by the aggrieved party and commissioned its own survey. As a result, the NRA imposed a suspended solids condition on the discharge consent of the cress farm in question and those of all other farms in that region. On a much larger scale campaigns by Greenpeace on environmental issues invariably use high quality expert evidence as the foundation of successful campaigns.

(5) Statutory consultees can assist in persuading an authority to alter its position. For example, under the WRA, the NRA is bound to create and consult with Regional Fisheries Advisory Committees (RFAC). These independent committees are designed to provide a dialogue between the NRA and the angling and other fishery interests in an area. Clearly support from the relevant RFAC will help to persuade the NRA to adopt a particular course of action.

Structure of regulatory bodies

8.26 Once a decision has been made to lobby a regulator it is important to ensure that representations reach the right person. The following brief descriptions of how the principal agencies operate may be of assistance. The addresses of all of these bodies are in Appendix 1.

National Rivers Authority

8.27   As Chapter 1 shows the NRA carries out a number of different functions, and this is reflected in the organisation's structure. Each region has departments dealing with pollution control, water resources, land drainage, fisheries and navigation. Any one problem may concern more than one department and it is important to notify all relevant departments.

Each region has a legal department which services all other departments, and has a general manager who is in overall charge of the region. Increasingly each region now divides responsibility by geographical area, and each area has its own manager.

Campaigners who feel that NRA officers are not dealing satisfactorily with a particular problem may find it helpful to communicate with area or general managers. Managers can also help to ensure that there is co-ordination between departments concerned with larger problems.

The NRA also has a national office situated in Bristol, which is concerned with matters of national policy in relation to its various functions. Campaigners should communicate with this office if national issues are being addressed, eg pollution of bathing beaches.

Her Majesty's Inspectorate of Pollution

8.28   The head office of HMIP is in London. It is concerned *inter alia* with policy issues, the issue of technical guidance notes and research. There are principal area offices, in Bedford, Bristol and Leeds. Each area office is responsible for a number of regions, each of which has its own office. Regional offices work in multi-disciplinary teams, which are responsible for all aspects of regulation, from consideration of applications through to monitoring and enforcement.

Local authorities

8.29 The structure of local authority departments varies from authority to authority. The two principal departments concerned with environmental matters are Planning, which deals with matters raised in Chapter 3 and Environmental Health, which deals with those matters, eg air pollution control, where the local authority is the regulatory authority.

INFORMATION

8.30 The Environmental Information Regulations, issued in 1992 and operative since 1 January 1993, are the government's response to the EC Directive on the Freedom of Access to Information on the Environment (90/313/EEC). Although not entirely free from inadequacies they nevertheless impose duties and thereby underpin rights and constitute an important step along the path of the right to know. (*See* Chapter 9 for further details of the Regulations.) The information available could have a bearing upon a variety of situations, but can be of particular value in monitoring events for which regulatory authorities have special responsibility.

THE MEDIA

8.31 The environment has a high public interest value, and accordingly attracts considerable media attention. Advising in environmental cases carries with it the need to be aware of how to relate to the media in a way that is in the best interests of those represented and in a manner that is fair and which avoids the risk of being in contempt of court.

MAKING CONTACT WITH THE MEDIA

8.32 Many environmental issues have a high profile, and therefore the media will come to the problem rather than vice versa. However, in some cases campaigners or practitioners need to establish contact with the media. The way to achieve this is to prepare a press release, and identify which sections of the media ought to be circulated. Clearly some issues will only be likely to interest local media, whereas others will be of national interest.

The press release need only identify basic details of the issue, since any journalist following up the story will ask for the necessary detail to develop his or her theme. If the release concerns an issue which is the subject of current court proceedings, then great care must be taken to ensure that both the release and any follow-up interview do not prejudice a fair trial (*see* below).

Statutory authorities and many of the larger pressure groups have their own press officers or use a press agent and will have a list of media contacts to circulate.

If a practitioner or campaigner is uncertain who to contact or how to go about it, then it may be worth contacting one of the pressure groups for advice. (*See* details of environmental pressure groups at Appendix 2.)

RELATIONS WITH THE MEDIA

Problems

8.33   There are some points about dealing with the media that ought to be borne in mind at all times. First is the fact that, however sympathetic a journalist may be to a particular story, his or her ultimate objective is likely to be different from that of the person who wants to publicise the issue. The journalist's aim is to produce a good story and preferably one which conforms to the editorial values and views of the newspaper. As a result how the practitioner or campaigning group and the journalist see the end-product (newspaper article or radio/TV programme) can be very different. The final decision as to the content of the product will be for the relevant editor. To avoid problems arising from this difference, it is advisable for practitioners or campaigners to endeavour to approve the final product where possible, or at least secure agreement on the points that will be covered. This is particularly relevant where the content of the product is the subject-matter of court proceedings (*see* below).

Coverage

8.34   Media coverage tends to comprise either news reportage of a particular case, or a broader documentary treatment of an issue under debate. In the latter case it is likely that the programme or article will want to present both sides of the argument. It is important, therefore, that campaigners or practitioners ensure, first, that the journalist fully understands their arguments, and, second, that those arguments will fit into the structure and balance of the programme and will be presented in the most positive light.

When giving interviews it is sensible for campaigners to try and find out what questions will be asked in advance, since the perceptions of interviewee and interviewer concerning the important points to bring out can often be very different. The problem remains that the interviewee has no real control over the finished product nor the extent to which views are reported fully, in the correct sequence and in context.

Media agenda

8.35 Within the press and broadcasting media, regional and national, there is an influential band of writers, broadcasters and journalists with strong environmental credentials whose espousal of a topic or exposure of an issue can be of particular importance. For them to take up a case, however, they need to be convinced of the issues at stake, the extent of local feeling, and its particular significance at local or national level. Inevitably the attractiveness of the argument and its broader implications will contribute to the newsworthiness of the topic and that, as they say, is what sells papers. In other words, the media have their own agenda to satisfy and campaigners must be aware of this in pursuing their own aims. In time, campaigners learn to be selective in those with whom they deal, and who can be trusted to report material in a reliable and sympathetic manner.

Media publicity and contempt of court

8.36 Whenever media releases are made concerning cases where court proceedings are in being, what is permissible for publication should be borne in mind. The recent judicial criticism of a British Nuclear Fuels representative in respect of comments made to the media during the judicial review proceedings brought by Greenpeace is a good example of the consequences of breaching the rules.

More generally, stepping the wrong side of the rules is likely to have the effect of alienating the court and can do more harm than good to the conduct of a case. Defendants in environmental cases, as in other cases, will take advantage of any line of attack available. The assertion that media coverage has prejudiced the chance of a fair trial is an easy line to follow even where the evidence is thin. Defendants in environmental cases are likely to use this tactic even if they know that the coverage falls well short of what could be construed as contempt.

It is nevertheless perfectly right and appropriate that the existence of proceedings of public importance should be highlighted, and those involved with important cases should not draw back from publicising legitimate information about the case.

CONTEMPT

8.37 Recognising the possibility of a problem is the means of avoiding it. Criminal contempt is a criminal offence punishable by a fine or imprisonment. There are two categories: contempt in the face of the court, ie in the court room itself, and contempts committed outside the court. This section is concerned with the latter. Within the category are the following types of contempt:
  (a) publications which are likely to prejudice a fair trial or prejudice issues in pending proceedings; and
  (b) publications which lower the authority of the court.
The first of these types is relevant to this discussion. A further subdivision is necessary between publications relating to criminal proceedings and those relating to civil proceedings.

As a matter of general principle, publications that might be prejudicial to a fair trial are more likely to be in contempt in criminal proceedings than in civil proceedings. The reason for this is the assumption that juries are more likely to be influenced by media coverage than judges.

Contempt in criminal proceedings

8.38 It is an offence to comment on pending proceedings in a manner which prejudices a fair trial. This may include:
  (a) imputing guilt;
  (b) any systematic parallel investigation of the facts of a case;
  (c) an interview with the accused or with witnesses;
  (d) reporting the nature of defence.

Equally it is an offence to report matters in such a way as to influence the manner in which evidence is presented to the court. Against this it is not an offence to report the occurrence of a crime, nor to report the proceedings themselves, provided that the report is fair and accurate.

Contempt in civil proceedings

8.39 Many of the same principles apply in relation to civil proceedings as to criminal. However, as pointed out above, where the proceedings are to be heard by a judge alone, the approach is more relaxed than if a jury is involved.

As well as the matters set out above, publication of pleadings has been held as a contempt, although it is now unlikely that that still applies except where such publication clearly prejudices a fair trial.

SUMMARY

8.40 Certain principles can be suggested that will help where media releases are planned.

(1) The rules on contempt relate only to pending or current proceedings. Although care has to be taken where the party publicising knows that proceedings are imminent, clearly there is much more scope for going into the facts of a case when no proceedings have been commenced.

(2) Greater care needs to be taken in criminal cases than in civil cases.

(3) As the media are responsible for publishing the materials, they are aware of the risk of contempt, and exercise their own self-censorship.

(4) Publication of material is more likely to prejudice a trial, the closer its publication is to the hearing of the action. Any press release or other comment close to a criminal trial should be limited to reporting the date and venue of the hearing and the charges brought or principal issues to be tried.

(5) All publications should make it clear when issues are in dispute, and in particular that matters are alleged rather than proven.

(6) Care should be taken to ensure that media contact is limited to as few people as possible. The more people available for

comment the greater the risk of prejudicial material being published. Thus where a lawyer represents a group of people in an environmental case, it is highly advisable that all media contact is strictly limited to one representative and/or the lawyer.

CONTRIBUTING TO CONSULTATIVE PROCESSES

INTRODUCTION

8.41   Those involved with pressure groups, or with commercial interests whose activities impinge on the environment, need to be aware of the processes by which environmental policies are made. At whatever level these policies emerge there is invariably a consultation period before the policies are determined.

Contributing to the consultative process is a further way in which to influence opinion on environmental issues. This section will look at the various organisations that issue consultative documents and the areas that they cover, and how campaigners may obtain access to the consultative process.

It is of course very difficult to determine what benefit contributions to such consultations make. It is likely in some cases that the issuing body is predisposed to a particular policy option and even the most persuasive representations are unlikely to change this. Even in those cases, however, access to the consultative process provides campaigners with an opportunity to broach new ideas which, if not accepted today, will make their mark in the future.

Consultation at European level is dealt with in Chapter 6.

CONSULTATION AT NATIONAL LEVEL

8.42   The DoE is responsible for the issue of consultation papers impinging on the environment. These fall into two categories: Green Papers issued prior to legislation; and consultation papers relating to matters of environmental policy.

Green Papers

8.43   Green Papers are prepared to allow a period of public consultation on the contents of legislation before a Bill is introduced to Parliament. They consist of a statement of government intentions and an outline of the proposed contents of the Bill. There is usually a reasonable period for making submissions.

Other consultation papers

8.44 Other papers are produced on an *ad hoc* basis to seek views on whatever environmental policy area is to be developed.

The DoE maintains a database of interested parties and circulates consultation papers to those who might have an interest in the issue on which views are sought. Anyone interested may apply to be included in the DoE list of potential consultees.

Many acts of consultation receive media publicity, and copies of any given paper will be supplied on request. The DoE also has a library which holds copies of past and current consultation papers.

NRA AND CONSULTATION

8.45 The NRA periodically issues consultation papers relating to policy for which it is responsible. Recent examples have been papers on the development of water quality objectives (WQO) under the WRA, and the imposition of charges for the issue of discharge consents.

Unless they relate to the creation of new regional byelaws, these consultation papers are issued by the NRA head office in Bristol. There is, however, no central office responsible for the issue of all papers. As explained above, the NRA operates through different divisions which are charged with various statutory functions. This divisional philosophy applies also to the head office. Thus each division issues consultation papers relevant to its own area of responsibility.

Interested parties who wish to be placed on the list of consultees should apply to the relevant division at the head office of the NRA.

HMIP AND CONSULTATION

8.46 HMIP also issues consultation papers relevant to policy in their area of responsibility. Recent papers have concerned the method of assessment used by firms in determining 'best practice', and the application by Nuclear Electric to commence operation of Sizewell 'B' Power Station.

Consultation papers are issued from HMIP's head office in London. HMIP will issue papers to non-statutory consultees on request. As with the other organisations it is possible to be placed on the list of potential consultees. Application should be made to the head office.

LOCAL AUTHORITY CONSULTATION

8.47 The principal opportunity to influence environmental policy at a local level is through contribution to the structure and local plans issued by local authorities. The increasing significance of these plans is dealt with in Chapter 3 above. That chapter also looks at the opportunity for public involvement in the determination of structure and local plans.

PRESSURE GROUPS

8.48 It will be evident from earlier parts of this chapter that environmental groups will often find that their cause is supported by other pressure groups concerned with environmental issues.

Chapter 10 looks at some of the problems that can arise with funding environmental cases. Given the potential community of interest and the lack of resources available to many action groups, it will often be the case that help can be obtained from an environmental pressure group to make progress in one way or another.

Appendix 2 lists active environmental pressure groups and provides a brief description of their objectives and, where relevant, of their current concerns. This list is not exhaustive. It will be evident from the descriptions of the various pressure groups that each has its own method of working and exercising influence. For this reason there are a number of ways in which these organisations may help to address particular problems that present themselves to individuals or those who advise them.

In some cases the particular issue may have a political significance that does not admit of any of the legal remedies that are referred to above. Groups such as Greenpeace and FOE are very effective at taking up environmental issues and achieving the changes in attitude that are needed to secure the prevention of environmentally damaging activities.

Where any of the remedies outlined in this book are available one of the pressure groups may be of practical help in applying that remedy, in such ways as:

(a) the provision of information;

(b) recommending experts in the field; or

(c) the provision of financial support.

In certain circumstances the various organisations will take an active role:

(a) by involving themselves in the legal remedies on their own behalf or on behalf of those whom they represent;

(b) by taking up a problem brought to their attention.

Alternatively, in the case of eg public inquiries, a pressure group may already be involved in presenting a case which substantially makes the point in issue.

OTHER STATUTORY BODIES

8.49 Mention should also be made of a varying group of bodies which have been created by statute, and whose activities have an impact on the environment separate from the regulatory authority. This section will give a brief description of each.

INDIVIDUAL BODIES

Natural Environment Research Council

8.50 The National Environment Research Council (NERC) is responsible for the planning, encouraging and carrying out of research into the physical and biological sciences relating to the human environment and its resources. Areas into which it researches include water pollution, acid rain, leachate from waste tips, leakage of radiation material into water and the gathering of radioactive dust by wind currents. It carries out this research and training through its own institutes and grant-aided associations.

As far as the public is concerned, the benefit of NERC lies in its provision of environmental information. Its Environmental Information Centre is a plentiful source of information and is primarily concerned with ecology and land use and holds some of the most extensive databases in the UK. It holds biological records of

305

British flora and fauna, an information system on the state of the
environment in the EC, a digital map of critical loads of acidic pollution and thresholds of sensitivity of soils and freshwaters, as well as
a geological information service. Its National Water Archive has
information on matters such as national river flow and national
groundwater levels, monthly catchment rainfall figures and UK
daily rainfall.

Countryside Commission

8.51   Although the members of the Countryside Commission are
appointed by the Secretary of State, it is not part of the DoE or a
Crown servant. It is responsible for the conservation and enhancement of the natural beauty of the countryside in England and
Wales. It has numerous other duties such as the designation of
areas of outstanding natural beauty (ONB) and national parks,
improving facilities for visitors to the countryside and advising
both local and central government on matters prejudicial to
natural beauty. The main duties of the Commission are contained
in the National Parks and Access to Countryside Act 1949,
Countryside Act 1968, Local Government Act 1972 and the
Wildlife and Countryside Act 1981 although it is mentioned in
many other statutes and regulations.

Individuals may approach the Commission with a view to finding
out whether a particular area is an area of ONB or a national park
and to apply for land to be so designated. The Commission's help
may be sought to oppose major developments in ONBs or national
parks and to deal with complaints from the public regarding footpaths.

Royal Commission on Environmental Pollution

8.52   This is a permanent body which exists to advise on environmental policy, the adequacy of research into such matters and on the
possibilities of danger to the environment. It has, however, established a reputation for independence. It holds inquiries during
which it considers evidence. It will then publish a report to which
the government usually issues a formal response. Its influence is
quite subtle in increasing public and government awareness of
environmental problems.

Office of the Director General for Water Services

8.53   The role of the Office of the Director General for Water Services (OFWAT) is that of an independent regulator of the water industry in England and Wales. It was set up in August 1989 under the Water Industry Act (WIA) of that year. Generally speaking, OFWAT must ensure that the water industry in England and Wales provides a fair and efficient service. As the water companies have an effective monopoly in their areas the aim of government policy in setting up OFWAT was to provide a body to control abuse of that monopoly.

If a member of the public experiences problems with his water company he may approach OFWAT, who may take the matter up on his behalf.

In March 1993 OFWAT's National Customer Council was set up. Based at the head office in Birmingham, it takes a national as opposed to regional view of the industry and it is also a lobbying group at both national and European level.

It must also monitor the effectiveness of the water industry's investment programme. Essentially this means balancing the cost of investment with water quality. At present, this involves the implementation of the Urban Waste Water Treatment Directive. *See* s 27ff of the WIA for details of the Director General's duties.

The Drinking Water Inspectorate

8.54   The Inspectorate, established in January 1990, has two bases—one in the DoE and the other in the NRA. The main task of the Inspectorate is to check that water companies supply water that is safe to drink and meets standards set for drinking water.

The Inspectorate also investigates every accident that takes place which might affect drinking water. Prosecution may follow if a company supplies water unfit for human consumption. It should be pointed out that environmental health officers of local councils may also visit water companies to take water samples. If the company does not respond satisfactorily to an individual's complaint, then he should ask the local council to investigate.

THE ADEQUACY OF THE SYSTEM

8.55 That in the mid-1990s efforts should be necessary to deal with environmental matters, that environmentally essential steps are left to public-spirited or locally desperate people and that many of these steps are dependent on extra-legal remedies, is in itself a comment upon certain weaknesses in the law and failures in the system. The Law Commission is currently identifying the need for legislative changes in substantive law, as well as examining the subject of law reform and investigating a number of procedural issues. Major impediments include *locus standi*, the right to start court proceedings, the rules relating to this and the restrictive interpretation by the judiciary. The EC Fifth Action Programme issued in 1993 made a number of valuable recommendations, and is referred to in Chapter 6.

The argument of public policy, of the balance of convenience, so often a judicial stratagem for maintenance of the *status quo*, deters reform, and reduces drastically the number of cases brought to court and certainly impedes the environmental cause. Similarly, the judicial review process, while infrequently innovative, and very much a creation of a select number of liberal judges, has become the victim of its own success and by sheer volume of casework is unwieldy and is not widely available. Restrictions on the availability of legal aid has similar consequences. *See also* Chapter 10.

Most of these criticisms really relate to an inadequacy in the making available of full and unfettered access to justice. This inadequacy applies to all areas of activity, but those of environmental concern are especially relevant here. It follows, as a consequence, that a number of problems are not *legally* challenged or investigated. It also means that areas of law go untested and the scope of the law is not extended.

ENVIRONMENTAL COURTS

8.56 The weakness of the system, combined with the special needs of environmental casework, has caused some lawyers to examine Australia's environmental courts, which comprise lawyers and experts, and to raise the question of their suitability in the UK. The most notable protagonist is Lord Woolf, whose contributions to reform have been, throughout his judicial life, most significant, and who, in the 1992 Garner Lecture of the United Kingdom Environmental Law Association (UKELA), espoused the concept of such a court. The need for this type of court reflects the fact that environmental issues are becoming more complex, cover a widening spectrum of factors and are increasingly intruding into all aspects of life of concern to the coming as well as the present generation. It is also recognition that all of these implications must be accorded sufficient weight and balance if a *complete* and *informed* judgment is to be made.

Adapting such a court to the UK experience and needs requires careful thought and preparation. Its jurisdiction, appellate considerations, evidential requirements and procedural policy are a few of the aspects under review. If one aim of such a court is a greater informality, it is hoped that the rules of evidence will be less inhibiting and more akin to those acceptable at public inquiries. The perpetuation of the adversarial system is also in question and it has been suggested (by Lord Woolf, among others) that something akin to the inquisitorial approach might get closer to issues. The costs and financial implication of such changes are more fully examined in Chapter 10, but it must be said that the present rules are a disincentive to taking risks through the established system. Equally, limitations in the provision of legal aid prevent our legal system from operating on an even-handed basis. It is out of these inadequacies that the extra-legal courses discussed above are tending to emerge, with increasing popularity and regularity.

CHAPTER 9

EXPERTS, KNOW-HOW AND ACCESS TO INFORMATION

INTRODUCTION

9.1 This chapter deals with three areas that are of particular relevance to the environmental practitioner. They are distinct subjects, but have connections with each other.

The first is the role of experts. There are almost no cases arising from the issues discussed in this book that do not involve a reference to experts in some form or another. In the vast majority of cases, a successful outcome depends on receiving good quality expert evidence. It is crucial therefore that those involved with environmental cases know how to find appropriate expertise; understand the relationship between such experts and lawyers or others instructing them; and how to establish a good working relationship.

The second area is know-how. Given the central role of experts, it is important that practitioners have effective lines of communication. For this they need some basic technical understanding of pollution, of the environmental media, how pollution is measured and the types of expertise that are available. This material will cross-refer to the consideration of environmental law as it relates to the various media, dealt with in Chapters 1–7.

Finally, access to environmental information, factual and reliable, is essential to environmental groups, their legal advisers and experts instructed by them. It is only on the basis of such information that they are able to assess the extent of a problem and the availability of any remedy to deal with it. The final section of this chapter first discusses the effect of the Environmental Information Regulations and then looks at the availability of information in respect of each of the media by way of public registers.

Experts

Selecting an expert

Recommendation

9.2   As a general rule the best practical way to select an expert is to talk to others who have been involved with a similar problem, and to obtain a recommendation.

Published tests and professional bodies

9.3   Failing this, a number of publications contain details of experts and professional bodies have lists of experts. These include the following:

(1) The Environmental Law Foundation (ELF) has a network of members, a significant number of whom are experts. ELF is able to advise whether a suitable expert exists for a particular problem. One particular advantage of the ELF network is that all members are willing to do some *pro bono publico* work and to become involved in legal aid cases. (*See* Appendix 2.)

(2) The Environmental Data Services group, more familiarly known as ENDS, publishes a directory of environmental consultants. The directory comprises an alphabetical list of consultants and is indexed by type. Each entry has a checklist to indicate the size and range of expertise of the consultancy in question. The ENDS directory is the best single-volume source of information on environmental expertise. At present the cost of the directory is £49.50. (*See* Appendix 2 for details of ENDS.)

(3) The UK Register of Expert Witnesses contains details of all experts with experience of legal work. Obviously environmental experts form only a small part of the total register. However, the company that operates the register can search it for particular types of expertise. The register is run by J.S.

Publications and the cost of a complete printout of the register is £70.00. Alternatively an annual subscription costs £120.00 and this offers updates and a free 'Expert Location Service'.

(4) The Law Society has a database of experts, known as the Legal Practice expert witness referral service. Again this is for all types of expert, not just environmental ones. The service is only available to solicitors and is free. Enquiries should be made to the Law Society at 50/51 Chancery Lane, telephone number 071–320–5993.

(5) The Industrial Environmental Services Directory is published by Environment Business and contains details of experts and lawyers who specialise in environmental law.

(6) The National Society for Clean Air publishes a pollution handbook which covers 'UK pollution control, British and European law on Air pollution, Waste Disposal and Noise'. (*See* Appendix 2 for further details.)

Professional bodies

9.4   Appendix 3 lists professional bodies which represent the types of expertise that may be required in environmental cases. In one way or another they will be able to assist in identifying suitable experts.

Criteria for selecting experts

9.5   A number of criteria need to be taken into account when selecting an expert.

(1) For many consultancies preparing reports and giving evidence comprises only a small part of their professional work. Practitioners contacting a consultancy for the first time would therefore be wise to check whether the individual concerned has any experience of giving evidence and being cross-examined. Successful expert evidence is often as much a function of the ability of the expert to communicate, often under pressure, as of the level of the expert's knowledge.

(2) Regard should be had to the underlying independence of a consultancy. Some consultancies, particularly larger ones, are owned by water companies or other large corporations.

In nearly all cases it is important that the expert is truly independent of any possible influence.

The number of experts in specialised fields is, inevitably, small. Conflicts can arise where a given expert has already been involved in the issue in question in a manner that could compromise his ability to give genuinely independent advice. Obviously practitioners should address these issues early in the relationship.

(3) Some thought needs to be given to the resources of the consultancy in the context of the case they are advising in. Problems can arise with both small and large consultancies. One-man bands or small consultancies can be flexible in making time available for a given project. However, their lack of resources can be a problem in larger cases.

Large consultancies have the necessary resources to generate reports and other material at short notice, and to provide replacement experts if needed. However, other work commitments of individuals within the organisation can be greater, and therefore problems can arise if a particular individual is required to devote large periods of time at short notice.

In selecting an expert the practitioner should bear in mind that litigation requires working to rigid time limits and that sustained input may be needed from an expert at short notice.

(4) Most experts have some form of brochure setting out their expertise. This will include details of projects undertaken, as well as the experience of individuals.

Given the issues involved it may be prudent for a practitioner to contact a number of consultancies and decide which one fits best into the brief to which he is working. The cost of experts is dealt with later in this chapter, but note that the charging rates of experts vary considerably. While, of course, cheapest is not necessarily the best, available funding is often a very relevant factor in running a case. Sometimes, one expert may be able to provide a range of skills that another cannot.

THE RELATIONSHIP BETWEEN LAWYER AND EXPERT

9.6 Whatever remedy one is seeking to apply, expert advice, as to the cause of the pollution or other environmental damage complained of and/or the effect of that pollution, either will be essential or at the very least will enhance the presentation of the case.

Expert evidence

9.7   As the court or tribunal or other decision-maker will need to apply the law, and exercise any available discretion, to the nexus of facts, it is crucial that the expert understands the scope of any discretion and the tests which the decision-maker will apply, and equally important that the legal adviser is able to understand the evidence that the expert produces.

Thus if negligence is being alleged in a civil action, the expert must understand the tests the court will apply when determining whether the defendant is liable. If an IPC consent is being opposed, the expert must understand the matters which HMIP can take into account when deciding whether to grant that consent and the conditions to which the consent may be subject.

It is of course easy to offer up a counsel of perfection as to how a case is run. In reality the focus of a case can change and sharpen as it goes along, perhaps after documents have been disclosed, perhaps because of what the expert himself reports. It may therefore be quite late into the proceedings before the expert evidence is concluded, hence the importance of the practitioner establishing a proper working relationship with the expert from the earliest possible stage to ensure an effective cross-fertilisation of ideas.

Duty of expert

9.8   It is important to emphasise that the duty of an expert is primarily to the court. Judicial comment has made it clear that the purpose of expert evidence is to assist in the fair determination of issues between the parties. Such evidence is a mixture of fact and opinion, and in this differs from lay evidence which is simply of fact.

The role of the expert is to express an opinion based on an analysis of the facts presented to him on the legal issues that fall to be determined. Such an opinion clearly ought to be objective.

This is not to say that opposing experts have to agree. There can be two opinions on the same issue. For example two experts may disagree whether a given act or omission was a breach of the duty of care in negligence, given prevailing industry standards, or two experts may disagree what the best available technology presently is.

It does mean that an expert should exercise objective judgment on the established facts. If that judgment does not support the case of those instructing him or her then the sooner that view is known the better. An expert who gives opinions that he or she believes the client wants to hear does no one any favours. An opinion that is not based on proper scientific methodology will invariably be exposed in a hearing.

Chapter 7 has already referred to the importance of instructing experts early in common law cases. This of course applies to any case where expert evidence is to be relied on.

Meetings of experts

9.9 Once an expert has become involved in a contested case then it is sensible for him to look out for possible areas of agreement between the parties so as to reduce the scope of a dispute when it arrives at court and minimise expense. In some fora, eg the Official Referees Court, there is a standard direction that experts should meet before reports are exchanged with a view to narrowing areas of dispute. Wherever there are opposing experts it is always advisable to ensure that they meet, whether by agreement or by order of the court for this purpose.

Comments on other experts

9.10 Once reports have been exchanged, it is essential that the other side's expert evidence is reviewed and evaluated. If necessary, supplementary reports should be prepared to cover issues raised.

Form of an expert's report

9.11 The report should focus as closely as possible on the issues in dispute and avoid inclusion of extraneous or peripheral matter. It is essential that the lawyer reads through the report in draft form to ensure that it covers the points that the case addresses. Such a reading will serve a second purpose of ascertaining the intelligibility of the language. The persons who make the decision on the case must be able to understand the evidence being given. If technical terms are used a glossary should be prepared. If the basic science is particularly complicated it may be desirable to have a preliminary presentation of the principles involved before turning to the problem the expert is addressing. If appropriate, that presentation should use audio-visual aids. This is particularly relevant in jury cases.

Cost of experts

9.12   As with any other service the cost of obtaining expert advice can vary a great deal. Most environmental cases are run on a limited budget or are subject to some other cost constraint such as legal aid conditions or the need to tax costs on completion of a case.

It is sensible therefore to be clear from the outset what the basis of the expert's charges will be. It is often sensible to agree a fee ceiling for a first report and any subsequent stages of an expert's involvement.

It is also important to agree a billing pattern. Some consultants try to impose a monthly billing regime. This is inappropriate for the majority of legal cases. Some agreement that ties in with the needs of the party who is ultimately paying is highly desirable.

Some experts charge on the basis of daily rates, and some on hourly rates. The daily rates may vary from £250 to £750. The fees for actually giving evidence are usually higher than preparation costs. Hourly rates are generally in the range of £30–£100. If prices are quoted much above these figures, then, unless the expert is of exceptional seniority or specialisation, it is unlikely that those fees would be recovered on taxation. Such prices are often an indication that the consultants in question do not really want expert witness type of work. (*See also* the section on costs in Chapter 10.)

Where it is important to keep costs to a minimum it is worth considering whether some or all expert evidence can be presented by officers from the relevant regulatory authorities, eg the NRA. Clearly this will be less desirable when an independent opinion is required. However, there may be factual evidence of a scientific nature that can or ought to be presented by those responsible for the collection of that evidence. If such officers are required, invariably the authority in question will require a subpoena to be served on the officers in question, to avoid any accusation of partiality. In most cases the authorities are co-operative in making officers available for interview and agreeing proofs of evidence before a hearing. A daily charge for officers' time is made but this is not usually substantial.

Contracts with experts

9.13 In most cases the initial contact between lawyer/layman and expert is by telephone or meeting and subsequent contacts are incorporated in correspondence. Whatever the form of that initial contact it is essential to agree on some basic matters, to define roles and areas of responsibility, to deal with costs, and set time limits for the delivery of preliminary comments and the preparation of reports.

Some consultants operate, or endeavour to do so, on standard terms and conditions. These should be read carefully as they are often prepared for types of work that operate to a very different pattern to litigation cases.

Copyright and confidentiality

9.14 These issues are generally not raised and should not cause a problem. Nevertheless it is as well to flag the issue, so that agreement can be reached if it arises. Basic law suggests that copyright of a report remains with the author (ie the expert), and to avoid any problem the recipient of the report should clarify with the author the extent to which the report can be freely disseminated. It is at times very important for the circulation of expert evidence to be limited, particularly when reports are still in draft form. When working with a consultant other than on standard terms, which cover the point, it is advisable to ensure that issues of confidentiality and copyright are dealt with. It is crucial that the recipient of a report has an unfettered right to use the expert's report and findings.

Insurance

9.15 Many experts do not carry mandatory professional indemnity cover in respect of the work they do. If they do have cover, the amount can be relatively low. If the case in question relies on expert advice, that, if negligent, may cause loss or damage to a client, then the extent of cover ought to be checked.

Types of expertise

Introduction

9.16   Earlier in this chapter and elsewhere in this book the central role of experts has been emphasised. Given the close relationship between environmental practitioners and experts, and the importance that the legal adviser should understand the expert evidence, some discussion is required of the types of expertise available and the scientific basis of evidence presented. This section examines the types of evidence that might be encountered in relation to each of the environmental media. The section following looks at the basic science.

Air

9.17   The range of specialist expertise available to advise on air pollution can be divided between gaseous and particulate. Specialists will include those competent in the following fields:

(a) measuring emissions, both at source and at some distance from a point of origin, where pollution may be occurring and environmental effects may be felt;

(b) the engineering of (gaseous) emission control, eg from factory chimneys to advise on best available techniques (BATNEEC);

(c) modelling of gaseous and particulate (dust) emissions from both point and area/line sources;

(d) the interpretation of the modelling results, ie the significance of the pollution to water, soil, plants, animals and humans of the actual and predicted levels of pollutants;

(e) measuring noise levels and the impact of such noise on quality of life.

There may well be different specialists for different types of pollutants, eg vehicle fumes, power station emissions, industrial sources etc. The nuclear industry tends to have its own specialists in radioactivity.

Water

9.18   Specialists in the aquatic environment may be divided broadly into those who concentrate on fresh water and those who deal with the marine environment, with some individuals concentrating on estuarine systems.

Specialisations include the following:

(a) hydrology, which covers the study of surface water flows, catchments, rivers, lakes and streams;
(b) water chemistry, aquatic biology and microbiology including flora, invertebrates and fisheries;
(c) water supply, both from surface water and groundwater, and potable water treatment;
(d) water treatment specialists, also known as public health engineers, covering sewage treatment and industrial process water treatment.

Hydrogeology should also be included here because of its relevance to water supply, groundwater quality and contaminant modelling, although there is obviously some overlap between this and land specialisations.

Land

9.19 There is a wide range of specialisations which may be relevant to land pollution studies, covering the broad disciplines of geology, geography, biology and some aspects of engineering.

Specialists may be divided into:
(a) those concerned with the land itself such as geologists, geomorphologists, geotechnical engineers, and soil scientists;
(b) those concerned with what is on the land surface, for example ecologists, botanists, zoologists, specialists in reptiles, amphibians, insects etc;
(c) those concerned with the use of the land such as agronomists and landscape architects;
(d) those concerned with contamination and reclamation of it ('brush land').

Ecology includes more specialist areas such as industrial ecology. Ecotoxicologists, epidemiologists (usually doctors) and chemists also have a role to play, particularly in assessing the hazards and risks posed by particular levels of contamination to animals and humans.

Planning

9.20 There are a number of types of expertise that may be needed in planning cases. Areas covered include traffic, listed buildings, financial viability, and broader economic implications. Planning experts often work in conjunction with lawyers.

BASIC SCIENCE

9.21   This section provides a brief introduction to the basic science behind the assessment and measurement of forms of pollution in each of the environmental media. This summary should assist practitioners to understand expert evidence. It concludes with some comments on analysing samples, which can be very relevant to private prosecutions.

DEFINITIONS OF POLLUTION

9.22   Various definitions of pollution (or equivalent words) have been given elsewhere in this book. In common law any activity or event that causes physical damage or interferes with enjoyment of property is actionable, subject to the neighbour test discussed in Chapter 2. In criminal cases, the actual word 'pollution' sometimes occurs as part of an offence. On other occasions a phrase such as 'dark smoke' will be used and the emission of this needs to be established in order to determine liability. In the case of statutory authorisations the impact of a discharge or emission on the receiving environment is always of critical importance in deciding whether an authorisation should be given, and if so, subject to what conditions.

It is helpful, therefore, to have some idea of how scientists define pollution, and how they identify and measure it.

Of the many definitions available, two are worth quoting:
(1) A. Porteous in the *Dictionary of Environmental Science and Technology* defines pollution as a substance or effect which adversely alters the environment, is toxic, or interferes with health, comfort, amenities or property values of people.
(2) The Environmental Protection Act defines pollution of the environment to mean 'pollution of the environment due to the release (into any environmental medium) from any process of substances which are capable of causing harm to man or any other living organisms supported by the environment'.

See also Chapter 6 for a discussion of how European law has defined pollution.

These definitions have in common two basic elements, namely that there is detectable effect on the environment and that there is some impact on man or on man's activities, resulting from the activity or event in question.

Having decided what pollution is, it is necessary to look at how it is identified and measured by reference to each environmental medium, although, as Fig 2 below illustrates (see page 327), polluting substances are not always limited to one environmental medium and there is considerable mobility of different forms of substances between air, land and water.

POLLUTION OF WATER

Introduction

9.23 The following comments are addressed primarily at fresh-water problems, but also apply to estuarine and coastal waters that may represent a problem to environmental groups. There are numerous definitions of water pollution, none of which is entirely satisfactory. In general terms, it is the introduction by man of substances (or heat) which are harmful to the organisms which live in water or to the organisms, including man, which depend on water. The key point is that it is caused by man and is perceived to be harmful to man—to his public health, to the ecology of natural systems that are considered worth conserving or to a resource exploited for recreation.

  (1) *Concentration.* Water pollution only occurs if the concentration of a substance after dilution by the receiving water is sufficiently strong to cause a harmful effect. Thus a small drop of a very toxic substance in a very large river is not pollution. On the other hand, a large quantity of a substance usually thought of as harmless (eg milk) introduced into a small stream can be highly polluting. Where a substance is added to the environment in quantities which do not have a noticeable harmful effect this is called contamination.

  (2) *Water abstraction.* Closely related to water pollution is water abstraction for drinking, power generation or irrigation. The abstraction can have an adverse effect similar to that of water pollution due to the reduced volume of water available for diluting any substances added to the water.

  (3) *Entry point.* Pollution can enter water at various stages of the water cycle. Thus sulphur dioxide from power station emissions or radiochemicals from nuclear power accidents can

enter the atmosphere and be washed down in rainwater far away from the source of the pollution. From the point of view of water pollution this can be considered a non-point source. Another example is the way nitrates in agriculture percolate through soil to the water table, eventually emerging in streams or water pumped from aquifers. Most water pollution, however, enters watercourses at point sources such as sewage or industrial effluent discharge pipes.

(4) *Continuous discharges.* Water pollution from continuous discharges of effluents may cause chronic pollution. Such continuous discharges are licensed by the NRA and standards are set to minimise the effect of the effluent on the environment (*see* Chapter 5). Accidental discharges are not licensed and may cause acute pollution which may be severe but, sooner or later, the receiving waters recover. Discharges at concentrations above consent limits and discharges which are not licensed may form the basis of legal action against the polluter.

(5) *Water quality objectives.* A single point source of effluent may not in itself be polluting but when considered with all the other sources of effluent in a catchment may result in a cumulative adverse effect. A river catchment needs to be considered as a whole.

The government intends to set water quality objectives for watercourses which have regard to the uses made of the water (*see* Chapter 1). These in turn will determine the standards set for effluents by the NRA and, of course, will determine the costs of meeting those standards.

Types of pollution

9.24 There are several different types of water pollution. The three main categories are direct in their effect, others are more indirect.

(1) The first category covers poisons which are directly toxic to organisms. They range from simple salts of heavy metals such as copper, lead and zinc, to more complex substances such as herbicides or pesticides. In the case of fish, the poison enters through the gills and if the concentration is sufficiently high the fish may die. The toxicity of many substances has

been established by a standard method called LC50 Test. This is the Lethal Concentration at which 50 per cent of the test fish died.

(2) A second category of pollution is suspended solids which is finely divided matter carried by water. It may originate, for example, from quarries or coal mines. The extent to which the solids are carried depends on the speed of flow of the water. The suspended particles which settle on the surface of a river may smother the plants and animals living there. The suspended solids prevent light reaching green algae and provide a habitat unsuitable for the invertebrates (eg aquatic insects), food or fish. This damages the food chain or renders it toxic to organisms higher up the chain. Moreover, in rivers inhabited by salmon and trout, the suspended solids may fill up holes between the river gravel so preventing a flow of oxygen-carrying water from reaching eggs laid there in the spawning season. Any eggs laid in this gravel would probably die.

(3) A third category of pollution is organic matter such as sewage, silage and milk. These provide nutrients for bacteria in the water enabling them to grow rapidly and multiply. In the process the bacteria absorb oxygen from the water. If organic matter degrades and becomes harmless and within the dilution capacity of the receiving water the process is called self-purification. If, however, more oxygen is removed from the water than can be replaced from the atmosphere, then there is likely to be an adverse effect on the aquatic life. Some kinds of invertebrates are more tolerant of reduced oxygen content than others and this has led to the use of biological indices to assess the pollution status of a river. Some fish, such as carp and tench, are adapted to live in water of a relatively low oxygen content whereas salmon and trout are adapted to the high oxygen content of fast-flowing rivers. The oxygen content of water may be measured as milligrams per litre. Because the amount of oxygen dissolved in water depends on temperature, the oxygen content is often given as a percentage which represents the concentration of oxygen compared with the concentration if it were fully saturated at that particular temperature. Another laboratory test for oxygen determines the demand for oxygen by the organic

matter in a sample of water. This is called the Biological
Oxygen Demand (BOD). This is a very useful and widely
used measure of water quality. A river in its natural state may
have a BOD of up to 3 mg/l whereas fully treated sewage
effluent may have a BOD of 20 mg/l before dilution in the
receiving stream. The BOD test takes five days and sometimes a quicker test is used to measure Chemical Oxygen
Demand (COD). This test involves the addition of an
oxidant and acid in order to estimate the amount of oxidiz-
able material present. The COD includes organic matter
which is not biodegradable but nevertheless it is usually a
good indication of BOD.

(4)   A fourth, and less direct, form of pollution is the enrichment
of bodies of water with the plant nutrients nitrogen and
phosphorus. This is called eutrophication. An increase in
nutrients may be caused by the use of fertilisers in agriculture, the disturbance and drainage of soils in forestry or the
effluent from sewage treatment works. The increased
concentration of nutrients in a lake, and the accumulation
and release of nutrients from sediments, can result in an
increased growth of algae to form blooms. This can affect the
food chain and species of fish, the recreational use of water
and the value of water for abstracting for drinking.

(5)   Other categories of pollution include the heated water effluent from power stations; oil pollution which may prevent
oxygen exchange at the water surface; and aesthetic pollution by non-degradable materials such as condoms and
tampons which are not harmful but are considered objec-
tionable. (Such pollution may be caused by eg storm sewage
overflows.) Aesthetic interference with private rights could
be actionable at common law.

Monitoring pollution

9.25   The effluents from permitted discharges are sampled and
analysed by the NRA for compliance with consent standards. The
NRA also samples rivers to assess the effect of effluents on the
watercourse. The results of both kinds of sampling are recorded in
a public register which is available for inspection with reasonable
notice. An example of the results of NRA monitoring of the River

Churnet, near Leek in Staffordshire, is shown in Fig 1 below. As the river flows down from its source the BOD increases from 2 mg/l to 10 mg/l due to self-purification. The biological index called Biological Monitoring Working Party (BMWP) score is based on sampling and identification of invertebrates from the bed of the river. In the River Churnet, the score reduces from about 100 to about 30 as a result of the sewage effluent. Then the score recovers downstream due to the atmosphere at the water surface. The data are now only of illustrative interest as effluent quality from Leekbrook Sewage Treatment Works has subsequently improved.

The monitoring of rivers by the NRA is limited by staff resources to, say, weekly or monthly inspections. The reporting of pollution incidents is, therefore, more likely to come from water bailiffs, anglers and general members of the public. Anglers are generally regarded as guardians of rivers and lakes. It is very important that they keep a careful written record of any pollution problem affecting their water. This will be more

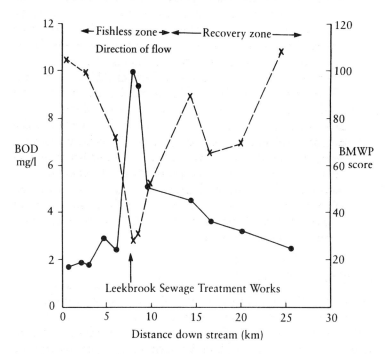

Fig 1: Mean BOD and mean BMWP scores for 1985 to 1991 for the River Churnet (from NRA public register)

accurate and credible than reliance on memory at a later date when improvements are negotiated or legal action contemplated.

POLLUTION OF LAND

Definitions of terrestrial pollution

9.26 Pollution has been defined at 9.22 above in its general sense; the term can be applied equally to the water, land and air environments. Terrestrial pollution has a number of sources, both natural and anthropogenic. As illustrated in Fig 2, polluting substances are not limited to one environmental medium and there is considerable mobility of different forms of substances between air, land and water.

Pollution of land may also be referred to as contamination, or the presence of substances at certain concentrations above a background level which may cause harm, directly or indirectly, to humans, animals, vegetation and structures. Contaminated land may also be described as 'land which represents an actual or potential hazard to health or the environment as a result of current or previous use' (DoE), or 'land containing substances, be they liquids or solids, which when present in sufficient quantities or concentrations, can cause harm directly or indirectly to man and the environment' (International Chamber of Commerce). Between 100,000 and 200,000 hectares of UK land is thought to be contaminated, of which between 1 and 4 per cent represents priority sites which are threatening the environment or human health.

The DoE issued in July 1994 an important Guidance Note entitled Planning and Pollution Control (PPG 23). This emphasised the role that planning policy is to have in 'tackling the UK's burden of land contamination'. The Department had previously issued Guidance on the Assessment and Redevelopment of Contaminated Land and is now participating in the publication of a new Guidance Programme which will be of considerable importance to all involved in land and property transactions as well as to all professional practitioners. The fact that best practice recommendations are fast emerging is of significance also to those who are occupiers of properties built on such sites or are living within the vicinity of polluted land whether or not built upon.

Sources of contamination

9.27 There are many sources of contamination, some occurring naturally, whereas others have become contaminants as a result of man's activities.

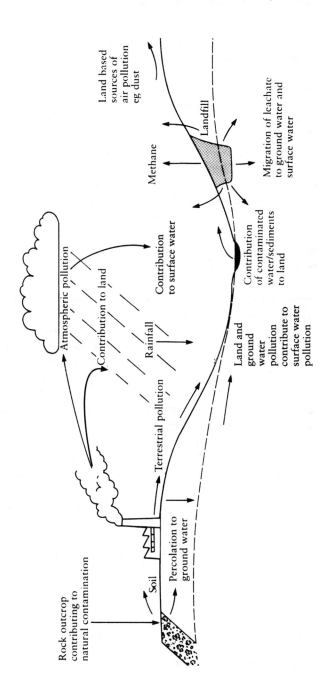

Fig 2: Sources and transport of pollutants

(1) Contamination may be due to the natural composition of the underlying rocks, which break down to form soils. For example, metals such as lead and zinc, which occur naturally, are mineralised in rocks that are exposed at the ground surface. The presence of natural contamination in the environment often leads to tolerances in animals and plants of levels higher than background levels of a particular substance. In some cases this phenomenon can be used as an indicator of the presence of particular substances, such as metals. Where plants are used in this way the process is known as geobotanical prospecting. The capacity of plants to absorb metals may also in future be utilised in programmes to clean up contaminated land, eg the use of reed beds, as may the capacity of micro-organisms such as bacteria and fungi to transform, destroy, fix or mobilise contaminants.

(2) Minerals and substances such as oils, natural gas and radon also occur naturally. It is often the extraction of these which accelerates the rate and increases the quantities of material released into the environment. For example, once lead is extracted from the ground as the mineral galena (lead sulphide) a significant amount will be available for release at the mine site in waste material from mining and processing; more will be released, possibly as particulate material, during smelting and refining; and the numerous end uses of the metal further distribute it in the environment: in lead pipes it may be released into drinking water, and as an additive to petrol it is widely dispersed to the atmosphere. The use of lead by man in coinage, industrial processes and in petrol in increasing quantities over the last few centuries is expressed *inter alia* in increasing concentrations in peat which have accumulated during that time in upland areas such as the Peak District. This is due to the increasing deposition rates of particulate lead from smelting, refining and the use of motor vehicles.

(3) Many more complex substances which occur naturally in small quantities have become important as pollutants, because man's actions have led to the much greater concentrations of these substances which are found in the environment today. Other sources of contamination are totally anthropogenic substances which do not occur in nature.

Many of the pollutants are dispersed by water, through

the hydrological cycle of rainfall, runoff and infiltration to groundwater (recharge) and surface water; by air, through wind-dispersed particulate and gaseous matter; and also by direct deposition by man, as in landfill sites and the uncontrolled dumping of waste or unwanted materials. These routes can all lead to pollution of land and groundwater or damage to the land surface.

(4) Landfill sites, as mentioned above, can prove a significant source of contamination, particularly older sites where management practices were less controlled than they are today. Sites are generally in old excavations such as sand and gravel or clay pits or quarries which have been operated according to two principles, either 'dilute and disperse' or 'containment'. Old sites were almost exclusively 'dilute and disperse', in which water percolating through the waste (which will initially absorb liquids up to its capacity) is allowed to move through the base and sides of the site away from the dumping area. This leachate frequently becomes grossly contaminated from contact with the waste, which may be of industrial or domestic origin, and migration of this causes pollution off site, in both ground and surface water. Methane is also produced as part of the ageing process of the waste, and can cause atmospheric pollution (methane is a gaseous hydrocarbon) and damage to surface vegetation as well as creating a hazard to development and nearby facilities due to its explosive properties at certain concentrations.

Significance of contamination

9.28 Pollutants are often described as phytotoxic or zootoxic, ie toxic to plants or to animals. The levels at which pollutants become hazardous will depend on the use of the land and the potential exposure and susceptibility of humans, plants, animals and structures to the pollutant, ie the risk of harm. The Interdepartmental Committee on the Redevelopment of Contaminated Land (ICRCL) has issued a number of guidance notes recommending 'threshold' and 'action' trigger concentrations for a number of contaminants and a range of end uses. The 'threshold' concentration is set at a level below which the site can be considered uncontaminated, but above which remedial action may be necessary. The 'action' concentration represents a level at which remedial action will be required or the form of development (end use) changed.

As mentioned above, the risk posed by a certain level of contamination depends to a large extent on the use of the land. For example, soil used for growing vegetables should generally have a lower level of contamination than ground which will be covered by a hard surface such as a road or a tennis court, as the potential for the contaminant to move into the food chain is much greater. In addition, different sorts of plant, different animals and human individuals respond differently to the same pollutant.

Identification of contamination

9.29 There are a number of methods by which to identify pollution of land from manmade sources. These include:

(a) a visual inspection of the land—often old buildings and structures and obviously non-natural landforms will provide information about the past uses of land and therefore the types of contaminants which may be found there;

(b) old maps and plans may reveal further detail about the activities carried on in a particular location.

There are of course exceptions, where no visual evidence or records exist, and buried materials are discovered on an apparently green field site.

A variety of site investigation methods exist for sampling potentially polluted sites for the presence of contaminants. These include:

(a) trial pits and trenches;

(b) surface soil samples;

(c) samples taken from depth by means of drilling or auguring.

The site investigations are usually logged, so that soil profiles and any unusual appearance or odour are recorded.

The levels of pollution are measured through the analysis of samples collected from across the surface of a site and also at depth, as mentioned above. Sometimes these pits or boreholes may intersect the groundwater level, which can become polluted as a result of the movement of surface contaminants down through the soil profiles as a result of rainfall recharging. Such substances may become more mobile on contact with groundwater, causing or allowing movement of the contaminants outside the original contaminated site boundaries. Uncontaminated land may thus become polluted by groundwater. Similarly, contaminated surface water may be a source of pollution to land which becomes inundated. For example, the flood plains of a river have been polluted by metals carried by the river from mining operations upstream.

Samples for analysis must be collected and analysed in different ways depending on the contaminants involved and the form in which they are present: as solids, absorbed into the soil particles, as a solution in groundwater, as a gas or vapour in the soil pores or as an immiscible liquid (one that cannot be mixed).

Measurements are usually expressed as a concentration, frequently the weight of a contaminant in a particular weight of soil, for example milligrams per kilogram (mg/kg) or micrograms per gram (µg/g). These measurements may also be expressed as parts per million (ppm), while greater concentrations of substances may be expressed as percentages. Results are often expressed as 'total' or 'available'. This is particularly important for some contaminants such as chromium, where one form of the metal (hexavelant in the case of chromium) is much more soluble and therefore available. Hexavelant chromium is approximately one hundred times more toxic than the non-soluble trivalent form. (*See* Chapter 10)

POLLUTION OF AIR

9.30 Most areas of human activity, from agriculture to transport and industry, produce a number of by-products which are released into the atmosphere. Thus anthropogenic releases into the atmosphere have often been responsible for degrading air quality, sometimes resulting in lethal local concentrations of airborne pollutants, as during the London smog episode in December 1952.

Sources of air pollution or contamination

9.31 Areas of potential concern in the field of air quality are broad and cover releases of a wide variety of material from a multitude of differing sources and producing various effects over a considerable range of distances. Major sources of releases into the atmosphere include, for instance, small- and large-scale industry, traffic and domestic sources. Airborne contaminants may consist of:

(a) gases (such as, sulphur dioxide, oxides of nitrogen or volatile organic compounds);
(b) particulate matter (such as fine dust);
(c) radioactive material.

The resulting nuisances include:

(a) increases in airborne concentrations of chemical species;

  (b) deposition of gaseous or particulate matter to the ground;
  (c) degradation in visibility due to particulate or water vapour;
  (d) odour;
  (e) noise.

If released in sufficient quantities, or over a protracted period, contaminant material released into the atmosphere may degrade the local environment or pose threats to human, animal or plant health in either the short or long term and would then normally be classified as a pollutant. Clearly, though, the distinction between a contaminant and a pollutant is based on an assessment of the adverse effects of each material and is often based on only a limited understanding.

Dispersal

9.32   Any species released into the atmosphere will be carried downwind and dispersed under the influence of atmospheric turbulence (the 'gustiness' in the wind). Thus the airborne concentration of the contaminant gradually decreases downwind as the pollutant becomes diluted. Where a source is elevated, the ground level concentration may be expected to reach a maximum value some distance downwind when the plume has broadened sufficiently to reach the ground. On passing downwind the pollutant may be washed out by rain or deposited to the ground or, in the case of coarser particulate matter, may gradually settle out under the influence of gravity.

Chemical transformation

9.33   Pollutants may also undergo chemical transformations to produce secondary species such as, for instance, the products associated with the photochemical smogs which may result from traffic emissions or the acidic products often classified as 'acid rain'. In the longer term, any pollutants which have not been washed out or deposited to the ground may be carried into the upper atmosphere as in the case of the CFCs which are responsible for ozone depletion. Many of the latter problems, of course, result in trans-national or global pollution and are principally the concern of negotiation at inter-government level.

Dispersal rate

9.34   The rate at which material is dispersed in the atmosphere is determined by the local terrain and also by the prevailing atmospheric structure and may vary quite considerably. Thus, the large local airborne concentrations associated with pollution episodes often result from specific, unusual atmospheric conditions rather than from exceptionally large releases of pollutant. The dispersion of material may also be dramatically altered by the presence of buildings (producing, in extreme cases, 'canyon' effects in urban areas) or by significant local physical features such as mountains. In many cases, of course, the resulting pollutant concentration is superimposed on a background value generated either by 'natural' or biogenic sources or by a variety of other, often unidentified, sources.

Table 1   Air quality guidelines specified by EC and WHO to protect human health

Guideline	Sulphur dioxide concentration (pg/m^3)	Nitrogen dioxide concentration (pg/m^3)
EC guide value annual mean	40–60	
98th percentile		135[b]
EC limit value 98th percentile	350[a]	200[b]
WHO guideline 1 hr mean	350	400

Notes

[a]: expressed as percentile of daily mean values throughout the year.
[b]: expressed as percentile of hourly mean values throughout the year.

Gaseous emissions

9.35   The major area of concern for gaseous emissions is the increase in airborne concentrations in areas relatively close to the source. This may result in potential damage to human or plant life or, in some cases, in damage to local structures. As the atmospheric concentrations resulting from even a constant emission may vary so much, it is normal to specify guideline limits for airborne concentrations of pollutants both in terms of an annual average and also some measure of the largest concentration of the pollutant likely to be encountered. The 98th percentile is often used for the latter purpose and represents the concentration of the specified pollutant that is not expected to be exceeded for 98 per cent of the time. Guideline limits for sulphur dioxide and nitrogen dioxide (both typical combustion products) set by the EC and WHO are shown in Table 1. Similar guidelines are available for other materials.

Particulate matter

9.36   The behaviour of particulate matter is largely determined by the size and density of the particles. Coarse particles, with a diameter greater typically than 30pm (1pm+1/1000 mm), will settle out under the influence of gravity and will be gradually deposited to the ground. Smaller particles, on the other hand, will remain suspended in the air and will be transported in a similar fashion to a gaseous contaminant. Of particular concern as regards air quality are particles with a diameter of less than 10pm. These may be readily inhaled and are often referred to as PM_{10} material or, occasionally, IPM (inhalable particulate matter).

The comprehensive monitoring of air quality throughout the country would be an impossible task. Continuous air quality records are, however, maintained at a number of sites. Urban air quality is currently an area of concern due to the increase in motor traffic, and pollutant levels are monitored at a number of sites in selected major cities, providing measurements of concentrations of PM_{10}, oxides of nitrogen and sulphur, ozone, carbon monoxide and various volatile organic compounds. The Commons Transport Committee has issued its own report on unleaded petrol ('Transport Related Air Pollution' HMSO) and the Royal Commission on Environmental Pollution has also separately confirmed its study of the impact of the car on the environment (both October 1994). Both reports highlight concerns over the discharge of pollutants into the atmosphere and the health consequences of this.

SAMPLING

9.37   In both common law and criminal cases considerable reliance is placed on samples taken and analysed for the purpose of demonstrating any given form of pollution.

This is of particular relevance in criminal prosecutions, where a single sample is relied on.

Chapter 5 looked at the question of evidence in private prosecutions. In some cases it is possible to rely on samples taken by regulatory authorities. In other cases an expert should be instructed to arrange for the analysis of samples. The best way to find a suitable analyst is through the advice of a relevant expert.

Wherever independent analysis of samples is to be undertaken, it is crucial to choose an analyst who has the expertise to analyse the sample effectively and reliably, and to ensure that he understands how the sample is to be taken, transported and analysed. It is also crucial that the degree of accuracy of the sample results is understood. Some methods of analysis are highly accurate whereas others have a considerable margin for error.

It should be borne in mind that an analyst is likely to be called to give evidence and be cross-examined. As with experts, an analyst must have the ability to give good quality evidence and must be independent.

Anyone employing an analyst should first ascertain whether he has approval from the National Measurement Accreditation Service for the specific type of analysis to be carried out.

ENVIRONMENTAL INFORMATION

INTRODUCTION

9.38   There have been numerous references in the text to the importance of securing good quality information as a prerequisite to preparing a case and working with experts. The remainder of this chapter is dedicated to describing what environmental information is available; what restrictions are placed on the release of such information and what powers exist to secure access to it; and where that information can be found. It looks first at the Environmental Information Regulations, which apply to all forms of environmental information, and then at the availability of information in respect of each of the environmental media.

Statutory or other bodies may hold information outside the scope specified in the Regulations. In many cases they are willing to supply that information provided it is not commercially sensitive or confidential.

Most institutions now make a charge for the supply of information. Often this is limited to photocopying charges, although sometimes an administration charge is made. Where extensive information is required, it is advisable to obtain at least an approximate indication of the charge.

Just as most cases are dependent on good quality expert evidence, they are equally dependent on collating the raw material that the experts need to prepare a report. In some cases it will be necessary for the expert to carry out sampling and survey work to build up the evidence needed to allow informed comment. In all cases, though, either exclusively or in conjunction with freshly obtained material, an expert will need to have access to historical raw data, reports, and other documents containing sufficient information to enable conclusions to be drawn. Clearly in many cases information will already be in the hands of those instructing the experts. Often, though, it will be necessary to obtain substantial amounts of information from other parties, particularly public bodies, as well as to secure information on discovery in civil actions.

The Environmental Information Regulations (**SI 1992 No 3240**)

Introduction

9.39   The Environmental Information Regulations 1992 came into force on 31 December 1992. They implemented the European Council Directive of 7 June 1990 (90/313/EEC). The government took full advantage of the period allowed for implementation, the deadline being the date they came into operation. The purpose of the directive, as stated in art 1, is to 'ensure freedom of access to, and dissemination of, information on the environment held by public authorities and to set out the basic terms and conditions on which such information should be made available'. In essence, it directs various bodies to make environmental information available to the public upon request.

Who is affected by the regulations?

9.40   The bodies covered by the regulations fall into two categories:
  (a) central government departments, ministers, local authorities and those carrying out the functions of public administration at a national, regional or local level which have responsibilities in relation to the environment;
  (b) bodies which have public responsibilities for the environ-

ment. This catches both public and private sector bodies placed under a statutory duty such as the NRA, English Nature, the Countryside Council for Wales and the Royal Botanic Gardens. The Regulations do not list the bodies themselves and, in the cases where such bodies refuse to divulge information, the courts will be called upon to decide. The *Griffin case* (*see* Chapter 6.26) considered the question of whether water companies were public bodies for the purpose of an EC Employment Directive. It was decided that the company fell within the parameters set out in *Foster v British Gas* (*see* Chapter 6). Since it is clear that water companies have public responsibilities for the environment, it is submitted that they are bodies that will be liable to disclose environmental information under this Directive.

What information must be released?

9.41 Environmental information is that which concerns 'the state of any water or air, the state of any flora or fauna, the state of any soil, or the state of any national site or other land' [and] 'any activities . . . which adversely affect . . . or are likely adversely to affect . . . [those matters and] 'any activities . . . which are designed to protect . . .' those matters. This includes information whether or not obtained as a result of the body's environmental responsibilities, information collected before the Regulations came into force, information held in written, visual, aural, or database form, documents, pictures, maps and records.

Who may request information?

9.42 Any person or company may apply for the disclosure of the information and the body supplying the information may make a charge for it so long as the charge does not exceed the cost reasonably attributable to the supply. The body must reply to a request for information within two months but it may refuse the request. There is no qualification which the applicant has to satisfy to become entitled to information. Thus if the body supplying the information is a relevant body and no ground exists for it to release the information, then the applicant does not have to establish any locus for the request.

Grounds for refusal

9.43 Regulation 4 lists the grounds upon which a body may refuse to disclose information:

(1) *Discretionary grounds.* There are five discretionary grounds:

  (a) information relating to matters affecting international relations: this includes any information or documents obtained from a state other than the UK, national defence and information affecting public security;

  (b) information which is or has been the subject-matter of any legal or other proceedings whether actual or prospective: examples include information collected and to be used for the purpose of criminal proceedings, or information which would deprive a person of a right to a fair trial;

  (c) information relating to the confidential deliberations of any body may be withheld: this includes the background deliberations, papers and reports leading to policy statements or decisions which would not normally be released but not those matters of a purely administrative or routine nature;

  (d) information contained in a document still in the course of completion;

  (e) commercially confidential information. There will be circumstances where the disclosure of information will prejudice the commercial interests of an individual or business. This will include information received from a third party under contract or by statute. In such circumstances there are no hard and fast rules but it will be appropriate to withhold information if disclosure might damage the reputation of the body supplying the information and, therefore, leave the third party open to legal action if it wrongfully releases information.

(2) *Mandatory grounds.* There are four cases where confidential information must be withheld:

  (a) where its disclosure would contravene any statutory provision or rule of law or would involve a breach of any agreement;

  (b) where it is personal information in relation to an individual who has not given consent to the disclosure;

  (c) where information has been voluntarily supplied and the person has not consented to its disclosure;

  (d) where disclosure may lead to the likelihood of damage to the environment.

If an individual is dissatisfied with the reasons given for non-disclosure then he may appeal to the head of the body concerned, or to the local government ombudsman if it is a local authority, to his MP or, if this fails, he may take an action through the courts.

These exceptions give a very broad discretion to bodies to refuse to disclose information. They are very wide-ranging and provide convenient and extensive grounds upon which to base a refusal. The basis of any legal challenge of a refusal to supply information would be by way of judicial review of the decision. It will take decided cases to clarify the breadth of some of the exceptions.

Chapter 7 considered the implications of the 'proceedings' exemption (1(b)) in the Regulations. It was submitted that there is much need for clarification of the impact of the directive in practical terms.

INFORMATION AND WATER

Water registers

9.44 Section 190(1) of the Water Resources Act (WRA) imposes a duty on the NRA to maintain a public register of information held by it. The register is governed by the Control of Pollution (Registers) Regulations 1989 (SI 1989 No 1660). The registers must be available for inspection free of charge by the public at all reasonable times. Copies of entries must be supplied on request, subject to payment of reasonable charges.

The register must contain, *inter alia*, the following categories of information:

(a) details of all applications for consents to the NRA;
(b) details of consents, including conditions to which they are subject;
(c) information relating to the analysis of all samples taken by the NRA, whether of effluent or waters, taken in connection with the authority's pollution control functions under the WRA;
(d) details of all authorisations granted by HMIP under the EPA.

Each of the eight NRA regions maintains its own register. (See Appendix 1 for the addresses of the NRA regional offices.) Most of the information is kept on computer. While the presentation of computer-generated information has improved, it is still often quite difficult to digest and members of the public may require some assistance in understanding abbreviations and generally decoding entries, from either experts or NRA officers. Officers are invariably helpful in discussing information and its implications.

Other information

9.45   The NRA holds a great deal of additional information, which may be invaluable in the preparation of a case. The NRA carries out surveys on a rolling basis on most watercourses, dealing with such matters as plant life, macroinvertebrates, water quality and fisheries. The NRA is usually co-operative in supplying data of this kind, and in any event it is of the type that is disclosable under the Environmental Information Regulations (*see* above).

The NRA has published a leaflet giving guidance on the register of trade and sewage effluent discharge consents open to public inspection. It gives information on what the register contains, when and how it may be inspected, and details of NRA offices. It should be noted that information concerning drinking water and trade effluent consents is held by the water undertakers, *see* Chapter 1.

Section 204 of the WRA prohibits the disclosure of information by the NRA which relates to the business affairs of any individual or company, except in the case of a series of exceptions listed at s 204(2). The most relevant of these are:

   (i) for the purposes of investigation of a criminal offence;

  (j) for the purposes of any civil proceedings brought under or by virtue of the Act; and

  (k) in pursuance of a community obligation.

PUBLIC REGISTERS AND IPC AND APC

9.46   Section 20 of the EPA requires the keeping of public registers of information. The register will be maintained by local authorities and HMIP but the local authority register must keep information relating to processes regulated by HMIP to ensure that the register information is available locally (s 20(2), EPA). The prescribed information includes:

  (a) applications for authorisations;

  (b) authorisations which have been granted;

  (c) variation, prohibition, enforcement and revocation notices;

(d) appeals under s 15;

(e) details of any convictions under s 23;

(f) monitoring information where the information is collected by the enforcing authority or the operator of the process and provided to the authority in compliance with a condition of an authorisation. In any case where monitoring information is exempted from the register by reason of commercial confidentiality instead a statement as to whether the monitoring indicates compliance with any relevant condition in the authorisation;

(g) particulars of any environmental assessment, carried out by the enforcing authority, of the consequences to a locality of carrying out a prescribed process in that locality;

(h) details of any directions given by the Secretary of State under the extensive retained powers in Part I of the Act.

The registers are maintained by HMIP at the offices shown in Appendix 1. HMIP also operates an automatic fax service whereby information can be transmitted automatically through the fax by keying in relevant digits on a press button phone.

Exclusions and exemptions

9.47 Information may be excluded from the register by direction of the Secretary of State for reasons of national security. In addition, and more importantly in view of the technical nature of authorisation and control, information may be excluded because it is commercially confidential. Commercial confidentiality may be claimed where its presence in the register would prejudice to an unreasonable degree the commercial interests of the person claiming the exemption (s 22(11), EPA). This seems to include a balancing of commercial prejudice against public interest.

If a business claims confidentiality, on application for an authorisation or at any other time (eg when monitoring information is submitted), it may request exemption from inclusion in the register. The enforcing authority has 14 days to determine whether information is confidential. If it fails to respond then it is deemed to be confidential. An appeal may be entered (within 21 days of the adverse decision) if an application for confidentiality is refused. If an appeal is made the information shall not be entered in the register until the Secretary of State has made his decision. On appeal the Secretary of

State may direct that information should be included in the register even though commercially confidential in the public interest (s 22(7), EPA).

Generally, if information is excluded from the register by reason of national security or commercial confidentiality it is not the subject of statutory consultation. There are, however, exceptions to this general rule in Reg 7(3) of the Environmental Protection (Applications, Appeals and Registers) Regulations 1991.

Chemical Release Inventory

9.48 This is not a statutory register but a proposed register of information to be held by HMIP and to be compiled from the IPC and APC registers and other information held by HMIP on radioactive substances. The inventory will provide useful information and analysis of the total amounts of chemical releases and radioactive substances releases.

Clean Air Act 1993

9.49 The Control of Atmospheric Pollution (Research and Publicity) Regulations 1977 require information specified in the Regulations and collated under Part V of the Clean Air Act 1993 (*see* Chapter 1) (formerly ss 79–84 of the Control of Pollution Act 1974) to be kept in a public register. The details to be placed on the register include information acquired under ss 35 and 36 of the 1993 Act and details of appeals under s 37 of the Act.

Control of Pollution Act 1974 and noise

9.50 Registers of information about noise abatement zones (*see* Chapter 1) are to be kept by local authorities. The register must include details of noise level measurements taken in accordance with the Control of Noise (Measurement and Registers) Regulations 1976. This sets the level of noise which may not be exceeded without consent or committing an offence.

Air quality monitoring

9.51 Air quality monitoring is required in respect of sulphur dioxide, nitrogen dioxide and lead by virtue of the Air Quality

Standards Regulations 1989. Although these regulations do not include rights to public inspection of the data it seems very likely that such information will be covered by the Environmental Information Regulations 1992.

Contaminated land registers

9.52   In March 1993 the Secretary of State for the Environment announced that in the light of widespread opposition the government was abandoning its proposals to introduce registers of contaminative land uses which had been provided for by s 143 of the EPA. The intention had been to establish a series of registers, held by local authorities and open to public inspection, which would record which land in their area was contaminated and by what. Opposition from surveyors, property developers, insurers, bankers and industry covered a number of areas:

(a)   the problem of blight: if a plot of land was included in the register this would deter potential purchasers and render the land unusable;

(b)   the definition of a contaminative use: although the DoE cut the number of such uses to 40, objectors were not reassured;

(c)   there was no provision to remove a site from the register if it was cleaned up;

(d)   there was no provision as to who should clean up a contaminated site, to what standard and who should bear the costs.

In the face of such objections the government decided not to proceed although it did confirm its intention to ensure that land contamination does not give rise to unacceptable risks to health and safety, to groundwater and the environment generally.

The recent series of commentaries and recommendations by DoE (*see* 9.26 above) does, however, indicate growing government awareness of the need to keep this topic well under review.

Registers held by waste regulation and waste collection authorities

9.53   While the contaminated land registers would have been a valuable source of information for the public, s 64 of the Act places a duty upon waste regulation authorities (WRA) to maintain a register of all current or recently current waste management licences. These registers will also contain information regarding modification of licences, supervisions, revocations, the imposition of requirements, appeals and convictions of licence holders and any action taken by the WRA under s 42 of the Act.

Information may be excluded on the basis of national security or commercial confidentiality. The Secretary of State has issued guidelines regarding the latter; the overriding principle is that an individual must show that the disclosure of such information would negate or significantly diminish the commercial advantage that he has over a competitor. Indeed, the person supplying the information may ask the WRA to exclude the information on the grounds that it is commercially confidential. The onus is also placed upon the WRA to inform a person that it thinks the information supplied is confidential.

Regulation 11 of the Waste Management Licensing Regulations 1994 provides for certain information to be excluded from the registers, such as information which is the subject-matter of criminal proceedings, any monitoring information obtained by a WRA after a period of four years has elapsed, or information on the exercise of a waste inspector's powers under s 69(3) of the Act. Where information has been excluded under s 66 of the Act, a statement based on that information showing whether there has been compliance with a condition of a waste management licence should be made.

Waste collection authorities which are not WRAs must keep registers relating to the keeping, treatment or disposal of controlled waste within their area.

Lastly, litter authorities must maintain a register of litter control areas and street litter notices. This register must be available for public inspection.

INFORMATION AND PLANNING

9.54 There are two principal sources of information in planning cases.

The planning register

9.55 Under s 69 of the Town and Country Planning Act 1990 every local authority is obliged to maintain a register of such information as is prescribed by a development order. Practically speaking, this will include copies of all applications for planning permission, of accompanying plans, and where applicable of decisions made.

Local Government Act 1972

9.56   Section 100 A–G sets out various categories of information that a local authority must make available to the general public. These are as follows:

  (a) copies of the agenda for a meeting of the council and of any reports submitted for that meeting (s 100 B);
  (b) copies of minutes of meetings once held (s 100 C);
  (c) copies of background papers relevant to the consideration of a given issue by the council when it met (s 100 D).

These obligations apply to meetings of the full council or a committee or a subcommittee. Section 100 A also contains details of the rights of the public to attend meetings of the council.

CHAPTER 10

FUNDING, FINANCE AND ECONOMICS

INTRODUCTION

10.1   The availability of funds and the cost of raising money affect both those who cause damage and those who suffer from damage. This chapter examines first the principles and elements of costs likely to be encountered by the prospective litigant or community group wishing to preserve or protect its amenities and those of the locality and discusses various fund-raising avenues. It then proceeds to an examination of the responsibility for damage, the burden of clean-up or compensation, how and where this does or should fall and the practical implications of this. Finally it looks at the question of priorities—those of the government and of society—and at the implications of the European influence, and offers some thoughts on future developments.

CONSTRUCTING THE ARGUMENT

PREPARATION

10.2   In order to present the issues of any campaign effectively, it is obviously necessary for a group to devote sufficient effort, and money, to fund-raising and enlisting support.

Information prepared with the intention of gaining the attention and support of those of like mind as well as those directing the regulatory authorities should comprise the essentials of the problem, its relevance to the locality, the likely consequences and, where possible, the legal implications as well as a preliminary view from experts. Such material is best prepared with the assistance of professionals and clearly the *pro bono* support of the practitioner members of ELF provides an immediate benefit. Other sources of free or low-cost advice are considered below.

Where possible, the material should include the results of a study or report, even though that presupposes some expenditure (on the expert, travel time, any surveying or testing for conclusions). Plans, photographs and models, if available, are well worth including, as these can produce a sense of immediacy. The legal view is generally dependent upon expert evidence and it could be that the early stage of an investigation produces an argument in principle rather than detail, but even to obtain that could involve the engagement of specialist counsel as well as solicitors.

It is important to recognise the cost to members of a campaign group, particularly the few who form the galvanising force, of supplying their time, as well as their reduced earning power. Additional costs include those for the preparation and distribution of material and information (telephone, postage, paper, and, increasingly, fax and word processing). The more that can be provided voluntarily the better and making such facilities available as part of the division of labour within a group can be invaluable.

FINANCIAL IMPLICATIONS

10.3 This section looks at the range of costs likely to be incurred in pursuing the various remedies dealt with in this book. The next section considers the principles upon which costs might be awarded. These differ, depending on where and how the issue is being argued.

It is important that those involved in campaigns, or practitioners advising them, remember that the charging rates of lawyers and experts vary throughout the country and are influenced by a number of factors. With this proviso, the authors suggest, with some hesitation, likely levels of costs in the belief that, whatever the national, or indeed local, variance, these do offer a yardstick for assessing the *sort* of range of costs involved even if it is only illustrative. In *all* cases, it is essential that those involved discuss and agree charges and, if an amount is agreed, that there is a clear understanding of *precisely* what work this covers.

County court and High Court costs

10.4   How costs develop, indeed accelerate, depends very much upon the forum that is used. The county court now has increased jurisdiction (see Chapter 2) and although proceedings in this forum are likely to be cheaper overall than High Court proceedings, it remains essential to establish the charging rate of all professionals involved. Assuming the use of one expert witness, counsel and, say, a two/three-day hearing, costs calculated on going rates (August 1994) could be anywhere between £3,000 and £10,000 depending upon the complexity of the case: legal aid charges should be one-third or so less.

This calculation assumes that the case goes to trial: experience shows, however, that whereas the initial steps in the proceedings have to be fully prepared and presented and, therefore, budgeted for, in most cases a settlement is reached before going to a hearing. In those circumstances the costs could be around 50 per cent or less of the figures given. This will depend, of course, upon the terms of the negotiated settlement and whether there is any contribution to be made by the other side. In any event, remember that all cases develop in stages and payment can be provided on a staged basis.

The costs of a similar case in the High Court, where the issues are likely to be more complex than those dealt with at county court level, and the remedy sought greater, could vary between £10,000 and £20,000. Such a case would obviously involve more witnesses and more court days. The cost figure assumes the interlocutory proceedings (ie the procedural steps leading up to the hearing) are straightforward and leading counsel is not needed. A complicated case requiring the employment of leading counsel could cost much more. Again, this assumes the case goes to trial.

Ex parte injunction applications, proceeding by way of affidavit, could cost around £3,000 in the county court and around £5,000 in the High Court, depending on the extent of expert involvement. It has to be borne in mind that if the injunction is refused at the actual hearing of the case then liability for the defendant's costs will also arise. Generally, but not always, the defendant's case will cost less to present than that of the plaintiff.

10.5 The costs of representation at a public inquiry, such as a planning inquiry, are more difficult to assess. Such representation necessitates preliminary work, early consultation with all the professionals involved, settlement of papers, the collation of information, co-ordination of the various persons involved and the different interests represented and final preparation of the case. The most difficult factor to assess is the length of the inquiry itself.

In principle, any person having a local interest can be heard at an inquiry, can ask questions and make representations. Such an objector can be professionally represented and give evidence but is then subject to cross-examination. The most desirable course is for a group of objectors to work through a single practitioner, namely a solicitor or other consultant. They are thereby recognised at the outset as having status in the inquiry and are entitled to receive copies of all papers as they are produced and they can be involved as one of the primary parties to the event.

Again, the costs depend on the number and nature of experts to be called, whether leading counsel needs to be employed. Another cost that is difficult to assess is that of expert evidence brought by the applicant for planning permission and the planning authority in its opposition. On average a planning inquiry lasts two or three days (although major inquiries can last three months and more). In the average case, costs will range from £9,000 to £12,000 but could well be more!

In most cases objectors have a fixed budget based on actual money collected and therefore have to decide what level of professional expertise they can afford and the precise role that those professionals are to play. The experience of ELF has been that groups can make progress if they concentrate upon a single aspect of the issues under debate and that money spent on co-ordinating the objectors' arguments is often the most productive. Chapter 3 deals more fully with the whole issue of inquiries.

10.6 Where possible and appropriate, the enforcement of rights should be argued through the regulatory authorities, rather than by private effort, as was recommended in Chapters 4 and 8.

There are many cases where this is not possible, but recourse to such an authority for part of a remedy or even as part of an overall strategy can often reduce cost and produce results.

Example

An example of a case where the regulatory authorities intervened is that of the Hillingdon Hospital incinerator. Here ELF support of a local action group resulted in the London Waste Regulatory Authority (LWRA) and HMIP intervening. The operating company was prosecuted, with certain officers of the company being joined as co-defendants. HMIP insisted on remedial work to the plant to improve emission levels.

Where a group aims to involve a regulatory authority, it is important, as indicated elsewhere, that the members of it get their facts right and enlist the support of professionals to ensure that their written representations are authoritative. An effective tactic that should ensure that a matter is not ignored is to send copies of letters to the local MP and the media and to state that this action is being taken. A good proportion of ELF casework in fact involves turning groups in the right direction and assisting in the drafting of letters and representations.

PLANNING AUTHORITIES

10.7   Objectors can sometimes provide information at an early stage which results in a refusal of planning consent, so putting the regulator at one with the objectors. Where there is a failure to comply with a licence for an authorisation or an operation is proceeding without any approval, then enforcement could involve prosecution and certainly result in the cessation of the operation. Objectors can also seek to press the authority to take steps through the courts by way of judicial review (usually in the High Court, for the costs of which see above), or they can initiate a private prosecution. A prosecution is generally in the magistrates' court but can move on to the Crown court, the cost of which, again, will vary but it is unlikely to be less than £2,000 and probably closer to £4,000/£5,000. It has to be recognised that the cost of a complex prosecution can be very high: the British Coal prosecution referred to in Chapter 5 involved a six figure claim for costs out of central funds.

10.8   None of these figures for costs include any allowance for the time of the members of the action group. Nor do they include opponent's costs which could be awarded (*see* below). Against that, costs could be awarded in favour of the applicant and such an award will offset a proportion of monies expended. It is usual for between 60 and 80 per cent of taxed costs to be recovered, leaving a shortfall that has to be funded.

The working out of a budget and keeping within its constraints is important as well as maintaining a dialogue with all professionals to ensure that they are adhering to this budget.

PRINCIPLES OF COSTS

INTRODUCTION

10.9   The ability to recover costs is a very relevant factor in initiating environmental litigation. Four broad categories of cases have been identified previously, and the principles governing the determination of costs of each category are as follows.

Common law cases

10.10   In common law cases the usual principle of costs will apply, namely, that costs follow the event. The benefit of this principle is that it ensures the recovery of the greater part of the costs if the case is successful; conversely, there is the risk of having to pay the costs of both sides if the case is lost.

Criminal prosecutions

10.11   In criminal prosecutions the same principle applies if the prosecution succeeds, but assessed costs in the magistrates' and Crown courts can often be less generous than civil taxations. However, if a case is unsuccessful, there is still a good chance that the court will order costs to be paid out of central funds even where the prosecution does not proceed beyond the committal stage.

The authority for this is s 17(1) of the Prosecution of Offences Act 1985 which provides that the court may order the payment of costs out of central funds in any proceedings in respect of an indict-able offence. Practice Direction (Crime: Costs) [1991] 1 WLR 498 provides that discretion ought to be exercised in favour of a private prosecutor except where there is a good reason for not so doing. Since the defence always has the opportunity to challenge the valid-ity of a prosecution on committal, it is submitted that it is very unlikely that costs would not be ordered out of central funds in a case that has been committed to the Crown court.

It ought, though, to be emphasised that the court has the power to order payment of defence costs by the prosecution. It will be evident from the above that this is only likely to happen in cases where a prosecution has been irresponsibly brought. The court can also order defence costs, as well as prosecution costs, to be paid out of central funds.

In statutory nuisance claims, s 82(12) of the EPA provides that the court shall make an order for costs where the alleged nuisance is proved. The Act does not state the position when the nuisance is not proved.

Planning and authorisation cases

10.12   In planning and authorisation cases the general rule is that there is no award of costs. There is some limited power vested in planning inspectors to award costs in inquiries and planning appeals. However, such awards are invariably made in favour of the applicant or the planning authority. It is very unlikely that any award of costs would be made in favour of objectors. In authorisa-tion applications and appeals there is no provision for awarding costs. Where planning or authorisations are referred to the High Court under statutory appeals procedures, the common law princi-ple of costs following the event apply. *See* Chapter 3 for further comment on awards of costs in planning cases.

Judicial review proceedings

10.13   In judicial review proceedings, the same principles apply as in common law cases. There are, however, signs that, when the issue raised is one of public importance, and where the applicant is, to some degree, acting *pro bono publico*, the courts are now more willing to exercise their discretion as to what order for costs should be made in favour of unsuccessful applicants. The recent application by Greenpeace for judicial review in relation to the Thorpe reprocessing plant is a good example. In this case no order for costs was made against Greenpeace.

A number of environmental groups made a joint submission to a recent consultation paper on the future of judicial review, and proposed that, where there is public interest in the outcome of a review which extends beyond the interest of the applicant itself then there should be a presumption that an award of costs against the unsuccessful applicant is unwarranted.

THE INDEMNITY PRINCIPLE

10.14 A case recently highlighted by the Law Society demonstrates the principle that the purpose of an order for costs made by a court is to indemnify the successful party for the expense it has incurred in fighting the case. This means that if there is no contractual liability on a client to pay his solicitor, then there is nothing to indemnify.

In that case a solicitor took on a statutory nuisance claim, for which legal aid is not available, knowing the client was not in a position to pay the fees, but on the basis that the chances of success were so great that the solicitor was content to settle his own fees from any costs order that was made by the magistrates. The defendants appealed the order for costs made by the magistrates on the basis that the complainant had no contractual liability to pay fees to the solicitor. Given the way in which the arrangement had been made with the client, the solicitor had to accept that there was no obligation to pay, and therefore the indemnity principle did not apply.

While the use of contingency fee arrangements remains unlawful, this situation remains a potentially dangerous trap. The Law Society is keen to see the question tried again since there is earlier case law which suggests that the issue is not as clearcut as it might appear.

In practice lawyers will, on occasions, find themselves drawn into proceeding with a case notwithstanding that the only prospect for payment will be from the defendant. In those instances there are precautionary steps that can be taken to avoid falling into the trap while maximising scope for acting for impecunious parties where legal aid is not available.

It is highly advisable to have clear agreement in correspondence as to the payment of fees and how they will be charged. It is quite proper to state in that agreement that, if the costs are not indemnified by the unsuccessful party, those fees can be paid by instalments to be agreed. It is always open to a solicitor to waive his contractual entitlement to collect fees, or to agree a reduction. The trap for the client still remains, however, because the solicitor cannot agree to waive or reduce the fees *before* the costs order is made because this would breach the indemnity principle.

GOOD HOUSEKEEPING AND COSTS

10.15   It will be readily apparent to anyone who has attended taxations of costs in the recent past that there is now a much heavier onus on those taxing bills to ensure that all sums claimed can be backed up with accurate records of time spent, and to justify that the work undertaken was necessary.

Sums recovered on taxation form a larger part of the total remuneration in many environmental cases than in commercial cases. In other words the profit costs recovered may well represent the remuneration to the solicitor without the addition of any solicitor and client element. There is therefore a high premium on the accurate recording of time.

In many environmental cases a significant part of the recoverable costs comprises experts' fees. Practitioners are advised to ensure that the experts they instruct keep an accurate record of time spent so that an adequate breakdown of fees can be presented if required. Many experts, particularly small operations, are not accustomed to keeping such records, and the matter needs to be resolved before work is commenced as it can be extremely difficult to try to put together details long after the event. *See* Chapter 9 on working with experts.

LEGAL AID

10.16   The foregoing discussion indicates the great value of the legal aid scheme where it is applicable and where it is available. The limits of its application and recent reduction in its availability have been the subjects of much adverse criticism.

GREEN FORM SCHEME

10.17 Legal aid is not applicable to issues decided by and pleaded before administrative tribunals. A public planning inquiry, therefore, will not admit of legal aid. There is, however, the Green Form scheme under which two hours' free advice is available. A plaintiff can thereby obtain general guidance and background assistance in anticipation of a planning problem or as a preliminary to a planning dispute. The assistance is an entitlement of considerable value and can extend to letter writing and even support for a reference to the European Court of Justice in situations where a preliminary ruling is appropriate.

JUDICIAL REVIEW

10.18 Testing a planning decision before the court by way of judicial review comes within its remit, as does a simple appeal on a matter of law brought to the appellate division. Endeavours to broaden the limit of jurisdiction by arguing questions of fact as points of law have, however, been more noted for their ingenuity than their success! *See* Chapter 3 for further comment.

APPROVAL BY LOCAL LEGAL AID BOARDS

10.19 Even with the above means of access to the scheme, however, it remains necessary to satisfy the local legal aid board that assistance should be provided. A board may frown upon novel elements or regard the evidence gathered as not sufficiently persuasive, and reject an application. Such rejection could trigger the legal aid appeal system which includes, as a last resort, an application for judicial review. Complying with all the requirements involves yet more work and time and this can have particular significance if the original remedy sought was itself by way of judicial review. With time running on both applications the risk of being out of time on the substantive issue is considerable. A plaintiff can try to find a more supportive board in another part of the country but that requires a broad knowledge of the arena known principally to a limited number of highly geared plaintiff law firms and again assumes continuation of the *pro bono* line. In this context the report (*The Times*, 2 July 1994) that Mr Justice Popplewell had quashed

the decision of the Northern Area Legal Aid Committee to refuse
financial support for the 28 test cases of smokers trying to sue the
tobacco industry, saying it was based on procedural irregularity, is
of interest. The judge's decision means that a different area board
will now hear the application.

OBJECTIONS TO MULTI-PLAINTIFF ACTIONS

10.20   A side consequence of the increase in recourse to legal aid
for multi-plaintiff actions is the complementary increase in objections raised by prospective defendants. This challenge to availability, whether by representations to a board before a decision or
appeal to the court by way of judicial review after a decision, adds
to the pressures upon prospective litigants and indeed upon their
advisers. The greater the novelty, or the perceived novelty in the presented cause of action, the greater is the likelihood of resistance to
it. Given the nature of environmental casework, however, practitioners have frequently to be innovative and it is the writers' firm
view that such issues should be the subject of adjudication by the
courts and not estoppel by local boards.

Legal aid is more likely to be granted in cases of tort or nuisance
where the civil remedy is by way of injunction or damages than in
the situations discussed above.

ELIGIBILITY FOR LEGAL AID

10.21   The key to the availability of legal aid is the financial standing of the applicant as identified by the levels of disposable income
and capital. The definition of 'disposable' allows for appropriate
deductions for living purposes. Legal aid is available where disposable income falls between £2,294 and £6,800 (£7,500 for personal
injury) and where capital is between £3,000 and £6,750 (for personal injury, £8,560). At the lower levels full legal aid is available,
and no financial contribution is required of the applicant. Above
those figures, aid is available on a graduated scale. Those in receipt
of income support are eligible for civil legal aid regardless of capital.
The limits are reviewed in April each year. The figures given are
those in force in July 1994.

10.22 When an application is made for legal aid, an area office has power to issue a temporary or provisional certificate, known as an 'emergency certificate', immediately without waiting for an assessment of means from the Benefits Agency's legal aid assessment office. A full application must be submitted at the same time. This is because an emergency certificate may only be granted if sufficient information is available to show the nature of the proceedings, the circumstances in which legal aid is required and that the applicant is likely to fulfil the conditions under which full legal aid may be granted.

LIMITATIONS ON THE AVAILABILITY OF LEGAL AID

10.23 Environmental cases, perhaps more than others, have an element of novelty and tend towards a conscious testing of boundaries. They therefore underline the importance of a liberal interpretation of legal aid schemes, but current cost-cutting exercises make such an interpretation unlikely. The initiation of representative actions is reduced by this and other factors, such as the following:

(a) the strict application of the rules of locus;
(b) the reluctance to grant legal aid where the cost of recovery could exceed the amount recovered; this is particularly relevant to claims involving damage to health; it is not so easily argued where property rights are in issue;
(c) the benefit to others argument, by which boards refuse aid to pursue a remedy from which others, who have neither initiated proceedings nor themselves applied for assistance, would arguably benefit (for obscure reasons, this rule does not appear to be enforced in Northern Ireland);
(d) the charging order based on any property in the ownership of the legal aid applicant to help defray expense is frequently seen as a discouragement to proceeding with an application. Given the cost rules in our courts, as elsewhere explained in this chapter, this could be a very serious impediment for the small householder.

10.24   Except in the case of a financial refusal based on the capital or income test, an applicant has a right of appeal against a legal aid board decision. This appeal is to the appropriate area committee for the decision to be reviewed (Legal Aid (General) Regulations 1989, Reg 34). The form of appeal is by way of reconsideration of the application. There is no appeal from the decision of the area committee which is final, unless by way of judicial review.

ORGANISING RESOURCES

10.25   The earlier part of this chapter illustrates how lack of funding frequently hampers the application of environmental remedies. Chapter 8 looked at the importance of extra-legal remedies. This lack of funding puts a high premium on the organisation of those addressing these issues. Shrewd use of human and financial resources is essential, particularly where they are limited. This section looks at matters which those advising action groups should bring to their attention.

THE WORK OF ACTION GROUPS

10.26   Many of the recommendations in earlier sections of this chapter, including those relating to control of expenditure and early consultation with professionals, are directly applicable to action groups.

Fund raising must be one of the primary functions of an action group (*see* below). The greater the enthusiasm, indignation and even anger that can be generated, the better the prospect of support funding. Self-interest inevitably plays a part and action groups are well advised to research and set out, fully and objectively, how their community will be directly affected, specifically what established amenities are under threat, whether this impacts upon children or the elderly, education, health and safety, as well as property values.

Action groups need to be advised of the importance of persuading their neighbours that a remedy is available or that representation, properly made and at the right time, can produce results. Groups which have had the benefit of ELF guidance at an early stage have been better equipped to set out the principles of law and procedures that are involved as well as to highlight areas where evidence is required. An indication of cost breakdown, specifying the stages and likely amounts required, can be important in preparing a group to anticipate its continued financial need, as well as to appreciate the convenience of providing this on an instalment basis.

ELF advice

10.27   It should be specifically noted here that ELF members make no charge for an initial interview and preliminary assessment, which is generally in written form, thereby providing the nucleus of the group with immediate documentary support, if appropriate, or at the very least a statement of evidence that is required or to be improved upon. Very often, experts will also give early assistance without immediate charge. ELF members have in any event agreed to limit their charging rates to legal aid levels once the matter proceeds. That too has obvious advantages.

Fund raising

10.28   The manner and style of collecting money is best left to the ingenuity of the local people. They must decide how best to gain attention and retain people's interest—often a difficult task. They must open a separate bank account in the name of the action group, providing for it to be operated by joint signatories, one of whom should be a professional person or local councillor able to offer independence as well as probity. Fund-raising events of all sorts, enlisting the support of a local (or national) celebrity, major or minor, involvement of the press, local radio and TV can all prove profitable.

Formation of a representative group

10.29   The need to raise public awareness and ensure recognition of a matter of local or regional interest has been previously stressed (Chapter 8) and this has the effect of producing alliances of interested parties to emerge. With environmental issues being so much to the forefront, there is much that such a grouping can do to influence existing as well as future environmental policy at local and national levels.

Where many parties are involved in a single cause of action or where a community or part of one wishes to be for example represented at an inquiry, then the formation of an action group to represent the interests of the component parts is clearly sensible.

It is important that such a group knows from the start to what extent it can bind the individual parts, and to that end there is merit in adopting some basic rules that set out the objects of the group, how it can take decisions and who is to speak on behalf of them all. For the practitioner it is far easier to progress a case if there are predetermined mechanisms for receiving instructions rather than having to consult with all concerned before any step can be taken.

The formation of a representative group embracing local people, local businesses, local enterprises and interest groups is also helpful in terms of augmenting fund-raising prospects. Where litigation is continuing a group can place funds in a central account to finance the continuing work, thus reducing multiple claims on individuals. Where the interests of the constituent parts of a group are unequal, it may be necessary to work out a formula for contribution of funds. Such an issue will only arise if damages are involved and care must be taken in setting up and then maintaining the group that all are working to one end. If there are differences these should be recognised at the outset and some accommodation for this built into the alliance. For a group to become fragmented as the case proceeds and become prey to orchestrated divisiveness is demoralising and generally fatal. By and large a policy of one for all and all for one has to be the best!

An action group is also an appropriate vehicle through which to put forward community-wide objections in relation to planning and authorisation applications and appeals. Clearly the greater the number of individuals a group represents the more effective it will be. It is sensible therefore for the group to obtain as many signatories as possible to a statement of its principal aims. Care in constructing such a statement and ensuring its support by local people, particularly those able to speak with authority, has been noted elsewhere.

Sustaining the sense of individual involvement can prove taxing and it is therefore important for action groups to provide regular updates on the progress of a campaign, covering both setbacks and advances. Meetings, whether in halls or homes, are helpful, particularly if advisers can be brought along from time to time to give encouragement and immediacy to the proceedings. Again, the value of working to a fixed budget must be emphasised.

It is inevitable that in financial terms an action group has much less power than the commercial interests seeking planning and authorisation consents. It is therefore important for such a group to work out very carefully what its objectives are and perhaps to focus on narrow issues rather than risk spreading its resources too thinly. As was indicated in Chapter 8, if there is more than one group appearing at an inquiry and taking the same or a similar line, it could be advantageous for each to concentrate upon different aspects of the argument. This is particularly important in working with a regulatory body, although an agreed division of labour must always be of benefit. In any event local action groups and their advisers should at the earliest possible stage look at the most effective ways of employing their resources, however limited these are.

OTHER SOURCES OF ASSISTANCE

10.30 Each action group is inevitably concerned with its own campaign and of necessity concentrates upon its particular problem. For that reason it may be difficult for such groups to enlist support from other bodies, but there are benefits to be derived from contacts with national organisations.

NATIONAL CAMPAIGN ORGANISATIONS

10.31 The national bodies such as Friends of the Earth, Greenpeace and the Worldwide Fund for Nature (WFN) have district and regional memberships and local action groups should establish contact with one or other of them. If a local issue can be shown to have relevance to problems experienced elsewhere, or to be part of a series of connected issues, then some financial assistance may be available from one of these organisations. A decision as to whether to make such a contribution is obviously a matter for those organisations to determine and will depend upon availability of funds or the extent to which they may be committed elsewhere at the particular time. The advice and guidance that such organisations can offer is of value in any event.

Although local people feel an understandable sense of 'owner-ship' in a dispute, if there emerges the means of having an issue fully ventilated as well as financially and professionally backed by a national organisation, a local body should consider permitting the national body to take over the handling of the local campaign. In those circumstances arrangements should be formalised with regard to liaison, local input and consultation.

Further information on national campaign organisations is given in Appendix 2.

LAW CENTRES

10.32   Law centres are likely to be a source of good guidance, rather than providers of funds, particularly if they have an environ-mental section, but again it is to be emphasised that help in the way of providing access to experience and administrative skills has itself a monetary worth.

Planning Aid of London can provide actual planning expertise. The Planning and Administrative Law Bar has a *pro bono* scheme in operation. The Bar also operates the Free Representation Unit (FRU), from which free advice and advocacy is available.

FUNDING FOR SUPPORT ORGANISATIONS

10.33   With the reduction in the level of legal aid available and limitation on its application for preliminary investigation, those with little funding have to depend upon the public-spirited attitude of lawyers and consultants. (The expertise available through ELF is valuable here.) The number of self-help organisations has increased as the availability of legal aid has reduced. The contingency fee approach based broadly on the American system only works (if at all) in cases where monetary compensation is sought and is appropriate. Preservation of the environment may have a price greater than pearls but it does not meet the costs of its protection nor those of its protectors!

The connection between the structure of our legal and adminis-trative systems, its composite parts, procedures and means of access on the one hand and the cost of such access and how it is borne, on the other, is very clear. One pioneering Lord of Appeal, Lord Woolf, is in the course of a fundamental rethink of the civil justice system at the behest of the government and his report is expected around 1996. Given his reputation and his previously canvassed views on law reform, one can be hopeful of the outcome.

The need for uninhibited access to justice for those committed to ensuring the conservation and protection of the environment is clear. The means provided are, however, quite inadequate. All but the most desperate or the most committed are deterred from embarking on the course of litigation.

PUBLIC-SPIRITED BENEFACTOR

10.34   Every local campaign group would ideally like to find a disinterested person of wealth who is concerned about the ecological balance and who would support local issues as part of the greater good. Such enthusiasm does exist and it can be tapped. Any group attempting this must devote much attention to its presentation which must set out a well-constructed description of the issue, an assessment of the prospect of success as well as a detailed estimate of cost.

ELF experience indicates that it might be necessary to fix a ceiling on expenditure, and that generally means requiring the experts, counsel and solicitors to agree a fixed sum for their services.

LEGAL COSTS INSURANCE

10.35   Legal costs insurance is available for actions including personal injury and nuisance (which would embrace pollution and trespass). It is doubtful that cover would be available for issues of a planning or land use nature although building disputes may be included. The policy must, of course, be in place before the problem itself.

It is essential that the policy cover leaves the choice of solicitor to the insured, so that he may have access to professionals with experience in environmental casework. It is also important to establish whether there is any limitation on expenditure on expert witnesses or even the need to demonstrate that a *prima facie* case exists before the policy is activated: this has overtones of the novelty objection that may be raised to legal aid applications (*see* above).

Such cover is certainly worth considering although each policy offered should be carefully reviewed. Premiums quoted (as at July 1994) are in the order of £200 plus VAT for £25,000 costs cover.

Self-help

10.36   The authors are two practising lawyers and the fact that they advocate doing without professional representation should be looked at with caution! In so doing, however, they recognise that in spite of best efforts, the raising of funds may be impossible or inadequate. They also recognise the view of some, namely, that in some circumstances professionals and experts are best avoided.

In terms of outlay, self-help must be the cheapest option: in terms of personal time and commitment it can be the most expensive. Dispensing with experienced advisers means a saving in fees, thereby dramatically reducing costs and fund-raising needs. With that, however, must go the attendant risks in presentation and prosecution of the argument in the face of the massed professionals and experts on the opposing side. It is conceded that employment of such skills is no certain route to success and that the inspired individual can still work wonders.

Whatever the inspiration, however, even on a self-help basis, it is desirable to seek as much voluntary assistance as possible from local like-minded people, other campaigning groups and organisations. Self-help involves a greater dependence upon *pro bono* assistance and makes it all the more important to impress upon the statutory authorities the need for their intervention in the desired manner. The authors recommend an approach that is coaxing without being supine, assertive without being adversarial, and should be delighted to hear from those who have been successful by using such a formula!

Conciliation and compromise

10.37   Alternative Dispute Resolution (ADR), which originated in the USA, has been operating in the UK since 1990. It involves the agreed intervention of an approved mediator to whom and through whom the various parties or their representatives can communicate. By a shuttle process involving a mixture of separate and combined meetings, the mediator endeavours, piece by piece, to reduce areas of conflict and finally to bring the parties to a position with which they both can live. For those wanting more details of the process, the names and addresses of the two main organisations appear in Appendix 4.

The key to the adoption of the ADR process is recognition by all parties that were their dispute to be conducted on traditional lines, each could be locked into a lengthy and costly battle. By following the ADR approach, they realise that they can achieve a solution which, while falling short of the 'best' result, has the merit of speed and reduced expense. That recognition, however, carries with it the parallel appreciation by each party of the other's determination and capacity to see the argument through to the court room or other forum of adjudication, equipped with good representation and sound supporting evidence.

The question must be posed whether a large corporation intent upon, say, a multi-million pound development, and faced with one or two local objectors, would accept the wisdom of resorting to ADR. There are doubtless public-spirited, though privately owned, companies and others in public ownership that would be attracted to the ADR approach regardless of the strength of the opposition. There can also be good practical reasons for accepting a lesser result in the interests of speed and lower costs. In the main, however, we must recognise that whereas Goliath may not have run for ADR upon meeting David for the first time, his surviving brother would. For those reasons, if a small action group can present itself as well equipped, well supported and well advised, it can be made to appear an opponent worthy of the recognition of a major organisation.

ELF, although not yet admitted to the ADR circle, urges its members to consider recommending ADR as a possible course of action to its clients. It must of course be recognised that intransigence is not the monopoly of wealth and power. There are points of principle in many issues and opportunity for compromise may be limited. The ADR system is, however, available and all parties to any dispute should at least have the opportunity for using it even if they do not take it.

The Centre for Dispute Resolution (CEDR) which operates ADR is a major organisation, membership of which is open to law firms and other professionals as well as commercial corporations. The fees (as at July 1994) are: a joining fee of £500; annual membership of £500 which entitles a member to utilise CEDR's services at a lower cost than a non-member (who is charged an arrangement fee of between £300 and £500 per party); the fees for the employment of a mediator vary according to the value of a claim, and range from £350 to £1,500 per day. Assuming even a concentrated ten dedicated days to reach a conclusion, that total cost at the highest level is something in the order of £15,000. The fees of the lawyers involved are of course additional but taken overall it compares favourably with the alternative of going through to a court hearing. Costs of each party in preparing for ADR must be added but should be far lower than those of a full trial.

It should be recognised that practising lawyers, even where conducting disputes in the adversarial style, will look for opportunities to propose compromise and conciliation to their client and for willingness on the part of the other side. There is a dynamic to the process of resolving disputes and within that cycle (quite apart from the door of the court syndrome) there will emerge moments when the unthinkable is thinkable and settlements emerge. The negotiating skill of the practitioner is then all-important since it must be remembered that, while it can be said that in a compromise conclusion there are no losers, there are also no winners!

It must be accepted, however, that in community terms it could well be difficult to seek compromise in resolving the problems caused by, say, the ill-advised siting of an incinerator, or the determination to run a multi-lane roadway through an area of scenic beauty and special scientific interest. How much better and more effective it would be if businesses, corporations, planners and other authorities regarded it as positive and desirable to take account of local interests and to offer consultation and advice on best practice, rather than seeing them as courses to be observed simply as a matter of form.

RESPONSIBILITY FOR DAMAGE AND COST OF CLEAN UP

INDUSTRY

10.38 Industry must set the costs of compliance and good practice and the impact of such measures upon their market share.

(1) Non-compliance can lead to civil litigation, damages and expense, or even a criminal prosecution, with the attendant financial as well as custodial risk to the officers of the company.
(2) Banks and other financial institutions are increasingly requiring companies to comply with good practice, as regards the products, the processes in use, the plant, its workers and care for neighbours.
(3) Lastly, well-conducted businesses wish to respond to and to be seen to be responding to the expectations of their community.

Historical pollution

10.39   Earlier discussion has touched upon the problem of historical pollution and the inherited liability that results. Of increasing significance are the problems that arise from land that has been so contaminated. In many instances it would be virgin ground. Such land may be acquired for a number of possible purposes, subject to the unknown time bomb ticking away beneath the surface. A serious problem could develop directly at the site itself or, as the result of a leaching process, some distance away.

A typical example is the construction of a housing estate on land which 20 to 30 years previously was used for landfill purposes consequentially beneath the surface a slow degenerative process occurs that produces ultimately a sudden emergence of methane gas, with all its consequential risks to health and safety, as well as the devastation caused to the houseowners.

The results of such an event are far-reaching:
(a) householders and their families could suffer ill-health and seek compensation for this;
(b) a blight on the property in terms of renting or sale and consequent problems with mortgagees;
(c) the developer could be pushed financially to the point of insolvency;
(d) the likelihood of the innocent house buyer being able to recover damages might be in doubt;
(e) the bankers to the developer could be left with a burdensome asset and a shortfall in value.

Therein lies the background to the advantage of enlightened self-interest: better a clean-up than a wind-up!

The practitioner must be alive to the prospect of such difficulties and ensure that the client (wherever it may be in the chain of interests previously referred to) is aware of and conducts full investigation into such possibilities. Heading off the problem rather than litigating the issue subsequently is clearly the preferred course.

Claims relating to the injudicious use of land

10.40   How land is used, as was pointed out in Chapter 9, is of the utmost significance to environmental protection. There are now large numbers of personal injury cases as well as claims for economic loss in the aftermath of injudicious use of land. With these, however, go the attendant strain upon families, the time lag in any conclusion, the whole gamut of the legal process, the questions of evidence and causal proof. The purpose of mentioning them here is to flag the significance of these matters and to emphasise the practitioner's obligation to raise full enquiries as well as advise the client of the implications. That applies equally to the buyer of a house or flat, a developer, the tenant of an industrial complex and his landlord.

There are cases where the innocent inheritors of a problem nevertheless stand directly in line as a prime target for the carrying of legal responsibility. In addition, of course, are those who have been directly involved in causing a problem and by their own actions bring themselves into the firing line.

Foreseeability

10.41   The foreseeability test highlighted in the *Cambridge Water* case has been the subject of much comment by lawyers and environmentalists and is dealt with more fully in Chapter 2. The offending party, namely Eastern Counties Leather PLC, was clearly responsible for bringing the 'foreign' substance on to the land, yet the Cambridge Water Company, the *wholly* innocent party, is left with a financial responsibility which makes nonsense of the 'polluter pays' argument. That concept has an attractive ring about it, but there is no legal force or doctrine involved. In coming to the decision, their Lordships clearly invited our legislators to address the dilemma of historical contamination emerging in later years, with all the damaging consequences, including in some cases the obligation to clear up someone else's mess! That the government of the day is not rushing to legislate (any more than it wished to initiate the register of contaminated land) is related to the financial implications and the burdens arising. It is, nevertheless, a nettle that has to be grasped.

BURDEN AND RESPONSIBILITY

10.42   The question of where the burden should lie in respect of historical and unforeseen pollution is a major problem. Those who suffer damage from pollution should be compensated. Those who cause it should pay—save that the real test as we have seen is not who caused it but who is *legally* responsible for it.

Moreover, the level of compensation awarded could have the consequence of forcing a guilty party into liquidation, thereby destroying a business without any commensurate relief to the victim.

The experience in the USA of the Super Fund has not proved satisfactory and yet some sort of equivalent to that arrangement seems the most practical approach. The authors do not pretend to have *the* answer, nor one that is fully tested or costed, but they feel that an attempt to suggest a solution or at least propose a principle for adoption in the search for one may be a sensible way through the dilemma.

A clean-up fund

10.43   The concept is that those who carry such liability should (subject to satisfying modest criteria as to their financial standing), have recourse to a national clean-up fund on a loan basis. Repayment would be over an extended period so as not to endanger the stability of the company.

The fund would need to be established by the Treasury in the first instance and could be supplemented through a charge of a kind similar to the Development Land Tax (DLT). How such a Clean-Up Tax (CUT) should be applied and charged requires careful balancing to avoid the sort of adverse impact on land prices of the old DLT. One suggestion is that the tax should fall equally on vendor and purchaser, with an absolute prohibition against one indemnifying the other by any means. That should ensure that land prices are kept under reasonable control. The tax should in any event be kept relatively low, rising perhaps on a stepped basis according to the value of the consideration. Brown land would be exempt. There would have to be regard to development areas and other concessionary needs.

The backing of such a resource makes the challenge to liability less important. The imposition of absolute strict liability on the occupier/user of the land *in situ* at the date when the act of pollution emanating from the land is first recognised avoids lengthy arguments over liability and the complication of causation. Means testing would be necessary, to establish what proportion of the compensation or cost should be borne by the company, what should be provided by way of loan and the level of interest to be charged. The difference in culpability, and therefore of the cost of a loan facility, between those actively and knowingly responsible for pollution, and those who have inherited an old problem not previously known, should be recognised.

It is clear that there is, as yet, no tested and generally proved or acceptable approach that satisfies all interests and all needs. While posing the problem does not produce *the* solution it does at least focus minds and contribute to the public debate as well as crystallisation of policies.

THE POLLUTER AND THE PAYER

10.44 To convert the slogan that the polluter pays into a legal argument, the injured party, ie the plaintiff, has the onus of demonstrating cause and effect. The plaintiff must prove:
  (a) that the defendant by its actions caused the problem;
  (b) that the defendant knew or should have known the likely consequences of its acts which have resulted in the problem complained of;
  (c) that the plaintiff has suffered damage;
  (d) that such suffering and damage flow directly from the act itself.

Encouraged by our adversarial system, as well as the financial and psychological pressures imposed upon litigants by protracted proceedings, the defendant company (and it is almost always a company with limited liability), and perhaps its insurer, if cover exists, will, save in the most blatant cases, force the plaintiff to prove all aspects of the claim fully and will put forward all available arguments against.

This reactive attitude arises principally because of the variations in the expectations of and the demands upon industry, both as to the manner in which it conducts its business and the legal responsibilities carried by so doing. Where there are prescriptive requirements, regulatory expectation and monitoring of clearly defined parameters of responsibility, all involved in industry have a precise set of standards within which to operate. Where there are transgressions, and provided causation is established, the only issue should be the nature of the remedy and the level of compensation.

Standard regulations

10.45 Such a result presupposes common regulatory requirements by which all are bound, thereby avoiding the fear of unfair competition save for those prepared to risk prosecution. Standard regulations obviate the uncertainties of voluntary regulation and provide a precise measure and target to which all can aspire. The imposition of such standards necessitates greater provision for start-up capital. Again there is the question of cost and the source of funding and the extra expense imposed upon the product is ultimately paid for by the consumer. Such a system only works, therefore, if the government sets obligatory standards, those standards are accepted and implemented by industry, the banks provide the money on affordable terms and the public re-enforce the will of government by supporting improved environmental levels and being willing to pay for such improvements.

Legislative settlement of liability

10.46 The Lords have clearly signalled that the question of liability has to be settled by Parliament. This acknowledges a political dimension to the environmental debate and underlines how inappropriate it is to impose upon the judiciary the task of determining the balance in society between one demand and another. The ecological argument is less likely to receive a satisfactory hearing than those of a juridical complexity or of economic substance. The forum of a court controlled by a judge, who (assuming there is no jury) determines issues of fact and law following an adversarial presentation, may be equipped to draw refinements on points of law but has demonstrated less ability to distinguish between competing claims for environmental protection on the one hand, and the economic argument on the other hand. The weight attaching to economics is generally determined by evidence relating to the level of financial benefit expected to accrue, coupled with the expense component (within which is frequently placed the argument of cost effectiveness). Where there is a gulf between the two schools is in the standards used in determining the expectation of benefit and the real value in assessing the quality of a cost. At Twyford Down, for example, there was resistance, on the grounds of expense, to the construction of a tunnel through a hill directly in the path of what was (in spite of objections) the insisted-upon line of the M3 extension. As a result a broad expansive elevation, constituting an essential sweep of this majestic landscape, a recognised area of scenic beauty and part of an SSSI, was literally hacked out and destroyed. Under the guise of saving money, a great price has in fact been paid.

The environmental courts discussed in Chapter 8 also bear upon these issues.

Cost-benefit analysis

10.47   The economic argument is frequently advanced as justification for reduction in environmental standards. Local employment, attraction of local industry, development of a local infrastructure, the benefit of an alleged planning gain are argued as matters to be put in the balance in the process of making choices.

What is often not incorporated into the equation is the underlying socio-economic costs, the short-term benefit that might arise set against the long-term detriment that results and the implications of easing problems in one district only to accentuate them elsewhere. Concern must be expressed at the misuse as well as the misreading of economic issues.

The authors advance the view that any cost analysis is incomplete if it limits itself simply to outlay and the adoption of a course based upon levels of expenditure alone. Tampering with the environment, whether in a minor or major degree, carries consequences all of which need to be brought into the equation so that the totality of what is involved can be fully assessed. One action will inevitably set up a series of reactions and interactions and all have relevance to the decision-making process. Accordingly, they are all part of the value judgements that are being made and should be brought into account in assessing the cost of any project.

That involves the bringing together of evidence relating to the social and ecological implications, the human and technological dimension. This requires receptiveness to change in political and jurisprudential terms: it involves improved participation in the making of the law and in its administration. It also warrants fuller examination than can be devoted here and it is hoped that the reader is sufficiently attracted by the principles to explore these propositions further.

POLICY AND PRIORITIES

10.48　At first sight, the devotion of a whole chapter to the issue of funding and economics may have appeared a surprising luxury in a book directed to the practicalities of environmental casework. The subjects raised in the preceding pages, however, demonstrate the essential part that the money factor plays in all aspects of this work. The private citizen and action groups can be hemmed in and see their rights become meaningless where remedies cannot be pursued because of lack of funds. Industry also has to elect whether to invest in good practice and minimise exposure to potential claims or to go for short-term advantage and argue the issue if the need arises.

Government needs to give a lead in investment for the future and in safeguarding future generations and to conduct policies that support current demands without damaging that awareness. Environmental groups must never cease to be vigilant and must seek proactive intervention rather than be reactive, while recognising that not all aims can be immediately satisfied and that there are times when priorities must be set.

THE EUROPEAN INFLUENCE

10.49　The proposals contained in the EC's Fifth Action Programme (1992) provide the answer to the citizen's prayer in the

373

matter of costs and expense. It recommends expanding the class of those entitled to initiate steps through the courts or administrative tribunals: it restates the right of access to justice for all, but in so doing recognises that this would be meaningless if such access is not supported by sufficient funding. It contemplates that public interest cases should therefore be paid for by central government. *See also* Chapter 6 on this point.

Those recommendations are not enshrined in obligatory directives and there is no sign of the present administration in this country wishing to adopt such programme voluntarily.

Recourse to Europe is in any event likely to be of a variable benefit. The quality aspirations of the EC have given way to the economic pressures upon the enlarged EU, with the result that standards set in European terms are being subverted to those acceptable to and affordable by individual countries. For example, there are no longer common standards for the purity of drinking water or for permitted discharges Thus, whatever the posturing of government, we find now (post-Maastricht) that, following the supposed virtues of subsidiarity, with the less exacting values and standards of national governments, more and more of our coastal waters fail to satisfy the former standards.

The EU has made a definite and increasingly important start in the establishment of standards and requirements. The United Nations Conference on the Environment and Development held in June 1992 in Rio de Janeiro produced a number of conventions and agreed aims towards 2000. Nevertheless, standardisation worldwide has a long way to go.

The approach of those systems which are for the first time establishing protective measures for the environment is of considerable interest. The Czech Republic is one instance where, until the overthrow of the totalitarian regime, few or no environmental regulations existed. Now under its list of fundamental rights and freedoms, citizens are constitutionally entitled to claim legally a 'right to life in favourable environment'. All have standing to test matters through the courts. Also the Environmental Act of 1991 serves a 'responsibility on the part of all persons to preserve a favourable environment for future generations' and identifies a favourable environment as a fundamental right of man. (See, 'Regulating the European Environment' by Tom Handler.)

THE FUTURE

10.50 It has been stated elsewhere that the community has higher expectations than in the past, and the system must be competent and appropriate for responding to those needs and aspirations. We must take note of the increasing expression of communal feelings instanced by the growing emergence of campaign groups and citizen organisations and a consequential increase in representative actions. Some hold that such activity reflects a disenchantment with our institutions, particularly as regards communicating and securing expectations.

In addition, it is necessary to examine who must carry the burden of establishing proof of responsibility and the possibilities for ameliorating its impact. An extension of the *res ipsa loquitur* principle would be in keeping with the current level of scientific and medical knowledge and the growth in the number of investigations and research bodies. The increasing awareness of the relationship between toxicity and physical as well as mental conditions, identified by epidemiologists and others in specialist fields, does contribute to the argument that, once a *prima facie* case has been established, the burden of proof should then shift so that whoever is under challenge has to demonstrate that it does not bear liability.

Such an approach should limit the opportunity for delay, it will certainly reduce costs, particularly to the legal aid fund, it will concentrate minds and it ought to produce a more equitable result.

Practitioners must learn to use the existing law and the system to its full advantage. As committed environmentalists we should approach the problem presented to us from the perspective expressed in these pages. The marriage of those two strands should enable a better understanding of the underlying issues and the needs of clients, so offering a broad perspective and overview. Practitioners may not be appointed to speak as advocates for the environment, but by advancing and championing the issues explored within this book they are gaining that status. In so doing there is an effective demonstration of the importance of preserving the four elements and adding that of professional integrity and commitment.

APPENDIX 1

REGULATORS

ENGLISH HERITAGE

Fortress House, 23 Savile Row, London W1X 1AB
Tel: 0171 973 3000

ENGLISH NATURE

Head Office: Northminster House, Northminster, Peterborough PE1 1UA
Tel: 01733 340345

FORESTRY COMMISSION

Headquarters: 231 Corstorphine Road, Edinburgh EU12 7AZ
Tel: 0131 334 0303

HER MAJESTY'S INSPECTORATE OF POLLUTION (HMIP)
OFFICES

HMIP (Headquarters): Romney House, 43 Marsham Street, London SW1P 3PY
Tel: 0171 276 8061
HMIP Anglian Region: Howard House, 40–64 St Johns Street, Bedford MK42 0DL
Tel: 01234 272112

HMIP Anglian Region: Mill House, 4th Floor, Brayford Side North, Lincoln LN1 1YW
Tel: 01522 512566
HMIP Midlands Region: Unit 15–17, Wren's Court, Lower Queen Street, Sutton Coldfield, West Midlands B72 1RT
Tel: 0121 362 1000
HMIP Monitoring Branch: Cameron House, White Cross Industrial Estate, South Road, Lancaster WA1 4XQ
Tel: 01524 842704/842708
HMIP North East Region: Stockdale House (1st Floor), Headingly Business Park, 8 Victoria Road, Headingly, Leeds LS6 1PF
Tel: 0532 786636
HMIP North East Region: Don House, Pennie Centre, 20–22 Hawley Street, Sheffield S1 1HD
Tel: 0114 270 0459
HMIP North East Region: Swan House, Merchants Wharf, Westpoint Road, Thornaby TF17 6PD
Tel: 01642 633753
HMIP North West Region: Mitre House, Church Street, Lancaster LA1 1BG
Tel: 01524 382100
HMIP North West Region: Kings Court, Unit 2, Manor Park, Runcorn WA7 1HR
Tel: 01928 579522
HMIP Southern Region: Millennium House, Unit 2, Fleet Wood Park, Barley Way, Fleet GU13 8UT
Tel: 01252 776600
HMIP Southern Region: 3 East Grinstead House, London Road, East Grinstead RH10 1RR
Tel: 01342 312016
HMIP South West Region: Highwood Pavilion, Jupiter Road, Patchway, Bristol BS12 5SN
Tel: 0272 319600
HMIP Technical Guidance Branch: Government Buildings, 2 Burghill Road, Westbury-on Trym, Bristol BS10 6NH
Tel: 0117 976 4150
HMIP Wales Region: Brunel House, 11th Floor, 2 Fizalan Road, Cardiff CF2 1TT
Tel: 01222 495558

NATIONAL RIVERS AUTHORITY OFFICES

Head Office: Bristol
Rivers House, Waterside Drive, Aztec West, Almondsbury, Bristol
BS12 4UD
Tel: 01454 624400
Head Office: London
Eastbury House, 30–34 Albert Embankment, London SE1 7TL
Tel: 0171 820 0101
Anglian NRA: Kingfisher House, Goldhay Way, Orton Goldhay,
Peterborough PE2 5ZR
Tel: 01733 371811
Northumbria and Yorkshire NRA: Eldon House, Regent Centre,
Gosforth, Newcastle upon Tyne NE3 3UD
Tel: 0113 244 0191 (Leeds) 0191 231 0226 (Newcastle)
North West NRA: PO Box 12, Richard Fairclough House,
Knutsford Road, Warrington WA4 1HG
Tel: 01925 653999
Severn Trent NRA: Sapphire East, 550 Streetsbrook Road, Solihull
B91 1QT
Tel: 0121 711 2324
Southern NRA: Guildborne House, Chatsworth Road, Worthing,
West Sussex BN11 1LD
Tel: 01903 820692
South Western NRA: Manley House, Kestrel Way, Exeter EX2 7LQ
Tel: 01392 444000
Thames NRA: Kings Meadow House, Kings Meadow Road,
Reading, Berkshire RG1 8DQ
Tel: 01734 535000
Welsh NRA: Rivers House, Plas-yr-Afon, St Mellons Business Park,
St Mellons, Cardiff CF3 OLT
Tel: 01222 770088

Appendix 2

Pressure Groups

Anglers Conservation Association

23 Castlegate, Grantham, Lincs NG31 6SW
Tel: 01476 61008.
This association was formed in 1948 with the purpose of fighting against water pollution. It operates by way of membership who pay an annual subscription. In return for that subscription the ACA will fund legal actions on behalf of members, any recovered costs being returned to the ACA. The organisation has been primarily involved with fighting common law cases, but has also brought criminal prosecutions and involved itself in planning and authorisation issues.

The Council for the Protection of Rural England

Warwick House, 25 Buckingham Palace Road, London SW1 0PP
Tel: 0171 976 6433.
The CPRE was established 66 years ago and, as a pressure group, campaigns for the preservation of the English countryside. It is a registered charity. Its work takes it into planning and development, agriculture and countryside management, transport, land use and natural resources. It therefore appears regularly at inquiries which threaten the countryside.

ENVIRONMENTAL DATA SERVICES

Finsbury Business Centre, 40 Bowling Green Lane, London EC1R 0NE
Tel: 0171 278 7624.
The principal function of ENDS is its monthly report, which contains comprehensive coverage of issues relating to environmental regulation. This includes case reports on recent legal cases. ENDS also publishes a directory of environmental consultants (*see* Chapter 9), the present cost of which is £49.50.

THE ENVIRONMENTAL LAW FOUNDATION

Lincoln's Inn House, 42 Kingsway, London WC2B 6EX
Tel: 0171 404 1030.
ELF was formed in 1992, reflecting the growing body of people who were affected by environmental problems, who needed expert advice in relation to those issues but who did not necessarily have the resources to fund substantial cases on their own. To this end ELF has set up a network of lawyers and scientific experts who are willing to undertake a limited amount of work *pro bono*, and to do legal aid work, or work at legal aid rates.

FRIENDS OF THE EARTH

26–28 Underwood Street, London N1 7JQ
Tel: 0171 490 1555.
FOE is a well-known organisation with a long pedigree as an environmental pressure group. FOE occasionally commences public interest litigation. Through local groups it takes up particular environmental issues such as the impact of motorway construction and often makes appearances at public inquiries as an objector. Details of local groups can be obtained from the local campaigns director at FOE head office in London.

Current campaigns include monitoring the implementation of waste regulation; pressing for the creation of contaminated land registers; continuing work on drinking water standards.

GREENPEACE

Canonbury Villas London N1 2PN
Tel: 0171 354 5100.
Greenpeace addresses many of the same issues as FOE although it has a greater focus on global issues. It is noted in particular for creating public consciousness of environmental issues through direct action.

Greenpeace is perhaps more willing to resort to litigation as a remedy. It has initiated criminal prosecutions for water pollution and it has been involved in highly publicised judicial review litigation in relation to the commencement of BNFL operations at Sellafield without the need for a public inquiry. Although ultimately unsuccessful, that litigation was ground breaking in establishing the locus of environmental groups to bring judicial review proceedings and altering judicial attitudes to the award of costs in such proceedings (*see* Chapter 4).

Other Greenpeace campaigns are mostly of an international nature but they have local implications. The global warming campaign has implications for industrial activity in this country, for car use and attitudes to planning issues. Another campaign relates to the dumping of toxic materials in the North Sea, which has relevance to the issue of sewage sludge dumping and chemical discharges from the North Sea coast.

NATIONAL SOCIETY FOR CLEAN AIR

136 North Street, Brighton BN1 1RG
Tel: 0273 26313
The Society campaigns for reductions of air pollution. It publishes an annual pollution handbook.

ROYAL SOCIETY FOR NATURE CONSERVATION

The Green, Witham Park, Waterside South, Lincoln LN5 7JR
Tel: 0522 752326
County Wildlife Trusts exist in all counties as pressure groups to protect the interests of wildlife. They will appear at inquiries and

make representations in planning and authorisations cases where there are relevant issues.

UNITED KINGDOM ENVIRONMENT LAWYERS ASSOCIATION

This organisation was formed in the early 1980s to reflect the emergence of environmental lawyers as a separate breed. It has established quite a substantial membership. At committee level it is dominated by representatives from the larger law firms, who tend to act for industry.

The association has formed a number of working groups covering, *inter alia*, each of the environmental media.

PROFESSIONAL INSTITUTIONS

THE ASSOCIATION OF CONSULTING ENGINEERS

Alliance House, 12 Caxton Street, London SW1H 0QL
Tel: 0171 222 6557

THE BRITISH ECOLOGICAL SOCIETY

26 Blades Court, Deodar Road, London SW15 2NU
The society has a directory of members and will assist in finding the right specialist. Not all members of the society are professional.
Tel: 081 871 9797

BRITISH SOCIETY OF SOIL SCIENCE

Department of Soil Science, University of Reading, Whiteknights, PO Box 233, Reading RG6 2DW
Tel: 0734 316 559

THE GEOLOGICAL SOCIETY

Burlington House, Piccadilly, London W1V 0JU
Tel: 0171 434 9944
The society's directory lists, *inter alia*, consulting geologists, geochemists, geophysicists, civil engineers, mining engineers, hydrogeologists, and environmental consultants.

INSTITUTE OF BIOLOGY

20 Queensbury Place, London SW7 2DZ

INSTITUTE OF BRITISH GEOGRAPHERS

1 Kensington Gore, London SW7 2AR

INSTITUTE OF CHEMICAL ENGINEERS

Davis Building, 165–171 Railway Terrace, Rugby CV21 3HQ

INSTITUTE OF FISHERIES MANAGEMENT

22 Rushworth Avenue, West Bridgford, Nottingham NG2 7LF

INSTITUTE OF WASTE MANAGEMENT

9 Saxon Court, St Peters Gardens, Northampton N1 1S

INSTITUTION OF CIVIL ENGINEERS

1–7 Great George Street, London SW1P 3AA

THE INSTITUTION OF ENVIRONMENTAL SCIENTISTS

14 Princes Gate, London SW11 1PU

INSTITUTION OF WATER AND ENVIRONMENTAL MANAGEMENT

15 St Johns Street, London WC1N 2EB

ALTERNATIVE DISPUTE RESOLUTION ORGANISATIONS

CENTRE FOR DISPUTE RESOLUTION

100 Fetter Lane, London EC4
Tel: 0171 430 1872

IDR EUROPE LIMITED

Three Quays, Tower Hill, London EC3
Tel: 0171 929 1790

KEY EC DIRECTIVES AND CORRESPONDING UK LEGISLATION

WATER

DIRECTIVE

80/778/EEC (OJ L229 30.8.80): Directive relating to the quality of water intended for human consumption

UK LEGISLATION

Water Resources Act 1991 and Water Industry Act 1991

DIRECTIVE

76/160/EEC (OJ L31 5.2.76): Directive concerning the quality of bathing water

UK LEGISLATION

Water Act 1989

DIRECTIVE

91/271/EEC (OJ L135 30.5.91): Directive concerning urban waste water treatment

UK LEGISLATION

Water Act 1989

DIRECTIVE

80/68/EEC (OJ L20 26.1.80): Directive on the protection of groundwater against pollution caused by dangerous substances

UK LEGISLATION

Water Resources Act 1991 and Environmental Protection Act 1990

DIRECTIVE

76/464/EEC (OJ L129 18.5.76): Framework Directive on pollution caused by certain dangerous substances discharged into the aquatic environment of the Community

UK LEGISLATION

Water Act 1989 and Environmental Protection Act 1990

WASTE

DIRECTIVE

78/319/EEC (OJ L84 31.3.78): Directive on toxic and dangerous waste

UK LEGISLATION

Control of Pollution Act 1974

DIRECTIVE

91/689/EEC (OJ L377 31.12.91): Directive on hazardous waste

UK LEGISLATION

Environmental Protection Act 1990

DIRECTIVE

84/631/EEC (OJ L326 13.12.84): Directive on the supervision and control within the European Community of the transfrontier shipment of hazardous waste

UK LEGISLATION

Transfrontier Shipment of Hazardous Waste Regulations 1988 (SI No 1562)

DIRECTIVE

75/442/EEC (OJ L194 25.7.75): Directive on waste

UK LEGISLATION

Environmental Protection Act 1990

AIR

DIRECTIVE

80/779/EEC (OJ L229 30.8.80): Directive on air quality limit values and guide values for sulphur dioxide and suspended particulates

UK LEGISLATION

Air Quality Standards Regulations 1989 (SI No 317)

DIRECTIVE

88/609/EEC (OJ L336 7.12.88): Directive on the limitation of emissions of certain pollutants into the air from large combustion plants

UK LEGISLATION

Environmental Protection Act 1990 and Environmental Protection (Prescribed Processes and Substances) Regulations 1991 (SI No 472)

DIRECTIVE

84/360/EEC (OJ L188 16.7.84): Directive on combating of air pollution from industrial plants

UK LEGISLATION

Environmental Protection Act 1990

MISCELLANEOUS

DIRECTIVE

1210/90/EEC (OJ L120 11.5.90): Regulation on the establishment of the European Environment Agency and the European Environment Information and Observation Network

UK LEGISLATION

No implementary legislation required

DIRECTIVE

85/337/EEC (OJ L175 5.7.85): Directive on the assessment of the effects of certain public and private prospects on the environment

UK LEGISLATION

Town and Country Planning (Assessment of Environmental Effects) Regulations 1988 (SI No 1199)

DIRECTIVE

90/313/EEC (OJ 158 23.6.90): Directive on the freedom of access to information on the environment

UK LEGISLATION

The Environmental Information Regulations 1992 (SI No 3240)

EC INSTITUTIONS

Information Office:	European Parliament UK Office 2, Queen Anne's Gate London SW1H 9AA Tel: 0171 222 0411
Headquarters:	European Parliament Offices Rue Belliard 97–113 B-1047 Brussels Tel: 010 32 2 284 2111
Secretariat:	Plateau du Kirchberg L-2929 Luxembourg Tel: 010 35 2 43001
Plenary Sessions:	Palais de l'Europe BP 1024 F 67070 Strasbourg Tel: 010 33 88 17 40 01
	European Court of Justice Centre Européen Plateau du Kirchberg L-2925 Luxembourg Tel: 010 35 2 43031

INDEX